D1035909

Dante and English poetry

Shelley to T. S. Eliot

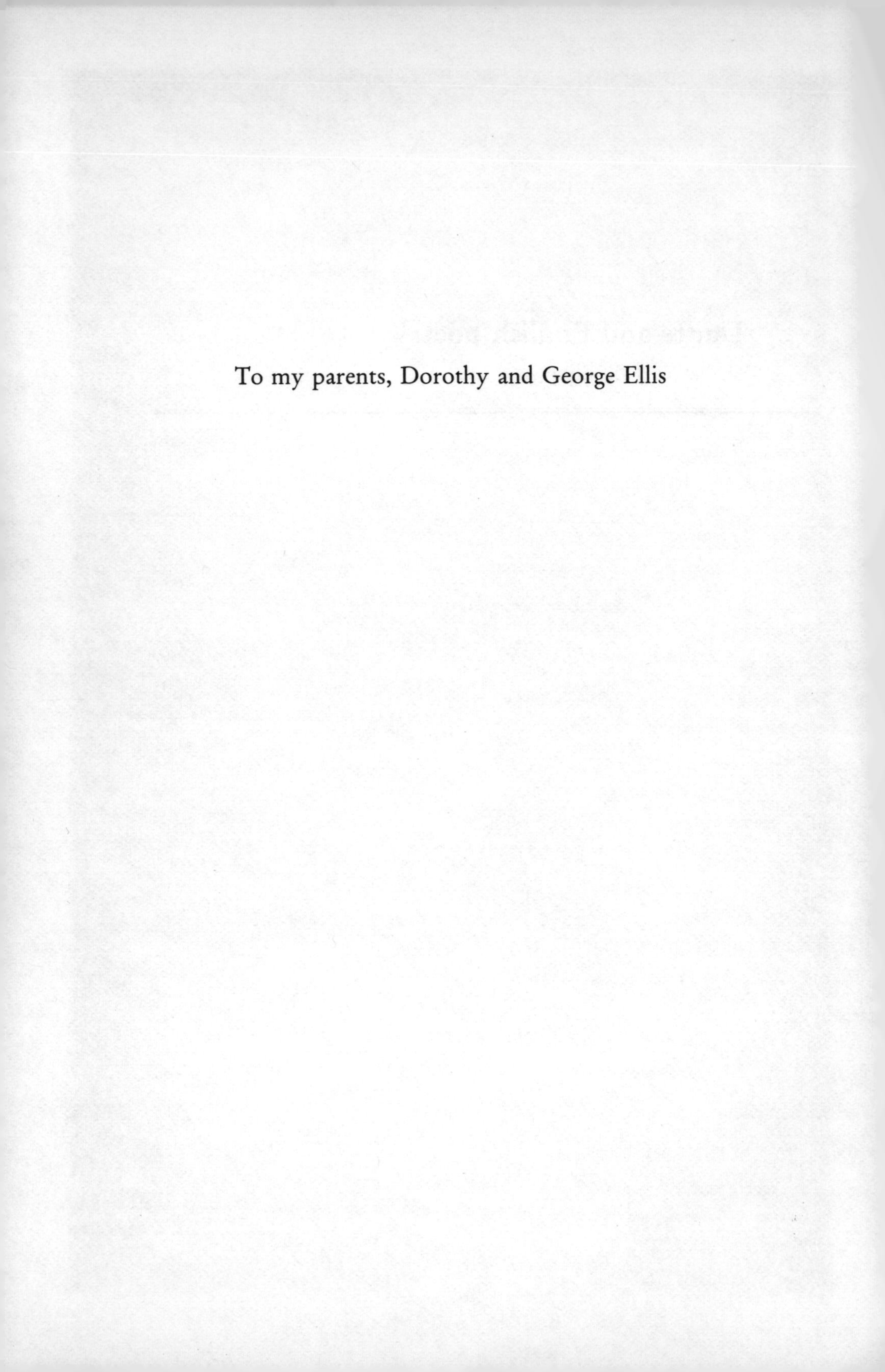

To my parents, Dorothy and George Ellis

Dante and English poetry

Shelley to T. S. Eliot

STEVE ELLIS

'sì mi fecer de la loro schiera . . .'

Cambridge University Press

Cambridge

London New York New Rochelle

Melbourne Sydney

Published by the Press Syndicate of the University of Cambridge
The Pitt Building, Trumpington Street, Cambridge CB2 1RP
32 East 57th Street, New York, NY 10022, USA
296 Beaconsfield Parade, Middle Park, Melbourne 3206, Australia

First published 1983

Printed in Great Britain at
the University Press, Cambridge

Library of Congress catalogue card number: 82-23650

British Library Cataloguing in Publication Data

Ellis, Steve
Dante and English poetry.
1. Dante Alighieri 2. English poetry
—Italian influences
I. Title
821'.8 PR595.I/

ISBN 0 521 25126 5

WV

Contents

Illustrations

Acknowledgements

This book originally began its existence as a doctoral thesis presented to the University of London in 1981. Its production was possible thanks to a three-year grant from the Department of Education and Science followed by a one-year Study Abroad Scholarship from the Leverhulme Trust, which enabled me to continue my research in Florence, Italy. I am indebted to the staffs of the British Library, the University of London Library at Senate House, and University College Library; and, in Florence, to those at the Biblioteca Nazionale, and at the libraries of the Società Dantesca Italiana and the British Institute. I wish to pay special thanks to Antonia Duffy at University College and Prue Shaw at Bedford College, who jointly supervised the thesis; and to Peter Caracciolo, A. C. Charity, Warwick Gould, Ian Haywood, A. D. Moody, John Took and Mary Baffoni for information and assistance. Acknowledgements are also due to the editors of *Comparative Literature* and *Paideuma*, in which earlier versions of parts of Chapters v and vi first appeared. I would like to thank all my friends who have put up with me during the lengthy production of this study; in particular Joanna Porter and Julie Thomas, whose typing and helpfulness have been vital. My final and largest debt remains however to my parents, to whom this book is dedicated.

Extracts from unpublished prose of T. S. Eliot are reprinted by permission of Mrs Valerie Eliot and Faber and Faber Ltd.

Editions and abbreviations used in the text

Editions

La Commedia, ed. Giorgio Petrocchi, *Le opere di Dante Alighieri*, Edizione nazionale, 7, 4 vols. ([Milan]: Mondadori, 1966–7).

Il Convivio, ed. Maria Simonelli (Bologna: Pàtron, 1966).

De Vulgari Eloquentia, ed. Pier Vincenzo Mengaldo, Vol. 1 (Padua: Antenore, 1968).

Epistolae, ed. Paget Toynbee, 2nd ed. (Oxford: The Clarendon Press, 1966).

Monarchia, ed. Pier Giorgio Ricci, Edizione nazionale, 5 ([Milan]: Mondadori, 1965).

Rime, ed. Gianfranco Contini, 3rd ed. (Turin: Einaudi, 1973).

Vita Nuova, ed. Domenico De Robertis (Milan: Ricciardi, 1980).

Abbreviations

(The *Commedia*)
Inf. *Inferno*
Purg. *Purgatorio*
Par. *Paradiso*

Conv. *Convivio*
DVE *De Vulgari Eloquentia*
Ep. *Epistolae*
Mon. *Monarchia*
VN *Vita Nuova*

Introduction

In this study I have attempted to show the ways in which a series of modern poets (and some critics) writing in English have regarded Dante, and how their assessments relate to the type of poetry they were themselves producing and seeing produced. This is not primarily a study of Dante's 'influence' on modern poets, if by influence we mean the production of poetry stylistically similar to Dante's own, or the imitation of specific turns of phrase or expressions in his work; a thorough, and indeed enormous, review of such influence was carried out long ago by A. R. Halley, at least for the nineteenth century, though the supposed derivations from Dante he puts forward are not always convincing.[1] In T. S. Eliot's words:

> the important debt to Dante does not lie in a poet's borrowings, or adaptations from Dante . . . The important debt does not occur in relation to the number of places in one's writings to which a critic can point a finger, and say, here and there he wrote something which he could not have written unless he had had Dante in mind.[2]

Although many such borrowings and adaptations are traced in the following pages, it will be seen that the 'important debt' the moderns owe to Dante will often involve us in discussion of his political, religious and ethical thought, of the way characters are presented in the *Commedia*, and of his relationship with Beatrice. These themes in his work have often been strangely interpreted in the light of modern theories of poetry, and several modern poems which in some ways attempt to emulate them have thereby turned out to be significantly different. Another major area of discussion concerns the various modern assessments of the relationship between Dante's work and that of his contemporaries, with the periodic attempts to close or widen the gap between them. Apart from his work, the events of Dante's life have exercised a considerable fascination in modern times, and the consequences of this are also presented here.

This does not pretend to be a complete study of Dante's significance for the nineteenth and twentieth centuries. Such a work would also have to take into account a great many prose writers, such as Ruskin, George Eliot, Forster and Joyce, to mention only obvious examples, although the first named has been admirably covered by Martin Bidney and the last by Mary T. Reynolds.[3] I feel justified, however, in largely confining my attention to the poets discussed here because of the conspicuous degree of interaction in their ideas about Dante. Such interaction can be positive or negative; that is, we cannot understand Yeats's approach to Dante without some knowledge of Shelley's, upon which it is largely based; nor can we appreciate Eliot's position unless we take into account the nineteenth-century uses of Dante that he repudiated. The work of the seven poets I have chosen to discuss shows, I believe, a greater debt to Dante, of one sort and another, than that of any other major poet during the past two centuries, though I have added comments on Keats and Tennyson where appropriate.

In a field as large as this much work has, of course, already been done, and I am particularly indebted to that of Paget Toynbee and Frank Kermode, as will be clear. As remarked, however, this book places a particular emphasis on the development, revision and rejection of ideas about Dante since the Romantic period; and by bringing the following poets into juxtaposition I hope to shed new light on these ideas and put into sharper focus the distinctive features of each poet's reaction to Dante. It is particularly the case with Yeats, Pound and Eliot that their respective attitudes to Dante can be explained in part in terms of how they understood their relationship with each other. Thus a good deal of the criticism referred to in the following pages is deficient in its ignoring of the wider context into which Dante's *fortuna* among modern poets may be placed. Dante was of fundamental importance to the seven poets we are concerned with with the sole exception, arguably, of Byron: it is hoped that this study will therefore illuminate some of the central issues of modern poetry over the last two hundred years.

I

Shelley, Dante and freedom

The works of His fingers have borne witness against Him.
(Notes to *Queen Mab*)

Shelley's response to Dante is an influential example of the recurrent modern practice of attending to Dante's 'poetry' while neglecting or discounting his beliefs, the most celebrated example of which is Croce's *La poesia di Dante*, with its distinction between Dante the poet and the far less important 'Dante filosofo e politico' ('Dante the philosopher and politician').[1] Rather than presenting Dante's beliefs, Shelley endows him with his own; and the powerful influence the *Commedia* had on him manifests itself in a poetry whose intention and philosophy is markedly different. The result is important for later writers like Rossetti and especially for Yeats, who tends to confuse the *Commedia* with Shelley's very dissimilar adaptations from it. None of the other poets we shall look at – not even Ezra Pound – had beliefs that were so opposed to Dante's; yet the *Commedia*'s influence on Shelley was arguably greater than on any of the others, excepting Eliot. This contradiction caused Shelley no undue alarm, as we shall see; his ability to negotiate it is typical of several modern writers' ignoring of Dante's philosophy, religion and poetic style in the interests of their own, often highly unusual, interpretations of him.

One of the major examples of Dante's influence is in the final act of *Prometheus Unbound*. Although specific reminiscences of the *Paradiso* – not all of them very convincing – have been pointed out here, the influence might be described as nothing less than the entire act itself.[2] The first three acts were finished by April 1819 and this last act added as an afterthought towards the end of the year;[3] in between Shelley had been reading the *Purgatorio* and the *Paradiso*,[4] and there seems little doubt that the decision to add a final act celebrating the universal happiness following the tyrant Jupiter's downfall, and, in words addressed to the Earth: 'The love which paves thy path along the skies' (IV.522),[5] was a direct outcome of Shelley's response to the *allegrezza* of the *Paradiso* with its 'amor che move il sole e l'altre stelle' ('love that moves the sun and the other stars') (XXXIII.145). Thus a passage like the following –

> And from the other opening in the wood
> Rushes, with loud and whirlwind harmony,
> A sphere, which is as many thousand spheres,
> Solid as crystal, yet through all its mass
> Flow, as through empty space, music and light:
> Ten thousand orbs involving and involved,
> Purple and azure, white, and green, and golden,
> Sphere within sphere . . .
>
> (IV.236–43)

– exhibits no specific source in the *Paradiso*; but that Shelley's 'mystic measure/Of music, and dance, and shapes of light' (IV.77–8) was inspired by Dante's *cantica* would seem undeniable. The fact that one Love centres on the Earth and the other on the stars indicates, however, a major divergence between them which we shall take up shortly, for the *Prometheus* adapts from Dante very much for its own political ideals.

Shelley's affection for the *Paradiso* is highly unusual for his day, especially among English writers; working through Toynbee's invaluable anthology we have to wait until 1825, three years after Shelley's death, before we find an appreciation of the *Paradiso* written in England akin to Shelley's own, namely John Keble's observation of the 'intense effect' the *Paradiso* produces 'by little more than various combinations of *three* leading ideas – light, motion, and music . . .', a statement that could as well be applied to the final act of Shelley's drama.[6] Among Shelley's contemporaries the sublime horrors of the *Inferno* exercised a fascination that the other two *cantiche* could not sustain, whereas Shelley himself regarded the *Purgatorio* as 'a finer poem' than the *Inferno*.[7] In his knowledge of the *Vita Nuova*, which he quotes from in the preface to *Epipsychidion* (p. 411), he belonged to an even more select group, and he even made some notes on the *Convivio*.[8] His greatest admiration was reserved however for the *Paradiso*, especially for its celebration of Beatrice:

> Dante understood the secret things of love even more than Petrarch. His *Vita Nuova* is an inexhaustible fountain of purity of sentiment and

language: it is the idealized history of that period, and those intervals of his life which were dedicated to love. His apotheosis of Beatrice in Paradise, and the gradations of his own love and her loveliness, by which as by steps he feigns himself to have ascended to the throne of the Supreme Cause, is the most glorious imagination of modern poetry . . . The [*Paradiso*] is a perpetual hymn to everlasting love.[9]

Even so, the poem unfinished at Shelley's death, *The Triumph of Life*, shows a new note of realism in Shelley's work derived from a fresh study of the *Inferno*.

We may turn then to a comparison of Shelley's 'love which paves' and Dante's 'amor che move', conceptions which may be said to be at the centre of each poet's work. In Mrs Shelley's words:

[Shelley] never mentioned Love but he shed a grace borrowed from his own nature, that scarcely any other poet has bestowed, on that passion . . . he spoke of it as the law of life . . . In his eyes it was the essence of our being, and all woe and pain arose from the war made against it by selfishness, or insensibility, or mistake.[10]

One can set beside this the famous Dantean declaration: 'I' mi son un che, quando/Amor mi spira, noto, e a quel modo/ch'e' ditta dentro vo significando' ('I am one who, when Love breathes in me, takes note, and goes affirming what he dictates to me inwardly') (*Purg.* XXIV.52–4), but, whereas the manifestations of *Amor* in Dante are gathered together into one great synthesis and, as Shelley points out, 'ascend' from the love of Beatrice to the universal love, Shelley's own work, indeed like his life, shows the problems of fitting love for an individual woman into a wider social and spiritual framework; problems which are exploited in *Epipsychidion* for their dramatic effect, as we shall see. This tension between the personal and universal love is also evident in *The Revolt of Islam*, where Shelley is as much occupied with the romance of Laon and Cythna as he is with the rebellion they are at the centre of: their isolated lovemaking deep in fantastic caverns is no less congenial a subject to him than the celebrations of fellowship among the liberated peoples at the end of canto V; and the eventual failure of the rebellion seems more than compensated for by the paradise the lovers sail to after death in 'The Temple of the Spirit', as the poem ends. We must not forget that Shelley had barely half the life-allowance of Dante in which to 'synthesise' his various ideals; one cannot calculate what he would have achieved had he lived on, though one of his most famous admirers posited his performing a complete *volte-face* and embracing Christianity.[11]

The Revolt of Islam takes us to the crux of the Shelley–Dante question, projecting as it does man's happiness and freedom on earth as the result of the abolition of all external authority and the forgiveness of one's enemies:

> the chastened will
> Of virtue sees that justice is the light
> Of love, and not revenge, and terror and despite.
> (V.XXXIV)

In Dante things are not so straightforward: the first time we come across justice and love referred to together in the *Commedia* is in the inscription above Hell-gate: 'Giustizia mosse il mio alto fattore;/ fecemi la divina podestate,/la somma sapïenza e 'l primo amore' ('Justice moved my high maker; the divine power, the consummate wisdom and the first love made me') (*Inf.* III.4–6). This conception of justice has frequently outraged readers of Dante, both in the Romantic period and since.[12] Shelley himself, however, nowhere expresses such a reaction, even though attacks on the concept of Hell – which he regarded as an authoritarian fiction – are loud and frequent in his work (see for example *Queen Mab* IV.208–17). He managed to enjoy the *Purgatorio* and *Paradiso* without being unduly worried by the *Inferno* because, as *A Defence of Poetry* shows, he worked out a theory of poetry that accommodated what he called such 'distorted notions' (*A Defence*, p. 289); and indeed the need to accommodate precisely the *Inferno* was probably an important stimulus in Shelley's theorising.

One might say that from the beginning, if we look at *Queen Mab* and its Notes, the need for such an accommodation is present in Shelley's blistering attack on Christianity: 'Milton's poem alone will give permanency to the remembrance of its absurdities' (Notes, p. 821). More specifically the defence of 'Necessity! thou mother of the world!' in the Notes against the 'advocates of free-will' (pp. 809–12), among whom Dante – whose work was unknown to Shelley at the time – is a major figure (see *Purg.* XVI.67–84), hardly points to a future rapprochement between the two. Love and authority of any kind are affirmed to be incompatible: 'Love withers under constraint: its very essence is liberty: it is compatible neither with obedience, jealousy, nor fear' (p. 806), whereas for Dante love has to be regulated by obedience, since man is liable to be attracted towards the wrong things 'se guida o fren non torce suo amore' ('unless guide or rein directs his love') (*Purg.* XVI.93). Dante's love, of course, is ultimately directed at a Being whose existence Shelley denied but whom he made use of as a personification of tyranny *against* whom love is pitted; this rebelliousness is suggested as the cause of Prince Athanase's 'mysterious grief':

> God's displeasure, like a darkness, fell
> On souls like his, which owned no higher law
> Than love; love calm, steadfast, invincible
>
> By mortal fear or supernatural awe . . .
>
> (ll. 94–7)

It must be said, though, that Shelley's unfavourable conception of a God 'Girt round with storms and shadows . . .' (*The Revolt of Islam* x.xl) is Miltonic; yet even the radiance of the *Paradiso* embodies a hierarchical system Shelley could scarcely have approved of, for his 'own heart' told him that 'Love makes all things equal' (*Epipsychidion* ll. 126–7). But there are degrees of nearness to God in the *Paradiso*, as Beatrice explains: the blessed 'differentemente han dolce vita/per sentir più e men l'etterno spiro' ('have different shares in the sweet life, through feeling the eternal breath less and more') (IV.35–6), and the 'dolce vita', as Piccarda has previously pointed out, involves precisely the acquiescence in a 'higher law' which Shelley's heroes reject unconditionally:

> Anzi è formale ad esto beato *esse*
> tenersi dentro a la divina voglia,
> per ch'una fansi nostre voglie stesse.

(Rather it is the essence of this blessed existence that we keep within the bounds of the divine will, so that our own wills are made one.)

(III.79–81)

Indeed, it is hardly necessary to spell out the absolute contrast between the poet whose major work insists on the necessity of political and spiritual authority and obedience to them and the one who adored 'Eldest of things, divine Equality!' (*The Revolt of Islam* v.li.3) and detested all obedience, seen as 'Bane of all genius, virtue, freedom, truth' (*Queen Mab* III.178). The contrast is clearest in *Queen Mab* and its Notes where Shelley's attention is firmly focussed on political denunciations and remedies: if man had followed 'the impulses of unerring nature', including a natural, that is vegetarian, diet (Notes, pp. 807, 826ff), then his 'freeborn soul' would never have fallen victim to the 'oppressors' heel' of priests and kings that tramples it in *The Revolt of Islam* (VIII.vii). Institutions like marriage and religion were the mechanisms of a tyrannical government and had no place originally in the uncorrupted natural order to which Shelley desired a return. As Shelley got older he had reservations about *Queen Mab*, arising in part no doubt from his reading of Plato and Dante: 'in all that concerns moral and political speculation, as well as in the subtler discriminations of metaphysical and religious doctrine, it is . . . crude and immature'. But he remained 'a devoted enemy to religious, political and domestic oppression', and thus held to the notion of the 'freeborn soul' (*Letters*, II, 304–5; quoted in *Poetical Works*, p. 838).

Dante, of course, believed the soul was freeborn too, but in a very specific way: it had the freedom to choose between right and wrong and thus to decide where it spent eternity. In order for the 'libero arbitrio' to exercise its choice wisely it needs law and instruction, the *freno*. Dante had no belief in the possibility of returning to 'unerring nature':

> Esce di mano a lui che la vagheggia
> prima che sia, a guisa di fanciulla
> che piangendo e ridendo pargoleggia,
> l'anima semplicetta che sa nulla,
> salvo che, mossa da lieto fattore,
> volontier torna a ciò che la trastulla.
> Di picciol bene in pria sente sapore;
> quivi s'inganna, e dietro ad esso corre,
> se guida o fren non torce suo amore.

(From the hand of him who delights in it before its creation the simple little soul comes, like a child both laughing and crying and knowing nothing except to turn willingly to that which pleases it, having been created by a happy maker. In trivial joys it first takes pleasure; here it falls into error, and runs after them unless guide or rein directs its love.)

(*Purg*. XVI.85–93)

Only under a universal emperor, as Marco Lombardo goes on to tell Dante, can the 'legge per fren porre' ('law that puts a rein') on the *arbitrio* be enforced properly, a theory spelt out much more fully in the *Monarchia* which stresses the need for a political system that preserves 'hec libertas [arbitrii] sive principium hoc totius nostre libertatis [quod] est maximum donum humane nature a Deo collatum' ('this liberty of the will or foundation of all our liberty which is the greatest gift assigned by God to humanity') (I.xii.6). Monarchy was a term that particularly attracted Shelley's loathing; although both poets shared an aversion to the crowned heads of their own day, Shelley also, of course, had no affection for the Dantean ideal of Imperial Rome.

Before turning to *A Defence of Poetry*, which also manages to be, in Corrado Zacchetti's words, a 'difesa di Dante' ('defence of Dante'),[13] we may look at *Epipsychidion*, which draws on Dante's presentation of Beatrice in the *Vita Nuova* and the *Commedia* in the interests of Shelley's own conception of love. The poem takes little note of the extended significance Beatrice comes to have for Dante in his mature work and has the effect of dislodging her from her Christian setting; though Dante feigned through her 'to have ascended to the throne of the Supreme Cause' as Shelley said in *A Defence*, Shelley's own hero founders on his journey, partly because he has no very clear idea where he might be going, his failure in this sense constituting the poem's tremendous, Icarus-type conclusion:

> Woe is me!
> The wingèd words on which my soul would pierce
> Into the height of Love's rare Universe,
> Are chains of lead around its flight of fire –
> I pant, I sink, I tremble, I expire!
>
> (ll. 587–91)

Emilia is a 'Seraph of Heaven!' (l. 21), just as Dante, to choose a quatrain from one of the most famous sonnets of the *Vita Nuova*, celebrated Beatrice –

> Ella si va, sentendosi laudare,
> benignamente d'umiltà vestuta;
> e par che sia una cosa venuta
> de cielo in terra a miracol mostrare.

(She goes along, hearing herself praised, clothed benignly in humility; and seems something come from heaven to earth to demonstrate a miracle.)

(XXVI.6)

– but there is a deliberate quality of excess in Shelley's descriptions which contrasts with the smooth control of Dante's 'dolce stil' as

Epipsychidion gets to work on raising both Shelley's lady and his own imagination to a pitch of ungovernable excitement:

> Seraph of Heaven! too gentle to be human,
> Veiling beneath that radiant form of woman
> All that is insupportable in thee
> Of light, and love, and immortality!
> Sweet Benediction in the eternal Curse!
> Veiled Glory of this lampless Universe!
> Thou Moon beyond the clouds! Thou living Form
> Among the Dead! Thou Star above the Storm!
> Thou Wonder, and thou Beauty, and thou Terror!
> (ll. 21–9)

In spite then of Shelley's references to the *Vita Nuova* in his preface to the poem, his rapturousness is based much more on the *Paradiso*:

> See where she stands! a mortal shape indued
> With love and life and light and deity,
> And motion which may change but cannot die;
> An image of some bright Eternity;
> A shadow of some golden dream; a Splendour
> Leaving the third sphere pilotless . . .
> (ll. 112–17)

This attempt to find 'in a mortal image the likeness of what is perhaps eternal' (which Shelley later confessed to be an 'error' – *Letters*, II, 434), and thus to invest, in Dante's terms, the Beatrice of the *Vita Nuova* with the full glory of the Paradisal Beatrice, is exploited for its dramatic qualities in the poem: there are no 'gradations' on the ascent into 'Love's rare Universe' but one headlong rush; and the hero is burnt up in the process. Witnessing his end one is reminded of T. S. Eliot's comment on the *Vita Nuova*, which goes some way towards suggesting the great difference between it and *Epipsychidion*: 'There is . . . a practical sense of realities behind it, which is anti-romantic: not to expect more from *life* than it can give or more from *human* beings than they can give; to look to *death* for what life cannot give.'[14] The women in Shelley's poetry are often several sizes larger than life however: one is reminded of that extraordinary scene in *The Revolt of Islam* where Laon, surrounded by entire battalions of the tyrants' army, is snatched to safety by Cythna:

When on my foes a sudden terror came,
And they fled, scattering – lo! with reinless speed
A black Tartarian horse of giant frame
Comes trampling over the dead, the living bleed
Beneath the hoofs of that tremendous steed,
On which, like to an Angel, robed in white,
Sate one waving a sword; – the hosts recede
And fly, as through their ranks with awful might,
Sweeps in the shadow of eve that Phantom swift and bright . . .
(VI.xix)

None of Beatrice's earthly appearances was ever quite like this!

Shelley in fact goes on to acknowledge in *Epipsychidion* that his love should have been firmly based in either the here or the hereafter –

in the fields of Immortality
My spirit should at first have worshipped thine,
A divine presence in a place divine;
Or should have moved beside it on this earth,
A shadow of that substance, from its birth;
But not as now . . .
(ll. 133–8)

– but given that it partakes of both the physical and the transcendental to an equally passionate degree, it is appropriate that the island-refuge envisaged towards the end of the poem is situated, somewhat like Dante's *paradiso terrestre*, ''twixt Heaven, Air, Earth and Sea' (l. 475); that is, both in and out of time and place. The poem's conclusion describes a mystical union that in fact rehearses the mounting excitement and sudden expiration of physical love-making; the poem is nearer by now to Donne's 'Extasie' or Marvell's 'To his Coy Mistress' than to anything in Dante:

our veins [shall] beat together; and our lips
With other eloquence than words, eclipse
The soul that burns between them, and the wells
Which boil under our being's inmost cells,
The fountains of our deepest life, shall be
Confused in Passion's golden purity,
As mountain-springs under the morning sun.
We shall become the same, we shall be one
Spirit within two frames, oh! wherefore two?
One passion in twin-hearts, which grows and grew,
Till like two meteors of expanding flame,
Those spheres instinct with it become the same,

Touch, mingle, are transfigured; ever still
Burning, yet ever inconsumable:
In one another's substance finding food,
Like flames too pure and light and unimbued
To nourish their bright lives with baser prey,
Which point to Heaven and cannot pass away:
One hope within two wills, one will beneath
Two overshadowing minds, one life, one death,
One Heaven, one Hell, one immortality,
And one annihilation. Woe is me!
The wingèd words on which my soul would pierce
Into the height of Love's rare Universe,
Are chains of lead around its flight of fire –
I pant, I sink, I tremble, I expire!

(ll. 566–91)

The climax of the poem is a magnificent rhetorical jumble of life, death, Heaven, Hell, and so forth, comprising an effort to find something large enough to define a love that would outweigh everything, just as a variety of rhetorical tropes were tried upon Emilia at the start of the 'flight': 'Thou Wonder, and thou Beauty, and thou Terror!' (l. 29). Whatever this love is, it is certainly anarchical: the hero expires amidst a defiant attempt to confound the distinctions of Christian cosmology. Shelley's 'unfortunate friend' would no doubt have been a great admirer of Paolo and Francesca.

Epipsychidion is then a good example of Shelley's use of elements from Dante's work to create a whole that is entirely dissimilar. Richard E. Brown has recently examined the question at greater length, but obscures the significance of Shelley's 'mis-handling' of the Beatrice theme by his own confusion about Beatrice's significance. Thus, discussing Shelley's translation of a stanza from 'Voi, che 'ntendendo il terzo ciel movete' ('You, who through understanding move the third heaven') (*Conv.* II) prefixed to the poem, he notes: 'Dante's third heaven is occupied, of course, by the blessed who practise the kind of love the Shelleyan speaker aspires to realize between himself and Emily; she, like Beatrice, is briefly figured as a native of this sphere who has temporarily descended to appear before the questing poet.'[15] 'The kind of love the Shelleyan speaker aspires to realize' is precisely what is in question in the poem, however; whatever it is, it is extremely unlikely that Dante's blessed practise it, and, although Emilia is addressed as 'a

Splendour/leaving the third sphere pilotless', it is certainly not the third sphere the hero has ambitions of returning to: Shelley may have 'borrowed' Dante's 'donna' but he has not borrowed his cosmology. Moreover, Shelley's own extremely impressive cosmological imagery in *Epipsychidion* (ll. 345–83) is an allegory of the *ménage à trois* or even *à quatre* Shelley posits in the poem, a proposal more obvious in the far more prosaic earlier drafts and prefaces (*Poetical Works*, pp. 424–30). It is in justification of wanting to extend his female household –

> I never was attached to that great sect,
> Whose doctrine is, that each one should select
> Out of the crowd a mistress or a friend,
> And all the rest, though fair and wise, commend
> To cold oblivion . . .
>
> (ll. 149–53)

– that Shelley uses Dante's description of love in the following section of the poem, in the lines beginning 'True Love in this differs from gold and clay,/That to divide is not to take away' (ll. 160–1), the lines that so 'gravelled' Eliot.[16] Shelley's statement is inspired by Virgil's description of the relationship between the blessed in *Purgatorio* xv: the 'caritate' they enjoy grows rather than diminishes with the growth in the number of those who partake of it, as opposed to what happens in the division of earthly goods:

> Perché s'appuntano i vostri disiri
> dove per compagnia parte si scema,
> invidia move il mantaco a' sospiri.
> Ma se l'amor de la spera suprema
> torcesse in suso il disiderio vostro,
> non vi sarebbe al petto quella tema;
> ché, per quanti si dice più lì 'nostro',
> tanto possiede più di ben ciascuno,
> e più di caritate arde in quel chiostro.

(Because your desires are centred where the divided parts are each less than the whole, envy prompts you to sigh. But if love of the highest sphere turned your desire upwards, there would be no such anxiety in your hearts, since there the more there are to say 'ours', the more good each individual possesses, and the more charity burns in that cloister.) (ll. 49–57)

Shelley's use of this idea in *Epipsychidion* seems hardly dissimilar to an adulterer's use of the text 'Love thy neighbour' as he climbs the garden-fence.

I believe, however, that the hero is consciously shown by Shelley as a sort of Dante in wild disarray, and that this use of a fictitious author for the poem enabled him to participate in its imaginative sexual assault while reserving judgement about the 'philosophy' of love the poem expresses; as soon as it was written he told Ollier it belonged to a portion of him 'already dead' (*Letters*, II, 262–3). In *The Triumph of Life*, the suggestion of passion's destructiveness found at the end of *Epipsychidion* (which forms an interesting contrast to the 'naturalism' of *Queen Mab*) is taken up again: Shelley witnesses 'Maidens and youths ... Bending within each other's atmosphere', who

> Kindle invisibly – and as they glow,
> Like moths by light attracted and repelled,
> Oft to their bright destruction come and go ...
> (ll. 152–4)

These are, like Paolo and Francesca, 'on ... rapid whirlwinds spun' (l. 144), but the destruction remains 'bright': Shelley had not quite relinquished his belief in the splendour of what Dante calls 'il folle amore' ('mad [i.e., sensual] love') (*Par.* VIII.2). And indeed it is this splendour, the hero's reckless, glorious and impossible attempt to 'Beacon the rocks on which high hearts are wrecked' (l. 148) that constitutes *Epipsychidion*; its function is clearly not to re-enact the Dantean love its preface refers us to. The last poem we shall be looking at that claims a connexion with the *Vita Nuova* is Eliot's *Ash-Wednesday*; the fact that this could hardly be more dissimilar to *Epipsychidion* shows the extraordinary variety of influences Dante's work has exerted.

Dante's understanding of 'the secret things of love' forms then a sizable part of Shelley's admiration for him, removed, however, from its Christian context. Because this context is absent in *Epipsychidion* one has difficulty in accepting Emilia as an 'authentic' Beatrice; that is, accepting her as the compounded incarnation of Christian–Platonic divinity the narrator would see her as in the first half of the poem; the tributes showered on her seem mainly a preparatory stage in the imagined seduction with which the poem closes. The Victorians, as we shall see, also found Beatrice difficult to resist, again as long as she was first deprived of her roles in the

Commedia as teacher and as representation of divine Wisdom, though the incorporation of her into their pictures of romance is devoid of *Epipsychidion*'s sexual–Promethean energy.

Another major component in Shelley's admiration for Dante centres round the question of 'freedom' already referred to. Whatever their vast differences in outlook, there were elements in Dante's thought Shelley could respond to without reserve: thus Dante's adoration of Beatrice is saluted in *A Defence* as a stage in the recognition of the equality of women (p. 289); Shelley also follows the Protestant tradition of describing Dante as 'the first religious reformer, [whom] Luther surpassed . . . rather in the rudeness and acrimony, than in the boldness of his censures, of papal usurpation'.[17] Dante was also 'the first awakener of entranced Europe; he created a language, in itself music and persuasion, out of a chaos of inharmonious barbarisms' (p. 291). Yet how, we may ask, in this 'difesa' of Dante does Shelley excuse Dante's Hell and his Christianity generally, in an essay which includes, for example, another attack on the idea of free-will (p. 285)? The following passage supplies the answer:

> The distorted notions of invisible things which Dante and his rival Milton have idealized are merely the mask and the mantle in which these great poets walk through eternity enveloped and disguised. It is a difficult question to determine how far they were conscious of the distinction which must have subsisted in their minds between their own creeds and that of the people. Dante at least appears to wish to mark the full extent of it by placing Riphaeus, whom Virgil calls *justissimus unus*, in Paradise, and observing a most heretical caprice in his distribution of rewards and punishments. (pp. 289–90)

Whether the placing of Riphaeus in Paradise, even taken with other examples of Dante's 'heretical caprice', can be said to outweigh his orthodoxy, never mind his Christianity, is hardly worth discussing; rather like the hero of *Epipsychidion*, Dante is seen as confounding the distinctions between Heaven and Hell, a game that satisfied his capriciousness. Dante's attacks on Pope and clergy, motivated by a desire for reform and hardly, of course, for abolition, have always lent themselves to those who would see a *Dante hérétique, révolutionnaire et socialiste*, to quote the title of Eugène Aroux's nineteenth-century study (Paris, 1854). One immediately thinks of Blake's comment on the Milton of *Paradise Lost*, 'a true Poet and of the Devils party without knowing it', an attitude that strikingly anticipates Shelley's position in *A Defence* and one that has been described by M. H. Abrams as 'the earliest instance of that radical mode of romantic polysemism in which the latent personal significance of a narrative poem is found not merely to underlie, but to contradict and cancel the surface intention'.[18] One can establish Dante as a 'true Poet' in this Romantic sense by attending to his denunciations in the *Commedia* rather than to its illustrations of his orthodoxy; thus one might highlight his severity to Pope Nicholas III in *Inferno* XIX (90–114) rather than his going down on his knees to Adrian V in *Purgatorio* XIX (127).

But Shelley's defence of Dante is not based ultimately on the idea of him as simply a heretic; it rather centres round the fundamental Platonism of *A Defence* whereby 'A poet participates in the eternal, the infinite, and the one; as far as relates to his conceptions, time and place and number are not' (p. 279). Thus,

> Every epoch, under names more or less specious, has deified its peculiar errors; revenge is the naked idol of the worship of a semi-barbarous age . . . But a poet considers the vices of his contemporaries as the temporary dress in which his creations must be arrayed and which cover without concealing the eternal proportions of their beauty . . . Few poets of the highest class have chosen to exhibit the beauty of their conceptions in its naked truth and splendour; and it is doubtful whether the alloy of costume, habit, &c., be not necessary to temper this planetary music for mortal ears.
>
> (p. 282)

Poetic compositions consist of both a 'temporary dress', or 'mask and mantle', and a naked, eternal truth; since for Shelley 'The great secret of morals is love, or a going out of our own nature and an identification of ourselves with the beautiful which exists in thought, action, or person, not our own' (pp. 282–3), whatever prompts to the beautiful can be considered eternal, and whatever does not the inevitable 'alloy' of poetry rather than the poetry itself. This leads to the splendid concept of 'that great poem which all poets, like the co-operating thoughts of one great mind, have built up since the beginning of the world' (p. 287), in which the unco-operating thoughts, as mere temporal alloy, have rusted away. A poet, by definition, belongs to a co-operative.

Of all this Dante may have been aware in writing the *Commedia*, though 'It is a difficult question to determine . . .' In any case it is not particularly important that he should have been:

The persons in whom this power [of poetry] resides may often, as far as regards many portions of their nature, have little apparent correspondence with that spirit of good of which they are the ministers. But even while they deny and abjure, they are yet compelled to serve the power which is seated upon the throne of their own soul. (p. 297)

Finally, since poetry participates in this eternal 'spirit of good' it must be variable under earthly conditions: 'Time . . . forever develops new and wonderful applications of the eternal truth which it contains' (p. 281); poets write 'the words which express what they understand not . . .' (p. 297).[19]

It is clear then that, whereas the *Paradiso* partakes of 'the eternal, the infinite, and the one', as Shelley specifically points out (p. 279), those elements of the *Commedia* he did not take to, its justice, its theology, its didacticism – 'Didactic poetry is my abhorrence'[20] – caused him no real concern. Rather, the *Commedia* offered him a prime example of the conjunction of the eternal and temporal, 'the planetary music' and its 'disguise'. There have indeed been some 'new and wonderful applications' of the matter of the *Commedia*, as we shall see; one thinks particularly of the 'symbolist' interpretation of W. B. Yeats, the origins of which have some connexion with Shelley's essay. It is also interesting to compare Shelley's position with Croce's attempt to divide the *Commedia* into two elements of temporary and permanent value, only the latter of which can again be termed 'poetry': certainly the conclusion of *La poesia di Dante* is strikingly Shelleyan:

. . . Dante non è piú Dante nella sua definita individualità, ma è quella voce meravigliata e commossa, che tramanda l'anima umana nella perpetuamente ricorrente creazione del mondo. Ogni differenza, a questo punto, svanisce, e risuona solo quell'eterno e sublime ritornello, quella voce che ha il medesmo timbro fondamentale in tutti i grandi poeti ed artisti, sempre nuova, sempre antica, accolta da noi con sempre rinnovata trepidazione e gioia: la Poesia senza aggettivo.

(. . . Dante is no longer Dante in his definite individuality, but is that marvelling and impassioned voice which the human soul transmits in the perpetually recurring creation of the world. Every difference, at this point, vanishes, and the only sound is that eternal and sublime refrain, that voice which has the same fundamental timbre in all the great poets and artists, always new, always ancient, received by us with a trepidation and joy that is always renewed: Poetry itself, with no adjective.) (p. 163)

If *A Defence* illustrates one method of regarding Dante as a 'progressive' poet, *Prometheus Unbound* includes another, and one which was widely diffused among Shelley's contemporaries. At the climax of Act III the Spirit of the Hour tells of man's regeneration after Jupiter's fall:

> The loathsome mask has fallen, the man remains
> Sceptreless, free, uncircumscribed, but man
> Equal, unclassed, tribeless, and nationless,
> Exempt from awe, worship, degree, the king
> Over himself; just, gentle, wise . . .
>
> (III.iv.193–7)

This alludes to a similar great moment of regeneration in the *Commedia*, when Dante has completed his understanding and rejection of the various types of sin and is thus ready to enter the *paradiso terrestre*. Virgil tells him:

> Non aspettar mio dir più né mio cenno;
> libero, dritto e sano è tuo arbitrio,
> e fallo fora non fare a suo senno:
> per ch'io te sovra te corono e mitrio.

(Expect no longer any words or signs from me; your will is free, upright and whole, and it would be a fault not to do as it judges; so that I crown and mitre you over yourself.) (*Purg.* XXVII.139–42)

It is the idea of self-kingship that is especially dear to Shelley in his poetry, together with its corollary demanding the abolition of all external authority. The vain insignia of Empire, the ruins of ancient Rome, the ambition of Napoleon who is one of those in *The Triumph of Life* whose 'lore/Taught them not this, to know themselves' (ll. 211–12), are contrasted throughout his verse with 'the kings of thought', who, unlike Empires and those who would set them up, are 'of the past . . . all that cannot pass away' (*Adonais* XLVIII.432), Keats's having died at Rome offering Shelley a marvellous opportunity to exploit such a contrast. The conclusion of the sonnet 'Political Greatness' is especially pertinent:

> Man who man would be,
> Must rule the empire of himself; in it
> Must be supreme, establishing his throne
> On vanquished will, quelling the anarchy
> Of hopes and fears, being himself alone.
>
> (p. 642)

Shelley's politicisation of Dante's concept of freedom here once more obscures its moral significance: Dante is again concerned with the 'libero arbitrio' and unlike Prometheus does not become exempt from 'awe, worship, degree' at the moment of liberation but in fact becomes precisely fitted for them, ready to take his place in God's 'vera città': ''n la sua volontade è nostra pace' ('in his will is our peace'), as Piccarda says in a famous line from a speech already referred to (*Par.* III.85); or as the paradox is stated in the second Collect of the Anglican service of morning prayer: 'O God . . . whose service is perfect freedom'. It would have been more convenient for the Promethean interpretation of the *Commedia* had Dante's journey concluded at the end of the *Purgatorio*, that is precisely in the earthly paradise, where the re-made individual has not yet been received into the hierarchy of Paradise proper; this would also have solved the plight of Rossetti and several of his contemporaries who were hurried on from an affecting reunion of lovers into a region where Beatrice takes on the role of Dante's theological instructor and is eventually relinquished by him anew. The two lovers being reunited on the top of a mountain after a ten-year separation provides the ideal Romantic scenario, a sort of mediaeval *Wuthering Heights*.

For Dante, as already remarked, the idea of the individual and the Empire were not mutually exclusive but complementary: only under the jurisdiction of the latter could the 'arbitrio' exist unimpeded and the greatest number of men reach the earthly paradise. One of his arguments in the *Monarchia* is based on the idea of man as microcosm: just as the 'vis . . . intellectualis est regulatrix' ('intellectual power is ruler') in him (I.v.4), so in the world there must be one force ruling the others. For Shelley, however, the Roman emperors were 'A race of despicable usurpers' and Caesar's assassins 'holy patriots',[21] a belief carried over into *The Triumph of Life* where he castigates

> the heirs
> Of Caesar's crime, from him to Constantine
> . . .
> And Gregory and John, and men divine,
>
> Who rose like shadows between man and God
> (ll. 283–9)

in a poem which encapsulates both Shelley's admiration for the stylistic features of Dante's poetry and his resistance to Dante's thought.

Prometheus then, representing the 'soul of man' (III.i.5), makes a journey parallel to Dante's, towards a freedom where

> men walked
> One with the other even as spirits do,
> None fawned, none trampled; hate, disdain, or fear,
> Self-love or self-contempt, on human brows
> No more inscribed, as o'er the gate of hell,
> 'All hope abandon ye who enter here'
>
> (III.iv.131–6)

and which is celebrated, as we began by saying, in the paradisal Act IV. Dante's own progress from Hell to Heaven takes on a similar dimension in much Romantic thinking, as long as his own definition of freedom is, as it were, 'de-Christianised'. As Ezra Pound put it, Dante's journey is 'a symbol of mankind's struggle upward out of ignorance into the clear light of philosophy',[22] an observation Dante would have had no quarrel with until, perhaps, he asked for a closer definition of what modern writers like Pound and Shelley understood as constituting 'ignorance' and 'light'. One might claim that the Romantic period 'discovered' Dante *personaggio* to the same extent that they ceased to be interested in the ideas of Dante *poeta*; as Eliot said, we have to go back to the eighteenth century to find a readership that was interested in a poem's ideas rather than in its imagery or its music, or, one might add, rather than in its hero.[23] In Mrs Shelley's words, 'the subject Shelley loved best to dwell on was the image of One warring with the Evil Principle' (*Poetical Works*, p. 271), and it is easy to see how the dramatic episodes of Dante's journey must have fired his imagination; for example, in the first stanza of the 'Ode to Liberty', his soul, like Ianthe's in *Queen Mab*, is 'rapped' up beyond 'the remotest sphere of living flame' by 'The Spirit's whirlwind' (ll. 10–13, p. 604), an episode reminiscent to my ears at least of Dante's vision of being borne aloft 'infino al foco' ('as far as the [sphere of] fire') by the eagle in *Purgatorio* IX (19–33), although it rises, as it were, to much greater altitudes. This kind of reaction to the *Commedia* is also implied in Foscolo's observation that 'in tanta moltitudine d'episodi, e di scene d'infinita diversità nella lunga azione della *Divina Commedia*, il primo, unico, vero protagonista è il Poeta' ('in such a great multitude of episodes, and of scenes of infinite diversity in the long action of the *Commedia*, the first, only, and true protagonist is the Poet').[24] Virgil's famous description of Dante's mission at the beginning of the *Purgatorio*: 'libertà va cercando' ('he goes seeking liberty') (I.71), puts in an epigrammatic form the irresistible opportunities the *Commedia* provided of turning Dante into a Romantic freedom-fighter.[25] If even Mont Blanc could be seen in this way (though only of course to the initiate) –

> Thou hast a voice, great Mountain, to repeal
> Large codes of fraud and woe; not understood
> By all, but which the wise, and great, and good
> Interpret, or make felt, or deeply feel.
> ('Mont Blanc' ll. 80–3, p. 533)

– then the rather more articulate monument of Dante's poem had little chance of having its 'voice' go unheard or uninterpreted. The narrator in Browning's *Pauline* describes his admiration for Shelley in words that can be applied to the Romantics' response to Dante: 'my choice fell/Not so much on a system as a man',[26] but in the *Commedia* the man at the centre of it can be said to co-exist with the Catholic system of thought, and the two can be divorced from each other only at the cost of impairing the poem's uniqueness.

All this is not to deny that the Romantics had every reason to see the great individuality of the *Commedia* and the great individual within it.[27] Dante entered the Romantic period with a reputation as one of history's great trouble-shooters, so to speak, with his *Monarchia* still on the papal Index and with eighteenth-century Jesuit commentaries on and editions of the *Commedia* heavily censorious and censored.[28] Foscolo's contrast between the popularity of Dante and Petrarch is especially memorable, the latter's poetry being

> admirably calculated for a Jesuits' college, since it inspires devotion, mysticism, and retirement, and enervates the minds of youth. But since the late revolutions have stirred up other passions, and a different system of education has been established, Petrarch's followers have rapidly diminished; and those of Dante have written poems more suited to rouse the public spirit of Italy. Dante applied his poetry to the vicissitudes of his own time, when liberty was making her dying struggle against tyranny; and he descended to the tomb with the last heroes of the middle age.[29]

'Poems more suited to rouse the public spirit of Italy'. This is of course the Dante of Byron's *The Prophecy of Dante*, though this poem again has its own misleading portrayal of Dante's politics. In the last resort, as in Byron's summing up of Dante's importance as 'the poet of liberty' for the age of revolutions ('Persecution, exile, the dread of a foreign grave, could not shake his principles'),[30] it is not exactly what Dante said but the spirit in which he said it that counts: the majestic, unbowed, indeed 'Promethean' personality-type who becomes, in a rather more 'fallen' form, the Byronic hero of the following chapter. This is the type of figure we find applauded in *Queen Mab*:

> him of resolute and unchanging will;
> Whom, nor the plaudits of a servile crowd,
> Nor the vile joys of tainting luxury,
> Can bribe to yield his elevated soul
> To Tyranny or Falsehood . . .
>
> (V.171–5)

Dante himself might not have been altogether out of sympathy with this hero-worship directed at his spirit rather than at his system. After all, in his own poem he elevates the republican Cato to the guardianship of Purgatory as an *exemplum* of fidelity to one's own ideals at the cost of death: in Natalino Sapegno's words, Cato's suicide is an 'exemplum . . . in nome di quell'idea di libertà, che nel poeta cristiano si dilata, dall'originario valore strettamente politico, fino a coincidere con la libertà dell'arbitrio' ('*exemplum* . . . in the name of that idea of liberty, which broadens in the Christian poet from its original strictly political significance until it coincides with the liberty of the will').[31] Behind the 'valore strettamente politico' of the *Commedia* we can find plenty of instances where the Romantics could discover adumbrations of their own ideal of personality, of man 'being himself alone', as in one of Virgil's reproofs to Dante, or rather, in one of Dante's self-reproofs:

> Vien dietro a me, e lascia dir le genti:
> sta come torre ferma, che non crolla
> già mai la cima per soffiar di venti.

(Follow after me, and leave people to talk: stand like the firm tower, which never bends its head when the wind blows.) (*Purg*. V.13–15)

Here we have an anticipation of one of the most famous of Romantic images, as expressed in *Queen Mab*:

> O human Spirit! spur thee to the goal
> Where virtue fixes universal peace,
> And midst the ebb and flow of human things,
> Show somewhat stable, somewhat certain still,
> A lighthouse o'er the wild of dreary waves.
> (VIII.53–7)

And as we noted, Dante even finds his liberty in that peculiarly hallowed spot of Romanticism, the top of a mountain.

Thus the first great individual is celebrated by a later individualistic age. In Hazlitt's words: 'Dante was the father of modern poetry . . . His poem is the first great step from Gothic darkness and barbarism; and the struggle of thought in it to burst the thraldom in which the human mind had been so long held, is felt in every page.'[32] Finally then, Dante's fight for freedom in the *Commedia* is not a question of religious or political affiliation but of historical evolution: it is the modern era casting off the tyranny of mediaeval anonymity. This position, which underlies *A Defence of Poetry* – 'the first awakener of entranced Europe' – marks out the ground on which the main battle between the various 'poets' Dantes' has been fought over the last two centuries; that is, over the questions of Dante's relation to his own age and the relation of that age to the modern one: was Dante the prototype of the modern or the quintessence of the mediaeval? Is his poem the first great step or the consummation of a series of prior steps? The answers to these questions have depended on the nature of the relationships the poets answering them have felt to exist between themselves and their own age and immediate predecessors: they have sought in Dante's situation a mirror for their own.

As far, then, as the Romantics are concerned, the monarchism of the *Commedia* fades into insignificance within the dramatic setting Dante has created for it, and Dante, with all his nostalgia for the authoritarian past, becomes the prophet of the radical future, from the Shelleyan ideas examined here to the *Risorgimento* movement in Italy.[33] Auerbach has presented the paradoxical outcome of the *Commedia*'s religious concerns in similar terms: by virtue of Dante's

> immediate and admiring sympathy with man, the principle, rooted in the divine order, of the indestructibility of the whole historical and individual man turns *against* that order, makes it subservient to its own purposes, and obscures it. The image of man eclipses the image of God. Dante's work

made man's Christian-figural being a reality, and destroyed it in the very process of realizing it. The tremendous pattern was broken by the overwhelming power of the images it had to contain.[34]

Or, in Eliot's peculiar emphasis, 'in Dante's Hell souls are not deadened, as they mostly are in life . . .'[35] Escaping from the Christian-figural framework that gave them their birth, Dante's characters – Francesca, Ulysses, Ugolino – become the inspiration and the idols of a modern literary realism whose interest centres on this life, not the next, and who have even been celebrated, with their context ignored or forgotten, as the heroes of the poem. And nowhere in this unwitting assertion of modern individualism did Dante have more success, and thus more failure, than in the creation of himself, Dante Alighieri. Hence the choice of epigraph for this chapter.

Any attempt to find specific similarities between the political positions of Dante and Shelley or Byron would seem unfruitful; it has however been attempted by Oswald Doughty who, although noting that 'Dante's political and religious beliefs, and especially the principles underlying them, were almost the extreme opposite of those held by the romantic poets', still feels the monarch Dante requires is so close in his 'idealistic' nature to the 'ideal populace of high-minded voters' desired by the 'democratic romantics' that 'the ultimate ideal result would be the same!' Dante and the Romantics only differed as to means rather than ends, since they both wanted man 'to enjoy the happiness which springs from the individual's freedom to realize his best potentialities . . . Ultimately then, Dante, though by no means in agreement with the romantics' faith in democracy, sufficiently shared their ideal political goal to justify their praise of him as a personification of their ideal of liberty . . .'[36] The problem remains, however, of believing that Dante and Shelley would have agreed over what man's 'best potentialities' are. Whatever the ambiguities of Dante's own position, in the *Commedia* at least one cannot divorce his politics from his religion: monarchical government would preserve that freedom in which man can properly attend to his religious concerns; without an imperial power to keep in check the squabblings over territory between cities, princes, kings and popes, and thus to keep the Church to its spiritual and educational roles, man falls into the idolatry of money-worship:

per che la gente, che sua guida vede
pur a quel ben fedire ond' ella è ghiotta,
di quel si pasce, e più oltre non chiede.

(so that the people, seeing their guide only trusting in that commodity they themselves are greedy for, feed on that and seek for nothing further.)
(*Purg.* XVI.100–2)[37]

Shelley never claims directly that Dante was a republican, though he certainly implies this and finds it convenient to suppress Dante's anti-republicanism.[38] Thus Dante was 'the Lucifer of that starry flock which in the thirteenth century shone forth from republican Italy, as from a heaven, into the darkness of the benighted world' (*A Defence*, p. 291). He considered Dante, Petrarch and Boccaccio as 'the productions of the vigour of the infancy of a new nation, as rivulets from the same spring as that which fed the greatness of the republics of Florence and Pisa, and which checked the influence of the German Emperors' (*Letters*, II, 122). There is nothing original in such an assertion: the three great *trecento* writers had often been welded together into a sort of literary triumvirate by Italian critics in the interests of various cultural or stylistic campaigns. For example, Martinelli describes the celebration of the triumvirate in the fifteenth century as part of a political programme developed by the Medici, to 'affermare l'importanza culturale fiorentina in Toscana' ('affirm the cultural importance of Florence in Tuscany') (*Dante*, p. 24); Florence's unwillingness to relinquish one of the jewels in its crown means, as it were, a posthumous recalling of Dante from exile and indeed a smoothing-over of the political differences between Dante and the city-state that that exile had produced; as everyone knows, far from 'check[ing] the influence of the German Emperors', Dante would have brought them into Italy to put a stop to the corruption and expansionism of Florence and the other powerful cities – see especially the famous apostrophe to 'serva Italia' in *Purgatorio* VI (76–151). But the qualities and ideas peculiar to each of the three writers were lost sight of in the celebration of their shared origin. Some lines by Poliziano, in a translation by William Roscoe which Shelley probably read, are a good expression of these Renaissance attitudes:

Nor ALIGHIERI, shall thy praise be lost,
Who from the confines of the Stygian coast,

As BEATRICE led thy willing steps along,
To realms of light and starry mansions sprung;
Nor PETRARCH thou, whose soul-dissolving strains
Rehearse, O love! thy triumphs and thy pains;
Nor HE, whose hundred tales the means impart,
To wind the secret snare around the heart,
Be these thy boast, O FLORENCE! these thy pride,
Thy sons! whose genius spreads thy glory wide.[39]

From the sixteenth century onwards the triumvirate tended to lose its political significance as Florence's power waned; it might be said that Dante's ideas became even more obscured as the three began to be celebrated as stylistic exemplars alone in controversy with those who would see the *quattro-* or *cinquecento* as the golden age of Italian style; thus Rolli in his reply to Voltaire upholds 'All three, the first, the best and the never-interrupted Standards of the [Italian] Language and the Stile'.[40] This is not to deny that simultaneously in the early nineteenth century the age-old polemic between 'Dantists' and 'Petrarchists' remained in a healthy state; this may be said to continue into the criticism of Pound, whose denigration of Petrarch is based on his weighing Dante in the opposite scale. This is no less true of his attacks on Milton, though the Romantics' verdict in this particular comparison was often given against Dante, unlike Pound's (and Eliot's).

When Shelley mentions the three writers together, as above, he is at bottom admiring Florence herself, who is addressed in 'Marenghi' as

. . . foster-nurse of man's abandoned glory
Since Athens, its great mother, sunk in splendour . . .

'The light-invested angel Poesy/Was drawn from the dim world to welcome thee', he adds (VII.29–34, p. 565).[41] Behind Florence lies Athens;[42] as opposed to Dante's belief in the practical Empire of Rome, Shelley's ideal in his poetry remains the 'intellectual empire' of Greece, as Mrs Shelley puts it in her notes to *Hellas* (p. 481):

. . . Greece and her foundations are
Built below the tide of war,
Based on the crystàlline sea
Of thought and its eternity;

Her citizens, imperial spirits,
  Rule the present from the past,
On all this world of men inherits
  Their seal is set.
(ll. 696–703)

Whether this empire is actually realisable in earthly terms is the question the conclusion of *Hellas* leaves us with:

Another Athens shall arise,
  And to remoter time
Bequeath, like sunset to the skies,
  The splendour of its prime;
And leave, if nought so bright may live,
All earth can take or Heaven can give.
(ll. 1084–9)

The fundamental difference that strikes one about Shelley's and Dante's productions as 'political poets' is in fact the division between poetry and practical politics in the one and their integration in the other. For Shelley it was not poetry's job to propose 'the direct enforcement of reform':

My purpose has hitherto been simply to familiarise the highly refined imagination of the more select classes of poetical readers with beautiful idealisms of moral excellence; aware that until the mind can love, and admire, and trust, and hope, and endure, reasoned principles of moral conduct are seeds cast upon the highway of life which the unconscious passenger tramples into dust, although they would bear the harvest of his happiness.
(Preface to *Prometheus Unbound*, p. 207)

As he states in the same Preface, he was planning 'a systematical history of what appear to me to be the genuine elements of human society', to be written, of course, in prose; and indeed no one who has read his *A Philosophical View of Reform*, for example, can doubt Shelley's interest in, and knowledge of, the practical questions he discusses there with his customarily formidable logic: parliamentary reform, the abolition of the national debt, the standing army, sinecures and tithes, the freedom of thought in religious affairs, and so on (*Shelley's Prose*, pp. 248–9). However, the beautiful egalitarian idealism of *Prometheus Unbound* forms a marked contrast to the *Commedia* which, frequently to the regret of modern writers who make shift to ignore Dante's didacticism, incorporates and makes explicit its author's monarchical beliefs, as, most obviously, in

Purgatorio xvi. Yet in the last resort the differences between Dante and Shelley go beyond their respective views about poetry's function towards an opposition that might be crudely labelled Aristotle versus Plato. That is, the 'immortal visitations' Shelley celebrates throughout his verse, the Fairy Queen in *Queen Mab*, the 'veilèd maid' of *Alastor* (l. 151), the 'Shape all light' in *The Triumph of Life* (l. 352), are images of 'the eternal, the infinite, and the one' manifesting itself under earthly conditions that can permit no more than a temporary vision of it, a fate also suggested for the renewed Athens in *Hellas*. Moreover, these visitations refer as much to Shelley's personal, as to his political, fantasies; they too can be termed 'images of solitude', to use Yeats's phrase:

Shelley . . . writes pamphlets, and dreams of converting the world or of turning man of affairs and upsetting governments, and yet returns again and again to these two images of solitude, a young man whose hair has grown white from the burden of his thoughts, an old man in some shell-strewn cave . . .[43]

In *The Revolt of Islam*, Shelley certainly seems more interested in the solitary lovers' 'warring with the Evil Principle' than in the state that is being warred for; more taken by the splendour of the morning-star amid darkness than by the day which is expected to follow it.

For Yeats, who read the *Commedia* very much under the influence of his reading of Shelley's poetry, Beatrice and the paradisal Rose of *Paradiso* xxx–xxxi functioned as 'images of solitude' for Dante too, but there is no sense of Dante seeking a refuge amongst his images in the same way as Mrs Shelley, rather exaggeratedly, describes her husband doing in her note on *The Witch of Atlas*:

Shelley shrunk instinctively from portraying human passion, with its mixture of good and evil, of disappointment and disquiet . . . he loved to shelter himself rather in the airiest flights of fancy, forgetting love and hate, and regret and lost hope, in such imaginations as borrowed their hues from sunrise or sunset, from the yellow moonshine or paly twilight . . . (p. 389)

Dante's court of Heaven is in no sense a 'shelter' where he may 'forget', but to the end forms a scathing contrast with the human society that should strive to resemble it:

> ïo, che al divino da l'umano,
> a l'etterno dal tempo era venuto,
> e di Fiorenza in popol giusto e sano,
> di che stupor dovea esser compiuto!

(I, who had come from the human to the divine, from time to eternity, and from Florence to a just and sane people, with what stupor must I have been filled!) (*Par.* XXXI.37–40)

Similarly, Beatrice is a different type of 'veilèd maid' from the apparition in *Alastor*: she may also be the mystical 'Being whom [the poet] loves' which the Preface to Shelley's poem describes, but beyond this Beatrice has what one may call a public, as well as a private, function, being the mouthpiece for a Theology which in its celebration of the kingdom of Heaven does not lose sight of earthly imperfections which indeed cause inhabitants of the *Paradiso*, like St Peter (canto XXVII), such concern. As Pound said, referring to the simple conviction of Dante's reply to Charles Martel's question in *Paradiso* VIII –

> 'Or dì: sarebbe il peggio
> per l'omo in terra, se non fosse cive?'
> 'Sì', rispuos'io; 'e qui ragion non cheggio'

('Now say: would it be an evil for man on earth if he were not a citizen?' 'Yes', I replied, 'and here I need no proof') (115–17)

– 'Dant' had it,/Some sense of civility . . .'[44]

Shelley had this sense too, but in his poetry he is always liable to present a very different kind of *Paradiso*, like the Elysian isle in *Epipsychidion*, or the 'windless bower . . ./Far from passion, pain and guilt' at the end of 'Lines Written among the Euganean Hills' (ll. 344–5, p. 558), together with endless descriptions of voyages in mystical seas and rivers by which these havens are reached. Dante in his younger days wrote the sonnet 'Guido, i' vorrei' (*Rime*, 9) which posits the magical voyage of a group of lovers away from the world's affairs; its effect on Shelley, who translated it (*Poetical Works*, pp. 725–6), is obvious from the mystical elopement and voyage with Emilia proposed in *Epipsychidion*, and Shelley actually quotes from the sonnet in a letter to her (*Letters*, II, 448). But Dante's mature *Paradiso* is not at all 'Shelleyan'; not solitary, pastoral and entranced, already half 'Pre-Raphaelite', but populous, civic and practical: 'tutta tua vision fa manifesta' ('make all your vision known'), as Cacciaguida tells Dante (XVII.128), a vision which is not something which severs Dante's involvement with the world, but one which emphasises and clarifies the fraud and corruption of one society from the illuminated viewpoint of another.

It is, however, important to realise that what one might term the 'Shelleyan Dante' becomes established in nineteenth-century thought, in part because Shelley himself comes to be seen primarily in terms of his apolitical concerns, in terms of his evocation of the 'Spirit of Solitude'. In this conception the *Paradiso* becomes a 'refuge' and Beatrice the 'solitary image' of the lost love of Dante's youth. This is so in Rossetti, and, as mentioned, in the much more sophisticated polemic of Yeats, and will involve us in some further discussion of the above issues in subsequent chapters.

In her note on *The Cenci*, Mrs Shelley expressed the wish that Shelley had continued his success with the drama by keeping to this more 'popular' type of production. However,

> the bent of his mind went the other way; and, even when employed on subjects whose interest depended on character and incident, he would start off in another direction, and leave the delineations of human passion, which he could depict in so able a manner, for fantastic creations of his fancy, or the expression of those opinions and sentiments, with regard to human nature and its destiny, a desire to diffuse which was the master passion of his soul.
> (p. 337)

The human passion of *The Cenci*, which Shelley's wife so much admired, seems to modern taste perhaps rather too clearly 'delineated'; but in Shelley's last poem, *The Triumph of Life*, we have a character who is arguably the most forceful of Shelley's dramatic creations precisely because of a certain dispassionate quality in his passion: Rousseau is similar to the souls in Dante's Hell who can have regrets but no repentance. It is here, as well as in the dialogue between Rousseau and the narrator, that we find the fruits of a fresh study of Dante in Shelley's verse, a study no doubt prompted by his reading of his friend Taaffe's *Comment* on the *Inferno* the previous year.[45] There is a new dispassionateness in Shelley's own survey of humanity in the poem, a 'sadder and wiser' Shelley perhaps less ready with his 'beautiful idealisms of moral excellence':

> Methought I sate beside a public way

> Thick strewn with summer dust, and a great stream
> Of people there was hurrying to and fro,
> Numerous as gnats upon the evening gleam,
>
> All hastening onward, yet none seemed to know
> Whither he went, or whence he came, or why
> He made one of the multitude, and so
>
> Was borne amid the crowd, as through the sky
> One of the million leaves of summer's bier . . .
> (ll. 43–51)

As Eliot put it, 'There is a precision of image and an economy here that is new to Shelley.'[46] When Eliot returned to the poem several years later as a testimony of 'what Dante has done, both for the style and for the soul, of a great English poet', he suggested it was Shelley's greatest work.[47] Whether or not one can accept this, it is certainly Shelley's most 'Dantesque' poem – and at bottom this is why Eliot judged it as he did. Yet even within this kinship the differences are notable. Thus Dante's meetings with Beatrice and Matelda (which latter Shelley translated, pp. 727–9) are the inspiration behind Rousseau's meeting in the April grove with the 'Shape all light' (l. 352), for the setting where the stream 'Bent the soft grass' on its banks (l. 316) – in imitation of Dante's Lethe which 'piegava l'erba che 'n sua ripa uscìo' ('bent the grass that grew from its bank') (*Purg*. XXVIII.27) – is obviously a *paradiso terrestre*. Rousseau, like Dante, has to fulfil the ritual of drinking from the stream, which is also labelled 'Lethean' (l. 463), but, whereas Dante's draught takes from him the memory of his sins (XXVIII.128), and is a prelude to Beatrice's unveiling her face completely to him, Rousseau finds 'the fair shape waned in the coming light', 'cold' and 'bright', of Life itself, which proceeds to wheel him off on its hideous triumph (ll. 412, 434). Thus Rousseau is on his way down the mountain, as it were, while Dante is bound in the opposite direction, though Rousseau's, or Shelley's, *paradiso* has no Christian significance of course: we have rather the *Alastor* theme of a soul who has experienced a visitation of immortal beauty being yet forced to live under earthly conditions. Thus Dante's meeting with Beatrice once more furnishes the inspiration for that visitation Shelley's various heroes spend their lives attempting to retrace, as the protagonist of *Epipsychidion*: 'In many mortal forms I rashly sought/The shadow of that idol of my thought' (ll. 267–8). If we compare Dante's description of Beatrice's first appearance to him on top of the mountain with Rousseau's similar moment in *The Triumph*, we find Shelley going beyond Dante's heightened naturalism –

> dentro una nuvola di fiori
> che da le mani angeliche saliva
> e ricadeva in giù dentro e di fori,
> sovra candido vel cinta d'uliva
> donna m'apparve, sotto verde manto
> vestita di color di fiamma viva

(within a cloud of flowers that rose from the angels' hands and dropped down both inside and outside [the chariot], a woman appeared to me girt with olive over a white veil, dressed in the colour of living flame beneath a green mantle) (*Purg.* xxx.28–33)

– to invest Rousseau's figure with all the transcendental glory previously bestowed on Emilia Viviani:

> '. . . there stood
>
> 'Amid the sun, as he amid the blaze
> Of his own glory, on the vibrating
> Floor of the fountain, paved with flashing rays,
>
> 'A Shape all light, which with one hand did fling
> Dew on the earth, as if she were the dawn,
> And the invisible rain did ever sing
>
> 'A silver music on the mossy lawn;
> And still before me on the dusky grass,
> Iris her many-coloured scarf had drawn:
>
> 'In her right hand she bore a crystal glass,
> Mantling with bright Nepenthe; the fierce splendour
> Fell from her as she moved under the mass
>
> 'Of the deep cavern . . .'
>
> (ll. 348–61)

If, however, Beatrice is transformed in Shelley's hands, the initial discovery of Rousseau and the narrator's opening words with him remain extremely similar to various other encounters in the *Commedia*:

Struck to the heart by this sad pageantry,
Half to myself I said – 'And what is this?
Whose shape is that within the car? And why –'

I would have added – 'is all here amiss? –'
But a voice answered – 'Life!' – I turned, and knew
(O Heaven, have mercy on such wretchedness!)

That what I thought was an old root which grew
To strange distortion out of the hill side,
Was indeed one of those deluded crew . . .
(ll. 176–84)

The vivacity of question and response here reproduces for me the typical eagerness and attention of Dante *personaggio* in the *Commedia*, the sudden interruption by a spirit he is unaware of and his consequent expression of surprise; it is not so much Dante's meeting with the metamorphosed tree-form of Pier della Vigna Shelley is drawing on (*Inf.* XIII.28–33), but rather the openings of his encounters with Farinata or especially Belacqua (*Inf.* X.22–30, *Purg.* IV.97–102). Similarly, in the dialogue of lines 188 to 224, where the intricacies of the *terza rima* do not impede the fluency of the narrator's questioning or Rousseau's responses, we are reminded of the natural rhythm of conversational episodes in the *Commedia*, as, for example – with differences of setting apart – Dante's meeting with Bocca degli Abati in *Inferno* XXXII (85–102). Shelley has managed to cope with the difficult task of writing English in *terza rima* without, as Eliot pointed out with much admiration, letting the rhymes obtrude themselves and thus halt the flow of the verse. It is natural to compare, as did Eliot himself, this passage from *The Triumph* (beginning at line 176) with Eliot's own 're-creation' of the *terza rima* in the air-raid passage from *Little Gidding*. Eliot concludes that Shelley's lines are a better imitation of Dante's style,[48] and one is tempted to agree with him, not simply because Shelley used rhyme where he did not, but in so far as Shelley re-creates one of Dante's great achievements in the *basso inferno* particularly, a dialogue squeezed out under the pressure of great excitement. The passage in *Little Gidding*, which we shall of course examine, is for the most part a stately monologue.

If we can accept that there is some truth in Mrs Shelley's statement that 'Shelley shrunk instinctively from portraying human passion, with its mixture of good and evil, of disappointment and disquiet', then *The Triumph* shows him attempting to overcome this antipathy: in Rousseau Shelley analyses his own regret and disquiet at the desiccation even the most elevated imagination is subject to; and Dante's poetry helped him to do this. Even so, later generations were left with the fruits, not of this more careful investigation of Dante, but of his earlier endeavours; that is, the balance of his poetical theory and practice leaves us not with the idea of the poet as a recorder of life and its triumphs, but rather, as Shelley says in *A Defence*, as 'a nightingale, who sits in darkness and sings to cheer its own solitude with sweet sounds' (p. 282). At the same time, Shelley wanted these 'sweet sounds' to have political influence, though any didacticism would impair their sweetness; thus they must move men not through the reason, but as the West Wind, Mont Blanc and the Skylark's song moved them, through the senses and intuitions. Thus in *The Revolt of Islam* Laon's songs of freedom are 'homeless odours' floating through the air (IX.xii), their thought as it were transubstantiated into sensory material. Similarly, the skylark is

> Like a Poet hidden
> In the light of thought,
> Singing hymns unbidden,
> Till the world is wrought
> To sympathy with hopes and fears it heeded not . . .
> ('To a Skylark' ll. 36–40, p. 602)

It is the light or music or even smell of thought that poetry communicates rather than the thought itself. And, even though Dante is presented in imagery that is more forceful than the comparison with the nightingale or skylark, Shelley's imagery relies on the same assumptions: '[Dante's] very words are instinct with spirit; each is as a spark, a burning atom of inextinguishable thought; and many yet lie covered in the ashes of their birth and pregnant with a lightning which has yet found no conductor' (*A Defence*, p. 291). We have heard a great deal about the 'spirit' or 'lightning' in Dante, but very little about what his thought actually was, an omission which allowed Shelley to contemplate the rather odd partnership of himself as the West Wind stirring up Dante's ashes and scattering Dante's words among mankind together with his own. 'The Lucifer of [the] starry flock' of Italian writers is thus enthroned in Shelley's own Empyrean, where the differences of thought are forgotten, but the thought *of* which heartens those who are left behind to battle on against the Evil Principle:

'...
A light of heaven, whose half-extinguished beam

'Through the sick day in which we wake to weep
Glimmers, for ever sought, for ever lost ...'
(*The Triumph of Life* ll. 429–31)

Thus, having achieved Shelley's highest symbolic accolade of the morning-star, Dante takes his place beside Christ, Adonais and all the others who beacon

from the abode where the Eternal are.
(*Adonais* LV.495)

Shelley's emphasis on Dante in *A Defence* as a radical and republican and his implicit identification of Prometheus' achievement of freedom with Dante's own, are not Shelley's legacy to the Dante tradition: each generation of poets has very much its own concerns which it attempts to find reflected in Dante's work, and by the time the final chapter is reached we shall have turned full-circle in discussing Dante's influence on a poet who, from a philosophical point of view, could hardly have had less in common with Shelley, T. S. Eliot.[49] What Shelley does pass on to future poets is the confusion outlined above between Beatrice and Shelley's own transcendental females which, combined with various 'Byronic' elements we shall now go on to discuss, enters into Yeats's re-creation of Dante. What has been referred to as the 'Shelleyan Dante' is then by no means a complete representation of Shelley's own ideas, for *A Defence* and *The Triumph of Life* show an attention to the polemical and stylistic features of Dante's work as well as to its 'romantic' elements. But ironically the polemical element in Shelley's own thought, with which he had confused Dante's, tended to be overlooked by later generations, in part because Shelley's fate was similar to Dante's in that his poetry was read and his prose neglected.[50] Even so, any imbalance in the resulting conception of Shelley seems more reasonable than the lacunae in the Romantic picture of Dante discussed in this chapter, for Dante's 'prose' philosophy is also clearly and systematically present in his major poetry in a way in which Shelley's is not.

II

Dante as the Byronic hero

But, as misfortune has a greater interest for posterity . . .
(Advertisement to 'The Lament of Tasso')

The question of how Dantesque a poet Byron was might be introduced by looking at a note in Zacchetti's book *Shelley e Dante*, which contains a furious objection to some observations on the relationship between Byron and Dante put forward by Arturo Farinelli in his *Dante in Spagna, Francia, Inghilterra, Germania.*[1] Farinelli had referred to 'il canto così poco dantesco che [Byron] chiamò "Profezia di Dante"' ('that poem which has so little of Dante about it that Byron called *The Prophecy of Dante*') (p. 280), and complained that Byron was 'practically obsessed by the fateful sentence' that Francesca speaks in *Inferno* v (121–3) – 'Nessun maggior dolore/che ricordarsi del tempo felice/ne la miseria; e ciò sa 'l tuo dottore' ('There is no greater grief than remembering happy times in misery, and your teacher knows that') – noting that Byron 'recalls it all the time'. He added, 'You would think he there found condensed the entire *Commedia*, of which, in truth, he knew few passages' (p. 310). Farinelli thus concludes that 'l'ammirazione per Dante [restava] sempre infeconda . . . nel bollente spirito di Lord Byron' ('admiration for Dante remained always unfruitful . . . in the turbulent spirit of Lord Byron') (p. 323). Zacchetti's outrage is aggravated by the fact that his own *Lord Byron e L'Italia*, which sustains an opposite viewpoint, is apparently unknown to Farinelli:

il prof. [sic] A. Farinelli, dicevo, *parlando del Byron in relazione a Dante*; il prof. Farinelli, dico, in tanta bibliografica farina, nella quale ha lasciato anche tutta la crusca del suo sacco, citando anche minuzie nulle o insignificanti; il prof. Farinelli, ripeto, (e concludo! – perchè mi son seccato) – , ignora . . . un libro che s'intitola *Lord Byron e L'Italia* . . . e che infine dedica un intero capitolo . . . all'argomento *Dante e Byron.*

(prof. Farinelli, I was saying, *speaking of Byron in relation to Dante*; prof.

Farinelli, I say, amongst so much bibliographical flour, which also contains all the chaff from his sack in the shape of citations of no significance or value; prof. Farinelli, I repeat (for the last time! – because I've had enough), is ignorant . . . of a book called *Lord Byron and Italy* . . . which after all dedicates an entire chapter . . . to the question of *Dante and Byron*.)

(*Shelley e Dante*, pp. 137–8)

This other work of Zacchetti's turns out, however, to be rather disappointing: the 'intero capitolo' is a mere eight pages, for the most part generalising about *The Prophecy of Dante*:

non è un grande capolavoro, ma in [Byron] dimostra, ripeto, una cosa essenzialissima: la capacità di intendere perfettamente gli spiriti e le forme della poesia dantesca, non solo, ma di capire e di sentire, come il migliore degli italiani, che Dante è l'anima stessa d'Italia; che Dante e Italia sono una cosa sola; che di nostra gente è Dante il simbolo, l'auspicio, il nume indigete; che in lui si riassumono il passato, il presente e l'avvenire del nostro paese . . . Vi è insomma, nella *Prophecy*, un senso di italianità, e di italianità inspirata a Dante, veramente meraviglioso per uno straniero.

(it is not a great masterpiece, but I repeat that it shows an essential feature of Byron: the capacity to understand perfectly the spirit and form of Dante's poetry; not only this, but to understand and to feel, like the best of the Italians, that Dante is the very soul of Italy; that Dante and Italy are one and the same thing; that Dante is the symbol, the guardian, the native deity of our race; that in him are gathered the past, the present and the future of our country . . . There is in fact, in the *Prophecy*, a sense of Italianness, and of Italianness inspired by Dante, absolutely miraculous for a foreigner.)[2]

Zacchetti's comparison is itself a good example of Romantic attitudes: again it is the *spirit* of the *Commedia* that speaks in Byron and certainly not the letter, since Italian nationalism is *The Prophecy*'s furthest political ambition, as summed up in the lines

What is there wanting then to set thee free,
And show thy beauty in its fullest light?
To make the Alps impassable; and we,
Her Sons, may do this with *one* deed – Unite.

(II.142–5; Vol. IV, 260)[3]

– though to make reservations about the *Prophecy*'s representation of Dante's politics is not to suggest that Dante would have had any sympathy with the type of imperialism that was practised after the Congress of Vienna in 1815.

Nowadays, when fewer critics among the Italians themselves would maintain, one imagines, that 'Dante e Italia sono una cosa sola', it is easier to side with Farinelli over this question of Dante's importance to Byron. One cannot however agree with him that Byron knew only 'pochi frammenti' ('few passages') of the *Commedia*: his annoyance with Friedrich Schlegel's accusation of Dante's want of 'gentle feelings' shows more than a cursory reading of Dante:

Of gentle feelings! and Francesca of Rimini – and the father's feelings in Ugolino – and Beatrice – and 'La Pia!' Why, there is gentleness in Dante beyond all gentleness, when he is tender. It is true that, treating of the Christian Hades, or Hell, there is not much scope or site for gentleness – but who *but* Dante could have introduced any 'gentleness' at all into *Hell*? Is there any in Milton's? No – and Dante's Heaven is all love, and glory, and majesty.[4]

It is true that Byron is also on record as indulging in a long tirade against the *Commedia* that ends: 'the poem is so obscure, tiresome, and insupportable that no one can read it for half an hour without yawning and going to sleep over it like Malagigi; and the hundred times I have made the attempt to read it, I have lost', but this, according to Medwin, occurred in a conversation with Shelley when the latter was warmly praising the *Commedia*, and I would think it quite within Byron's powers to take up an extreme and opposite position for the fun of it.[5] Otherwise we might accept Zacchetti's explanation: 'chi non è cieco, vede facilmente che il Medwin referisce come giudizi di Byron le stupidaggini e le schiocchezze ch'esso Medwin aveva lette nelle *Lettere Virgiliane* del Bettinelli' ('you would have to be blind not to see that Medwin adduces as judgements of Byron the stupidities and foolishness that he himself had read in Bettinelli's *Virgilian Letters*') (*Shelley e Dante*, p. 140).[6] And perhaps in any case consistency was not Byron's forte.

Looking through Byron's poetry we find a greater restriction in his range of references to Dante than in Shelley's. There are, for example, recollections of one of the Romantics' favourite passages from the *Commedia*, the Ugolino episode, in *Parisina* (l. 241; Vol. III, 546; cf. *Inf.* XXXIII.62–3) and in *Don Juan* (II.lxxxiii; Vol. VI), an episode which may also have helped prompt Byron's decision to write *The Prisoner of Chillon*; there is Ulysses (*Don Juan* II.xxxvi; cf. *Inf.* XXVI. 119–20); and there is the translation of the opening six lines of *Purgatorio* VIII at *Don Juan* III.cviii, in Byron's long passage celebrating twilight, though the hour 'in which the Heart is always full' (II.cxcii) generally sees it full of a different sentiment to that which Dante describes, as in the awakening passion of Juan and Haidée. This brief list of references to Dante is not of course exhaustive; but putting *The Prophecy of Dante* on one side it is fair, I think, to suggest a certain sort of casualness in Byron's responses: he labels Dante 'The Bard of Hell' in *Childe Harold's Pigrimage* (IV.xl; Vol.II. 359), and this indicates the restricted nature of his interest in him, as far as we find it illustrated in his poetry. And even this Hell can hardly be said to be always taken seriously, as when Juan's bedroom door opens mysteriously at Norman Abbey: '"Lasciate ogni speranza,/Voi, ch'entrate!" The hinge seemed to speak,/ Dreadful as Dante's rima, or this stanza . . .' (XVI.cxvi). It was useful in providing a little Gothic atmosphere or, as here, comedy.

There is, however, one part of the *Commedia* which, as Farinelli pointed out, engrossed Byron, the Paolo and Francesca episode, which he translated (Vol.IV, 317–22).[7] The theme of incestuous love, Cain's with his sister Adah, Manfred's and Astarte's, and, more approaching the situation we have in Dante, Hugo's for his father's wife Parisina, recurs throughout Byron's poems and seems to be condemned in the latter two cases. That is, Manfred accepts both his guilt and the agony of remorse that proceeds from it as just punishment; he accepts, in fact, the Hell he finds himself in, the 'Hell on earth' which is one of Byron's favourite dramatic themes and which this chapter will be largely concerned with; and there is no suggestion in the following passage from *Manfred* that Byron would interpret Francesca's 'questi, che mai da me non fia diviso' ('this one, who will never be divided from me') (*Inf.* V.135) as any consolation:

> Thou lovedst me
> Too much, as I loved thee: we were not made
> To torture thus each other – though it were
> The deadliest sin to love as we have loved.
> Say that thou loath'st me not – that I do bear
> This punishment for both – that thou wilt be
> One of the blesséd – and that I shall die . . .
> (II.iv.120–6; Vol.IV,117)

In *Parisina*, though Hugo claims that Azo tricked him out of Parisina's hand in marriage (ll. 252–5), we are told by the narrator 'Dark the crime, and just the law' by which Hugo was put to death (l. 428), and Azo's action is again defended at lines 575–7. What indeed strikes one immediately about Byron's translation of the

Francesca episode is the small changes he makes that emphasise her guilt and remorse, translating 'menò costoro al doloroso passo!' ('brought these to the woeful pass!') (V.114) as 'Led these their evil fortune to fulfill!', and, more interestingly, 'Galeotto fu 'l libro e chi lo scrisse' ('A Gallehault was the book and he who wrote it') (l. 137) as 'Accurséd was the book and he who wrote!' It is important then to realise that Paolo and Francesca were not 'heroes' in quite the same way to Byron as they were to many readers in the nineteenth century;[8] there is not, as in Shelley's *Prince Athanase*, an admiration for that God-defying love which 'owned no higher law' but rather an interest, as with Manfred, in the writhings of the conscience that accepts its guiltiness; Manfred is also, it is true, a hero, but Byron feels no need to protest against God on his behalf. Similarly, in *The Two Foscari*, Byron accepts the claims of judgement to be taken as seriously as the claims of love for the opportunity this offers in presenting the turbulent state of mind of the old Doge, called upon to participate in the council's condemnation of his son:

DOGE ...
Methinks we must have sinned in some old world,
And *this* is Hell: the best is, that it is not
Eternal.
MAR. These are things we cannot judge on earth.
DOGE And how then shall we judge each other,
Who are all earth, and I, who am called upon
To judge my son? (II.i.364–9; Vol.V, 150)

Occasionally, we even find a wholehearted piety in Byron, as in the Mortal's prayer to God at the end of *Heaven and Earth*: 'Yet, as *his* word,/Be the decree adored!' (I.iii.886–7; Vol. V,319).

Apart from the Paolo and Francesca story as a 'vision of judgement', Byron was also interested in the *nature* of their punishment, presented, in Dante, as more a torture of mind than of body, and one similar to that which his own heroes often suffer. Thus we might compare the lines already mentioned –

Nessun maggior dolore
che ricordarsi del tempo felice
ne la miseria ... (V.121–3)

– with Manfred's:

... there is no future pang
Can deal that justice on the self-condemned
He deals on his own soul. (III.i.76–8)

Byron in fact uses these lines from Dante for the epigraph to canto I of *The Corsair*; for canto II, 'Conosceste i dubbiosi disiri?' ('You knew dubious desires?') and for canto III 'Come vedi, ancor non m'abbandona' ('As you see, it still doesn't abandon me'), all taken from this same meeting between Dante and Francesca. It would seem that the first epigraph refers to the sorrow of Conrad and Medora after their parting, and the second to the attraction, 'dubbioso' indeed, Conrad sees in Gulnare at the end of canto II:

> Oh! too convincing – dangerously dear –
> In Woman's eye the unanswerable tear! . . .
> By this – how many lose not earth – but Heaven!
> Consign their souls to Man's eternal foe,
> And seal their own to spare some Wanton's woe!
> (II.1149–60; Vol.III,268–9)

Again, a reference perhaps to the fate of Paolo; indeed, to Conrad's horror Gulnare later turns out to be a homicide, where one would have expected him to sympathise rather more with her situation (III.1598ff). The final epigraph is in some ways the most interesting; it refers to Conrad's grief at the death of Medora and the memory of their love he must bear forever – 'Come vedi, ancor non m'abbandona':

> Full many a stoic eye and aspect stern
> Mask hearts where Grief hath little left to learn;
> And many a withering thought lies hid, not lost,
> In smiles that least befit who wear them most.
> (III.1804–7)

The remainder of life being blasted by some hidden emotional catastrophe: this is indeed the *sine qua non* of the Byronic hero, as again in Lara – 'some deep feeling it were vain to trace/At moments lightened o'er his livid face' (I.83–4; Vol.III, 327).

Don Juan is rather different, however, even though Juan and Haidée again bring Paolo and Francesca to Byron's mind –

> Alas! they were so young, so beautiful,
> So lonely, loving, helpless, and the hour
> Was that in which the Heart is always full,
> And, having o'er itself no further power,
> Prompts deeds Eternity cannot annul,
> But pays off moments in an endless shower
> Of hell-fire – all prepared for people giving
> Pleasure or pain to one another living;
> (II.cxcii)

– and although he light-heartedly casts his own poem as a 'Galeotto' –

> if you'd have them wedded, please to shut
> The book which treats of this erroneous pair,
> Before the consequences grow too awful;
> 'Tis dangerous to read of loves unlawful,
>
> (III.xii)

– the pair are in the end exculpated: '. . . Love was born *with* them, *in* them, so intense,/It was their very Spirit – not a sense' (IV.xxvii). It is a golden-age love, existing outside the pale of the social and marital hypocrisies which are Byron's recurrent target in the poem, and the catastrophe it leads to is not a moral one, for after her death Haidée 'sleeps well/By the sea-shore' (IV.lxxi), unlike that other shore-dweller (but, unlike Haidée, adulteress) Francesca.[9] Although Love is indeed 'soon or late . . . his own avenger' (IV.lxxiii), the religious significance Love is given in the poem seems entirely tongue-in-cheek:

> Oh, Love! Of whom great Caesar was the suitor,
> Titus the master, Antony the slave,
> . . .
> Oh, Love! thou art the very God of evil,
> For, after all, we cannot call thee Devil.
>
> (II.ccv)

What Dante treats seriously, Byron does lightly: thus the above stanza might recall Francesca's famous words on love beginning 'Amor, ch'al cor gentil ratto s'apprende . . .' ('Love, which is quickly kindled in the noble heart . . .') (*Inf.* V.100–7), but of course the irony of her situation – her ignorance of how impoverished a conception of 'Amor' hers is, compared with its manifestations in the *Paradiso* – finds an equivalent nowhere in *Don Juan*, where Byron shows little faith in the majority of its forms:

> The noblest kind of love is love Platonical,
> To end or to begin with; the next grand
> Is that which may be christened love canonical,
> Because the clergy take the thing in hand;
> The third sort to be noted in our chronicle
> As flourishing in every Christian land,
> Is, when chaste matrons to their other ties
> Add what may be called *marriage in disguise.*
>
> (IX.lxxvi)

Thus, then, though love – or its absence – might be said to be at the centre of *Don Juan*, the Paolo and Francesca theme has no real relevance to it. I doubt if many readers take Byron's statement seriously that 'that's the moral of this composition,/If people would but see its real drift'; that is, that the poem is a morality on 'those/Whose headlong passions form their proper woes' (VI.lxxxvii–viii). Of course the poem ends very much *in medias res* with its 'real drift' uncertain; my own bet is that Juan would have ended his days comfortably ensconced in an archbishop's seat. The morality of war, in the siege of Ismail cantos VII and VIII, seems to me to be more seriously examined than the morality of love, and raises a certain double-sidedness in Byron's nature; that is, a powerful imaginative response to what he there condemns; rather as, in spite of his republicanism, he differs from Shelley in being strongly affected by the 'glory' of Imperial Rome (see for instance *Childe Harold*, IV.xlvi, cvii–cviii). As remarked, consistency seems not to have been his most conspicuous virtue.[10]

This type of inconsistency is in fact one of the central elements in the aspect of 'Byronism' we shall be examining in this chapter. Byron refers to his 'orthodoxy' lightly and in passing in *Don Juan* (XI.vi), but we can find adequate expression in his writings, as well as in the recollections of those who knew him, of some religious belief: the Byronic hero, with his prototype of course in Milton's Satan, labours under a *just* punishment, or curse.[11] Of course, the fact that we are concerned with poets rather than philosophers explains why Dante's influence on Byron is far smaller than it was on the 'heretic' Shelley, even though a certain measure of religious agreement unites them. But if the gap between Byron's poetry and Dante's remains wide, we can now turn to the fascinating phenomenon of the Romantics' attempt to bridge it, to conjure up, that is, the Byronic Dante.

To begin with, we have Dante's account of his life in exile from the *Convivio* (I.iii. 4–5) included in Cary's 'Life' of Dante prefixed to his translation of the *Commedia*:

> Wandering over almost every part, to which this our language extends, I have gone about like a mendicant; showing, against my will, the wound with which fortune has smitten me, and which is often imputed to his ill-deserving, on whom it is inflicted. I have, indeed, been a vessel without sail and without steerage, carried about to divers ports, and roads, and shores, by the dry wind that springs out of sad poverty . . .[12]

Dante is a proto-Childe Harold then; it seems hardly necessary to quote:

> Once more upon the waters! yet once more!
> And the waves bound beneath me as a steed
> That knows his rider. Welcome to their roar!
> Swift be their guidance, whereso'er it lead!
> Though the strained mast should quiver as a reed,
> And the rent canvass fluttering strew the gale,
> Still must I on; for I am as a weed,
> Flung from the rock, on Ocean's foam, to sail
> Where'er the surge may sweep, the tempest's breath prevail.
> (*Childe Harold* III.ii)

But what is notable for our purposes about the *Convivio* is that, apart from the passage Cary translates, Dante hardly refers to his own situation at all, unlike the *Pilgrimage*, where the narrative continually oscillates between what the Childe sees, and the state of his own emotions on seeing it. Dante, for whom exile was a bitter reality, differing from the Childe's 'thirst for travel' (I.xxviii), wrote the *Convivio* in a spirit motivated by an eminent practicality, in the hope of repairing a reputation damaged by the poverty of exile, since, as he says above, most men judge by external appearances: 'Quando è l'uomo maculato . . . d'alcuno colpo di fortuna . . . queste macule alcuna ombra gittano sopra la chiarezza de la bontade, sì che la fanno parere men chiara e men valente' ('When a man is besmirched . . . by some reverse of fortune . . . the stain obscures the brightness of his excellence, making it appear less conspicuous and worthy') (I.iv.10–11). Nothing really contrasts more with Dante's getting down to work to retain his status among men in this way than Byron's exploitation of the dramatic possibilities of exile: 'Self-exiled Harold wanders forth again . . .' (III.xvi), a voluntary but marvellously ironic act on Harold's part since it is precisely himself he is trying to escape from, or 'the Demon Thought' (I.lxxxiv: 'Song to Inez', 6).

Such obvious dissimilarities between the Childe and Dante would need no comment had not critics been determined to confuse Dante with both Byron's creations and Byron himself. A good illustration of this is in Hazlitt's *Lectures on the English Poets* (1818), in which the opening lecture includes the following assessment of Dante:

> Dante seems to have been indebted to the Bible for the gloomy tone of his mind, as well as for the prophetic fury which exalts and kindles his poetry

. . . His genius is not a sparkling flame, but the sullen heat of a furnace. He is power, passion, self-will personified . . . there is a gloomy abstraction in his conceptions, which lies like a dead weight upon the mind; a benumbing stupor, a breathless awe, from the intensity of the impression; a terrible obscurity, like that which oppresses us in dreams; an identity of interest, which moulds every object to its own purposes . . . The immediate objects he presents to the mind, are not much in themselves, they want grandeur, beauty, and order; but they become everything by the force of the character he impresses upon them. His mind lends its own power to the objects which it contemplates, instead of borrowing it from them . . . Dante's only object is to interest; and he interests only by exciting our sympathy with the emotion by which he is himself possessed. He does not place before us the objects by which that emotion has been excited; but he seizes on the attention by showing us the effect they produce on his feelings; and his poetry accordingly gives the same thrilling and overwhelming sensation, which is caught by gazing on the face of a person who has seen some object of horror. (pp. 34–6)

The passage contains an implicit identification of Dante with Milton's Satan, who is also, we learn later, 'the principle of . . . the abstract love of power, of pride, of self-will personified . . .' (p. 126); this is a development of an idea already mooted in the eighteenth century by Thomas Warton: 'There is a sombrous cast in [Dante's] imagination: and he has given new shades of horror to the classical hell. We may say of Dante, that "Hell/Grows darker at his frown".'[13] Dante's mind is then a 'lamp', and an infernal one at that, rather than a 'mirror': it lends 'its own power to the objects which it contemplates'. When we pass on to Hazlitt's discussion of Byron we find a recognisably similar type, though now in a state of some degeneration; no doubt this is what Hazlitt particularly means when he calls Dante 'the father of modern poetry' (p. 34); or what he had meant by a statement of 1815: 'Dante is a striking instance of the essential excellences and defects of modern genius.'[14] In the *Lectures* he continues:

Lord Byron shuts himself up too much in the impenetrable gloom of his own thoughts . . . The Giaour, the Corsair, Childe Harold, are all the same person, and they are apparently all himself . . . the passion is always of the same unaccountable character, at once violent and sullen, fierce and gloomy. It is not the passion of a mind struggling with misfortune, or the hopelessness of its desires, but of a mind preying upon itself, and disgusted with, or indifferent to all other things . . . There is nothing more repulsive than this sort of ideal absorption of all the interests of others, of the good and ills of life, in the ruling passion and moody abstraction of a single mind, as if it would make itself the centre of the universe, and there was nothing worth cherishing but its intellectual diseases . . . But still there is power, and power rivets attention and forces admiration. 'He hath a demon': and that is the next thing to being full of the God. His brow collects the scattered gloom: his eye flashes livid fire that withers and consumes.

(pp.302–3)

It is true that Hazlitt indicates the major difference between, say, the Childe and Dante that has already been suggested (Byron's 'is not the passion of a mind struggling with misfortune'); but it is, in Hazlitt's eyes, a mind of a similar cast to Dante's in its gloomy but fiery egotism. Again, if we look as far ahead as Eliot, the vicissitudes of Dante's reputation are striking: for Eliot Dante's poem is precisely *not* an indulgence of what he dismissively calls ' "personality" in the romantic sense of the word' ('Lancelot Andrewes', *Selected Essays*, p. 352), but a record of experiences that 'seemed to [Dante] of some importance; not of importance because they had happened to him and because he, Dante Alighieri, was an important person who kept press-cutting bureaux busy, but important in themselves . . .' (*Dante*, *Ibidem*, pp. 272–3). Moreover, Dante 'not only thought in a way in which every man of his culture in the whole of Europe then thought, but he employed an [allegorical] method which was common and commonly understood throughout Europe' (*Dante*, p. 242). The Romantics' correlation of Dante with the heroes of their own day was abetted by a kind of felicitous ignorance about what 'the whole of Europe then thought' however; it is only in the next generation that an interest in Dante's contemporaries, and in what he shared with them, becomes common. Hazlitt's complaints about Byron's continual self-intrusion sound similar to objections Bettinelli had voiced about the *Commedia*: 'A molti dispiace quell'egoismo di superbia, con cui [Dante] fa se stesso centro e fine del gran poema, parlando sempre di sé, fattosi eroe ed argomento di sí lungo lavoro, e delle cose sue . . .' ('Many dislike that egoistic pride which led Dante to make himself the centre and occasion of the great poem, always speaking of himself as hero and theme of a work of such length, and of his own affairs . . .').[15]

One might wonder when reading Hazlitt's words on Dante where, if at all, the *Purgatorio* and *Paradiso* figure in his estimate, for the above comments are based solidly on an over-attention to the gloom and horror of the *Inferno*, which is typical of the period.

Hazlitt's extraordinary suggestions, together with his rather careless mistakes, suggest not only that he had not read the *Inferno* very attentively and the rest of the *Commedia* perhaps not at all, but that what he did read was enveloped for him in a sort of pre-existing Byronic miasma: here, he became aware, was 'the father of modern poetry' and of some aspects of that poetry he did not very much like though was yet overcome by, for 'still there is power, and power rivets attention and forces admiration'. Perhaps it is this riveted attention on Byron that led Hazlitt to the lengths he had to go to to make Dante's mind into a 'furnace', that led him to statements like, 'The immediate objects [Dante] presents are not much in themselves, they want grandeur, beauty and order' – which even a cursory reading of let us say *Purgatorio* XXVIII and XXIX must surely dispel – and like, 'He does not place before us the objects by which that emotion has been excited . . . He affords few subjects for picture' (pp. 35–6). This extreme denial of Dante's 'objectivity' runs counter to one of the standard observations of the time on Dante's style, and one which is surely much more reasonable, as in Cary:

> He is said to have attained some excellence in the art of designing; which may easily be believed, when we consider that no poet has afforded more lessons to the statuary and the painter, in the variety of objects which he represents, and in the accuracy and spirit with which they are brought before the eye. ('Life', p. xxx)

To return to 'the gloomy tone of his mind', we find that 'grim Dante', as Byron refers to him in *Don Juan* (x.xxvii), was one of the most fashionable literary figures of the period; the opening of the Childe's song 'To Inez' might have been put in his mouth –

> Nay, smile not at my sullen brow;
> Alas! I cannot smile again

– and its close:

> Smile on – nor venture to unmask
> Man's heart, and view the Hell that's there.
> (I.lxxxiv. 1–7)

Dante's exile, together with the profound inner woe resulting from the loss of Beatrice, fitted him beautifully for the Byronic role:

> Whate'er he be, 'twas not what he had been:
> That brow in furrowed lines had fixed at last,
> And spake of passions, but of passion past . . .
> (*Lara* I.66–8)

Thus it is that the *Inferno* Dante visited came to be regarded as an exteriorisation of his inner state, as Hazlitt suggests, and so he keeps company with Manfred or the Childe:

> I *have* thought
> Too long and darkly, till my brain became,
> In its own eddy boiling and o'erwrought,
> A whirling gulf of phantasy and flame . . .
> (III.vii)

Byron himself did not quite fall for this identification; indeed what we have said of his interest in the 'emotional torture' of Paolo and Francesca might indicate that he found his own conception of the 'inner Hell' distinguishable from, and indeed more sophisticated than, much of Dante's infernal vision. 'Those sufferings Dante saw in Hell alone', he says in *Don Juan* (IV.CV), which suggests his interest in them was limited precisely by their location: the drama of this life's torments sufficiently satisfied Byron's imagination to leave him free of attending to those in the next, which indeed tend to become, as remarked, Gothic stage-trappings or mere points of (jocular) comparison, as in Byron's lines on 'Monk' Lewis –

> Even Satan's self with thee might dread to dwell,
> And in thy skull discern a deeper Hell,
> (*English Bards and Scotch Reviewers*,
> ll. 281–2; Vol I, 319)

– or as in *Parisina*, where the news of his wife's infidelity sounds in Azo's ears more terrible than the trump of the Last Judgement (ll. 83–90). This is not to deny that the mediaeval concept of Hell is something one is not sad to see fall into disuse; but the idea of Dante seeing sufferings 'in Hell alone' implies a separation between life and death which does no justice to Dante's fundamental ambition to insist on the relationship between the two; the sufferings he sees in Hell, as we never forget, are for the most part a result of the various kinds of tragic ignorance he had already found permeating Italy.

The modern, individual 'Hell on earth' is presented as greater than the mediaeval one then, its heroes more heroic, as when Manfred, who suffers 'Remorse without the *fear* of Hell' (III.i.71, my italics), drives off the demons:

> Back to thy hell!
> Thou hast no power upon me, *that* I feel;
> Thou never shalt possess me, *that* I know:

> What I have done is done; I bear within
> A torture which could nothing gain from thine:
> The Mind which is immortal, makes itself
> Requital for its good or evil thoughts . . .
> (III.iv.124–30)

Seeing Dante's Hell as something internal, in the way we have been looking at, is an attempt to modernise it, to bring it up to date, to remedy its 'crudities', these last nowhere more felt than in Dante's presentation of Satan compared with Milton's, a stock comparison during the nineteenth and twentieth centuries. Whereas the former is often associated with the frescoes of the middle ages, a mere 'outward' representation of evil, the 'deformity of [Milton's] Satan is only in the depravity of his will; he has no bodily deformity to excite our loathing or disgust. The horns and tail are not there, poor emblems of the unbending, unconquered spirit, of the writhing agonies within' (Hazlitt, *Lectures*, pp. 127–8). Coleridge noted Dante's 'occasional fault of becoming grotesque from being too graphic without imagination' (*Notes and Lectures*, II, 108); he creates with his Satan a caricature or 'emblem' of evil rather than its 'essence', as Eliot was later to complain (*Dante*, p. 251).[16] But what consequence does all this have for the *Paradiso*? Here is Macaulay's comment:

> those religious hopes which had released the mind of the sublime enthusiast from the terrors of death had not rendered [Dante's] speculations on human life more cheerful . . . He hoped for happiness beyond the grave: but he felt none on earth. It is from this cause, more than from any other, that his description of Heaven is so far inferior to the Hell or the Purgatory. With the passions and miseries of the suffering spirits he feels a strong sympathy. But among the beatified he appears as one who has nothing in common with them, – as one who is incapable of comprehending, not only the degree, but the nature of their enjoyment. We think that we see him standing amidst those smiling and radiant spirits with that scowl of unutterable misery on his brow, and that curl of bitter disdain on his lips, which all his portraits have preserved, and which might furnish Chantrey with hints for the head of his projected Satan.[17]

This extraordinary passage testifies to the overwhelming power of the 'Byronism' under discussion in this chapter, the more so because Macaulay's article is the best short essay on Dante – he is particularly good on Dante's style – that had been written in English to date. The massiveness of Macaulay's blind spot – the idea that the

Paradiso is vitiated by Dante's inability to believe in it – is all the more surprising bearing in mind that Macaulay has no republican axe to grind in the essay; that is, he is not looking out for a Dante who thinks it 'Better to reign in Hell, than serve in Heaven' (*Paradise Lost* 1.263). He is simply captivated by the Romantic fashion for the 'sullen brow'. It was indeed rare at the time to find unreserved applause for the *Paradiso*, as remarked in Chapter 1, but even in the eighteenth century it did exist, at least outside England: 'nella *Cantica* del *Paradiso*, la calma, la serenità, l'estasi, il sublime della Religione sembrano essere entrate nello spirito e nello stile di questo Poeta. Egli prende parte alle beatifiche visioni: ebro n'è il suo spirito, ebra n'è l'anima sua: l'universo tutto sembra arridergli intorno' ('in the *Cantica* of *Paradise*, the calm, serenity, ecstasy and sublimity of religion seem to have entered the spirit and the style of this poet. He participates in the beatific visions: his spirit is drunk with it all, as is his soul, and the entire universe seems to be smiling around him').[18] Shelley would have seconded this and, by a rather mighty irony, so would Byron himself, to judge from his comment above on the 'love, and glory and majesty' of the *Paradiso*. He deserves some apology for the way we have been using his name to represent the interest in the 'infernal' personality, even if his own poetry formed the main fuel for this interest. He could never have agreed, for example, with an absurd comment like the following, from an unsigned review of 1818, which may be regarded as typical of the period:

> The brief outline of Dante's history will account for, and excuse the gloomy and sarcastic spirit apparent in his poetry, which, though softened occasionally, by a tender and affecting melancholy, never brightens into the radiance of cheerfulness and joy . . . the *Purgatorio* and *Paradiso*, like the *Paradise Regained*, though containing passages of great beauty, cannot be read with interest or pleasure.
>
> (*Monthly Magazine*, February 1818, quoted in Toynbee, II, 263)

We note again how Dante's biography – his 'history' – is being used as a basis for the reading of his poetry, and hopelessly interferes with it in the process. Indeed, in Macaulay's comment, we saw how the exile from Florence had been transformed into a Byrono-Satanic exile from his own *Paradiso*.

We also saw Macaulay making a significant appeal to the surviving portraits of Dante in support of his judgement, and we remember Hazlitt had seen the *Commedia* as it were reflected in 'the face of a person who has seen some object of horror'. This obsession with Dante's physiognomy – grim Dante – is part of what one might call the physiognomical craze of the time; all Byron's heroes are automatically endowed with the same type of features:

> Dark and unearthly is the scowl
> That glares beneath his dusky cowl:
> The flash of that dilating eye
> Reveals too much of times gone by
> . . .
> Not oft to smile descendeth he,
> And when he doth 'tis sad to see
> That he but mocks at Misery.
> How that pale lip will curl and quiver!
> Then fix once more as if for ever;
> As if his sorrow or disdain
> Forbode him e'er to smile again.
> (*The Giaour*, ll.832–56; Vol.III,125–6)

Byron's and Shelley's friend Taaffe, who in his laborious *Comment* mixes much useful information with a great deal of legendary and anecdotal nonsense, noted that 'scarcely once, during full thirty years that [Dante] survived [Beatrice] was he ever known to smile' (p. 110), though all we need to do to come across Dante smiling several times (as at Belacqua) is to read his poetry. Taaffe's observation may have derived from Boccaccio's 'Life' of Dante, which we shall discuss shortly.

The Byronic physiognomy is reflected in the landscape settings of the time as well, with all their 'frowning' crags and towers, or where the 'sweet brow' of Italy suffers 'sorrow ploughed by shame' in *Childe Harold* (IV.xlii). Indeed, in saying as above that the *Pilgrimage* 'oscillates' between the Childe and what he sees, one overlooks the fact that there is little distinction between them: the frowning crags are an externalisation of the Childe's inner state, the ruins of Rome the individual writ large: 'Among thy mightier offerings here are mine,/Ruins of years – though few, yet full of fate' (IV.cxxxi). By canto IV the Childe has indeed become a ruin, 'dropped' by Byron as the protagonist of the poem. The balance between the inner and outer does not remain constant; now the individual is exalted, now the Empire: 'Upon such a shrine/What are our petty griefs? – let me not number mine' (IV.cvi), though this is what the narrator can never refrain from doing. This search for a congenial habitat, the individual's making himself 'the centre of the universe' in the way Hazlitt complained of, is precisely what we are asked to believe Dante originated, and that he found his habitat only in the *Inferno*.

But to return to Dante's face – although one can be more specific: it is the *brow*, the frown, the mark of Cain as in Byron's drama (*Cain*: *A Mystery* III.i.500–1; Vol.v,273), that particularly denotes the inner Hell ('Hell/Grows darker at his frown') – there were two 'portraits' of Dante that the Romantics generally had in mind when visualising him: one by Stefano Tofanelli (Plate 1) and another by the English artist Thomas Stothard (Plate 2), engravings of which were used as the frontispieces for Cary's translation of the *Inferno* (1805–6) and Boyd's translation of the entire *Commedia* (1802) respectively. Both engravings indeed show a rather gloomy figure: Stothard's might be with justice described as 'grim' while the epithet 'melancholy' would seem more appropriate for Tofanelli's. A reviewer noted in 1806 that Dante's profile 'is almost as supernatural as his poem' (Toynbee, II, 56) which indicates in an innocent way that according of equal status to both face and poem which we have already seen play such havoc with criticism of the *Paradiso*. The reviewer was doubtlessly referring to Stothard's portrait with its absurdly exaggerated aquiline nose and furrowed forehead. Something of a cult grew up around Dante's face; witness Thurlow's sonnet (1820), 'On Seeing the Head of Dante':

> Thy mournful face, expressive of keen thought
> ...
> Is full of grief, oblivion and despair.
> (Quoted in Toynbee,II,149)

(I quote the first and last lines only.) The history of the reactions to the portraits of Dante is immensely important for an understanding of his significance for Rossetti and especially for Yeats, as we shall see. Neither portrait can possibly be original, but in the Romantic period they were wholeheartedly welcomed as additions to the various grim galleries adorning real or fictional Gothic mansions, as the one Byron is writing in at *Don Juan* xv.xcvii – 'Old portraits from old walls upon me scowl' – or as in the abode of Lara (I.181–200).[19]

Apart from the portraits, the Byronic critics of Dante had another string to their bow: the description of Dante given by Boccaccio in his 'Life' of the poet, and quoted from by Cary in the preface to his translation: 'il suo volto fu lungo, e 'l naso aquilino, e gli occhi anzi grossi che piccioli, le mascelle grandi, e dal labbro di sotto era quel di sopra avanzato; e il colore era bruno, e i capelli e la barba spessi, neri e crespi, e sempre nella faccia malinconico e pensoso' ('his face was long, his nose aquiline, his eyes big rather than small, his jaw large and with the bottom lip sticking out further than the upper. He had a dark complexion, with hair and beard that were thick, black and curly; his expression was always melancholy and pensive').[20] It is this last detail of course that particularly interests us, whilst other of Boccaccio's remarks, as for instance that Dante 'dilettosi . . . d'essere solitario e rimoto dalle genti acciò che le sue contemplazioni non gli fossero interrotte' ('he loved . . . to be on his own and away from people so that no one could interrupt his contemplations') (p. 466), again anticipate Childe Harold, 'sunk . . . in thought as he was wont' (II.xli). I doubt, however, whether many readers of Dante would be willing to put a great deal of trust in Boccaccio's picture of him, precisely because this centres round an ideal of the philosopher as thus studious, retired and contemplative, to which he makes Dante's life approximate, as far as its upheavals would allow:

Gli studii generalmente sogliono solitudine e rimozione di sollecitudine e tranquillità d'animo disiderare . . . In luogo della quale rimozione e quiete, quasi dallo inizio della sua vita infino all'ultimo della morte, Dante ebbe fierissima e importabile passione d'amore, moglie, cura familiare e publica, esilio e povertà.

(Studying generally requires privacy, the absence of worry and a calm state of mind . . . But instead of this seclusion and quiet Dante, practically from the beginning of his life to the day of his death, experienced fierce and intolerable feelings of love, a wife, family and public responsibilities, exile and poverty.) (p. 444)

And Boccaccio goes on to suggest that had Dante had a normal run of luck his achievement would have been even greater: 'io direi che egli fosse in terra divenuto uno iddio' ('I would say that he would have become a god on earth') (p. 457). Whatever damage the above disasters (including the 'moglie') did to Dante's philosophical studies, surely we are justified in thinking that his poetry could not have been written without them, especially without the 'fierissima e importabile passione d'amore', an assumption central to Yeats's ideas. An Italian critic notes Boccaccio's ideal here 'dell'uomo di lettere e di scienza che agli studi ha dedicato una intera esistenza, figura cara alle aspirazioni del Boccaccio e chiaramente precorritrice degli ideali umanistici' ('of the man of letters and of science who has devoted his entire existence to study, a figure dear to Boccaccio's aspirations and a clear forerunner of humanist ideals').[21] We shall have to return to the *Trattatello* in our discussion of Yeats, but for the moment, if one adduces the anecdote Boccaccio quotes about the feast at Siena (p. 467), where Dante stood the entire day reading a book without realising that games and dancing were going on in front of him, one has to put in the opposite scale the rather more credible evidence of the entire *Commedia* in deciding whether Dante had an eye for the life around him or not. This is not to deny that there were periods in his life when Dante was veritably buried in his books: he tells us in the *Convivio* of his damaging his eyes from over-studying (III.ix.15–16), but in the *Convivio* itself Dante is not a man hopelessly wrapped up in his own solitary contemplations but one passionately concerned to pass his knowledge on, to give others the benefit of his studies, just as in the *Commedia*. In everything he wrote he showed himself a good Aristotelian: 'la necessità de la umana civilitade . . . a uno fine è ordinata, cioè a vita felice; a la quale nullo per sé è sufficiente a venire sanza l'aiutorio d'alcuno . . . E però dice lo Filosofo che l'uomo naturalmente è compagnevole animale' ('the necessity of human civility . . . is directed to one end, namely happiness in life. No one can obtain this by himself but only with the help of other people . . . That is why the Philosopher says that man is by nature a social animal') (*Conv.*IV.iv.1). The *Convivio* is written out of a belief in social man, in citizenship; and Dante invites to his banquet especially those whose civic duties have left them no time for 'ozio di speculazione' ('the leisure of speculation') (I.i.4), the fruits of which he now wants to share. Hardly a greater injustice has been done to Dante than the identification with the Byronic figure who can say

> Fain would I fly the haunts of men –
> I seek to shun, not hate mankind;
> My breast requires the sullen glen,
> Whose gloom may suit a darken'd mind.
> ('I would I were a careless child', Vol.I, 207–8)

Even Shelley's association of him with the West Wind, if more complimentary, derogates from the practical nature of Dante's involvement with his kind; while Byronism also indicates a complete inattention to the stylistic features of Dante's poetry; that essentially *childlike* delight in, or fear of, what he sees in the

Commedia; that absolute absorption in what he describes and the spontaneity of his reactions to it.[22] All the works of Dante's maturity were written with a public intention which might be summed up in words he himself applied to the greatest of them: 'finis totius et partis est, removere viventes in hac vita de statu miseriae et perducere ad statum felicitatis' ('the aim of the whole and the part is to remove those living in this life from a state of wretchedness and to lead them to a state of felicity') (*Ep.* x.15); yet he becomes the much less 'applied' Shelleyan rebel or, much worse, the image of sullen misanthropy.

Another frequently repeated tale concerning Dante refers to Can Grande della Scala and his court-jester, whose levels of intelligence Dante (supposedly) slightingly compared. Cary again quotes it in his 'Life', explaining that Dante 'was at times extremely absent and abstracted; and appears to have indulged too much a disposition to sarcasm' (p. xxvi). And so 'it is believed that he left Verona in disgust at the flippant levity of that court, or at some slight which he conceived to have been shown him by his munificent patron Can Grande, on whose liberality he has passed so high an encomium' (p. xiv). At least Cary does make mention here of Dante's tribute to Can Grande in *Paradiso* xvii.76–92; other critics preferred to ignore this and use the anecdote – originally recorded by Petrarch[23] – to show Dante's complete inability to make a success of court life; his inability, that is, to live among people who were enjoying themselves. One is again taken to parallels in Byron, Childe Harold for instance:

> To such the gladness of the gamesome crowd
> Is source of wayward thought and stern disdain:
> How do they loathe the laughter idly loud,
> And long to change the robe of revel for the shroud!
> (ii.lxxxii)

And such a figure is at the centre of Rossetti's poem 'Dante at Verona'. The morose, unsociable Dante degenerates during the nineteenth century into something of a stock joke, as in Emerson's 'Dante was very bad company, and was never invited to dinner'.[24] The earliest serious protest against this impression comes, as far as I am aware, from the man who can be said to have founded Dante scholarship in England, Henry Clark Barlow, in his attack on a picture exhibited by Lord Leighton in 1864 entitled *Dante in Exile*

(Plate 4). Dante is seen emerging from a shadowy vestibule at Can Grande's court, severely aloof from the lovers on one side and the jester on the other. Barlow urged that the Dante of poets and painters

> should be Dante, the author of the *Divina Commedia*, such as his writings declare him to have been . . . the poet, the artist, the musician, the orator, theologian and philosopher, the man of universal sympathies, whose art was ever warmed by the genial influence of love, and whose spirit rejoiced in all that was great or good . . . he would not have gone with a sour face to a feast. He, who had doomed, along with suicides, the ungrateful wretch who is sad when he ought to rejoice,
>
> 'E piange là dov'esser dee giocondo',
>
> (*Inf.*XI.45)
>
> would not have condemned himself by wearing the aspect of melancholy at a public festival.[25]

This really seems an immensely significant confrontation between artist and academic: one might say that the Romantics were free to create their versions of Dante because no one knew him well enough to object; but certainly twentieth-century 'poetical' responses to Dante have been aware of the vast amount of scholarship at their backs tending to impede their freedom. This is one of the reasons why Yeats 'safeguards' his conception of Dante – which is Romantic in all its essentials – by wrapping it up in the near impenetrability of *A Vision*. In Pound's discussions of Dante there is frequently a polemical element directed against the universities: if Yeats retreats into his visions Pound attempts to establish his ideas about Dante through sheer forcefulness, while with Eliot the problem is not so acute, partly because his ideas are more orthodox and because he comes to concentrate more and more on the implications of Dante's style, an area in which he was well qualified to make observations.

Armed then with the portraits, the anecdotes, and the facts of Dante's biography, Romantic critics had little difficulty in creating the Byronic Dante, and the fascination of such a personality was too strong not to intercede between them and Dante's work. Another comment by Macaulay represents the consummation of the ideas discussed so far:

> In every line of the *Divine Comedy* we discern the asperity which is

produced by pride struggling with misery. There is perhaps no work in the world so deeply and uniformly sorrowful. The melancholy of Dante was no fantastic caprice. It was not, as far as at this distance of time can be judged, the effect of external circumstances. It was from within. Neither love nor glory, neither the conflicts of earth nor the hope of heaven could dispel it. It turned every consolation and every pleasure into its own nature. It resembled that noxious Sardinian soil of which the intense bitterness is said to have been perceptible even in its honey. His mind was, in the noble language of the Hebrew poet 'a land of darkness, as darkness itself, and where the light was of darkness'. The gloom of his character discolours all the passions of men and all the face of nature, and tinges with its own livid hue the flowers of Paradise and the glories of the eternal throne. All the portraits of him are singularly characteristic. No person can look on the features, noble even to ruggedness, the dark furrows of the cheek, the haggard and woeful stare of the eye, the sullen and contemptuous curve of the lip, and doubt that they belong to a man too proud and too sensitive to be happy.[26]

As remarked in the previous chapter, there are obvious elements in Dante's life and work that do connect with the Romantic picture of him; it is not difficult to see how the one is transformed into the other even if one is amazed by the extent of the transformation. We have witnessed the Romantics' ignorance of the *Monarchia*, and one might repeat that the more one reads of Dante's various works – and here the *Convivio* seems especially important – the more absurd these Byronic notions become, founded as they are upon a rather sensationalised reading of the *Inferno* and on odd scraps of biography. Still, Dante's pride, for example, is well documented, as in the famous letter to the 'Amico Florentino' refusing what he saw as the dishonourable terms under which Florence would repeal his exile: 'Non est haec via redeundi ad patriam, Pater mi; sed si alia per vos antecedenter, deinde per alios invenitur, quae famae Dantisque honori non deroget, illam non lentis passibus acceptabo. Quod si per nullam talem Florentia introitur, nunquam Florentiam introibo' ('There is no way here of returning to my native country, Father; but if you to begin with, and others afterwards, can find a way which does not derogate from the reputation and honour of Dante, I will tread it with no slow steps. But if Florence can be entered by no such path, I shall never enter Florence') (*Ep.*IX.4). We can say of him, with the Childe, 'He would not yield dominion of his mind/To spirits against whom his own rebelled.' (III.xii). As Byron has him say in *The Prophecy*: 'mine is not a nature to be bent/By tyrannous faction, and the brawling crowd' (I.34–5). Dante, like Byron's Lara, impresses by the sheer power of his personality –

> So much he soared beyond, or sunk beneath,
> The men with whom he felt condemned to breathe
> (I.345–6)

– by his soaring and sinking to both Heaven and Hell. In the Victorian period we shall find a reaction to all this and the rather audacious attempt to cut Dante down to size.[27]

Turning to *The Prophecy of Dante* itself, we find Dante's Byronism handled with comparative restraint, which again suggests Byron deserves some apology for the way his name has been used in this chapter. He described the inspiration behind the poem as arising from his residence in Ravenna, adding an interesting afterthought about common destinies:

> The place of Dante's fifteen years' exile, where he so pathetically prayed for his country, and deprecated the thought of being buried out of it; and the sight of his tomb, which I passed in my almost daily rides, – inspired me. Besides, there was somewhat of resemblance in our destinies – he had a wife, and I have the same feelings about leaving my bones in a strange land.
> (Medwin, *Conversations*, p. 158)

In *The Prophecy* Dante goes rather with the more mellowed Childe of canto III of the *Pilgrimage* than with the wild, brooding outcast of cantos I and II; for instance, Byron makes Dante battle with, and finally overcome, his dreams of revenge against Florence, described luridly and then cast off with horror:

> Great God!
> Take these thoughts from me – to thy hands I yield
> My many wrongs, and thine Almighty rod
> Will fall on those who smote me . . .
> (I.118–21)

It is true that there is a sting in the tail; he cannot quite say with the Byron of *Childe Harold* IV, 'And pile on human heads the mountain of my curse! . . . That curse shall be Forgiveness' (cxxxiv–cxxxv), but he is presented as one who will yield up his own frustration and ire to God's tribunal, one of those 'Who could resist themselves even, hardest care!' and is thus emblemed as the 'Alp's snow summit' which 'nearer Heaven is seen/Than the Volcano's fierce eruptive crest' that suffers 'The Hell which in its entrails ever dwells' (III.181–93). 'So be it: we can bear', he says quite simply of his tribulations (IV.20). We have not quite the Dante of the *Paradiso*; but at least he repudiates (or claims to) his 'infernal' portion. The concept is similar to the Dante who represented 'self-Empire' in Chapter I, as opposed to, to take another example, Byron's judgement on Napoleon: 'An Empire thou couldst crush, command, rebuild,/But govern not thy pettiest passion' (*Childe Harold* III.xxxviii).

In *The Prophecy* Dante is imagined as speaking 'shortly before' his death (Preface), between

> the retrospect
> Of half a century bloody and black,
> And the frail few years I may expect
> Hoary and hopeless, but less hard to bear,
> For I have been too long and deeply wrecked
> On the lone rock of desolate Despair,
> To lift my eyes more to the passing sail
> Which shuns that reef so horrible and bare;
> Nor raise my voice – for who would heed my wail?
> (I.134–42)

But this heroism of hopelessness is really only a more discreet falsification of some of the ideas we have looked at; Dante's biographers mostly agree that, especially in his last years, he found some consolation in exile, namely a refuge at Ravenna in the court of Guido da Polenta, who raised the famous tomb after Dante's death.[28] Again, the above reflects the fatal influence of *Childe Harold*:

> Self-exiled Harold wanders forth again,
> With nought of Hope left – but with less of gloom;
> The very knowledge that he lived in vain,
> That all was over on this side the tomb,
> Had made Despair a smilingness assume . . .
> (III.xvi)

Byron makes Dante mourn his lot in words reminiscent of the passage from the *Convivio* quoted above (p. 43) –

> To live in narrow ways with little men,
> A common sight to every common eye,
> A wanderer, while even wolves can find a den
> (I.161–3)

– but the *Convivio* was written at least fourteen years before

Dante's death, when exile was still relatively fresh upon him;[29] in any case, it is the idea of Dante irrevocably and permanently stranded on 'the lone rock of desolate Despair' that one objects to particularly; could he ever have composed the *Commedia* in a state of resignedly waiting for death to put an end to his misfortunes? One need not minimise the hardships Dante experienced in exile, but again we know from the *Commedia* that he found some affection and concern after 1302, that someone 'heeded his wail'; if we doubt that Dante is referring to some such case with the mysterious reference to 'Gentucca' (*Purg.*XXIV.37), possibly his hostess in Lucca, we can always return to the verses on the della Scala family already mentioned. But references to these alleviations would spoil the plot of *The Prophecy*; for instance they would discredit Dante's address to Beatrice in the poem –

Thou sole pure Seraph of my earliest love,
Love so ineffable, and so alone,
That nought on earth could more my bosom move,
And meeting thee in Heaven was but to meet
That without which my Soul, like the arkless dove,
Had wander'd still in search of . . .

(I.20–5)

– not to mention the undesirable mitigating effect they would have on what I have described as the Byronic hero's *sine qua non*, the hidden woe of the lost loved one who 'ancor non m'abbandona'. We in fact know very well that other things *could* Dante's bosom move after he lost Beatrice; indeed, this is the entire point of Dante's undertaking his journey in the *Commedia*, for the pursuit of various types of 'falso piacer' ('false pleasure') after Beatrice's death led him into the dark wood that she rescues him from, upbraiding him thus on their reunion in the *paradiso terrestre*:

Alcun tempo il sostenni col mio volto:
mostrando li occhi giovanetti a lui,
meco il menava in dritta parte vòlto.
Sì tosto come in su la soglia fui
di mia seconda etade e mutai vita,
questi si tolse a me, e diessi altrui.

(I sustained him for some time with my countenance, showing my youthful eyes to him and leading him with me, turned in the right direction. As soon as I was on the threshold of my second age and changed lives, this man took himself from me and gave himself to another.)

(*Purg.*XXX.121–6)

'He gave himself to another.' And whether Beatrice means here another woman, or an over-infatuation with 'la donna Filosofia' (which would be the last thing to interest the Byronists), or something other than both, does not particularly matter: Dante *did* find other love after Beatrice's death, and declared it himself for *Filosofia*: 'io, che cercava di consolarme, trovai . . . a le mie lagrime rimedio . . . Sì che in picciol tempo, forse di trenta mesi, cominciai tanto a sentire de la sua dolcezza, che lo suo amore cacciava e distruggeva ogni altro pensiero' ('I, seeking to console myself, found . . . a remedy for my tears . . . So that in a short while, perhaps thirty months, I began to feel her sweetness so much that love for her drove out and destroyed all other thoughts') (*Convivio* II.xii.5–7). But, although the Romantic critics (and their Victorian successors) could look certain harsh facts of Dante's existence in the face, such as his exile, and indeed rhapsodise over them, one harsh fact they consistently smooth over: this 'infidelity' to Beatrice, the anything but romantic reunion in *Purgatorio* XXX and XXXI. Instead, we are asked to believe, as in Macaulay, that 'all love, excepting the half mystic passion which he still felt for his buried Beatrice, had palled on the fierce and restless exile' ('Essay on Dante', p. 614).

The premise of *The Prophecy* then is Dante's inhabiting 'the lone rock of desolate Despair' with Promethean heroism, the rock being the entire earth, and he, with no chance of ever being unbound –

> An exile, saddest of all prisoners,
> Who has the whole world for a dungeon strong,
> Seas, mountains, and the horizon's verge for bars
> (IV.131–3)

– an assertion that exactly contradicts, incidentally, Dante's letter to his Florentine friend, refusing Florence's conditions: 'nonne solis astrorumque specula ubique conspiciam? Nonne dulcissimas veritates potero speculari ubique sub coelo . . .?' ('will I not be able to look at the mirrors of the sun and stars everywhere? Will I not be able to speculate on the sweetest truths beneath any sky . . .?') (*Ep.*IX.4). In fact, the opening lines of *The Prophecy* immediately strike a dubious chord: 'Once more in Man's frail world! which I had left/So long that 'twas forgotten . . .' But Dante never forgets this world; the aim of the *Commedia* is to teach man a religious *and* a political morality which indeed are complementary in his thought. Byron might not then have thought 'privately' that Dante was especially Byronic; but a poem treating him thus was too good an opportunity to miss. It is a good poem too, I think, showing an accomplished handling of the *terza rima*, though this is not, compared with *The Triumph of Life*, particularly 'Dantesque'.

Yet Byron's Dante has some concern for the world, some 'fight' left in him; we perhaps only realise how much after reading Rossetti's poem on the exile, 'Dante at Verona', where the protagonist has been utterly drained of any resistance whatsoever to the misery of his situation (see Chapter IV). Dante can still indulge in another frequent Byronic activity, the curse:

> Florence! when thy harsh sentence razed my roof,
> I loved thee; but the vengeance of my verse,
> The hate of injuries which every year
> Makes greater, and accumulates my curse,
> Shall live, outliving all thou holdest dear . . .
>
> (IV.111–15)

But the general tone of the poem is more one of sorrow than anger; rather more muted indeed than Dante's own invectives against Florence as in *Purgatorio* VI.127–51.[30]

After all the above, it might be refreshing to quote two comments from a Romantic critic of greater authority as a Dantist than those we have looked at: Foscolo. In his *Essays on Petrarch* he includes a long comparison between Dante and Petrarch which is extremely interesting for the purposes of our discussion. For Foscolo, it was Petrarch who 'entice[s] us into a morbid indulgence of our feelings, and withdraw[s] us from active life', while Dante 'calls into action all the faculties of our soul', a formulation nearer to Shelley's response than to Byron's. Moreover, Foscolo notes that Petrarch was actually 'more unhappy than Dante, who never betrayed that restlessness and perplexity of soul which lowered Petrarch in his own estimation . . .' (pp. 183–4, 205). Yet Petrarch would not particularly have answered the Romantics' needs, for, as Foscolo suggests, his 'gloom' was something approaching a more modern *ennui* than the Titanesque misery the Romantics found in Dante and of which they could say 'there is power'.

The final, and indeed fullest, treatment of Dante the Byronic hero is in the third of Carlyle's lectures *On Heroes* of 1840, 'The Hero as Poet'. The lecture is really a compendium of all the secondary material on Dante we have referred to: it again starts out, not from Dante's poetry, but from a long exordium on Dante's face:

After all commentaries, the Book itself is mainly what we know of him. The Book; – and one might add that Portrait commonly attributed to Giotto, which, looking on it, you cannot help inclining to think genuine, whoever did it. To me it is a most touching face; perhaps of all faces that I know, the most so. Blank there, painted on vacancy, with the simple laurel wound round it; the deathless sorrow and pain, the known victory which is also deathless; – significant of the whole history of Dante! I think it is the mournfulest face that ever was painted from reality; an altogether tragic, heart-affecting face. There is in it, as foundation of it, the softness, tenderness, gentle affection as of a child; but all this is as if congealed into sharp contradiction, into abnegation, isolation, proud hopeless pain. A soft ethereal soul looking out so stern, implacable, grim-trenchant, as from imprisonment of thick-ribbed ice! Withal it is a silent pain too, a silent scornful one: the lip is curled in a kind of godlike disdain of the thing that is eating out his heart, – as if it were withal a mean insignificant thing, as if he whom it had power to torture and strangle were greater than it! The face of one wholly in protest, and life-long unsurrendering battle, against the world.[31]

One might suggest as a specific source for this Satano-Promethean hero Byron's description of Parisina's husband in old age, living with the fact of his son's execution at his own hand:

> never tear his cheek descended,
> And never smile his brow unbended;
> And o'er that fair broad brow were wrought
> The intersected lines of thought;
> Those furrows which the burning share
> Of Sorrow ploughs untimely there;
> Scars of the lacerating mind
> Which the Soul's war doth leave behind.
> He was past all mirth or woe:
> Nothing more remained below
> But sleepless nights and heavy days,
> A mind all dead to scorn or praise,
> A heart which shunned itself – and yet
> That would not yield, nor could forget,
> Which, when it least appeared to melt,
> Intently thought – intensely felt:
> The deepest ice which ever froze
> Can only o'er the surface close;
> The living stream lies quick below,
> And flows, and cannot cease to flow.
> (ll. 537–56)

One needs, however, no specific source to demonstrate the

provenance of Carlyle's observations above; and it is remarkable how he ignores his own hint that the portrait might not be 'genuine' and proceeds to base his entire meditation upon it. One might note, however, the increased sentiment in Carlyle's picture, with its 'softness, tenderness, gentle affection as of a child', an emphasis reminding us, I think, that we are in 1840 rather than in 1820. The rest of the lecture is a familiar *pot-pourri*: Dante's miserable marriage (p. 141), his misery at Can Grande's – 'Such a man, with his proud silent ways, with his sarcasms and sorrows, was not made to succeed at court' (p. 144), his miserable end, dying 'broken-hearted' (p. 145), the Satanic quality of his imagination which leads to Carlyle's exclusion of two-thirds of the *Commedia*: 'You remember that first view he gets of the Hall of Dite: *red* pinnacle, redhot cone of iron glowing through the dim immensity of gloom; – so vivid, so distinct, visible at once and forever! It is an emblem of the whole genius of Dante' (p. 150; later he calls Dante 'deep, fierce as the central fire of the world' (p. 164), cf. Hazlitt's 'furnace'); and finally the pathos of Dante's fidelity towards Beatrice: although 'The earthly world had cast him forth to wander, wander; no living heart to love him now; for his sore miseries there was no solace here' (p. 144), yet:

> I know not in the world an affection equal to that of Dante. It is a tenderness, a trembling, longing, pitying love: like the wail of Aeolean harps, soft, soft; like a child's young heart; – and then that stern, sore-saddened heart! These longings of his towards his Beatrice; their meeting together in the *Paradiso* [sic]; his gazing in her pure transfigured eyes, her that had been purified by death so long, separated from him so far: ah, one likens it to the song of angels; it is among the purest utterances of affection, perhaps the very purest, that ever came out of a human soul.
> (p. 153)

The idea of the 'sore-saddened heart' is again Byronic –

> They did not know how Hate can burn
> In hearts once changed from soft to stern
> (*The Siege of Corinth*, ll. 322–3; Vol.III, 462)

– but this last comment of Carlyle's is really the preliminary design for the softer, pastel colours of the 'Pre-Raphaelite' Dante.

After all this, one can be excused for thinking Dante never had a fair chance in Carlyle's subsequent comparison of him with Shakespeare: 'Withal the joyful tranquillity of [Shakespeare] is notable. I will not blame Dante for his misery: it is as battle without victory; but true battle, the first, indispensable thing. Yet I call Shakespeare greater than Dante, in that he fought truly, and did conquer' (p. 175). But probably the most bewildering statement in the essay is this: 'I do not agree with much modern criticism, in greatly preferring the *Inferno* to the other two parts of the Divine *Commedia*. Such preference belongs, I imagine, to our general Byronism of taste, and is like to be a transient feeling' (p. 154). Can Carlyle really be unaware that his own lecture is one of the most prominent examples of 'Byronism of taste' on record? And we are justified, I think, in claiming that Carlyle's taste in this respect is predominantly a means of self-expression rather than a means of genuinely approaching Dante; a means of establishing a rapport which a friend of his suggested between

> l'âme de Dante et celle de Carlyle, qui chemine aussi, lui, dans ce monde comme une âme en peine douée de toutes les susceptibilités les plus douloureuses. Il n'a aucune sympathie pour ceux qui veulent faire de la vie humaine une fête et un enchaînement de jouissances, lui qui n'y voit qu'une lutte dont il a conscience à toutes les heures de son existence.[32]

However, Carlyle was at least right that the overwhelming influence of the *Inferno* was a transient phenomenon. And, indeed, only a few weeks after his lecture was delivered occurred an event of great significance for our story, the uncovering of another 'portrait' of Dante in the Cappella della Podestà in the Bargello in Florence (Plate 3); indeed, the celebrated long-lost portrait by Giotto which Vasari had recorded and which Carlyle thought he was discussing, when in fact he was referring to the Tofanelli portrait showing Dante with the 'simple laurel'.[33] The new portrait, which soon became widely popular, showed no crabbed old man or sullen speculator but a figure in the flower of youth whose influence on Rossetti and his contemporaries was considerable. But before we go on to examine this, we have to take in another important event of 1840: the appearance of Browning's *Sordello*.

III

Browning, Dante and the two Sordellos

'that help was prematurely thrust
'Aside, perchance! . . .' (*Sordello*, final version)

'Dante and Shakespeare are a peculiar Two. They dwell apart, in a kind of royal solitude; none equal, none second to them: in the general feeling of the world, a certain transcendentalism, a glory as of complete perfection, invests these two' ('The Hero as Poet', p. 138). During the 1840s, however, the kind of interest that Dante arouses is rather different from Carlyle's adulation: he is dethroned from his solitude and the connexions are stressed between him and his contemporaries, though a fuller discussion of this interest in 'Dante and his circle' will have to wait till the following chapter. Browning's own approach to Dante has also little in common with that of the writers discussed so far; indeed, his belief in the gradual evolution of poetry as a mechanism for the ever more thorough analysis of human nature and its relationship with the Divinity – as outlined in *Sordello* and the 'Essay on Shelley' – ensures automatically that Dante's 'glory' is diminished somewhat compared with its extent in Romantic criticism. It is true that in *A Defence of Poetry* one can trace a similar idea of a social and in some senses poetical progress through the ages; but it can be claimed that the amount of attention Shelley pays to Dante in *A Defence*, taken together with *The Triumph of Life*, indicates that Shelley came to see Dante's mastery as less and less superseded in any way. I believe, as will become apparent, that a similar process of revision can be detected in Browning's own career, but, in his early and middle years at least, his belief that Shelley himself most nearly approached what he terms 'the whole poet' than 'any other writer whose record is among us' guarantees a lower rung for Dante on 'that mighty ladder, of which, however cloud-involved and undefined may glimmer the topmost step, the world dares no longer doubt that its gradations ascend' ('Essay on Shelley', pp. 9–11).

The best place to examine the complexities of Browning's attitude to Dante is in *Sordello*, where he makes several direct references to him. The subject of the poem is part of this new interest in Dante's contemporaries and near-contemporaries and, although its notorious difficulties have always prevented it from being widely read, it has had, one might say, some important admirers: Rossetti pays tribute to it in the preface to his translations,[1] and part of Pound's admiration for it is doubtless a result of his own desire to see Dante as 'heralded' by an important forerunner, in his case Cavalcanti. Lionel Stevenson noted:

> When Shelley was at school, the dominant geological hypothesis was 'catastrophism', with its impressive concept of violent transformations. By the time Tennyson and Browning were inquiring into cosmology, the 'uniformitarianism' of Hutton and Lyell had established the belief in an imperceptibly slow evolution.[2]

Whether Dante himself was 'evolved' or violently precipitated remains an extremely active question until well into the twentieth century, as we shall see. Part of the complex inadequacy of Browning's own Sordello is his inability to work by stages, his desire to have historical transformation brought about overnight by this 'Promethean' catastrophism; by 1840 he might be regarded as himself an anachronism. One feels that, as Browning saw him, the unfortunate fellow is something of an anachronism for the thirteenth century too, so that it seems a little hard to accept one critic's claim that '*Sordello* has an important bearing . . . on the steady pushing back of the dating of the "Dark Ages"', since its hero's historical authenticity seems so doubtful;[3] as Stewart W. Holmes has clearly shown, Browning has taken vast liberties with his historical sources,[4] and surely *Sordello*'s readers can never have imagined they were being shown a character with anything other than very nineteenth-century preoccupations. What we are concerned with in this chapter is not so much the contrast between the 'heralded' Dante and the figure whose poem Hazlitt saw as 'the first great step from Gothic darkness and barbarism' (quoted above, p. 23) but rather with the relationship Browning sets up between his own Sordello and the Sordello found in cantos VI to VIII of Dante's *Purgatorio*.

At first sight the two seem to be in a totally unqualified opposition. The theory of poetic evolution referred to above is described in Book v:

> I covet the first task
> And marshal yon Life's elemental Masque,
> Of Men, on evil or on good lay stress,
> This light, this shade make prominent, suppress
> All ordinary hues that softening blend
> Such natures with the level: apprehend
> Which evil is, which good, if I allot
> Your Hell, the Purgatory, Heaven ye wot,
> To those you doubt concerning: I enwomb
> Some wretched Friedrich with his red-hot tomb,
> Some dubious spirit, Lombard Agilulph
> With the black chastening river I engulf;
> Some unapproached Matilda I enshrine
> With languors of the planet of decline –
> These fail to recognize, to arbitrate
> Between henceforth, to rightly estimate
> Thus marshalled in the Masque! Myself, the while,
> As one of you, am witness, shrink or smile
> At my own showing! Next age – what's to do?
> The men and women stationed hitherto
> Will I unstation, good and bad, conduct
> Each nature to its farthest, or obstruct
> At soonest in the world: Light, thwarted, breaks
> A limpid purity to rainbow flakes,
> Or Shadow, helped, freezes to gloom: behold
> How such, with fit assistance to unfold,
> Or obstacles to crush them, disengage
> Their forms, love, hate, hope, fear, peace make, war wage,
> In presence of you all! Myself implied
> Superior now, as, by the platform's side
> Bidding them do and suffer to content
> The world . . . no – that I wait not – circumvent
> A few it has contented, and to these
> Offer unveil the last of mysteries
> I boast! Man's life shall have yet freer play:
> Once more I cast external things away,
> And Natures, varied now, so decompose
> That . . . but enough!
>
> (pp. 196–8)[5]

Progress in poetry is established as an increasingly sophisticated analysis of human nature which gradually rids itself of the 'external' devices it had earlier depended on to present humanity; in Dante's case the theological classification of vice and virtue (the Emperor Friedrich is indeed referred to as one of the entombed Epicureans in *Inferno* x.119), and in the case of the poet of the 'Next age', the stage or 'platform' on which character is presented through the interaction of dramatic roles, Browning then suggesting that the form he has himself adopted in *Sordello* is, though evolving from these earlier stages, a progressively 'purer' analytical tool. This last point is clearer in the amended version of the poem where Browning alters and interrupts the above speech of Sordello thus:

> 'Once more I cast external things away,
> 'And natures composite, so decompose
> 'That' . . . Why, he writes *Sordello*!
> (v.618–20)[6]

This idea of what is essential in literary history – that is, the presentation of man – being scaffolded by external forms that can afterwards be dismantled, is again referred to earlier in Book v in more political terms, where Hildebrand's contribution to the history of civilisation is seen as built up from what can then be regarded as the 'scaffold' for it: that is, Charlemagne's refounding of a social ideal (pp. 178–80). It is, I believe, a rather melancholy fact that Browning is the last poet we shall be looking at who does not regard his own verse as in some measure a 'falling-off' from Dante's, because this is what the various twentieth-century ideas of a 'dissociation of sensibility' all imply; while there seems to be, as will be argued, a certain undervaluing of Dante in Browning's approach to him, it may well be that Dante himself would have had more sympathy with Browning's concerns to adjust the human to the Divine than with the more fulsome praises of later poets whose interests have had less direct connexions with his own.

The advance towards the 'freer play' of man's life sets out then from Dante and leads to *Sordello* itself: by 'unstationing' one of the *Commedia*'s own characters and then refashioning him, Browning can show how far poetry has come in the contrast between the two Sordellos. Before examining them it will be as well to point out that there are passages in Browning's poem expressing an obvious admiration for Dante. In the passage already quoted, his achievement is indeed stated rather in passing, which might lead us to miss its significance: Dante's recording of 'Life's elemental Masque,/Of *Men*' (my italics) contrasts with Sordello's failure to observe an earlier injunction in Book II, or at least to persevere in the attempt:

> present us with ourselves, at least,
> Not portions of ourselves, mere loves and hates
> Made flesh . . .
>
> (p. 68)

Thus Browning would agree with Erich Auerbach, let us say, about the importance of Dante's poem in the evolution of *mimesis*. Even so, Browning's eyes remained fixed on the future rather than on the past; he could say with his Paracelsus, 'these things tend still upward, progress is/The law of life, man is not Man as yet' (*PW*, V.743–4), and this rather leads him into taking Dante's work for granted.

On the other hand, there is the tribute to Dante in Book I, where Sordello himself is first introduced to the reader. It again needs to be quoted at length:

> for he – for he –
> 'Gate-vein of this hearts' blood of Lombardy'
> (If I should falter now) – for he is Thine!
> Sordello, thy forerunner, Florentine!
> A herald-star I know thou didst absorb
> Relentless into the consummate orb
> That scared it from its right to roll along
> A sempiternal path with dance and song
> Fulfilling its allotted period
> Serenest of the progeny of God
> Who yet resigns it not; his darling stoops
> With no quenched lights, desponds with no blank troops
> Of disenfranchised brilliances, for, blent
> Utterly with thee, its shy element
> Like thine upburneth prosperous and clear:
> Still, what if I approach the august sphere
> Named now with only one name, disentwine
> That under current soft and argentine
> From its fierce mate in the majestic mass
> Leavened as the sea whose fire was mixt with glass
> In John's transcendent vision, launch once more
> That lustre? Dante, pacer of the shore
> Where glutted Hell disgorgeth filthiest gloom,
> Unbitten by its whirring sulphur–spume –

Or whence the grieved and obscure waters slope
Into a darkness quieted by hope –
Plucker of amaranths grown beneath God's eye
In gracious twilights where his Chosen lie,
I would do this! If I should falter now –
(pp. 15–17)

The expression 'consummate orb' used here for Dante is especially significant, for the orb is used throughout the poem for historical figures who, through achieving a certain personal completeness (somewhat similar to Yeats's concept of 'unity of being', discussed in Chapter v) mark the crucial stages of civilisation's advance (see especially Book v, p. 195). Sordello's failure is represented as an inability to round into an orb, to unify certain antitheses, for instance the 'Man-part' with the 'Poet-part' (II, pp. 71–3); this internal incoherence leads him in turn to be unable to complete the larger unity with the people by espousing the Guelph cause on their behalf. Progress is seen ideally then as a pattern of widening concentric circles, like the rings of a tree, leading in time – if we look again at the 'Essay on Shelley' – to this latter's 'spheric' poetical faculty which most nearly shows the 'whole poet' (pp. 10–11). And since the outer growth-rings, if larger, depend on the existence of the inner – 'The sphere though larger, is not more complete ' (VI, p. 227) – then Browning's talk of Dante's 'consummate orb' emphasises that his success, in contrast with Sordello's failure, was a willingness to perform the circumscribed role history had assigned him, and thereby suggests that Dante himself was an evolutionist. Sordello of course wants to complete all the circles at once; having been 'Goito's God of yore', he is unable to respond to the call to 'dwindle to a Guelf' (v, p. 186), and, because he sees the sphere does not become more complete, he can see no reason for bothering to enlarge it, in that great final duty-evading soliloquy in Book VI (pp. 222–35). The orb–sphere–circle image (anticipating the Ring) recurs constantly in *Sordello*; Sordello's despair at the 'concentricity' of history is compounded at the point of death by the realisation that this may be the condition of eternity too; that the circle he could not complete in life, with the 'Soul's no whit/More than the Body's purpose under it' (VI, p. 239), might be the demand of a series of successive spheres after death where some 'new bond/In place of flesh' might again impede Mind's 'flight' beyond the allotted boundary (VI, p. 236). We may be forgiven for anticipating at this point since this is exactly how we find Sordello in the *Purgatorio*, stranded as it were at the foot of the seven terraces. But there his condition is ameliorated by Grace; and indeed in Browning's poem he is rescued from his agonising meditations by the Christian revelation just as he dies (VI, pp. 240–2).

To return to the orbs of civilisation, we find that the work of Charlemagne and Hildebrand described in Book V (pp. 178–80) is seen as leading ideally to the work of the great poets, beginning with Dante. The first two, as men of action, imposed social progress by force, by 'stress/Of Strength' (pp. 178, 180), but the aim is a more civilised mechanism of change:

> Thought is the soul of act, and stage by stage,
> Is soul from body still to disengage
> As tending to a freedom which rejects
> Such help and incorporeally affects
> The world, producing deeds but not by deeds,
> Swaying, in others, frames itself exceeds,
> Assigning them the simpler tasks it used
> As patiently perform till Song produced
> Acts, by thoughts only, for the mind . . .
>
> (p. 196)

Sordello then goes on, in the passage we began by quoting, to refer to Dante as the first one to show 'Men'. The suggestion that Dante himself was dependent on the earlier 'inner rings' of the two men of action is novel; thus Browning would doubtless have agreed with the first, but rejected the second, of Hazlitt's two propositions: 'Dante was the father of modern poetry . . . His poem is the first great step from Gothic darkness and barbarism' (quoted above p. 23). Sordello himself is Dante's forerunner too; but Browning makes little of his actual 'success' in this respect; that is, though he states that Sordello 'rewrought . . . Language' – acknowledging Dante's tribute to him in the *De Vulgari Eloquentia* as 'tantus eloquentie vir existens, non solum in poetando sed quomodocunque loquendo patrium vulgare deseruit' (' a man of great eloquence, who deserted his native tongue not only in writing poetry but in all types of discourse') (I.XV.2) – he rapidly passes on to his failure to do anything effective with it (II, pp. 68ff). He points out that Sordello did indeed pass with posterity for a 'God' (VI, p. 250), but Browning's evolutionary theory posits this kind of success as a ghastly irony compared with the cosmic proportions of his failure.

This is because he has located Sordello at the most crucial point in the chain. It is again where two antitheses should be reconciled: power and poetry, the stage of working 'part by Strength and part/by Knowledge' (v, p. 182), the junction between Hildebrand and Dante falling plumb on Sordello's shoulders; 'The moment's the great moment of all time!', as Strafford says in Browning's play.[7] Sordello is 'He whom fortune wafts/This very age her best inheritance/Of opportunities' (v, p. 185). He is already a poet who has found his songs to have considerable influence on men (as for example Salinguerra informs us, IV, p. 163); he then gets the chance to become a political leader and thus realise the complete 'Apollo', 'Half minstrel and half emperor' (I, p. 38). At this point it is perhaps a good idea to take a breath before embarking on the magnitude of what Browning is suggesting in this extraordinary poem. Beneath all the obscurities the evolutionary thesis that commits him to this crucial focal point in the thirteenth century is clear enough; to maintain it he has abused his historical sources by making Sordello Salinguerra's son (and thus giving him the real opportunity of leadership), and by having Sordello die young under the awful burden of his historical significance. What we have in *Sordello* is a modern myth of the Fall, a specific point in history where the evolution went wrong and which Browning is calling attention to for the first time:

lo, a step's awry, a bulge
To be corrected by a step we thought
Got over long ago – till that is wrought,
No progress!

(v, p. 182)

But of course there is no going back; the imperfection of Sordello's orb or 'ring' has thrown all the subsequent rings out of true too; what Sordello

should have been,
Could be, and was not – the one step too mean
For him to take, we suffer at this day
Because of; Ecelin had pushed away
Its chance ere Dante could arrive to take
That step Sordello spurned, for the world's sake:
He did much – but Sordello's step was gone.
Thus had Sordello ta'en that step alone,
Apollo had been compassed . . .

(VI, pp. 250–1)

What 'we suffer at this day' is not, as has been suggested, the lack of Italian unity alone[8] but, through Sordello's failure, a universal imperfection in society; on one level the 'sad disheveled [sic] ghost' of Book III (p. 115) represents all humanity suffering the consequences. As remarked above, civilisation started to go wrong within the private circle of Sordello himself, where man and poet, soul and body could not be harmonised; this left him unfit to round into the larger circles by combining with Palma, who brought love (the need for which is stressed in Book VI, pp. 217–18), or with Salinguerra, who brought power; and one might also add with Eglamor, who brought a sense of duty and devotion to the poetic art. The infection, as it were, spread outwards: the largest and most important circle, his combination with the people, to work on their behalf, was recognised by Sordello in theory –

> the new body, ere he could suspect,
> Cohered, mankind and he were really fused
> (IV, p. 140)

– but was not actually achieved. And so the troubles of Browning's own day are seen as radiating from the flawed personality of a thirteenth-century poet–magnate to whom history had hitherto felt little need of paying much attention. Sordello's mission was finally to combine the great social antithesis of Guelph and Ghibelline by submitting himself to the former cause as head of the latter; to anticipate again we remember that if, on earth, this union proved impossible, we find Sordello after death in Dante's poem introducing pairs of erstwhile enemies now reconciled in the Valley of the Rulers (*Purg.* VII.91–136). It will be clear, I think, that we need not accept Browning's declaration of 1863 that the historical detail was only the 'background' to his story of 'the development of a soul';[9] rather early thirteenth-century Italy provided him with a suitable setting to study a soul whose divisions are a microcosmic copy of a wider political polarisation into opposite camps.

Poor Sordello is then largely responsible for the continuing variance on earth as opposed to the unity in *Purgatory*; but given that we had the right place and right time in history to amend this variance, Browning adds the observation that Dante, and not Sordello, was the right man for the job. It is typical of Browning to be attracted to the idea that a perfect conjunction of circumstances was missed only by Dante's having been born fifty years or so too late; his characters are tantalised by the 'near miss' throughout his poetry. Although Hildebrand 'groaned', as Sordello says, at a task 'Paul had moaned,/[And] Moses failed beneath' (v, pp. 181–2), he still accepted it; Dante did so too, after his initial alarm at being singled out to visit the afterlife – 'Io non Enëa, io non Paulo sono' ('I'm not Aeneas, I'm not Paul') (*Inf.* II.32). But it must be said in fairness to Sordello that the burden Browning gives him is even greater than Dante's or Hildebrand's, or at least utterly ill-suited to his capacities. Since he is the type of character who wants to build Rome in a day, he is especially vulnerable to the prophetic powers Browning forces on him; that is, his prior knowledge of how history will 'turn out', revealed in the passage already quoted where he more or less predicts Browning's poem on him, impedes him from making his proper contribution to it: the more he realises what he should do, the less he feels inclined to do it, as stressed in lines added to the later edition –

> 'God has conceded two sights to a man –
> 'One, of men's whole work, time's completed plan,
> 'The other, of the minute's work, man's first
> 'Step to the plan's completeness . . .'
>
> (*PW*, v.85–8)

The two sights are yet another duality that conflict, rather than harmonise, in Sordello, though this problem is really at the root of the poem's form, which takes stupendous leaps from the thirteenth to the nineteenth century and back again. It seems that Browning has deliberately wrapped his claim for Sordello's would-be importance in a cloak of confusions, as if he could not trust either his reader or himself to accept it were it stated directly; not only does he distort historical fact, as remarked, but he adds to the confusion with the rather bewildering changes of locale, time-span and grammatical subject introduced continuously throughout the poem. Thus his 'remedy' for having taken liberties with his subject is to take even more: he anticipates the charge of changing the identity of a character found in Dante by brazenly meeting it head-on:

> Strange that three such confessions so should hap
> To Palma Dante spoke with in the clear
> Amorous silence of the Swooning-sphere.
> Cunizza, as he called her!
>
> (v, pp. 213–14)

I think the bravado ultimately induces one to accept the poem as myth rather than history. Sordello can be regarded as fallen man generally, and 'into one face/The many faces crowd' (III, pp. 117–18); he is indeed another version of the 'sad disheveled ghost' who represents the bulk of humanity unable to complete their spheres, an emblem of human failure under the control of another figure Browning describes in *The Ring and the Book* as 'a dusk misfeatured messenger,/No other than the angel of this life' (I.594). Indeed, Browning's own attitude to Sordello has as much contradictory duality as any of Sordello's own, whose inaction is both condemned and smiled upon: as Festus told Paracelsus, 'The weakness you reveal endears you more' (III.865, p. 101). Browning's 'disentwining' of Sordello from Dante's sphere is a stand for all those history has judged adversely or forgotten, that 'luckless residue we send to crouch/In corners out of sight' (III, p. 117), who might have achieved success had they found

outward influence,
A soul, in Palma's phrase, above his soul,
Power to uplift his power . . .
(VI, pp. 217–18)

At the same time, Browning does not wish to endorse the evading of one's duty, or 'yoke'. The poem's Christianity is of course fundamental here: Sordello's hapless floundering after leaving his 'Paradise' (I, p. 27) at Goito is ended by a vision of the Incarnation, but the price of this is his death; as both Paracelsus and Guido Franceschini find, it is a common trick of the 'angel of this life' in Browning to grant understanding too late. The Incarnation in *Sordello* –

Ah, my Sordello, I this once befriend
And speak for you. A Power above him still
Which, utterly incomprehensible,
Is out of rivalry, which thus he can
Love
. . .
[and] a Power its representative
Who, being for authority the same,
Communication different, should claim
A course the first chose and this last revealed –
This Human clear, as that Divine concealed
(VI, pp. 240–1)

– is of course an exemplar for human behaviour, a course of action revealed to man. The task Sordello shirks of submitting his soul to earthly conditions, of 'Fit[ting] to the finite his infinity' (VI, p. 237) and thus doing his 'minute's work' in life, was accepted by Christ who, in Dante's lovely words, 'non disdegnò di farsi sua fattura' ('did not disdain to make himself into what he had made') (*Par.* XXXIII.6). Sordello's last-minute illumination in Browning's poem, together with the complete absence of any religious notions in his outlook until then, tallies, as we have remarked, with Dante's locating him in the *Antipurgatorio* as one of the late (and very late) repentant. In a letter to Elizabeth of December 1845, Browning quoted the lines from *Purgatorio* V.52–7 –

> Noi fummo tutti già per forza morti,
> e peccatori infino a l'ultima ora;
> quivi lume del ciel ne fece accorti,
> sì che, pentendo e perdonando, fora
> di vita uscimmo a Dio pacificati,
> che del disio di sé veder n'accora

(We all at some time died by violence, and were sinners up to our last hour; then, light from heaven gave us understanding, so that, repenting and forgiving, we left our lives at peace with God, who pierces our hearts with the desire to see him)

– and added 'Which is just my Sordello's story'.[10] In spite, then, of its extreme political or social claims the poem is, theologically, rather orthodox, another fundamental duality in Browning. To his explanation of the poem's theme in Book III, 'what I sing's the fate of such/As find our common nature . . . Cling when they would discard it' (p. 127), he added what I take to be a rather reluctant hint in 1863 that Sordello's fate indeed has this orthodox outcome after all its earlier enigmas: 'But that's the story – dull enough, confess!' (III.985).

Not that Sordello's story can be summed up with just those six lines from Dante. Indeed, to quote Festus's words to Paracelsus again –

> I call your sin exceptional;
> It springs from one whose life has passed the bounds
> Prescribed to life. Compound that fault with God!
> I speak of men; to common men like me
> The weakness you reveal endears you more
> (III.861–5)

– is to realise that this duality of vision, systematised by Browning in the 'Essay on Shelley' as 'what man sees' and 'what God sees' (pp. 6–7), is also fundamental to *Sordello*, and, indeed, to all Browning's poetry; as Mason says, 'It takes several forms, involving related questions; it is the dilemma of religious or realistic, expressive or dramatic, didactic or descriptive, and even of withdrawal from or involvement in the world' ('A Study', p. 222). The important connexion, which we shall go on to explore, that exists between how Dante saw Sordello and how Browning saw him, taken together with the fact that the two are manifestly widely different, has, not surprisingly, led some critics to claim that Dante's figure is also at the centre of the later poem and others that he has nothing at all to do with it.[11] Both propositions are, to an extent, true: if we concentrate on Browning's attempt to see 'what man sees' in *Sordello* then it is already clear that his hero 'challenges' Dante's picture of him: the *Commedia*'s religious classifications 'scaffold' the presentation of various humanity but permit no prolonged analysis of men's inner states. It is here that Browning parts company with the Romantics, for many of whom, as we have seen, Dante had here and there allowed the 'scaffold' to slip into the background in his sympathy (conscious or otherwise) with certain figures like Francesca and Ulysses who came to be regarded as practically heroine and hero of the *Inferno*; as Auerbach said, the paradoxical outcome of Dante's ability to 'show Men' resulted in the pattern being broken 'by the overwhelming power of the images it had to contain' (*Mimesis*, p. 202). Browning saw the Men there in Dante too, but he still saw the pattern as very much intact; his lack of interest in such Romantic favourites as Paolo and Francesca is symptomatic of this; and indeed only a poet desirous of creating men and women of an unprecedented subtlety could, one feels, have regarded Dante as primarily a classifier, an unusual emphasis we shall be coming back to.

It becomes, however, increasingly apparent that Browning's attitude to the classification in Dante is far from dismissive, whatever his doubts about it as an 'external thing' to poetry. Indeed, the difficulties of doing without it had already been presented in the hectic, disorganised inspiration that afflicts Aprile in *Paracelsus*:

> Didst thou . . .
> Ne'er range thy mind's extent, as some wide hall,
> Dazzled by shapes that filled its length with light,

Shapes clustered there to rule thee, not obey,
That will not wait thy summons, will not rise
Singly, nor when thy practised eye and hand
Can well transfer their loveliness, but crowd
By thee forever, bright to thy despair?
(II.574–81)

Although Browning might 'outdo' Dante by showing one character in infinitely greater complexity, he remained aware that at some stage 'what man sees' has to be related to 'what God sees' and that this last involves an unavoidable element of judgement; the 'subjective' poet has to take over from the 'objective', to use terms from the 'Essay on Shelley' that remain to be discussed. As Mason says: 'the problem of whether the new analytical and pluralistic poetry could really achieve a fresh moral synthesis occupied Browning throughout his life' ('A Study', p. 145). Aprile's gargantuan, indiscriminate love – 'I would LOVE infinitely, and be loved!' (II.385) – ruins him; the contrast with Dante is spelt out most importantly in 'One Word More' –

Dante, who loved well because he hated,
Hated wickedness that hinders loving
(ll. 42–3, *PW*, p. 768)

– and indeed Dante can be seen as unifying the two halves of Aprile and Paracelsus, whose inordinate desires 'to love' and 'to know' need to be mutually regulated, a conclusion we are left with at the end of *Paracelsus* itself, together with the idea that 'even hate is but a mask of love's' (V.874). This reads somewhat like an endorsement of those harsh lines over Hell-gate about the involvement of ''l primo amore' in the creation of Hell (*Inf.* III.6), and this marks a real break between Browning and Shelley, who attempts, as we have seen, a sort of obliviousness to the condemnations meted out in the *Commedia*. For him, 'from the lowest depths of hell,/Through every paradise and through all glory,/Love led [Dante] serene . . .' (*The Triumph of Life* ll. 472–4); but the rather fearsome Dante of 'One Word More' illustrates that Love's judicial function necessarily upsets its serenity; moreover this characterisation of 'Love' receives its final endorsement in Browning's admiration for the extraordinary extremes of love and hate that go to make up Caponsacchi. And it is in *The Ring and the Book* that one senses most obviously a return to something like a 'Dantesque' presentation of humanity where judgement is outspokenly present, a completing of the circle back towards Dante which on one level Browning seems to be setting out on in *Sordello*, where the poetic value of the 'scaffold' has been discounted and its moral value not yet, one may say, fully appreciated. As already remarked, the fact that one can choose to concentrate on either the 'Men' or the 'system' in Dante is due to his extraordinary success as a creator of both, whatever doubts may remain about even his ability to finally synthesise the two.

It has been suggested above that Browning was not particularly interested in, for example, Francesca or Ulysses themselves; but it is certainly possible that the form of their speeches in the *Commedia* influenced Browning's ideas about the dramatic monologue, especially since they had been quoted out of context so often in Romantic criticism by writers who did not relish the *Inferno*'s 'scaffold' as to take on the status of independent poems. Thus Ulysses' speech in *Inferno* XXVI has fifty-two lines, compared with that in 'My Last Duchess' which has fifty-six (*PW*, pp. 367–9). Indeed, the speaker in this last poem might so easily have told his story (with a few modifications) from one of Dante's *bolge*. Here one should of course mention Tennyson's 'Ulysses', like 'My Last Duchess' one of its author's 'first tries' at the monologue form.[12] No poem is a better illustration of Dante in Romantic costume. Dante's Ulysses is a man of the world, 'del mondo esperto' (*Inf.* XXVI. 98), and he sets out on his final voyage to seek further acquaintance with 'vizi umani' ('human vices') and 'valore' ('worth') (l. 99); this involves him in the 'cento milia/perigli' ('hundred thousand dangers') he experiences in the Mediterranean before reaching the Pillars of Hercules, and it is only *then*, in contrast with Tennyson's hero, that he describes himself and his companions as 'vecchi e tardi' ('old and slow') (l. 106). Moreover, there is no indication that he had any intention of sailing beyond the Pillars at the outset of the voyage. His nine-line speech exhorting the sailors to do this seems to be acknowledged by Ulysses himself, in the somewhat wry title he gives it – 'orazion picciola' ('little oration') (l. 122) – to be an example of the fraudulent counsel he is damned for, for there is no glamour about the final part of the journey: five months on the open sea was clearly, as he says, a 'folle volo' ('mad flight') (l. 125). In Eliot's words, 'The story of Ulysses, as told by Dante, reads like a straightforward piece of romance, a well-told seaman's yarn'

(*Dante*, p. 250). Tennyson, in projecting a much more 'heroic' Ulysses, thereby helps us to realise how far Dante is from in any way succumbing to the spell of his Ulysses' adventurousness, in the reserve with which he treats it; the 'orazion picciola' expands in the later poem to become a defiant self-assertiveness, typically Byronic, in the face of the imminence of death and decay which prey on the narrator's mind throughout:

> Though much is taken, much abides; and though
> We are not now that strength which in old days
> Moved earth and heaven; that which we are, we are;
> One equal temper of heroic hearts,
> Made weak by time and fate, but strong in will
> To strive, to seek, to find, and not to yield.[13]

But the main difference is, as Eliot continues, that 'Tennyson's Ulysses is primarily a very self-conscious poet'. Dante's figure tells his story factually; his descriptions of the 'alto mare aperto' ('the deep open sea') (l. 100) are totally unadorned, whereas the later Ulysses loads his speech with a sensuous melancholy that is purely, so to speak, 'Tennysonian':

> Through scudding drifts the rainy Hyades
> Vext the dim sea . . .
>
> (ll. 10–11)

It is not easy to imagine this Ulysses wielding an oar; indeed, it is not easy to imagine him stepping into any boat other than that supplied by the imagination and piloted by the viewless wings of poesy:

> The lights begin to twinkle from the rocks:
> The long day wanes: the slow moon climbs: the deep
> Moans round with many voices. Come, my friends,
> 'Tis not too late to seek a newer world.
>
> (ll. 54–7)

This voyage is the typical Romantic flight into a fulfilment that cannot be possessed or even defined, expressed through images that transfer the concomitant languor onto the environment, whereas the simplicity of Dante's style befits his own Ulysses' hard-headed curiosity. Eliot's stress on the simplification of Dante's style is very much a reaction to poems like 'Ulysses' which invite a comparison with Dante and then turn out in the comparison to be 'too *poetical* . . . to be the highest poetry' (*Dante*, p. 248).

In Browning's monologues, the author has been true to his word in *Sordello* – 'The men and women . . ./Will I unstation' – but one feels that the stationing has never been completely abolished but is rather in abeyance. 'Browning the Simple-Hearted Casuist', as Hoxie N. Fairchild entitles his article, *does* suggest judgements on his men and women, for 'The poet . . . must faithfully render all the tangled phenomena of mental life, [but] must also apprehend God's truth and impart it to others.'[14] As Mason adds, 'the problem is never solved, if only because subtle relativism and oracular truth are mutually exclusive' ('A Study', p. 223). The desire for a 're-stationing' is occasionally voiced by Browning's own characters, like Paracelsus –

> to know my place,
> My portion, my reward, even my failure,
> Assigned, made sure for ever!
>
> (II.72–4)

– and Guido Franceschini:

> Oh, how I wish some cold wise man
> Would dig beneath the surface which you scrape,
> Deal with the depths, pronounce on my desert
> Groundedly!
>
> (XI.945–8)

However, 'An absolute vision is not for this world, but we are permitted a continual approximation to it' ('Essay on Shelley', p. 10). *The Ring and the Book* represents the furthest point in this approximation.

But it cannot, I believe, rival *Sordello* as Browning's most nearly perfect solution to reconciling the duality here under discussion. We can pursue a little further the poem's contrasts with Dante and with Dante's Sordello first. Francesco De Sanctis posited the same relation between Dante and nineteenth-century literature as that we find in *Sordello*; in the *Commedia*:

> Tutto è succo; tutto è cose, cose intere nella loro vivente unità, non decomposte dalla riflessione e dall'analisi. Per dirla con Dante, il suo mondo è un volume non squadernato . . . Là vive involto ancora e nodoso e pregno di misteri quel mondo, che sottoposto all'analisi umanizzato e realizzato, si chiama oggi letteratura moderna.

(Everything is substance; everything is actuality, things complete in their living unity, not decomposed by reflection and analysis. We can say with Dante that his world is an unscattered book . . . Inside it, still enfolded and unravelled and full of mysteries, lives that world which, subjected to a realised and humanised analysis, we call today modern literature.)[15]

In Croce's words some of Dante's figures appeared to De Sanctis as 'accenni di qualcosa che dovesse svolgersi nell'avvenire, che aspettasse la sua piena vita dallo Shakespeare e dalla letteratura moderna in genere' ('suggestions for something which would have to unfold in the future, which would await its full life from Shakespeare and modern literature in general') (Appendix to *La poesia di Dante*, p. 187). We clearly have Sordello's 'piena vita' in Browning's poem, in that extraordinarily courageous attempt to present complex moods of mental frustration without the slightest simplification. It is in the resolute adherence to a truth however complicated that Browning felt *Sordello*'s service to mankind to lie, poetry's function throughout the poem being stressed as a communication to its audience of greater powers of perception:

how I rose,
Or rather you advanced since evermore
Yourselves effect what I was fain before
Effect, what I supplied yourselves suggest,
What I leave bare yourselves can now invest . . .
(v, p. 198)

It had been Browning's intention to present more idealised figures in his poetry, 'Peasants . . . Queens', and so on (III, p. 117); but at some point, like his Sordello, he noticed the 'dim vulgar vast unobvious grief' around him (VI, p. 222) and decided to present Sordello as, on one level, a kind of embodiment of it; the painstaking analysis of his failure is a warning against facile optimism and an appeal for understanding, and indeed celebration, of the differences between men; all men cannot be Dante, as it were:

but if one can't eschew
One's portion in the common lot, at least
One can avoid an ignorance increased
Tenfold by dealing out hint after hint
How naught is like dispensing without stint
The water of life . . .
(III, p. 120)

It is a great pity that *Sordello* came to be regarded as a hopelessly incomprehensible piece of self-indulgence and that its deep and constant sense of public service came to be obscured, its touching belief in an audience ready to be educated:

> And therefore have I moulded, made anew
> A Man, delivered to be turned and tried,
> Be angry with or pleased at.
>
> (III, p. 125)

One might recall Cacciaguida's words to Dante on the *Commedia*:

> se la voce tua sarà molesta
> nel primo gusto, vital nodrimento
> lascerà poi, quando sarà digesta.

(but if your words are harsh on a first tasting they will leave vital nourishment after being digested.) (*Par.* XVII.130–2)

But the contrast with Dante is that, where he plucked 'amaranths grown beneath God's eye/In gracious twilights where his Chosen lie' (I, p. 16) – an image I take to refer to his systematic and economical presentation of the various shades he met, as in the twilit encounter with Sordello himself – Browning observes 'a pompion-twine afloat':

> Pluck me one cup from off the castle-moat –
> Along with cup you raise leaf, stalk and root,
> The entire surface of the pool to boot.
>
> (II, p. 76)

These are words Sordello himself speaks, but unlike Browning he is completely baffled by his inordinate, labyrinthine imagination; not the least of the poem's many marvels is the sense that Browning has wrung success out of an analysis of his own potential for failure; his dogged determination to finish it was no doubt sustained by his conception of a God-decreed 'yoke' laid on him (III, p. 119), though one shudders at the 'price of blood and brain', to use Paracelsus' words (V.169), it must have cost to remain under it. Of course, the complexities of the poem, the historical setting, the natural and architectural mazes and the involuted imagery used in setting them forth, must have been congenial to him; the poem accepts the challenge facing the Guelph cause in Book I of creating 'A surface solid now, continuous, one' out of the 'twine and tangle' of the 'chokeweed' (pp. 10–11). One cannot fail to notice the difference here with the *Commedia*, in spite of the nineteenth-century practice of comparing Dante's poem with a Gothic cathedral:[16] *Sordello* highlights the unsatisfactoriness of the Gothic appellation to Dante in itself meriting it much more, for with its regular divisions, measurements and chronology the *Commedia* should be compared with the buildings of Dante's own Tuscany, with their clear and simple ground-plans, broad areas of carefully organised fresco and restrained architectural ornament. It is rather in *Sordello* we find the complex galleries and mysterious recesses that characterise north-European Gothic building. How on earth, one wonders, would Dante have reacted to *Sordello*'s famous font (I, pp. 18–19) if the sight of a corbel in the shape of a bent human being upset him so much (*Purg*. X.130–4)? The recesses are not simply spatial: for the Victorians time had its sliding doors too and we shall see examples in the next chapter of Rossetti's chronology being no less fantastic than his mediaeval furniture and staircases. This is also a feature of 'One Word More' where the pen Dante uses to draw the angel (*Vita Nuova* XXXIV.1–2) has *already* been used to write the *Inferno*, though this is for important reasons we shall have to return to. As for *Sordello*, the temporal and descriptive maze, if one ever threads it, leads to a simple and preposterous suggestion: Sordello is to blame for the way things are in the nineteenth century.

If then we have Sordello's 'piena vita' in Browning's poem in intentional contrast with Dante's restricted presentation of him, we must also realise – and this is crucial – that the two Sordellos can be accepted as one and the same. In Dante's poem there is something undefined about him, something indeed already 'unstationed' that would have caught Browning's eye. As one of the last-minute repentants, he has to spend a period outside Purgatory proper equal to the length of his life, unless aided by prayers on earth, as Belacqua explains in canto IV.127–35. Thus he has not yet entered on his posthumous 'classification': Dante does not find him expiating any particular vice but set apart in a regal solitude that has yet a certain kind of haplessness –

> vedi là un'anima che, posta
> sola soletta, inverso noi riguarda

(see over there a soul seated completely on his own looking towards us)
(VI.58–9)

– for, as Sordello himself informs us,

> Loco certo non c'è posto;
> licito m'è andar suso ed intorno

(There is no fixed place appointed to us; I am permitted to go up and around) (VII.40–1)

He can wander up and down outside Purgatory, then, but he cannot get in, a state he has a sort of vision of in Browning's poem as suggested above (p. 72). One of the significant differences about Dante's Sordello is, however, his concern for political responsibility; he is the mouth-piece through whom Europe's negligent rulers are castigated. Whereas for Dante this is a natural extension of Sordello's earthly career, his poem on the death of Blacatz being a kindred piece of castigation,[17] for Browning it could only be part of the last-minute Revelation which rectifies his Sordello's understanding. This 'disagreement' between Dante and Browning does not then really tell against the other evidence that shows Browning bore in mind throughout *Sordello* his hero's eventual destination in the *Purgatorio*. There, cantos VI to VIII are imbued with a kind of waiting-room sadness: the constant return of night impeding any possibility of going further up the mountain (VII.49–60); the melancholy of the princes (for example VII.106–8) or of judge Nino – 'Non credo che la sua madre più m'ami' ('I don't think her mother loves me any more') (VIII.73); the *tristezza* of the famous pilgrim-hour passage opening canto VIII. The fact that Dante's Sordello has the consolation of eventual bliss, and also has an appearance 'a guisa di leon quando si posa' ('like a lion when it couches') (VI.66) – thus having finally 'united' after death with Browning's lion-faced (IV, p. 148) Salinguerra – does not distract the reader from this over-riding atmosphere of crepuscular melancholy; and this is Sordello's customary habitat in Browning's poem too where 'la notturna tenebra . . . [che] col nonpoder la voglia intriga' ('the darkness of night . . . which entangles our wills in powerlessness') (*Purg.* VII.56–7) can be regarded as a metaphor of his inaction. Browning introduces Sordello as a child visiting the penitential caryatids of the font at sunset, which is a kind of dumb-show for his posthumous appearance with the Rulers as ''l poco sole omai s'annidi' ('the setting sun now enters its nest') (VII.85); this ritual he repeats every evening (I, p. 19). Later, 'The evening star was high/When he reached Mantua' (II, p. 64); later still we watch him at dusk contemplating the ruins of his newly-hatched visions of Rome (v, pp. 173–4), visions that had been conceived in the 'grey twilight' of the previous dawn (iv, p. 172); and finally he undergoes his great self-examination at the end 'while evening sank' (vi, p. 216) and he sinks into death with it. He is, one feels, doomed from the start, attended by images of failure that gain greatly in significance if we know the *Purgatorio*. And indeed Browning has to reprimand himself for anticipating Sordello's outcome as early as Book i:

> Fool, who spied the mark
> Of leprosy upon him, violet-dark
> Already as he loiters?
>
> (p. 25)

There is, then, a struggle to disengage his Sordello from Dante's, caused by the fact that the one leads to the other; his warning against Sordello's inclination towards 'Thrusting in time eternity's concern' (i, p. 25) is also a self-reminder not to allow the Sordello Dante saw *sub specie aeternitatis* to overwhelm the earthly manifestation that prefigures him. What was seen under the aspect of time as the inexplicable paralysis of wasted potential, Sordello's 'strange disbelief that aught/Was to be done' (vi. p. 247), is seen after time, in Dante, as God's will; in the passage from the poem quoted above (p. 70) the evening-star has become, in God's scheme, the morning-star heralding Dante. Thus, in telling Sordello's story as far as the 'ultima ora', Browning has taken pains to establish a continuity with what Dante saw afterwards.

Yet understanding Sordello's failure as God's will in no way excuses it; no more than Dante did Browning accept predestination as a defence of negligent or evil behaviour. Already present in *Sordello*, and emphasised in *The Ring and the Book*, is an attempt to insist on that most difficult balance of commitment to right action in this world together with an awareness that the life 'men call years' is simply 'God's instant', as Pompilia puts it (vii.1841). We are frequently reminded in *Sordello* that earthly progress can only go so far, that a perfect union 'is not for this world':

> In short,
> When at some future no-time a brave band
> Sees, using what it sees, then shake my hand
> In heaven, my brother!
>
> (iii, p. 125)

When Sordello realises the provisionality of life on earth he discounts any obligation to it; this position, which might be regarded as a sort of moral death, is actually reached at the point of death itself which brings with it another duality, the splitting-off of soul from body:

> So seemed Sordello's closing-truth evolved
> In his flesh-half's break up – the sudden swell
> Of his expanding soul showed Ill and Well,
> Sorrow and Joy, Beauty and Ugliness
> Virtue and Vice, the Larger and the Less,
> All qualities, in fine, recorded here,
> Might be but Modes of Time and this one Sphere,
> Urgent on these but not of force to bind
> As Time – Eternity, – as Matter – Mind,
> If Mind, Eternity should choose assert
> Their attributes within a Life . . .
>
> (VI, pp. 235–6)

But he does not actually die in this faith: as we have said, and as Dante said too, there is just time for the great Exemplar of how Eternity should stoop to serve Time to be revealed to him; and the metaphor Browning uses to describe Sordello's appearance in death –

> A triumph lingering in the wide eyes,
> Wider than some spent swimmer's if he spies
> Help from above in his extreme despair
>
> (VI, pp. 241–2)

– recalls, perhaps deliberately, Dante's looking back on the dark wood he has escaped from near the beginning of the *Commedia*:

> come quei che con lena affannata,
> uscito fuor del pelago a la riva,
> si volge a l'acqua perigliosa e guata . . .

(like him who with troubled breath, having got from the sea to the shore, turns round to stare at the dangerous water . . .)

(*Inf.* I.22–4)

Sordello's location on Dante's mountain has been used by Browning as an image of his own Sordello's lack of application, and of his attempt to justify it to himself; thus Sordello asks:

> Whom palled Goito with its perfect things?
> Sordello's self; whereas for Mankind springs

Salvation – hindrances are interposed
For them, not all Life's view at once disclosed
To creatures sudden on its summit left,
With Heaven above and yet of wings bereft –
But lower laid, as at the mountain's foot . . .
(VI, p. 227)

He has, as it were, no belief in the earthly paradise on the mountain's top, which previously palled him at Goito; so he evolves the idea that the abolition of evil is actually harmful: what this would lead to would soon satiate whoever experienced it. It is vital, I think, to distinguish Sordello's position here from Browning's own, as stated in Book III:

'Tis Venice, and 'tis Life – as good you sought
To spare me the Piazza's slippery stone,
Or stay me thrid her cross canals alone,
As hinder Life what seems the single good
Sole purpose, one thing to be understood
Of Life . . .
(III, pp. 116–17)

This 'one thing to be understood' is clearer in the later version –

'T is Venice, and 't is Life – as good you sought
To spare me the Piazza's slippery stone
Or keep me to the unchoked canals alone,
As hinder Life the evil with the good
Which make up Living, rightly understood
(III.726–30)

– namely, the acknowledgement that life is a mixed bag, which leads to Browning's rejection of the 'dispensing without stint the water of life' attitude (above, p. 83); but this does *not* absolve us from our duty to keep climbing the mountain or ladder. As the Pope puts it in a great passage from *The Ring and the Book*,

I can believe this dread machinery
Of sin and sorrow, would confound me else,
Devised, – all pain, at most expenditure
Of pain by Who devised pain, – to evolve,
By new machinery in counterpart,
The moral qualities of man – how else? –
To make him love in turn and be beloved . . .
(X.1374–80)

At the same time it must be apparent – and this is Browning's great dilemma – that he can sympathise with Sordello's evasions; that he himself might have found a certain 'want of human interest' in the earthly paradise where creatures like Sludge and Blougram would have been left behind. In *Sordello*, the contrast between its hero and Dante –

> ere Dante could arrive to take
> That step Sordello spurned, for the world's sake:
> He did much – but Sordello's step was gone.
> Thus, had Sordello ta'en that step alone,
> Apollo had been compassed – 'twas a fit
> He wished should go to him, not he to it
>
> (VI, pp. 250–1)

– has also been powerfully imaged in the *Purgatorio*, in Dante's triumphant passage up the mountain in the arms of Lucia while, as Virgil says, 'Sordel rimase' ('Sordello remained') down below (IX.52–60). The reference to the all-important 'step' might have been determined by the episode from the *Purgatorio* where Sordello draws a line on the ground:

> Vedi? sola questa riga
> non varcheresti dopo 'l sol partito . . .

(See? You would not even cross this line after the sun has gone down . . .)
(VII.53–4)

Only a step, but to achieve it one needs the sun, or Grace, or love. The contrast with Dante who had, as it were, all three, is obvious; and also with Browning who in his 'sad disheveled ghost' has a kind of anti-Beatrice. But poor Sordello

> loves not, nor possesses One
> Idea that, star-like over, lures him on
> To its exclusive purpose
>
> (II, p. 60)

> years and years the sky above
> Held none, and so, untasked of any love,
> His sensitiveness idled . . .
>
> (VI, p. 218)

Compare Brunetto's prophecy to Dante: 'Se tu segui tua stella,/non puoi fallire a glorïoso porto' ('If you follow your star you cannot fail to reach a glorious port') (*Inf.* xv.55–6). In projecting Sordello's life as completely loveless Browning may have substituted Palma for Cunizza to suppress any recollection of the latter's actual elopement with Sordello. This is not recorded in the *Commedia* but any annotated edition would have supplied the information, as, for example, Cary's: '[Cunizza] eloped from her first husband, Richard of St Boniface, in the company of Sordello . . . with whom she is supposed to have cohabited before marriage'.[18] Finally, Sordello's basic problem, the inability to harmonise soul with body –

> a Soul's no whit
> More than the Body's purpose under it
> (A breadth of watery heaven like a bay,
> A sky-like space of water, ray for ray
> And star for star, one richness where they mixed . . .)
> (VI, p. 239)

– forms, as McCrory points out ('Browning and Dante', pp. 110–11), an interesting comparison with Dante's note that 'homo solus in entibus tenet medium corruptibilium et incorruptibilium; propter quod recte a phylosophis assimilatur orizonti, qui est medium duorum emisperiorum' ('alone among beings man occupies a middle ground between corruptible and incorruptible; on account of which philosophers rightly compare him with the horizon, which is the middle of two hemispheres') (*Monarchia* III.xv.3); indeed, all Dante's work strives to harmonise heaven and earth into a massive synthesis, *corruptibilia* with *incorruptibilia*, which is Browning's target too; Sordello's fitful wavering between the two spheres finds, as it were, its 'reward' in the *Antipurgatorio* where he remains in a sort of half-way house between earth and heaven.

However, God's supervision of the earthly process – the fact that Sordello was not 'resigned' by Him even though he failed badly – explains in part why Browning's poem, though centring on a particularly serious omission, strikes one as exuberant rather than tragic; its sheer descriptive energy suggests the world is no less interesting a place in spite of Sordello's inadequacy, which can thus be seen as another *felix culpa*. Browning's extraordinary spiritual stamina enabled him to sustain such a duality in his loyalties throughout his career: in *Sordello* itself one catches him 'siding' with Sordello as remarked, while at other moments the pressure of the duality between *felicitas* and *culpa* seems to overwhelm him and a great cry is the result:

> Alas, my friend – Alas Sordello! whom
> Anon we laid within that cold font-tomb –
> And yet again alas!
>
> (VI, p. 242)

This is not occasioned by Sordello's failure alone since, as we have said, that failure is illustrative of all mankind's deficiencies, of the operations of 'the angel of this life'. On the whole, however, the anguished questioning of the 'Dost thou well, Lord?' type (*Paracelsus* v.60) receives an affirmative answer in Browning through the mouths of his failures themselves, who, like Paracelsus and Sordello, die in states of triumphant illumination. It is only occasionally that one feels a frustration in Browning that the illumination did not come earlier. *Sordello* is certainly Browning's most serious attempt to come to terms with this life's innate deficiencies; having set up a scapegoat responsible for them he was able to proceed more securely to a portrayal of his other men and women that is divorced from the rest of *Sordello*'s philosophical considerations. And this advantage at least balances, I think, any distress he felt from sympathising with his scapegoat's case.

Browning's Sordello can be regarded then as an intended *figura* of Dante's, complete with all the excrescences of personality which are, in the next life, stripped away to leave us with the individual in his essentials, the Christian judgement being inevitably a simplification, a dividing ultimately into camps. It is here one feels how marvellously Dante's Sordello suited Browning's purpose: Dante had not simply enabled Browning to describe a character as 'man sees' him who could be automatically synthesised, thanks to the *Commedia*, with the figure God sees, but he had created a figure who, rather than illustrating a particular vice or virtue, seems to image a peculiarly modern isolation and inefficacy which allowed Browning plenty of scope in his prefiguration of him. The belief that man can and will be ultimately defined, together with a delight in his definition-eluding complexity: these are of course the components of that extraordinary synthesis Browning attempts in *The Ring and the Book*:

> learn and love
> Each facet-flash of the revolving year! –

Red, green and blue that whirl into a white,
The variance now, the eventual unity,
Which make the miracle.

(I.1360–4)

Here, Browning's fascination with the windings of the delinquent mentality, announced in *Sordello* –

ask moreover, when they prate
Of evil men past hope, don't each contrive,
Despite the evil you abuse to live?
Keeping, each losel, thro' a maze of lies,
His own conceit of truth?

(III, p. 119)

– is coupled with an admiration for the simple sincerity of the virtuous soul, as in Pompilia and Caponsacchi. As opposed to the author's delight in the tortuous sophistry of, say, the two lawyers, we have his belief that the heroes' case resides in their simple *look*, offsetting the treachery of language whereby truth's whiteness is toned down to grey or even turned black:

while you profess to show him me,
I ever see his own face

(VII.1185–6)

(as Pompilia tells Caponsacchi's detractors). This truth that comes undilutedly from the countenance rather than adulteratedly from the tongue suggests the kinship between Caponsacchi and the spirits of Dante's *Paradiso*:

The broad brow that reverberates the truth,
And flashed the word God gave him, back to man!

(VII.1796–7)

But the essence of most men remains wrapped in the earthly miasma it is yet vital we penetrate, as the Pope says:

Never again elude the choice of tints!
White shall not neutralise the black, nor good
Compensate bad in man, absolve him so:
Life's business being just the terrible choice.

(X.1234–7)

The choice however is only easy for those like Caponsacchi who are themselves clear vehicles of the truth; thus he can read hell's 'Large-lettered . . . masterpiece of print' on Guido's countenance

(VI. 1794) without realising that others cannot. He illustrates exactly the same moral zeal that characterises the Dante of 'One Word More':

> his left-hand i' the hair o' the wicked,
> Back he held the brow and pricked its stigma,
> Bit into the live man's flesh for parchment . . .
>
> (ll. 37–9)

The 'terrible choice' is terrible not only because of its difficulty but also because it tends to make morally irrelevant what is seen as poetically fundamental: 'Our interest's on the dangerous edge of things,/The honest thief, the tender murderer' says Blougram in his *Apology* (ll. 395–6, *PW*, p. 656), whereas the Pope states quite simply that 'good [shall not] Compensate bad in man'. *The Ring and the Book* can be said then to quite emphatically re-introduce the 'stationing' which we have seen to be indirectly present in *Sordello*: Guido's action is condemned quite openly by Browning himself in the first book, as is his character by being brought into juxtaposition with that holy pair who stand like a religious diptych at the poem's centre. The reader is invited to both love and hate, remembering in any case that the latter is but a 'mask' of the former (above, p. 79). A similarly virile Victorianism is in Carlyle:

> Infinite pity, yet also infinite rigour of law: it is so Nature is made; it is so Dante discerned that she was made . . . a man who does not know rigour cannot pity either . . . [Dante's] scorn, his grief are as transcendent as his love; – as indeed, what are they but the *inverse* or *converse* of his love?
>
> ('The Hero as Poet', pp. 153–4)

No doubt Carlyle, like the Pope, would have applauded Pompilia's sudden switch from acquiescence to action on learning she was pregnant, 'not/To longer bear, but henceforth fight, be found/ Sublime in new impatience with the foe!' (X.1057–9).

One feels that by the time Browning wrote *The Ring and the Book* he was ready for this more didactic stance. He had produced creatures, like Sludge and Blougram, who thwart our condemnation of them; their skills in self-justification lead us further and further away from faith in any standards of absolute right and wrong being able to do them 'justice'; and, while the 'stationing' takes on a more and more tenuous connexion with them, the more imperative the need for it becomes. It is as if Browning came to realise that his creatures might, like Frankenstein's, get disastrously out of hand; but that in *The Ring and the Book* he was able to indulge them and re-classify them at the same time. Thus he achieves a unity of the two categories of poet he discusses in the Shelley essay: as a 'Maker of quite new men' he had already fulfilled the role of the 'objective poet', who gets at 'new substance by breaking up the assumed wholes into parts of independent and unclassed value, careless of the unknown laws for recombining them' (pp. 8–9); and now he moves over to fill the role of the 'subjective poet', who recombines the new substance, since 'its very sufficiency to itself shall require, at length, an exposition of its affinity to something higher, – when the positive yet conflicting facts shall again precipitate themselves under a harmonizing law' (p. 9). 'The positive yet conflicting facts' are, of course, the views and characters of Guido and Pompilia; the 'harmonizing law' is the Christian judgement.

To return to *Sordello*, and its hero's figural relation with Dante's Sordello. The concept of *figura* is taken, of course, from Erich Auerbach:

The world beyond . . . is God's design in active fulfillment. In relation to it, earthly phenomena are on the whole merely figural, potential, and requiring fulfillment. This also applies to the individual souls of the dead: it is only here, in the beyond, that they attain fulfillment and the true reality of their being. Their career on earth was only the figure of this fulfillment. In the fulfillment of their being they find punishment, penance, or reward . . . man's existence on earth is provisional and must be complemented in the world beyond . . .[19]

This involves us in the paradox that, to return to Croce's phrase, Sordello's 'piena vita' in Browning's poem remains the mere preface to his assuming 'the true reality' of his being in Dante's. In *Sordello* itself there seems to be an awareness of what one might call the provisionality of human complexity with regard to the morally simplified essence or reality it will assume after death: I am thinking of Browning's presentation of Eglamor, who corresponds to Pompilia in *The Ring and the Book*, and who 'All along . . . lived Sordello's opposite' (II, p. 52). It is he, and not Sordello, whose triumph is featured at the end of the poem when Browning has a kind of vision of him in glory:

And Naddo gone, all's gone; not Eglamor!
Believe I knew the face I waited for,

> A guest my spirit of the golden courts:
> Oh strange to see how, despite ill-reports,
> Disuse, some wear of years, that face retained
> Its joyous look of love!
>
> (VI, p. 249)

Thus, after the divine revelation, Sordello's self-bafflement can be seen as a prior stage on the road to this simplified beatification:

> What has Sordello found?
> Or can his spirit go the mighty round
> At length, end where our souls begun?
>
> (VI, p. 241)

In the later version the last line becomes 'End where poor Eglamor begun?' (VI.605). And the question is, one feels, also directed at the poem itself: can it set out from the *Commedia* and, via the mighty round of a sophisticated modern awareness of self, return to it again?

The simplified reality of post-Judgement man has frequently caused great problems in the relationship between the Christian poet and his readers; many of Dante's figures in Hell have been popular because of the mixture they represent of nobility-in-sin. We may not find any of Blougram's 'tender murderers' but we do find Francesca, Farinata and Ulysses. Indeed, the fact that they preserve this life-like mixture after death is, as Auerbach says, 'part of the judgement which God has pronounced upon them' (*Mimesis*, p. 192). Yet how many times has Dante been accused of having failed to make his beatified 'interesting'! Whether Browning could have made Eglamor the centre of a poem is open to question; but in *The Ring and the Book* he has taken the risk of introducing at least one 'beatified' character much more overtly amongst his rogues and equivocators.

This poem, with its heightened atmosphere of good and evil, presents a case which, again like the Incarnation, is meant to be a permanent exemplar of the triumph of the one over the other, even if history subsequently proceeds to forget or falsify it. Every battle between these two forces, however small – 'the sphere though larger is not more complete' – is part of a continuous, cosmic campaign:

> there is passion in the place,
> Power in the air for evil as for good,
> Promptings from heaven and hell, as if the stars
> Fought in their courses for a fate to be.
>
> (X.660–3)

The desire to provide a golden Ring, an incontrovertible, irrefragable instance that 'tells for once' 'dead against the world,/ The flesh and the devil' (I.437–8) involves a procedure whereby Pompilia is unambiguously posited as 'the perfect soul' (VI.1162) and frequently compared with the Virgin, while Guido is subjected to the extravagant hatred of Caponsacchi:

> One great good satisfying gripe, and lo!
> There had he lain abolished with his lie,
> Creation purged o' the miscreate, man redeemed,
> A spittle wiped off from the face of God!
>
> (VI.1476–9)

Guido is also envisaged by the same speaker in a grotesque infernal consorting with, of all people, Judas:

> Kiss him the kiss, Iscariot! Pay that back,
> That smatch o' the slaver blistering on your lip –
> By the better trick, the insult he spared Christ –
> Lure him the lure o' the letters, Aretine!
>
> (VI.1945–8)

As we have said, Caponsacchi is obviously 'Dantesque', not only in his love for the *donna angelicata* Pompilia but also in the quality of his hatred; the two are inseparable. But the switch in scale from the immense 'ring' of Dante's poem to the domestic tragedy at the core of Browning's may involve the reader in some difficulties at this point; after all, the murderers Dante grouped with Judas were, as he saw it, betrayers of an entire civilisation. The danger is that Caponsacchi will appear fanatical, and that our glimpse of the 'eventual unity', in the shape of his and Pompilia's ardent mutual admiration, will be a little too bright to bear.

The Ring and the Book confirms then that what Browning saw in the *Commedia* was love and hate of a similarly straightforward robustness, the Dante who 'loved well because he hated'; indeed, saw primarily the scaffold, as we have maintained. Drawing the angel and writing the *Inferno* with *the same pen* – this is a schematisation of Dante's responses. Not only is this 'anti-

Shelleyan', as remarked, it is also totally foreign to Rossetti's ideas about Dante, even though the latter's drawing of *Dante Drawing the Angel* is often regarded as a sort of illustration to 'One Word More'. Rossetti practically forgot about the *Inferno*'s existence altogether, as we shall see.

This 'schematisation' obviously affects the way we regard Pompilia in comparison with Beatrice. The cost of seeing the former as the *donna angelicata* (and one notices more than one reminiscence of Shelley's descriptions of Beatrice Cenci and of Emilia) –

> The glory of life, the beauty of the world,
> The splendour of heaven . . .
>
> (VI.118–19)

– is, as remarked, the equation of her husband with Satan as vehicles of a cosmic battle. Nowhere in Dante, though, is Beatrice found with a similar antagonist: there is no independent force contrasting with, and thus throwing into greater relief, her 'whiteness'. This suggests that Dante's conception of evil is rather different from that of Caponsacchi, who seems to resemble him, or even from the Pope's: Dante seems very reluctant to admit any 'promptings from heaven and hell' into his world of human affairs: for example, Guido da Montefeltro has only his own conscience to urge him when he makes that difficult decision about whether to advise the Pope (*Inf.* XXVII.61ff); it is only after death that the good and bad spirits appear on either side of him. Browning's poem in fact evokes very successfully the atmosphere of the period in which it is set; that is, it suggests the violent *chiaroscuro* of Baroque art where the 'forces of darkness' seem to make a much more powerful contribution to the spiritual life than they were allowed to do in the middle ages. Browning's positing of the love–hate, good–evil balance in both Dante and *The Ring and the Book* would mislead one if it were allowed to suggest that the *Commedia*'s inert, impotent Devil has any significant part to play in men's lives, or that God's spokeswoman Beatrice has any enemy other than man's own carelessness and stupidity, the fault, as Marco Lombardo announced well before Shakespeare's Cassius did, being in ourselves, not our stars (*Purg.* XVI.67–84). It might be replied that Dante saw good and evil in their perfect state, where the one is clearly vanquished by the other, and that in *The Ring and the Book*'s business with this life they have a much more mixed aspect. But nowhere outside the *Commedia* does Dante show much alarm about what one would ordinarily call 'evil'; alarm about sin and ignorance of course, but all of this is man-made. This is what makes Dante such an inspiration: his belief in the significance of human responsibility, and the results that could be achieved if this were taken seriously. As Eliot said, Dante had faith in 'an ordering of the world more or less Aristotelian',[20] and one feels in Browning (and indeed in Eliot himself) a certain obscuring of Dante's humanism, an over-concentration on the Christian moralist; a tendency that goes in the opposite direction to Shelley's. Thus Guido's blackness is necessary to ensure the pathos of Pompilia's triumph; as a very Victorian angel in distress she seems poles apart from the Beatrice who embodies Dante's delight in God's purposes.

These distinctions have been attempted here as a proviso to claims like J. E. Shaw's that try to see Pompilia occupying an equivalent position in Browning's philosophy of love as Beatrice does in Dante's;[21] as suggested in our analysis of *Epipsychidion* it is extremely easy to pick up on a modern poet's use of a term like 'angel' and decide immediately that Beatrice has been authentically revived. This procedure becomes, I think, genuinely disastrous in McCrory's chapter on *Pauline*, whose heroine's *dolce stil nuovo* origins are suggested (pp. 161–83). But it takes more than the appellation 'pitying angel' (l. 711, *PW*, p. 25) to turn Pauline into a sister of Beatrice; indeed it seems difficult to turn her into anything other than an obedient pair of ears attending the egoism of the poem's narrator.

Although Dante's importance for Browning was fundamental, it was perhaps too fundamental to have a specific influence on his poetry over and above the ways we have examined. Thus Ruth Elizabeth Sullivan's claim for Dante's influence on the imagery of '"Childe Roland to the Dark Tower Came"' seems totally unconvincing, even though McCrory had already made most of the same points ('Browning and Dante', pp.121–60).[22] It may be said that Browning's attitude to Dante was based on an essential recognition: that Dante was a Christian poet who believed in the truth of what he was describing; a simple enough belief but one which, as we have already had occasion to see, not all modern poets seem willing to accept. But within this acceptance Browning's impression of Dante may be regarded as rather partial: he comes across as rather too much the poet of the other world, too much the

Dante *poeta* who judges and not enough the Dante *personaggio* whose participation in the narrative brings out all the drama of the various encounters; too much the Christian moralist, and not enough the political campaigner.

Returning for a final time to *Sordello*, we have seen that Browning there sets up a relation between this world and the next through the beautiful subtlety of his use of a *figura*, and that in *The Ring and the Book* the next world is not indirectly present in this way but is rather starkly thrust on the reader in the form of embodiments of virtue and vice who already seem too absolute to be convincing. On the other hand, since Sordello filled no exact moral category in Dante, Browning had a vaguer, and therefore easier, destiny to align him with. *Sordello* then is an answer to the dilemma between this life and the next because it removes the opposition between them.[23] But *Sordello* is not a complete answer: one of its hero's failings is a flinching from the process of allocation:

> nor if one man bore
> Brand upon temples while his fellow wore
> The aureole, would it task us to decide –
> But portioned duly out, the Future vied
> Never with the unparcelled Present! Smite
> Or spare so much on warrant all so slight?
> The Present's complete sympathies to break,
> Aversions bear with, for a Future's sake
> So feeble? Tito ruined through one speck,
> The Legate saved by his sole lightish fleck?
> (VI, p. 225)

It is quite clear he is not without Browning's sympathy in this, but Browning did not forget it was a failing; his picture of Dante's zeal to go round branding his associates in 'One Word More' –

> his left-hand i' the hair o' the wicked,
> Back he held the brow and pricked its stigma
> (ll. 37–8)

– is an uncompromising reading of the *Commedia*, but shows what Browning felt had to be done. The unenviableness of the task is responsible for much of Browning's greatest poetry, much of which is in *Sordello* itself:

> But how so order Life? Still brutalize
> The soul, the sad world's method – muffled eyes

To all that was before, shall after be
This sphere – and every other quality
Save some sole and immutable Great and Good
And Beauteous whither fate has loosed its hood
To follow? Never may some soul see All
– The Great before and after, and the Small
Now, yet be saved by this the simplest lore,
And take the single course prescribed before,
As the king-bird with ages on his plumes
Travels to die in his ancestral glooms?

(VI, p. 240)

IV

Rossetti and the cult of the *Vita Nuova*

That face, of Love's all-penetrative spell
Amulet, talisman, and oracle, –
Betwixt the sun and moon a mystery.
('Astarte Syriaca')

'By the 1830's', writes C. P. Brand, 'the favourite themes of Ugolino and Francesca were exhausted . . . the extent of the interest [in Dante] has diminished'; he adds 'Critics now asserted that this was not a suitable age for the study of Dante', and refers to two reviews of 1833 that indicate this.[1] Whether intentionally or not, Brand's chapter on Dante ends on the unwarrantable suggestion that interest in him was predominantly a Romantic affair. There may indeed have been a certain lull in this interest in the thirties; for example, only one new translation of the *Commedia* appeared, by I. C. Wright (its three parts published in 1833, 1836 and 1840)[2] though Cary's *Vision* was reprinted in 1831. On the other hand the appearance of works like Gabriele Rossetti's *Sullo spirito antipapale che produsse la Riforma* (1832; English translation 1834), Lyell's translation of the *Canzoniere* (1835, new editions 1840, 1842 and 1845) and Carlyle's *On Heroes* hardly shows the study of Dante underwent any diminution. And Toynbee has no difficulty in finding plentiful references to Dante from the thirties for his anthology. Once into the mid-century, the interest intensifies: in 1854 alone three new translations of the whole or part of the *Commedia* appeared and one was reprinted;[3] indeed, from 1850 onwards each decade of the nineteenth century, and particularly the 1880s, saw an extraordinarily sustained output of new translations.[4] A survey of nineteenth-century art shows a similarly constant attention to Dante; *pace* Professor Brand, the 'exhaustion' of the Francesca theme is an illusion: in the years 1837–8 four separate paintings of her – together with Paolo in three of them – were exhibited, and from 1850 till the end of the century sculptures or paintings on this theme are recorded on over twenty occasions.[5] Of course it might be maintained that most of the artists who handled the theme had no more than a routine interest in a Dante undergoing the process of becoming a household classic, a process doubtlessly aided by the popularity of Doré's engravings; but that Dante's gradual absorption into English culture did not preclude the intensity of his appeal is shown by Ruskin, for whom Dante was 'the central man of all the world, as representing in perfect balance the imaginative, moral, and intellectual faculties, all at their highest . . .'[6] As Toynbee says, Ruskin's works 'probably contain more quotations from the *Divina Commedia* than those of any other English writer . . .' (*DEL*, I, xlix). And, finally, Henry Clark Barlow's first article on Dante was published in 1849, inaugurating, one might say, the native tradition of Dante scholarship (listed in *Britain's Tribute*, p. 103).

Nevertheless, an extremely important change in the nature of the interest in Dante starts to emerge in the 1830s and becomes apparent in the next two decades. It is a rejection of the 'Promethean' Dante, and for our purposes may be summed up in one word: Beatrice. We shall see how the new-found interest in her involves a turning away from Romantic ideas a little later in the chapter. That she was a specifically Victorian favourite is again illustrated by Toynbee's list of artworks: the theme of *Beatrice*, or *Dante and Beatrice*, is found only twice before 1840, but between then and the end of the century there are again over twenty such examples, distributed fairly evenly through the decades; and these figures do not include Rossetti's works. The discovery of Beatrice was synonymous with that of the *Vita Nuova*: Shelley is really the only major English writer of the first quarter of the century to display any cognisance of Dante's 'libello', but by the early 1830s references to it occur with some frequency in Toynbee's anthology. At this time Arthur Hallam began a translation of it that was left unfinished, and Lyell's translation, never published, was later utilised for his version of the *Canzoniere*.[7] It is in Hallam's work that we find the first sustained appreciation of Beatrice: apart from his translations, there is the extended tribute to her in his long poem in *terza rima*, *A Farewell to the South* (1830), and his forceful defence of her historical reality in his reply to Rossetti's *Sullo spirito* (1832) (*Writings*, pp. 15–17, 255–60).[8] In Landor's *Pentameron* (1837), Boccaccio and Petrarch are pictured as shaking their heads over Dante's unfortunate political entanglements to remark: 'Ah! had Dante remained through life the pure solitary lover of Bice, his soul had been gentler, tranquiller, and more generous' (p. 40), an observation that rejects much in Dante that Shelley and Byron had found noteworthy. Landor continued in this vein in two 'Imaginary Conversations' of 1845 and 1846, 'Dante and Beatrice', and 'Dante and Gemma Donati', this latter being a eulogy of Beatrice put into the mouth of Dante's wife: 'Brave, brave Dante! I love you for all things; nor least for your love of her. It was she, under God, who rendered you the perfect creature I behold in you.'[9] One imagines Byron turning in his grave.[10] In 1846 a translation of the complete *Vita Nuova* appeared, published in Florence by the American Joseph Garrow, but its influence in England was naturally limited. The publication of Rossetti's translation in 1861 and of Theodore Martin's in 1862 finally introduced Dante's 'libello' to the general public; a reviewer noted that the original had 'hitherto met with comparatively little attention', but that little, as we shall see, was highly significant.[11]

The Byronic Dante, as we saw, was closely associated with the so-called portraits that confirmed the misery of his post-exilic life; the association emphasises the importance of the new 'portrait' of Dante (Plate 3) uncovered in the Bargello in 1840.[12] This certainly played a crucial part in developing the new interest in Dante's early life. Seymour Kirkup, who had a large hand in the find, sent excited and speculative letters to Gabriele Rossetti along with a watercolour copy:

> The poet looks about 28 – very handsome – un Apollo colle fattezze di Dante [an Apollo with the features of Dante]. The expression and character are worthy of the subject, and much beyond what I expected from Giotto . . . Add to which it is not the mask of a corpse of 56 – a ruin – but a fine, noble image of the Hero of Campaldino, the Lover of Beatrice . . . A parchment book under his arm – perhaps the *Vita Nuova*.[13]

Kirkup's hypothesis about the parchment book is especially interesting: the portrait and the *Vita Nuova* were to become inseparable in the minds of many readers. The contrast between the young man and the 'ruin' is echoed by Theodore Martin, writing in 1847: 'Were [the *Vita Nuova*] known as it ought to be, we should hear less of the sternness, the bitterness, and even ferocity, which are taken for granted by many as the leading features of his mind.'[14] The real victim of these 'anti-Byronic' developments is not Francesca but *is* Ugolino, whose story was immensely celebrated during the Romantic period but only infrequently attended to afterwards.

Apart from its pathos, the encounter in *Inferno* XXXIII had been held to exhibit the full ferocity of Dante's imagination.

Once Beatrice had been discovered, the Victorians had no difficulty in equating her with the heroines of contemporary romance. Landor, as we have already seen, supplements the tantalising incompleteness of the *Vita Nuova*'s account of the love-affair with one of his 'Conversations': Dante and Beatrice are seated together while the latter explains the impossibility of their marrying, adding: '. . . I think you would better not put your head against my bosom; it beats too much to be pleasant to you'.[15] This may have stimulated Martin, who was the worst culprit in these attempts to make the *Vita Nuova* more accessible to a modern audience; in the Introduction to his translation he expands on the after-effects of Beatrice's marriage:

> it is contrary to human nature that a love unfed by any tokens of favour should retain all its original force; and, without wrong either to Beatrice or Dante, we may conclude that an understanding was come to between them, which in some measure soothed his heart, if it did not satisfy it . . .[16]

Martin was not allowed to get away with this, being roundly trounced by Matthew Arnold in a review of the translation for creating out of the *Vita Nuova* 'something involving modern relations in social life between the two sexes'; Martin

> insist[s] upon making out of Dante's adoration of Beatrice a substantial modern love-story, and [arranges] Dante's real life so as to turn it into a proper sort of real life for a 'worshipper of woman' to lead . . . [Beatrice] must become
>
> The creature not too bright and good
> For human nature's daily food,
>
> of Wordsworth's poem . . .

As Arnold goes on:

> To have had his relations with Beatrice more positive, intimate, and prolonged, to have had an affection for her into which there entered more of the life of this world, would have even somewhat impeded, one may say, Dante's free use of these relations for the purpose of art.[17]

But this astute suggestion is carried too far, towards a conclusion that has a Carlylean flavour about it: 'the real truth is, that all the life of the world, its pleasures, its business, its parties, its politics, all is alike hollow and miserable to Dante in comparison with the inward life, the ecstasy of the divine vision' (p. 669). Arnold's little essay was known to Yeats, as we shall see, and had a strong influence on his ideas.

On one level, then, the Victorians took Beatrice to their hearts because they could associate the 'angiola giovanissima' ('youthful angel') of the *Vita Nuova* with, let us say, Patmore's *Angel in the House*. Again, in Martin's words: 'Earth has many such [Beatrices] – pure, patient, gentle, wise and helpful spirits – who minister strength, and guidance, and consolation . . .'[18] George Eliot associates Beatrice with Dorothea by prefixing the sonnet 'Ne li occhi porta la mia donna Amore' ('My lady bears Love in her eyes') (*VN* XXI) to Chapter LIV of *Middlemarch*: it is her love and consolation that redeem both Ladislaw and Lydgate. Poems with titles like 'Dante to Beatrice' became popular: for instance Palgrave's two sonnets of 1854 and Dinah Maria Mulock's sonnet of 1859, this latter accompanied by a companion piece 'Beatrice to Dante', which ends

> 'Look on me, Beatrice . . .
> more happy in this happy place
> That thou alone art hers and she is thine.'[19]

Here we have, of course, a re-enactment of the meeting in the *paradiso terrestre* – '"Guardaci ben! Ben son, ben son Beatrice"' ('"Look closely here! I am, indeed I am, Beatrice"') (*Purg*. XXX.73) – but with the disharmonious elements of that meeting carefully ignored in the interests of 'a substantial modern love-story' (see Chapter II, p. 61). We shall find Rossetti doing exactly the same thing when he handles this scene, his attitude to the Beatrice of the *Commedia* being wholly determined by the Beatrice he sees in the *Vita Nuova*. Although Rossetti goes too far in confusing the two works, the popularity of the 'libello' was a potential help to a fairer understanding of the *Commedia* in adjusting the great imbalance set up by the Romantic fascination with the *Inferno*. It may be that a reviewer already quoted goes too far, with regard to the poem, in his assertion that 'The idea of Beatrice pervades the most magnificently conceived and the most wonderfully executed work of the human imagination . . . It begins and ends with Beatrice',[20] but this sounds a good deal less like nonsense than the kind of account of the poem given a century earlier in say Michel Chabanon's *Vie du Dante* (Amsterdam, 1773), which gives forty-three pages to a description of the *Inferno* (concentrating almost entirely on Francesca and Ugolino), six to the *Purgatorio*, and one paragraph to the *Paradiso* prefaced with the remark that 'Nous épargnerons au Lecteur l'ennui d'en lire davantage' (p. 96)! There seems little doubt that the mid-century insistence on a very human Beatrice was provoked by Gabriele Rossetti's final work on Dante, *La Beatrice di Dante*, of 1842.[21] Martin, who could see Beatrices all around him – one of whom, as the dedicatory sonnet to his translation shows, was his wife – has hostile things to say against those who would see Beatrice as pure allegory in his Introduction. And, finally, Carlyle's lecture must be mentioned again for its rhapsody over Dante's 'longings . . . towards his Beatrice' (see Chapter II, p. 64).

This is the context then into which we should fit the most prominent of Beatrice's Victorian worshippers, Dante Gabriel Rossetti, who was working away on his translation of the *Vita Nuova* and penning his sketches based on it during the late 1840s. It is important to note that he is not the originator of the 'Beatrice cult'; it is only towards the end of the century that his name starts to become synonymous with this aspect of Dante's work, thus provoking Eliot's comment that 'Rossetti's *Blessed Damozel*, first by my rapture and next by my revolt, held up my appreciation of Beatrice by many years' (*Dante*, p. 262). One must also note that Rossetti differs sharply from several of his contemporaries in seeing in the *Vita Nuova* an atmosphere of mystery and secrecy which is also characteristic of the love-themes in his own painting and poetry; the idea of Dante's work as a prototype of the modern romance, which one could, like Martin, cheerfully interpret according to contemporary notions of 'human nature', must have been repellent to him. To Gabriele Rossetti the *Vita Nuova* had been 'un complesso di cifre arcane' ('a complex of arcane cyphers') (*La Beatrice di Dante*, p. 80); Rossetti acknowledged his father's influence on him in the sonnet 'Dantis Tenebrae':

> And didst thou know indeed, when at the font
> Together with thy name thou gav'st me his,
> That also on thy son must Beatrice
> Decline her eyes according to her wont,
> Accepting me to be of those that haunt
> The vale of magical dark mysteries
> Where to the hills her poet's foot-track lies . . .[22]

Rossetti was never particularly willing to enlarge upon what these 'magical dark mysteries' were: in his Introduction to part I of *Dante and His Circle* he excuses himself from dwelling on Dante 'of whom so much is known to all or may readily be found written' and hurries on to spend far more time discussing, for example, Cavalcanti (*Works*, p. 296). He half explains one of the enigmas to his patron MacCraken in a letter of 14 May 1854, in connexion with his watercolour of *The First Anniversary of the Death of Beatrice*:[23]

I had an idea . . . that the lady in my drawing should be Gemma Donati whom Dante married afterwards . . . The visitors are unnamed in the text [*Vita Nuova* XXXIV. 1–3]. But I had an idea also of connecting the pitying lady with another part of the *V.N.* and in part the sketch is full of notions of my own in this way, which would only be cared about by one to whom Dante was a chief study.[24]

Nothing could contrast more with the fuss the Romantics made over the new planet that swam into their ken. One can, I think, explain the long interval between Rossetti's finishing his translation and its publication in 1861 as part of this desire to keep Dante's mysteries to himself, whereas his father spent much of his life trying to publicise them.[25] During the 1850s, then, whatever interest in Dante there was outside Rossetti's circle owed little to a man who still tended to think in terms of arcane brotherhoods and secretive love, though one should note that this circle involved Ruskin, and, by letter, Charles Eliot Norton, whose own part translation of the *Vita Nuova* came out in the United States in 1859 (complete translation 1867).

The most convenient introduction to Rossetti's attitude to Dante is offered by a comparison between Byron's *The Prophecy of Dante* and Rossetti's 'Dante at Verona', composed according to William Rossetti between *c.* 1848 and 1852 (*Works*, p. 647) but not published until Rossetti's first volume of *Poems* in 1870. Although we saw in Chapter II that Byron's Dante was inundated with misfortune, we remember he could still say 'they have not yet/Quenched the old exile's spirit, stern and high' (I.41–2), and that he proceeds to harangue the Italians with the prospect of approaching calamity unless they take his rousing advice 'To make the Alps impassable', and to 'Unite' (II.144–5). Rossetti's poem is also set in Dante's exile, but his hero is, one fears, much more 'Quenched'. Even though Rossetti versifies part of Dante's letter to his Florentine friend rejecting Florence's terms for revoking his exile, and indulges in a diatribe against 'RESPUBLICA' as illustrated by Florence, 'A shameful shameless prostitute' (*Works*, pp. 12–13), Dante's overall bearing is not one of passionate resistance. Rather he is a miserable, moping figure, trapped in the rounds of a hateful court life presided over by Can Grande, and feeling generally 'perplexed/If any day that could come next/Were worth the waiting for or no . . .' (p. 11).

The reason he feels like this is because of his love for Beatrice; the melancholy separation both lovers experience in 'The Blessed Damozel' is precisely what afflicts Dante here:

> the voice said in his heart,
> 'Even I, even I am Beatrice';
> And his whole life would yearn to cease:
> Till having reached his room, apart
> Beyond vast lengths of palace-floor,
> He drew the arras round his door.
>
> At such times, Dante, thou hast set
> Thy forehead to the painted pane
> Full oft, I know; and if the rain
> Smote it outside, her fingers met
> Thy brow; and if the sun fell there,
> Her breath was on thy face and hair.
>
> (pp. 9–10)

Every element in the *Commedia* converges, in Rossetti's picture, on Beatrice –

> Each hour, as then the Vision pass'd,
> He heard the utter harmony
> Of the nine trembling spheres, till she
> Bowed her eyes towards him in the last,
> So that all ended with her eyes,
> Hell, Purgatory, Paradise
>
> (p. 14)

– and here this leads him to falsify what happens, for example, at the end of the *Paradiso*. But what is really significant about 'Dante at Verona' is the determining influence it shows, not of the *Commedia*, but of the *Vita Nuova*: Dante avoiding the life of the court to shut himself up in his room – a deliberate re-creation of the 'solingo luogo d'una mia camera' ('the solitude of my room') (*VN* III.2) – to meditate undisturbedly on Beatrice:

Then, weeping, I think certainly
  Thou hast beheld, past sight of eyne, –
  Within another room of thine
Where now thy body may not be
  But where in thought thou still remain'st, –
  A window often wept against:

The window thou, a youth, hast sought,
  Flushed in the limpid eventime,
  Ending with daylight the day's rhyme
Of her; where oftenwhiles her thought
  Held thee – the lamp untrimmed to write –
  In joy through the blue lapse of night.

(p. 10)

And Rossetti suggests near the end of the poem that it is the Beatrice of the 'libello' rather than of the *Commedia* who continued to hold the rock of Dante's mind –

Ah! haply now the heavenly guide
  Was not the last form seen by him:
  But there that Beatrice stood slim
And bowed in passing at his side,
  For whom in youth his heart made moan
  Then when the city sat alone

(p. 15)

– the very idea of a retrospective vision being suggested by Dante's vision near the end of the *Vita Nuova* itself of the Beatrice he had met as a child (XXXIX.1).

It is no wonder then that Rossetti's Dante is a failure at Can Grande's: all he wants is to be left undisturbed to think on the lost beloved, and he accordingly goes round telling the musicians to keep quiet, like a blight on all joyfulness. Dante the philosopher, Dante the politician, is unrecognisable from Rossetti's poem: the man who wrote the *Commedia*, *Monarchia* and *Convivio* remains for Rossetti the man who shut himself up in his rooms and wept for a year over Beatrice's death. His ignoring of all that had happened to Dante since his youth – 'where in thought thou still remain'st' – affords an interesting reflection on what one feels justified in claiming as Rossetti's own lack of intellectual development. I do not think it is unfair to Rossetti to suggest that his interests remain largely static after the early 1850s: many of the poems published in 1870 were written twenty years earlier, and, although the later poems of *The House of Life* show a new concentration on death and a natural tendency to review the past, they still show, as one critic has noted, a 'striking resemblance' to sonnets Rossetti produced before 1850;[26] and, although Rossetti turned to oils and relinquished watercolour about 1860, there is a constant repetition of themes: *The Salutation of Beatrice* turns up in 1880–1 as it did in 1849 (Surtees Cat. 260, 116A), *Dante's Dream* in 1871 as in 1856 (Cat. 81, 81R1). This forms a marked contrast with the increasingly panoramic scope of Dante's writing as his experience widened, an experience which helped him to fulfil quite dramatically his own dictum that 'altro si conviene e dire e operare ad una etade che ad altra' ('one should act and speak differently at different stages of one's life') (*Conv.* I.i.17). He could, unlike Rossetti, move beyond the *Vita Nuova*, but in Rossetti's conception he has had his ideas and passions whittled down into something Rossetti himself could cope with. Rossetti's writing of 'Dante at Verona' is contemporary with his translating the *Vita Nuova* and other early Italian poetry; when the translations came out in 1861 the volume included an announcement on the back end-paper that 'Shortly will be published, *Dante at Verona and other poems*', an intention forestalled by Rossetti's burying the manuscript of the poems with his wife. This association of the Dante of the *dolce stil nuovo* and the 'post-exilic' Dante remained in Rossetti's mind to exclude much of what was characteristic of the older Dante.

As for the sources of 'Dante at Verona' other than the *Vita Nuova*, we have already examined the popularity of the anecdotes about Dante in Chapter II; it is no surprise to find Can Grande's jester figuring in Rossetti's poem. William Rossetti suggested that 'a thorough relish for "Dante at Verona" can only be attained by readers who come to it well imbued with the subject-matter' (*Works*, p. 647), but one wonders whether these are not in fact the readers it is *least* likely to attract: after coming across such biographical make-believe again and again in the first half of the nineteenth century one begins to weary a little of the kind of subject-matter Rossetti draws on. The main inspiration for Rossetti's poem seems to have been Carlyle's lecture which, as we saw, was a sort of reservoir of secondary information about Dante; 'The wretched are not cheerful company', as Carlyle says (p. 143).[27]

This picture of Dante can be regarded as a sort of diluted Byronism, with the fierceness gone but the sorrow remaining. Even Ruskin is drawn into this tradition, noting that the Bargello portrait is 'in its quiet, earnest, determined, gentle sadness, the very type of the spirit of the good men of his time . . . you cannot conceive a smile on such a face'.[28] Yet the fact that the portrait did give a less harrowed physiognomy than was generally recognised before 1840 may have influenced Tennyson in a small change he made to 'The Palace of Art' between the 1832 and 1842 printings: originally the paintings of wise men around the royal dias included one in which 'Grim Dante pressed his lips'; in 1842, 'the world-worn Dante grasped his song [the 'parchment book' from the new portrait?],/And somewhat grimly smiled'.[29]

For Rossetti, all roads lead back to the *Vita Nuova*. He painted only one subject from the *Inferno*, *Paolo and Francesca* (Surtees Cat. 75), and none at all from the *Paradiso*; the subjects he chose from the *Purgatorio* are its various 'belle donne', which connect most obviously with the subject-matter of Dante's early poetry. Surtees's catalogue lists Rossetti's subjects from Dante as follows, some of them painted several times: *The First Anniversary of the Death of Beatrice* (*Dante Drawing the Angel*) (*VN* xxxiv, Cat. 42, 58); *Beatrice Meeting Dante at a Marriage Feast* (*VN* xiv, Cat. 50); *Giotto Painting the Portrait of Dante* (Cat. 54); *Dante at Verona* (Cat. 55); *Dante's Vision of Matilda Gathering Flowers* (*Purg.* xxviii, Cat. 72); *Dante's Vision of Rachel and Leah* (*Purg.* xxvii, Cat. 74); *Dante's Dream at the Time of the Death of Beatrice* (*VN* xxiii, Cat. 81); *The Salutation of Beatrice* (*VN* iii and *Purg.* xxx, Cat. 116, 260); *Dantis Amor* (based on *VN* xli, Cat. 117); *Beata Beatrix* (based on the death of Beatrice, *VN* xxviii, Cat. 168); *La Pia* (*Purg.* v, Cat. 207); *Madonna Pietra* (*Rime*, 43–6, Cat. 237); *The Boat of Love* (*Rime*, 9, 'Guido, i' vorrei', Cat. 239); and the *Donna della Finestra* (*VN* xxxv–xxxviii, Cat. 255).[30] It is probable, however, that Rossetti *was* well acquainted with the *Commedia*; indeed his sonnet 'On the *Vita Nuova* of Dante' tells us that he only turned to the 'libello' after having been 'long bound within the threefold charm/Of Dante's love sublimed to heavenly mood', and that he turned to it in pursuit, as it were, of Beatrice's biography (*Works*, p. 195); and there are several references in his poetry to the poem. Thus his sonnet 'After the French Liberation of Italy' castigates Europe as 'a loveless whore' with France as her 'paramour' (*Works*,

p. 205) in an obvious reminiscence of the Papal 'puttana' ('whore') and her 'drudo' ('lover') at the end of *Purgatorio* XXXII (148–60). Similarly, his sententious 'Soothsay' bases the following stanza –

Let lore of all Theology
Be to thy soul what it *can* be:
But know, – the Power that fashions man
Measured not out thy little span
For thee to take the meting-rod
In turn, and so approve on God
Thy science of Theometry
(*Works*, p. 222)

– on the eagle's words to Dante in *Paradiso* XIX:

Or tu chi se', che vuo' sedere a scranna,
per giudicar di lungi mille miglia
con la veduta corta d'una spanna?

(Now who are you to get on your high seat and judge lengths of a thousand miles with the short span of your sight?) (79–81)

But recollections of the *Commedia* are not frequent. It is as if Rossetti's interest in the poem was completely submerged by his enthusiasm for the *Vita Nuova*.

Whereas we saw Shelley in *Epipsychidion* seeking 'in a mortal image the likeness of what is perhaps eternal', and thus investing Emilia with the full glory of the Beatrice of the *Paradiso*, Rossetti goes in precisely the opposite direction. Just as Dante's life at Verona becomes 'Vita-nuovized', so does the *Divine Comedy*. This is clearest in his painting of 1859, *The Salutation of Beatrice*, in the National Gallery of Canada, Ottawa (Plate 5). The left-hand panel shows Beatrice greeting Dante 'In Terra' (*VN* III), the right-hand one 'In Eden' (*Purg.* XXX); the scenes are separated by a figure of *Dantis Amor* painted onto the frame. In order to make the two greetings as parallel as possible Rossetti has thoroughly modified Dante's description of the reunion 'In Eden'. He has indeed painted the following verses from *Purgatorio* XXX onto the frame –

sovra candido vel cinta d'uliva
donna m'apparve, sotto verde manto
vestita di color di fiamma viva

(a woman appeared to me girt with olive over a white veil, dressed in the colour of living flame beneath a green mantle) 31–3 and

Guardaci ben! Ben son, ben son Beatrice

(Look closely here! I am, indeed I am, Beatrice) (73)

– but the fact that Dante's spirit 'd'antico amor sentì la gran potenza' ('felt the great power of old love') (39) seems to have inspired Rossetti in making this meeting an exact continuation of the state of things 'In Terra'. In his scene there is no procession, no twenty-four elders, no virtues, no chariot, no griffin, no Matilda, no Statius and no river Lethe. The only difference between earth and Eden in the two scenes is that the street is replaced by a field and the 'due gentili donne' ('two noble ladies') who accompanied Beatrice in the *Vita Nuova* (III.1) give way to two more aetherial-looking maidens playing small harps. Beatrice has already lifted her veil and looks softly at Dante: it is clear that no reproval – 'Come degnasti d'accedere al monte?/non sapei tu che qui è l'uom felice?' ('How did you deign to come to the mountain? Didn't you know that man is happy here?') (XXX.74–5) – is taking place here. What we have is rather an illustration to Rossetti's own 'Blessed Damozel' than to the *Commedia*, where Paradise is precisely a trouble-free continuation of love on earth:

There will I ask of Christ the Lord
Thus much for him and me: –
Only to live as once on earth
With Love, – only to be,
As then awhile, for ever now
Together, I and he.

(*Works*, p. 5)

With this in mind Rossetti has cut out all the heavenly procession attending on Beatrice in accordance with his idea of what Love is: a private affair between man and woman with a minimum of unwelcome onlookers.

It is clear that this painting is a complete reduction of Beatrice's proper significance; yet it exhibits more than simple 'romantic' leanings. It is a clear rejection of Rossetti's father's ideas about Beatrice, Rossetti's resistance to which has been described by his brother: 'it would have been contrary to his very nature to contemplate [Beatrice] as any other than a woman once really living in Florence, and there really loved by Dante as woman is loved by man'.[31] In *Sullo spirito antipapale*, Gabriele had been able to use

Beatrice's allegorical significance in the *Commedia* as an argument against accepting her real existence in the *Vita Nuova*; Rossetti seems to have made the former figure so excessively un-allegorical partly to turn the tables. In this he would have been warmly applauded by Martin, for whom 'The Beatrice of the *Paradiso* is the Beatrice, whom men turned round and crowded to gaze at, as she glided past them on the streets of Florence' (*Dublin University Magazine*, p. 414).

A final point about the *Salutation* concerns the *Dantis Amor* on the frame, accompanied by the date of Beatrice's death, 9 June 1290, and the inscription 'Quomodo sedet sola civitas!' ('How doth the city sit solitary!') (*VN* XXVIII–XXIX).[32] He is portrayed as a youth with wings holding a sundial recording the hour of Beatrice's death, and Rossetti's independent painting of *Dantis Amor* (Cat. 117) shows him to be a conflation of the 'giovane' ('young man') introduced to us in *Vita Nuova* XII.3 and the 'peregrino spirito' ('pilgrim spirit') of the sonnet 'Oltre la spera' who journeys to see Beatrice in glory (*VN* XLI). His presence here on the frame confirms, of course, the painting's complete bias towards the *Vita Nuova*, for it is not the 'amor che move il sole e l'altre stelle' ('love that moves the sun and the other stars') that Beatrice leads Dante to which interests Rossetti; it is rather the love between man and woman that suffers separation, a constant theme in Rossetti's poetry and one which, in the guise of the above kind of personification, we shall discuss in the second half of this chapter.

Leaving Beatrice aside for the moment, we find the other main attraction the *dolce stil nuovo* phase in Dante's career had for Rossetti is associated with his membership of the Pre-Raphaelite Brotherhood. While Rossetti was working on the translations of poems produced in the late middle ages by one 'Pre-Raphaelite' Brotherhood, he was himself helping to form another. The exchanges of sonnets between Dante, Cavalcanti, Guido Orlandi, Cino da Pistoia, *et al.*, undoubtedly stimulated Rossetti's attempts to get his own circle – his brother, Scott, Woolner, Collinson, Deverell – involved in writing, and exchanging, poetry.[33] The interest in Dante's relations with his contemporaries is stressed by Rossetti in his rearrangement and republication of *The Early Italian Poets* (1861) under the new title *Dante and His Circle* (1874):

my object has been to make more evident at a first glance [the collection's] important relation to Dante. The *Vita Nuova*, together with the many among Dante's lyrics and those of his contemporaries which elucidate their personal intercourse, are here assembled, and brought to my best ability into clear connection . . . (*Works*, p. 282)

This is again a complete reversal of Romantic attitudes. The solitary exile, the Promethean freedom-fighter and, in the long run, the *Divine Comedy* itself – everything which stresses the gap between the genius of Dante and his contemporaries – tends to be discounted in the mid-century, and not only by Rossetti. The latter's translations are skilful enough to show that Dante's fellow-poets were indeed men of talent and individuality, particularly Cavalcanti and the man Rossetti calls the 'scamp' of the circle, Cecco Angiolieri (*Works*, p. 305). We have seen a certain similarity of aim in Browning's choice of hero in *Sordello*.[34] Rossetti's emphasis on Dante's circle is an important influence on Ezra Pound. Whereas Rossetti noted 'That [Cavalcanti's] poems dwelt in the mind of Dante is evident by his having appropriated lines from them (as well as from those of Guinicelli) with little alteration, more than once, in the *Commedia*' (*Works*, p. 303), Pound is content with no less than the assertion that '*Il Paradiso* and the form of *The Commedia* might date from this line', the line in question being Cavalcanti's 'Vedrai la sua virtù nel ciel salita' ('You will see her *virtù* risen into heaven'), from his *ballata* 'Veggio negli occhi de la donna mia' ('I see in the eyes of my lady').[35] Again one feels that, had the *Convivio* been better known, a surer picture of the transitions in Dante's thought would have resulted: his explanation there of the significance of the 'donna della finestra' for him as 'Filosofia' (II.xii.6) prepares one for the transition from the *Vita Nuova* to the much more complex ingredients and levels of meaning in the *Commedia*. Otherwise one may be left with the Rossettian method of handling the development between the two works; that is, with the pretence that no development exists.[36]

Rossetti's interest in the men of the late *duecento* as prototypes of his own circle was further increased by their activity in several fields: both Giotto and Dante could be claimed as poet–painters, for a *canzone* by the former is included in Rossetti's collection (*Works*, pp. 404–5) and Dante, as we know, drew angels on the anniversary of Beatrice's death. In his Introduction Rossetti mentions the tradition that Dante studied drawing with Giotto's master Cimabue (*Works*, p. 308), and the friendship between Giotto and Dante –

recorded by Vasari in his 'Life of Giotto' (p. 58) – received an added 'confirmation' from the Bargello discovery. In his picture of *Giotto Painting the Portrait of Dante* Rossetti wished to illustrate the famous lines from *Purgatorio* XI.94–9 on the 'vana gloria de l'umane posse' ('empty glory of human powers'), as he explained to Woolner (*Letters*, I, 122–3). Thus he has Cimabue looking over Giotto's shoulder watching the progress of the work while Cavalcanti leans on Dante's chair reading a volume of Guinizelli's poetry.[37] But Rossetti is greedy for incident: he again conflates *Vita Nuova* and *Commedia* by having Beatrice pass by in procession and Dante watching her. As he explains in the same letter:

> I have thus all the influence of Dante's youth – Art, Friendship and Love – with a real incident embodying them. The combination is, I think, the best which has yet occurred to me in illustration of this period of the poet's life, and the design is certainly about the best I have made.

The 'real incident', however, involves some stretching of the imagination: since Rossetti accepted Vasari's dating of Giotto's birth to 1276 (see Vasari, 'Life of Giotto', p. 57; Rossetti, *Works*, p. 308), then if Beatrice was still alive Giotto would have been at most fourteen when he painted the portrait.[38] In the unfinished watercolour replica (Surtees Cat. 54R1, plate 48) chronology is thrown to the winds with the heavily bearded Val Prinsep posing as Giotto, a realistic study which forms an odd contrast with the generalised features of the Dante Rossetti has copied into the painting from the Bargello portrait.

The doubtful chronology of Rossetti's painting has not been pointed out as an attack on him: one does not necessarily begrudge an artist's sacrificing historical accuracy for the sake of picturesqueness. Rather I have introduced it to illustrate a common nineteenth-century method of handling the events of Dante's life. In Landor's *Pentameron*, for instance, Dante is pictured as seated on his famous 'sasso' by the side of Florence Cathedral chatting with Giotto as the latter's tower is being built, even though this was not begun till 1334, over thirty years after Dante's exile and thirteen years after his death (p. 222). This kind of practice probably originated in Germany: in Ignaz Kollman's drama *Dante* (1826) the curtain falls on Beatrice dying in the presence of Dante, Giotto and Gemma Donati with Dante already due to go into exile confiding his children to Giotto's care.[39] Foscolo's suggestion that at the court of

Guido da Polenta, Dante's patron and Francesca da Rimini's father, Dante 'vide la stanza ove [Francesca] abitò giovinetta felice e innocente; udì forse narrato il caso dal vecchio Guido' ('saw the room where Francesca had lived as a happy and innocent young girl; he perhaps heard the aged Guido tell her story'),[40] is taken up by Carlyle who means to extract a much fuller emotional irony: 'Strange to think: Dante was the friend of this poor Francesca's father; Francesca herself may have sat upon the Poet's knee, as a bright innocent little child' ('The Hero as Poet', p. 153).

This rather cavalier manipulation of dates becomes, in Ruskin, a serious symbolical interpretation of the middle ages:

all great European art is rooted in the thirteenth century; and it seems to me that there is a kind of central year about which we may consider the energy of the Middle Ages to be gathered; a kind of focus of time, which, by what is to my mind a most touching and impressive Divine appointment, has been marked for us by the greatest writer of the Middle Ages, in the first words he utters; namely, the year 1300, the 'mezzo del cammin' of the life of Dante. Now, therefore, to Giotto, the contemporary of Dante, and who drew Dante's still existing portrait in this very year, 1300, we may always look for the central mediaeval idea in any subject . . .[41]

Whereas Kirkup would date the portrait to about 1293 – 'The poet looks about 28' – and Rossetti to before 1290, Ruskin brings it forward to 1300 in the interests of his 'central year'. The portrait for him is a symbol of that simultaneous perfection in the painting and poetry of the middle ages as expressed by its greatest artist and greatest writer; it is the keystone of a symmetrical arch. One senses that Giotto and Dante are well on the way to becoming allegorised into those buxom maidens who represent 'Art' and 'Letters' on the façades of Victorian buildings. This seems to be the idea behind their association, to take one example, in a stained-glass window in the south nave-aisle of the Victorian cathedral at Truro, where they appear with Innocent III (Plate 6).[42] Certainly mediaeval Florence represented to Ruskin an ideal of the State where the sister-arts go hand-in-hand: his 'mediaevalism' is of a much more serious nature than Rossetti's. But this is another reason for concentrating on the *Vita Nuova* rather than on the *Commedia* and for the reaction against the Romantics' interest in the exiled Dante in favour of the Dante of the 1290s: the desideratum is a kind of Giotto–Beatrice–Dante Utopia in which, in Rossetti's words, 'Art, Friendship and Love' flourish in mutual interaction.

Thus it is that Rossetti's first surviving drawing based on the *Vita Nuova*, *The First Anniversary of the Death of Beatrice* (Cat. 42, plates 27–8), commemorates not only Dante's 'Love', but also 'Art' (Dante drawing the angel) and 'Friendship' (as opposed to Browning's suggestion that Dante's visitors in *Vita Nuova* XXXIV were 'the folk of his Inferno'), since the visitors are clearly members of Dante's artistic brotherhood. We saw how in the later watercolour of this incident (plate 51) Rossetti 'inserted' Gemma Donati, and it is more than likely that the principal visitor in the Birmingham drawing is Cimabue or Cavalcanti.[43] This is confirmed, I think, by Rossetti's having produced the drawing for a fellow-member of the PRB: it is inscribed 'Dante G. Rossetti to his PR Brother John E. Millais'. Millais, as far as we know, had no interest in Dante and Beatrice but would certainly have responded to this illustration of the brotherhood's forerunners. In Rossetti's other paintings from the *Vita Nuova* we can trace further suggestions of the book's 'mysteries'. Thus the unnamed friend who takes Dante to the wedding feast in *Vita Nuova* XIV is clearly recognisable in Rossetti's painting of the scene (plate 33) as the Cavalcanti from the sketch of *Giotto Painting Dante's Portrait* (plate 45).

Before looking at the influence of the *Vita Nuova* on Rossetti's poetry we may conclude with a further word on the Bargello portrait. According to William Rossetti, 'The receipt of this portrait [that is, Kirkup's copy] probably put the mind and feelings of Dante Rossetti as much *en rapport* with the Florentine poet as any incident which had preceded it . . .' (*Family Letters*, I, 65). This statement has been unnecessarily contested by B. J. Morse, who bases his case on the fact that Rossetti did not begin his Dante studies till about five years after the portrait was received, that is till around 1845.[44] But a determining influence need in no sense be an immediate one, and the case for the portrait's importance has been made out in this chapter. What is indisputable is the immense interest aroused by the portrait on its discovery: Toynbee records notices of it by, amongst others, Landor, Mrs Shelley, Fitzgerald and Charles Eastlake (*DEL*, II, 122–4, 284–5, 562, 666). It was first published in England in the 1842 edition of Lyell's *Poems of the 'Vita Nuova' and 'Convito'* (Plate 4), together, interestingly enough, with the first reproduction in England of the so-called Torrigiani 'death-mask' (Plate 7), which aroused far less attention, picturing, as it did, the grim, 'ruined'

Dante then going out of fashion.[45] What is again indisputable is that Rossetti nearly always uses the Bargello copy as the basis for his own pictures of Dante.

Turning to Rossetti's poetry, we find a good deal of it displaying an intimate connexion with certain features of the early Italian work he translated. This is especially true of his sonnet-sequence *The House of Life*, which drew the following comment from Swinburne:

There has been no work of the same pitch attempted since Dante sealed up his youth in the sacred leaves of the *Vita Nuova*; and this poem of his name-child and translator is a more various and mature work of kindred genius and spirit.[46]

Commentators have not been slow to provide illustrations of the kinship between the two works, and indeed it is obvious that the first part of Rossetti's sequence, 'Youth and Change', shows a particularly 'Dantesque' inspiration; a series of sonnets reflecting the vicissitudes in the story of the narrator, his lady, and their personified Love was encouragement enough for Swinburne's comparison.[47] Recollections from Dante are particularly strong near the beginning of the sequence: in sonnet II the birth of Love in the lady's heart derives from the process described in 'Amore e 'l cor gentil sono una cosa' ('Love and the noble heart are one thing') (*Works*, p. 75, *VN* XX); the heart 'Clothed with [Love's] fire' of sonnet III from Dante's vision in *Vita Nuova* III.3–7, which also probably suggested the idea of 'proud Love . . . weep[ing]' in sonnet VII; while 'the spirits of mine eyes' worshipping the lady's face, 'their altar', in sonnet IV, is a conceit that came to Rossetti through the early Italians if not especially from Dante. Later in the sequence, the opening of sonnet XXXIII: 'Could Juno's self more sovereign presence wear/Than thou, 'mid other ladies throned in grace?' clearly harbours a recollection of 'Vede perfettamente onne salute/chi la mia donna tra le donne vede' ('He sees to perfection all salvation who sees my lady among other ladies') (*VN* XXVI); and sonnet XXXVII is a 'battaglia de' pensieri' ('battle of thoughts') re-enacting the divided loyalty Dante experienced between Beatrice and the 'donna della finestra'.

As we have seen, however, Rossetti's Love aims at a type of fulfilment utterly unlike Dante's, and it is tempting to apply Mario Praz's criticism of 'The Blessed Damozel' to the whole range of

Rossetti's poetry and suggest that he has merely taken over scenery and props from the *dolce stil nuovo* to stage a drama totally foreign to it.[48] Graham Hough sums up the contrast between the two writers thus:

Perpetually tormented by the irreconcilability of the unsensual love he had idealised and the love of the senses, [Rossetti] tries to identify them. Knowing that Dante's ideal love became in some way identified with the highest spiritual values, but blankly unaware of the austere scholastic method, the exact analysis and definition by which the transformation was accomplished, he simply turns his own confused and all too human conception of love into the highest value, and calls it God.[49]

The fullest critique of Rossetti's presumption in borrowing from Dante has been provided by Nicolette Gray. She has spotted that Rossetti failed to understand Dante's explanation in the *Vita Nuova* that 'Amore non è per sé sì come sustanzia, ma è uno accidente in sustanzia' ('Love is not at all itself a substance, but is an accident in a substance') (xxv.1); and that in the gloss Rossetti gives on this passage in his Introduction he claims Dante enters into the argument 'as if to show us that the Love he speaks of is only his own emotion' (*Works*, pp. 297–8 note). This has the effect, as Mrs Gray suggests, of completely 'de-universalizing' Beatrice's significance and drawing her within the circle of privacy and secrecy celebrated in Rossetti's own love-poems.[50] The idea of Beatrice's virtuous operation on all those about her gives way to an emphasis, again in Rossetti's words, that to each reader Beatrice will seem 'the friend of his own heart' (*Works*, p. 297). This has the further effect of muting the Christian ideology of the *Vita Nuova*; and Mrs Gray points out, for example, that Rossetti's translation of 'Vede perfettamente onne salute' (*VN* xxvi) has for the line 'La vista sua fa onne cosa umile', 'Merely the sight of her makes all things bow', which is, as she says, 'quite a different thing' from saying 'the sight of her makes all things humble . . . with the virtue of humility' (p. 36).

Rossetti's love-poetry is really so different from Dante's as to make the similarities appear the more spurious. 'The Song of the Bower' portrays a typical fulfilment:

Kindled with love-breath, (the sun's kiss is colder!)
  Thy sweetness all near me, so distant to-day;
My hand round thy neck and thy hand on my shoulder,
  My mouth to thy mouth as the world melts away.
(*Works*, p. 207)

This possessiveness is of course completely foreign to the *Vita Nuova*, Dante's ambition being first Beatrice's 'dolcissimo salutare' ('sweetest salutation') (x.2) and, after this is denied, the celebration of Beatrice with 'quelle parole che lodano la donna mia' ('those words which praise my lady') (XVIII.6). Part of Dante's 'mirabile letizia' ('wonderful happiness') is precisely Beatrice's public function, the 'onestade' ('worthiness') she creates in thosc around her (XXVI.1). The beloved's 'universality' that Rossetti celebrates –

> Sometimes thou seem'st not as thyself alone,
> But as the meaning of all things that are
> (*HL* XXVII)

– sees the woman not as the vehicle of a divine force but as the replacement for it, with love for her representing a complete abnegation of everything else: in the same sonnet the world is 'staked', or wagered, against the woman's heart, or else 'melts away' while the lovers kiss (see above). In the sonnet 'Heart's Haven' (*HL* XXII), the poet seeks the 'refuge' of his beloved's 'deep embrace', while

> Love, our light at night and shade at noon,
> Lulls us to rest with songs, and turns away
> All shafts of shelterless tumultuous day.
> (*Works*, p. 82)

Similarly, the 'fleshliness' of Rossetti's poetry removes it completely from the orbit of Dante's; the kiss that creeps 'Up your warm throat to your warm lips' of 'Youth's Spring-Tribute' (*HL* XIV) serving as one of many possible examples.[51]

It would be wrong, however, to claim that Rossetti had a purely secular mentality, for, although the conception of Paradise in several of his poems is an earthly consummation writ large, there can be no doubt of the genuineness of his desire to believe in the life after death. In a sonnet like 'Bridal Birth' (*HL* II) the anticipations of eternity may be no more than a soothing fancy –

> Now, shadowed by [Love's] wings, our faces yearn
> Together, as his full-grown feet now range
> The grove, and his warm hands our couch prepare:
> Till to his song our bodiless souls in turn
> Be born his children, when Death's nuptial change
> Leaves us for light the halo of his hair

– but in the two sonnets 'Love and Hope' and 'Cloud and Wind' (*HL* XLIII–XLIV) we have a sincere anxiety as to whether 'Our hearts shall wake to know Love's golden head/Sole sunshine of the imperishable land' in the next world; what Rossetti seems to fear in these sonnets is not an adverse Christian judgement after death but rather the state of simple non-existence. We have already noted the Blessed Damozel's desire 'only to be,/As then awhile, for ever now/Together, I and he'. These notions have again been criticised by Mrs Gray: 'Is the Blessed Damozel not Beatrice, only Francesca?' she asks. 'Is not this soul choosing union with another soul before union with God and is not that rejection and idolatry and Hell?' (pp. 40–1). Mrs Gray writes from an explicitly Christian standpoint, but all readers can see that the fate of Paolo and Francesca contains for Rossetti a vital attraction that is missing from Dante's relationship with Beatrice: that is, an eternal inseparability within a 'darkling close embrace', as 'The Stream's Secret' expresses it (*Works*, p. 116). The actual location of that embrace seems to be secondary to the fact that 'questi . . . mai da me non fia diviso' ('this one . . . will never be divided from me') (*Inf.* V.135).[52] Rossetti's painting of Paolo and Francesca brings to mind his phrase in the sonnet 'Farewell to the Glen', namely 'The bliss of being sad' (*HL* LXXXIV), in common with his other paintings of lovers like *Carlile Wall* or *The Wedding of St George and the Princess Sabra* (Surtees plates 52, 132). Hueffer noted of the *Paolo and Francesca* (plate 87):

> it is impossible to suppose that when Rossetti painted [this work] he, or any of his admirers, thought that the two lovers were really suffering . . . the flakes of flames were descending all over the rest of the picture, but they did not fall upon Paolo and Francesca. No, the lovers were protected by a generalized, swooning passion that formed, as it were, a moral and very efficient macintosh all over them.[53]

Not that Rossetti ever envisages in his poetry a consummation amid such a setting, however powerless the flames might be. The habitat Rossetti customarily chooses for his love lies within the 'breathless bowers' of *The House of Life*'s first sonnet, or the 'deep dim wood' of 'The Portrait' –

> In painting her I shrined her face
> 'Mid mystic trees, where light falls in
> Hardly at all; a covert place
> (*Works*, p. 169)

– where the world is shut out; a *paradiso terrestre* that recalls the 'ombra perpetüa, che mai/raggiar non lascia sole ivi né luna' ('perpetual shadow, which never lets the sun nor moon shine there') of Dante's (*Purg.* XXVIII.32–3). And as we have seen, it was at this point in the *Commedia*, with the lovers tenderly united, that Rossetti's interest ceased. One may conclude this brief survey of his ideal of consummation by quoting four stanzas from 'The Stream's Secret', a poem that conveniently illustrates most of the themes discussed so far:

> Oh sweet her bending grace
> Then when I kneel beside her feet;
> And sweet her eyes' o'erhanging heaven; and sweet
> The gathering folds of her embrace;
> And her fall'n hair at last shed round my face
> When breaths and tears shall meet.
>
> Beneath her sheltering hair,
> In the warm silence near her breast,
> Our kisses and our sobs shall sink to rest;
> As in some still trance made aware
> That day and night have wrought to fullness there
> And Love has built our nest.
>
> And as in the dim grove,
> When the rains cease that hushed them long,
> 'Mid glistening boughs the song-birds wake to song, –
> So from our hearts deep-shrined in love,
> While the leaves throb beneath, around, above,
> The quivering notes shall throng.
>
> Till tenderest words found vain
> Draw back to wonder mute and deep,
> And closed lips in closed arms a silence keep,
> Subdued by memory's circling strain, –
> The wind-rapt sound that the wind brings again
> While all the willows weep.
>
> (*Works*, p. 115)

The presence of the wind in this final stanza again carries the hint of a Paolo-and-Francesca-like dolorousness; and the third stanza quoted contains one of Rossetti's favourite devices, the equation of the loving heart with the leaf-concealed bird taken over from the opening of Guinizelli's famous *canzone*: 'Al cor gentil rempaira sempre Amore/come l'ausello in selva a la verdura . . .' ('Love always makes its abode in the noble heart, like a bird in the foliage of the wood . . .')[54]

To return to Rossetti's religion, we find frequent references to a Divinity in his poetry:

> Lady, I fain would tell how evermore
> Thy soul I know not from thy body, nor
> Thee from myself, neither our love from God.
> (*HL* v)

Mrs Gray has a perceptive comment on these lines: 'That is precisely Rossetti's position; he does not know Love from God. Of love he had a vivid experience, of God no clear conscious experience at all; he therefore tended to think of Love as God – clearly very different from thinking of God as Love. And so Love becomes an end' (p. 39). This is not however quite fair to Rossetti: in *The House of Life* there are three sonnets (LXVI, LXXII, LXXVI) that feature the biblical God rather than Rossetti's usual deity:

> O Lord of work and peace! O Lord of life!
> O Lord, the awful Lord of will! though late,
> Even yet renew this soul with duteous breath:
> That when the peace is garnered in from strife,
> The work retrieved, the will regenerate,
> This soul may see thy face, O Lord of death!
> (LXVI)

Here the lady is absent from Rossetti's hopes. In sonnets LXIII, LXXII, LXXXV and LXXXVI he imagines in no half-hearted manner the punishments of Hell, and in the last of these, 'Lost Days', the accusations those days, 'Each one a murdered self', will level at him 'to all eternity'. Nevertheless, the religious position in *The House of Life* remains enigmatic: William Rossetti has not unreasonably interpreted 'The One Hope' of the final sonnet to be 'the woman supremely beloved upon earth' so that what Mrs Gray terms Rossetti's 'idolatry' is reaffirmed at the last.[55]

The problem with those critics who dismiss Rossetti's 'Amore' as a complete impostor compared with Dante's is that they judge him altogether by the supreme standards of the *Commedia*. One must however keep to the *Vita Nuova* – which among Dante's works Rossetti was almost exclusively obsessed by – to make the comparison more realistic. What Rossetti thought of as the *Dantis*

Amor was, as we have seen, the *giovane-peregrino* of the *Vita Nuova*, who is re-created in *The House of Life* as a young man with wings and (on occasion) a lute.[56] In his paintings from Dante, Rossetti often fits Love out with what he considers suitable accessories: in the two versions of *Dante's Dream*, for example, Love carries a large bow and arrows, and actually bends over to kiss the dead Beatrice, a detail Dante nowhere mentions (*VN* XXIII). Thus it must be said that the *giovane* is adapted for Rossetti's purposes rather than taken over directly. In a sketch for the 1880–1 painting *The Salutation of Beatrice* (Cat. 260C, plate 391), Dante and Love are seen seated together on the edge of a well, a scene illustrating nothing in the *Vita Nuova* but rather the opening of Rossetti's own 'Willowwood' (*HL* XLIX). The *Dantis Amor* also functions more specifically in Rossetti's poetry as the personified 'Love's hour': we remember him from the 1859 *Salutation* painting recording the hour of Beatrice's death on a sundial; in Rossetti's poetry he rather represents the magical hour of reunion:

> Stands it not by the door –
> Love's Hour – till she and I shall meet
> . . .
> Its eyes invisible
> Watch till the dial's thin-thrown shade
> Be born, – yea, till the journeying line be laid
> Upon the point that wakes the spell . . .
> ('The Stream's Secret', *Works*, p. 117)

The personified hour appears again and again in *The House of Life*, in sonnets XIX, LV – where it waits after death as a fulfilment denied to the lovers in life – and in XXV, 'Winged Hours', where 'Each hour until we meet is as a bird/That wings from far his gradual way along/The rustling covert of my soul . . .', where it is conflated with the Guinizellian bird-image.

The drama of the *Vita Nuova*, love, separation, the hope of an eventual reunion, stimulated Rossetti's imagination far more than anything in the *Commedia*, including the reunion itself. It may be that much of the anguish in *The House of Life* sprang from Rossetti's enforced separation from Jane Morris; but, long before this relationship, or indeed any of Rossetti's relationships, began, he was writing a somewhat melodramatic poetry of separation obviously inspired by the *Vita Nuova*:

God, too, I know will sever
Our souls, even there: for she'll be in the full
House of his Saints, at peace; but I not so.
[Oh God!] I am quite sure that I shall never
See her again! that mine own hands will pull
Me down from her! No, much remains to know.[57]

Compare God's answer to the desires of the blessed for Beatrice in 'Donne ch'avete intelletto d'amore':

Diletti miei, or sofferite in pace
che vostra spene sia quanto me piace
là 'v'è alcun che perder lei s'attende,
e che dirà ne lo inferno: O mal nati,
io vidi la speranza de' beati.

(My loved ones, now suffer it in peace that your hope should stay as long as I please where there is one who waits to lose her, and who will say in hell: O you evil born, I saw the hope of the blessed) (*VN* XIX.8)

Here, one might say, is the kernel of Rossetti's interest in the *Vita Nuova*. If Beatrice is the 'speranza de' beati' and her absence from Heaven its sole 'difetto' ('defect') ('Donne ch'avete', l. 19), then the elevation of the woman to a level of 'idolatry' in Rossetti's poetry begins to look less like a misrepresentation of Dante's position:

And I said, 'Ah me! what art
Should win the immortal prize,
Whose want must make life cold
And Heaven a hollow dream?'
('Three Shadows', *Works*, p. 225)

Of course one cannot claim Dante's position is represented by one stanza from 'Donne ch'avete', and even if one could, there would remain the sensual element in Rossetti's 'idolatry' which is totally absent from the *Vita Nuova*. If we look at the very end of the 'libello' –

E poi piaccia a colui che è sire de la cortesia, che la mia anima se ne possa gire a vedere la gloria de la sua donna, cioè di quella benedetta Beatrice, la quale gloriosamente mira ne la faccia di colui *qui est per omnia secula benedictus*

(And then may it please him who is the lord of courtesy that my soul may travel to see the glory of its lady, that is of that blessed Beatrice, who looks in glory on the face of him *who is blessed through all ages*)

(XLII.3)

– we find Dante's attention remaining fixed on Beatrice rather than on the God whose representative, to be sure, she was on earth. The *Vita Nuova* ends on a note of adoration so different from that at the conclusion of the *Commedia* that it is no wonder a reader steeped in it as Rossetti was could consider his own poetry, where the beloved is often raised to the level of an absolute value, as in some ways emulating it. And what he emulates are not the theological elements that link the 'libello' with the great later work – the fact that Beatrice was 'uno nove' ('a nine') with her root in the Trinity bringing uncomfortably to mind his father's researches (*VN* XXIX.3) – but what the book shared with the other early Italian poetry Rossetti was interested in: a Love who in the early part of the *Vita Nuova* is the traditional master of the 'fedeli d'Amore' ('liegemen of Love'), at times tyrannous, at times oppressive to the heart that houses him, a Love who, in the havoc he creates among Dante's 'fearful spirits' on seeing Beatrice – as in 'Con l'altre donne mia vista gabbate' ('With other ladies you mock my appearance') (*VN* XIV) – has nothing to do with the Christian *Amore*. Thus, on Beatrice's death, Love is as powerless and miserable as Dante is; earlier in the book he and Dante rejoice or weep together in turn, depending on the course of events. This is the situation Rossetti takes over in his poetry: in the 'Willowwood' sonnets, for example (*HL* XLIX–LII), the picture of himself and Love both mourning the lost lady, the idea of Love's having 'pity and grace' for his 'fedele' but, as it were, no transcendental influence –

> her face fell back drowned, and was as grey
> As its grey eyes; and if it ever may
> Meet mine again I know not if Love knows
>
> (LII)

– derives from Dante's statement that Beatrice 'si n'è gita in ciel subitamente,/e ha lasciato Amor meco dolente' ('Beatrice has gone suddenly into heaven, and has left Love grieving with me') ('Li occhi dolenti', *VN* XXXI), a passage that accompanied Rossetti's earliest drawing of the *Dantis Amor* (Surtees plate 173).

Charles S. Singleton has described the conflict found in the work of Dante's predecessors between ideas of fidelity towards Christian and towards non-Christian *Amore*.[58] In Guinizelli's 'Al cor gentil', for example, the lover's obedience to his lady is compared with that of the angels to God, a presumption the poet is reprimanded for before God's throne in the last stanza: 'desti in vano amor Me per semblanti' ('you used Me as a comparison for your vain love'); the poet replies that his lady looked so much like an angel herself as to justify his love for her (Marti, *Poeti* . . ., p. 62). We are not told whether God is satisfied with the answer, however, and the conflict is left unresolved. Another poem translated by Rossetti, and one which Morse suggested may have inspired 'The Blessed Damozel' (pp. 239–42), is a sonnet by Jacopo da Lentino which Rossetti entitles 'Of his Lady in Heaven' (*Works*, p. 440). It is worth giving the translation in full:

> I have it in my heart to serve God so
> That into Paradise I shall repair, –
> The holy place through the which everywhere
> I have heard say that joy and solace flow.
> Without my lady I were loth to go, –
> She who has the bright face and the bright hair
> Because if she were absent, I being there,
> My pleasure would be less than nought, I know.
> Look you, I say not this to such intent
> As that I there would deal in any sin:
> I only would behold her gracious mien,
> And beautiful soft eyes, and lovely face,
> That so it should be my complete content
> To see my lady joyful in her place.[59]

Singleton believes that only in the *Vita Nuova* do we have a solution to the impasse: since Dante makes it clear that Beatrice not only looks like an angel but is one, there can be no doubt about her heavenly destiny or about the congruence of Dante's service to God and to her. Yet one may feel that Dante's desire for salvation shares with the above sonnet by Jacopo an obsession with his lady which is regulated in the *Commedia* by Beatrice's occasional reminders that 'non pur ne' miei occhi è paradiso' ('paradise is not only in my eyes') (*Par*. XVIII.21), and that only in this last work is the love towards the lady perfectly synthesised with the Christian love. *The House of Life* itself follows in what one might call the pre-Dante tradition whereby God and the beloved remain at odds with each other with the latter gaining the upper hand, for in the second part of the sequence, 'Change and Fate', the religious sonnets like the one quoted above (p. 125) cannot be reconciled with Rossetti's more familiar declarations that 'True Woman . . . were Paradise all uttermost worlds among' ('Her Heaven', sonnet LVIII). And, although 'Love, the lord of all' (sonnet XXXIV) receives less worship in this second part, Rossetti's turning to a different master, the 'Lord of work and peace!' in sonnet LXVI, does not remain constant, as the final sonnet, 'The One Hope', would seem to emphasise. The fact that Rossetti seems less willing, as the sequence progresses, to maintain the *Vita Nuova*-like Love in an absolute lordship that, in Dante's terms, is only occupied by the *Amore* of the *Commedia*, is certainly not due to a similar transition in him from the one to the other: if 'Love, the child once ours' is described as dead in the penultimate sonnet, then Rossetti did not find anything to replace him with. The sonnet 'Through Death to Love' (XLI) restates the argument of Jacopo's sonnet: Love is pitted against a salvation represented, in part, by Dante's description of the entry into Purgatory (IX.76–81):

> Howbeit athwart Death's imminent shade doth soar
> One Power, than flow of stream or flight of dove
> Sweeter to glide around, to brood above.
> Tell me, my heart, – what angel-greeted door
> Or threshold of wing-winnowed threshing-floor
> Hath guest fire-fledged as thine, whose lord is Love?

In spite of the examples given of the *Vita Nuova*'s influence on *The House of Life*, one is forced to conclude that the two works are not very similar. Several of Rossetti's sonnets deal with themes extraneous to that of the 'fedele d'Amore'; as Baum says in the Introduction to his edition, the sequence 'has little unity of a formal kind; on the contrary, its unity is the unity of Rossetti's life' (p. 46). There is, for example, a group of sonnets on art; and several on the wastage and misfortune of a life that has heavily, and to a large degree fruitlessly, invested in anticipations of 'Love's Hour'. No doubt Swinburne had these in mind when describing the sequence as 'more various and mature' than the *Vita Nuova*. The religious background to Rossetti's poetry often seems to be no more than a splendid *metaphor* of eternal fulfilment:

> Even so, where Heaven holds breath and hears
> The beating heart of Love's own breast, –
> Where round the secret of all spheres
> All angels lay their wings to rest, –

How shall my soul stand rapt and awed,
When, by the new birth borne abroad
Throughout the music of the suns,
It enters in her soul at once
And knows the silence there for God!
('The Portrait', *Works*, p. 170)

It is only fair, though, to Rossetti to note that, just as Shelley was aware of the liberties he had taken with Dante in *Epipsychidion*, so he himself probably realised the highly restricted absorption of Dante his work reflects. When he sent some early poems off to Leigh Hunt who replied commending his 'Dantesque heavens (without any hell to spoil them)', Rossetti informed his aunt, '[Hunt] refers to one or two of the poems the scene of which is laid in the celestial regions, and which are written in a kind of Gothic manner which I suppose he is pleased to think belongs to the school of Dante'; one of the poems was probably 'The Blessed Damozel'.[60]

The dissatisfaction one feels ultimately with the 'Pre-Raphaelite' Beatrice is the abnegation she involves of the whole pattern of Dante's career and beliefs. Dante was careful not to allow Beatrice to become an absolute value and to re-set her in the *Commedia* within the context of a Christian belief that allows her a substantial but ultimately secondary role: it is in a vision of God's glory that the poem ends and not, as in the *Vita Nuova*, of 'la gloria de la sua donna, cioè di quella benedetta Beatrice'. Thus Rossetti's statement in 'Dante at Verona' that 'all ended with her eyes,/Hell, Purgatory, Paradise' is a downright falsification. Yet in his ideas Rossetti is only continuing a tendency we saw in Shelley, whose hero in *Alastor* experiences a vision of a mystical female who is the consummation of 'all of wonderful, or wise, or beautiful, which the poet, the philosopher, or the lover could depicture' (Preface to *Alastor*, p. 14). Although the lady discourses to the poet in the vision of 'Knowledge and truth and virtue . . ./And lofty hopes of divine liberty' (ll. 158–9), she is unable to lead him to them, for awaking from his vision 'He seeks in vain for a prototype of his conception. Blasted by his disappointment, he descends to an untimely grave' (Preface, pp. 14–15). One may compare the episode with Rousseau's meeting with the 'Shape all light' in *The Triumph of Life*. Beatrice is certainly one element in that 'all of wonderful, or wise, or beautiful' which go to make up the perfection of the 'single image' in *Alastor*, but, as we saw, Shelley never produced a poetry where that 'image' is explicitly harmonised with his philosophy of liberty and truth: the relationship between them remains intuitive, or mystical. In Rossetti this problem does not arise, because Rossetti has no philosophy: the woman is purely and simply an end in herself. But during the nineteenth century, as Frank Kermode explains, 'The beauty of a woman . . . [becomes] the emblem of the work of art or Image', an Image that is 'a means to truth, a truth unrelated to, and more exalted than, that of positivist science, or any observation depending upon the discursive reason'; that is 'resistant to explication; largely independent of intention, and of any form of ethical utility'.[61] Shelley's abhorrence of didactic poetry explains why his women have to be this 'Imagistic' means to truth rather than *explain* truth as Beatrice does to Dante in canto after canto of the *Paradiso*. Romantic thinking then transforms Beatrice into its utterly dissimilar ideal of the Image: the classic example is in Keats's 'The Fall of Hyperion – A Dream', where the veiled priestess Moneta uncovers herself to the poet after he has climbed the steps to her raised altar:

> Then saw I a wan face,
> Not pined by human sorrows, but bright-blanched
> By an immortal sickness which kills not;
> . . .
> But for her eyes I should have fled away.
> They held me back, with a benignant light,
> Soft-mitigated by divinest lids
> Half-closed, and visionless entire they seemed
> Of all external things . . .
>
> (ll. 256–68)[62]

This may seem a very different unveiling from that of Beatrice to Dante in the *paradiso terrestre*; but it has been suggested that this is Keats's prime source in the above lines.[63] Moreover, as Kermode says,

> Moneta's face haunts many later poets as well as Keats . . . The knowledge it represents is not malign, but it is unrelated to 'external things'; the eyes express nothing, looking inward to the 'high tragedy In the dark secret chambers of the skull'. To prostrate himself before this figure is the privilege of the artist's joy and the reward of his suffering. (p. 22)

The female faces in Rossetti's poetry and painting are adduced by

Kermode as continuing the tradition of the Image (pp. 71–81), as in 'Astarte Syriaca':

> That face, of Love's all-penetrative spell
> Amulet, talisman, and oracle, –
> Betwixt the sun and moon a mystery.
> (*Works*, p. 226)

The woman's face as index to some ineffable knowledge is again presented in 'The Dark Glass' (*HL* xxxiv):

> Yet through thine eyes [Love] grants me clearest call
> And veriest touch of powers primordial
> That any hour-girt life may understand.

As with Moneta, the eyes are especially important, and it is here that the contrast between the Romantic Image and Dante's Beatrice is neatly pointed. For, as Kermode says, with a glance at Pater's description of the *Mona Lisa*, 'the inward-looking countenance, whether of drilled eyeball or *sfumato*' is crucial to the Image's mystical self-involvement; but when Beatrice unveils her eyes to Dante in the *Purgatorio* they are not 'visionless . . . Of all external things' but reflect the griffin to him:

> Mille disiri più che fiamma caldi
> strinsermi li occhi a li occhi rilucenti,
> che pur sopra 'l grifone stavan saldi.
> Come in lo specchio il sol, non altrimenti
> la doppia fiera dentro vi raggiava,
> or con altri, or con altri reggimenti.

(A thousand desires hotter than flame held my eyes on her sparkling eyes, which still rested firmly on the griffin. Just like the sun in a mirror the two-fold beast shone inside them, now in its first, now in its second nature.) (xxxi.118–23)

Moreover, the eyes reflect to Dante Christ's double nature, now as man, now as God. One of Beatrice's functions here, as is well known, is to represent allegorically divine Wisdom, or Theology, as she stands within the chariot of the Church;[64] and, although the ultimate end of Theology, namely God, can be said to share with the mystical truth represented by the Image the quality of ineffability, Theology itself remains a discursive activity with an explicit and in many areas explicable subject; as we see in the *Paradiso* when Beatrice sets about explaining.[65]

The transformation of Beatrice into Image was aided in Rossetti's case by his ignoring of the *Paradiso* and concentration on the *Vita Nuova*, a preference Mrs Gray sums up in her contention that 'The image therefore remains to us our ultimate starting point potentially always a way, so apt to present itself out of darkness as an end, an idol' (pp. 45–6). Buchanan's attack on Rossetti also traces his 'idolatry' back to the 'affectation, foolishness, and moral blindness' of the early Italian poets' adoration of woman:

In the ways of these poor devils Dante walked a little; and he has left us, in his *Vita Nuova*, a book which carries the system of individual fantasy about as near perfection as possible, and (of course) invests a radically absurd line of thought with a fictitious and tremendous interest . . . What was great and potent in Dante remained in the *Divine Comedy* and bore no seed. What was absurd and unnatural in Dante, mingling with foul exhalations from the brains of his brother poets, formed the miasmic cloud which obscured all English culture, generated madness even as far north as Hawthornden and Edinburgh . . . and generally bred in the very bones and marrow of English literature the veriest ague of absurdity ever known to keep human creature crazy. (*The Fleshly School*, pp. 10–11)

From this point on in his pamphlet, Buchanan refers to the malady simply as 'the Italian disease', and finds its presence in Victorian England the result of 'a fresh importation of the obnoxious matter from France' (p. 15), with the Baudelairean 'Femmes Damnées' as its source and Swinburne as its carrier (pp. 22–3). It may seem unfair to thus link Dante with Baudelaire in connexion with what Kermode calls the Image's 'pathological aspect' (p. 74), but for Buchanan even Beatrice remains a *femme fatale* if no attempt is made to justify the *Vita Nuova*'s 'absurd line of thought' with the fruit it bore in the *Commedia*. At the same time, other critics, like Martin, saw the 'libello' as sanctifying the highest Victorian ideals of womanhood, of those 'pure, patient, gentle, wise and helpful spirits – who minister strength' and so on. With regard to Rossetti, one might note finally that his sense of the woman as a repository of ultimate values is not an act of defiant idolatry but comes rather from his sheer religious uncertainty: he clung to what he knew. Beatrice was a real woman for him seen against a religious background Rossetti neither accepted nor rejected but could see only dimly through the female vehicle herself; a region

Whose peace abides in the dark avenue
Amid the bitterness of things occult.[66]

Appendix to Chapter IV: a note on Tennyson's *In Memoriam*

Hallam's enthusiasm for Dante was not carried over into Tennyson's great elegy on him which was begun in 1833 and published in 1850.[67] The joy of the reunion between Dante and Beatrice in the *Commedia* is of course something which *In Memoriam* can only uncertainly aspire to amid its predominant tone of 'honest doubt' (XCVI); and even Dante's distress on first losing Beatrice, as recorded in *Vita Nuova* XXXI–XXXIX, does not deepen into the intellectual confusion and nightmarish vision of a formless universe which Tennyson is subject to in Hallam's loss (LXX). The last two chapters of the *Vita Nuova* show, so to speak, that Dante knows exactly where Beatrice is and what she is doing; moreover, he has access to her in spiritual visions and she is with him as he studies as hard as he can in his promise to write something that will be worthy of her. Thus the loss of Beatrice is set within the secure confines of a Christian world-picture.

The opening section of *In Memoriam*, dated 1849, makes formal professions of Christianity which the *Commedia* had already substantiated in its monumental fashion. Thus the 'little systems' of man are 'but broken lights' of God (compare, for example, *Paradiso* XIII.52–4), and Hallam, who now lives in Christ, is there 'worthier to be loved', just as Beatrice's 'bellezza e virtù' grew in passing from the flesh to the spirit and her own lovableness increased accordingly (*Purg*. XXX.124–9). Tennyson is however denied access in his poem to the kind of Dantesque vision in which these propositions become certainties; indeed they are offset, even as he makes them, by the reiterated emphasis in this opening section that 'we cannot know', that uncertainty is the natural tenor of the spiritual life. The conclusion of the poem indeed strikes us as more assertive, passing like the *Commedia* from a celebration of the lost one to praise of 'That God . . . To which the whole creation moves', which echoes Dante's reference to the divine will as 'quel mare al qual tutto si move/ciò ch'ella crïa' ('that sea towards which everything it creates flows') (*Par*. III.86–7); yet we feel even here that Tennyson can come to terms more easily with the idea of Hallam as a prototype of the nobler race of men that will evolve on earth than he can with the idea of Hallam as a spirit.[68] This 'awful thought', the spiritualisation of that which was tangible (XIII), is at the core of Tennyson's brooding; he has no notion of how to envisage the 'something strange' his friend has been turned into (XLI), and as his self-confessed 'earthly Muse' is mainly concerned to 'render human love his dues' he has enormous difficulties apprehending a superhuman dimension (XXXVII). Hence his own comparison of *In Memoriam* with the *Commedia* ('It begins with a funeral and ends with a marriage – begins with death and ends in promise of a new life – a sort of *Divine Comedy*, cheerful at the close')[69] transposes Dante's story to a secular setting.

In between these opening and closing declarations of reliance on the divine will there is no straightforward movement from doubt to affirmation but an increasing emotional calm; spiritual uncertainties are not resolved but they become less pressing, and in his final address to Hallam Tennyson is able to state:

> Far off thou art, but ever nigh;
> I have thee still, and I rejoice;
> I prosper, circled with thy voice;
> I shall not lose thee though I die.
>
> (CXXX)

He senses, in the same section, that Hallam is 'mixed with God and Nature', and, as remarked, it is this latter mixture he finds easier to grasp. In the last sonnet of the *Vita Nuova* a 'thought' of Dante's ('pensero') passes 'Oltre la spera che più larga gira' ('Beyond the sphere with the broadest orbit') to see the heavenly Beatrice in glory, but Tennyson's occasional thoughts of

> wing[ing] my will with might
> To leap the grades of life and light
> And flash at once, my friend, to thee
>
> (XLI)

are vitiated by the uncertain worry about what he will find beyond 'the grades', such as being 'evermore a life behind' his friend (XLI), or being reunited with Hallam only to have to part once more: '"Farewell! We lose ourselves in light"' (XLVII). It seems then that Dante's picture of life beyond the grades is of no comfort to Tennyson and even, as this last quotation suggests, antipathetic to him;[70] the reunion of Dante and Beatrice is a preliminary stage in Paradise to the all-absorbing worship of the 'etterna fontana' ('eternal fountain') Beatrice turns towards in the last view we have of her (*Par.* XXXI.93), whereas Tennyson's hopes of heavenly consummation centre, like Rossetti's, on the re-establishment of human intimacy, a 'Love on earth' writ large:

> And we shall sit at endless feast,
> Enjoying each the other's good:
> What vaster dream can hit the mood
> Of Love on earth?
>
> (XLVII)

In Memoriam attempts to apprehend a concept of design in the universe – 'That all, as in some piece of art,/Is toil cöoperant to an end' (CXXVIII) – that will accommodate the destruction of a friendship that had itself seemed to be the clearest evidence of a providential design. Dante of course pinned no such significance on his earthly relationship with Beatrice; it seemed natural to him that a woman with her qualities should die young, an attitude termed by Eliot, as we have seen, 'the Catholic philosophy of disillusion' (*Dante*, p. 275), for God

> fella di qua giù a sè venire,
> perchè vedea ch'esta vita noiosa
> non era degna di sì gentil cosa.

(made her come to him from down here, because he saw that this noxious life was not worthy of something so noble.) (*VN* XXXI. 10)

But the intimate reciprocity of Tennyson's friendship with Hallam is presented in the poem as having seemed itself like an assurance of divine supervision:

> Nor could I weary, heart or limb,
> When mighty Love would cleave in twain
> The lading of a single pain,
> And part it, giving half to him.
> (XXV)

Moreover the perfecting of this design seemed to be augured in the imminent marriage, when 'thou shouldst link thy life with one/Of mine own house' and 'boys of thine/Had babbled "Uncle" on my knee' (LXXXIV). Thus all could be envisaged as leading to a harmonious consummation:

> Till slowly worn her earthly robe,
> Her lavish mission richly wrought,
> Leaving great legacies of thought,
> Thy spirit should fail from off the globe;
>
> What time mine own might also flee,
> As linked with thine in love and fate,
> And, hovering o'er the dolorous strait
> To the other shore, involved in thee,
>
> Arrive at last the blessèd goal,
> And He that died in Holy Land
> Would reach us out the shining hand,
> And take us as a single soul.

This parallel destiny is of course overturned in Hallam's death, and Tennyson's sense of the imbalance between heaven and earth is all the keener set against his memories of the earlier harmony; now he envisages Hallam in the 'blissful climes' while he remains 'To wander on a darkened earth' (LXXXV), or has doubts about a Lethean division between life and death which permits 'the happy dead' to forget those left behind (XLIV).

Tennyson's attempts to reconnect the shattered links of his universe result in the celebration of an evolutionary chain of being in the final section of the poem, but the background to this is an acute consciousness of the 'boundless shores' of space and time in which human identity threatens to be overwhelmed (LXX). The recurrence of Christmas and of the anniversary of Hallam's death gives some structure to this vast expanse; similarly the invocation to Hallam in XCIII –

> O, therefore from thy sightless range
> With gods in unconjectured bliss,
> O, from the distance of the abyss
> Of tenfold-complicated change,
>
> Descend, and touch, and enter . . .

– attempts, perhaps, to allay this bewildering sense of vastness with a reference to the ten heavens of the Ptolemaic universe, and, as with his reference to 'the grades' of light, it would doubtless be Dante's picture of that universe which Tennyson had particularly in mind. He remains, however, extremely conscious of the universe of modern science, of the 'rising worlds by yonder wood' (CV), and it is here he has to locate Hallam:

> So many worlds, so much to do,
> So little done, such things to be,
> How know I what had need of thee,
> For thou wert strong as thou wert true?
>
> (LXXIII)

Throughout the poem there is no clear positing of a second dimension, no distinction (or relation) between the superhuman and the extra-terrestrial. Tennyson thinks of Hallam 'In vastness and in mystery' (XCVII), and the two nouns have largely identical values for him. Thus, whereas Beatrice was 'disiata in sommo cielo' ('desired in high heaven') ('Donne ch'avete', *VN* XIX.9), Hallam is, in the verse just quoted, *needed*; the sense is of work to be done and progress to be effected in a Heaven that thereby remains an earth writ large. A kind of cosmic work-ethic is then incorporated into Tennyson's *Paradiso* in which the promise of Hallam's earthly career is salvaged and aggrandised but not essentially changed:

> So here shall silence guard thy fame;
> But somewhere, out of human view,
> Whate'er thy hands are set to do
> Is wrought with tumult of acclaim.
>
> (LXXV)

That affirmation of contact between Tennyson and his departed friend in section CXXX depends then on Hallam having heeded the repeated injunctions to 'Descend, and touch, and enter' rather than Tennyson having undertaken, in Dantesque fashion, a journey upwards into the vast, uncharted regions of the spirit. In *A Farewell to the South* Hallam had asked Dante:

> Who 'mid strife
> Of spiritual tempests bade thee moor
> Fast by Urania's isle thy peaceful bark?
> (ll. 250–2)

In *In Memoriam* Tennyson's Melpomene admits the justice of Urania's rebuking her for having 'loitered in the master's field':

> 'For I am but an earthly Muse,
> And owning but a little art
> To lull with song an aching heart,
> And render human love his dues;
>
> . . .
>
> 'I murmured, as I came along,
> Of comfort clasped in truth revealed;
> And loitered in the master's field,
> And darkened sanctities with song'.
> (XXXVII)

That field had in any case become much more spatially and spiritually problematic in the nineteenth century, and the result is that points of contact between Dante's poetry and *In Memoriam* are far fewer than, one is tempted to say, they should be.[71] Moreover, we should note that *In Memoriam* was begun and continued under the immediate shock of Hallam's death; by the time Dante described his reunion with Beatrice in the *paradiso terrestre* he had done a great deal of thinking on other topics that would need to be synthesised with it.

V

W. B. Yeats and Dante's Mask

Befitting emblems of adversity

('Meditations in Time of Civil War')

Yeats's career, rather like Ezra Pound's, shows a movement away from a certain 'Pre-Raphaelite' idealising towards a verse that incorporates a much wider and much more mixed range of experience. Rossetti's influence is obvious in several of the poems from the 1890s, the clearest instance being arguably 'He bids his Beloved be at Peace';[1] and Rossetti's rather misleading employment of Dante was certainly responsible for the kind of poetic aspirations Yeats and his early associates shared: 'If we spoke of love poetry we preferred the love poetry when one sang at the same moment not the sweetheart but some spiritual principle – "all must be vita nuova".'[2] Whether or not it is always clear what the spiritual principle is, Yeats's early work elevates the beloved to a position of symbolic intangibility that differs markedly from Rossetti's visions of consummation; the beloved may not greatly resemble Beatrice, but she is not open to any charge of 'fleshliness':

> You need but lift a pearl-pale hand,
> And bind up your long hair and sigh;
> And all men's hearts must burn and beat;
> And candle-like foam on the dim sand,
> And stars climbing the dew-dropping sky,
> Live but to light your passing feet.
> ('He gives his Beloved certain Rhymes', p. 158)

One can compare Rossetti's description of Beatrice and her effects from his translation:

> She hath that paleness of the pearl that's fit
> In a fair woman, so much and not more;
> . . .

> Whatever her sweet eyes are turned upon,
> Spirits of love do issue thence in flame,
> Which through their eyes who then may look on them
> Pierce to the heart's deep chamber every one.
>
> (*Works*, p. 324)

This indeed seems to be the source of that favourite Yeatsian epithet 'pearl-pale', a rather loose rendering of Dante's original which is simply 'Color di perle' ('Colour of pearl') ('Donne ch'avete', *VN* XIX.11). Yeats's achievement of what was denied to Rossetti, that is, a development in his verse reflecting the increasing complexity of his experience, is associated in his own mind with the final achievement of Dante: 'such men are able to bring all that happens, as well as all that they desire, into an emotional or intellectual synthesis and so to possess not the Vision of Good only but that of Evil'.[3] It may be that at the end of 'Meditations in Time of Civil War' Yeats could say: 'The half-read wisdom of daemonic images,/Suffice the ageing man as once the growing boy' (p. 427), but Yeats's commitment to these images is achieved in the later work under the pressures of political upheaval and self-questioning that are accepted and analysed in the poetry itself. This kind of synthesis between what the poet desires and what 'happens' does, needless to say, make the commitment all the more impressive.

This chapter will explore, more or less chronologically, Yeats's search for 'not the Vision of Good only but that of Evil', the fruits of which were published in 1925 under the title *A Vision* – a search in which Yeats felt that only Dante amongst modern writers had preceded him. We shall be mainly concerned with Yeats's writings between roughly 1915 and 1930; the second version of *A Vision*, published in 1937, shows that Yeats had reorganised his thoughts considerably with respect to spiritual states after death; but his attempt to systematise the course of history and the types of human personality – which is what primarily concerns us – is complete by 1925, and indeed in the later version deprived of one or two significant parts. One needs, however, to glance at Yeats's earliest writings on Dante to see how certain underlying assumptions, however sophisticated they later become, remain constant in his thinking.

In 1896 he published three articles in the July, August and September numbers of the *Savoy* on 'William Blake and his Illustrations to the *Divine Comedy*'.[4] One of the most striking characteristics about them is the serious ignorance Yeats occasionally shows about Dante, who 'symbolised the highest order of created beings by the fixed stars, and God by the darkness beyond them, the *Primum Mobile* . . . [Blake's God] took always a human shape . . . to imagine Him as an unpeopled immensity was to think of Him under the one symbol furthest from His essence . . .' (p. 133). There is no indication here that the Empyrean (not of course the *Primum Mobile*) is the climax of Dante's description of *light* in the *Paradiso*, the seat of the 'rivera/fulvido di fulgore' ('river of golden brilliance') (XXX.61–2) which is later transformed into the 'candida rosa' ('white rose') of the heavenly court; and there is no reference to Dante's final vision, in this place of 'pura luce' ('pure light'), of 'la nostra effige' ('our image') in the second of the three circles of the Trinity (XXXIII.131). In his essay 'Magic' (1901), Yeats mentions his meeting with a young man who had had a vision of Eden 'not by the wilderness he had learned of at the Sunday-school, but upon the summit of a great mountain' (*EI*, p. 45). Years later he commented: 'I had not at the time read Dante's *Purgatorio*, and it caused me some trouble to verify the mountain garden . . .'[5] The mistakes in the essays on Blake's Dante, written five years before 'Magic', are not then very surprising; no doubt Yeats knew some of the *Commedia*'s more celebrated episodes, but obviously had no clear idea of its overall structure, although he must have known something of the *Purgatorio*, since he refers to it in his second article (p. 135).

It is a tribute to Yeats's extraordinary genius that, although his knowledge of Dante's work remains the most inadequate of any of the poets in this study, his interpretation of Dante is in some ways the most interesting. He could not, for example, read Italian: 'I am no Dante scholar, and I but read him in Shadwell or in Dante Rossetti',[6] and there is no reason to believe he ever managed to read the *Commedia* in its entirety; what he did know, however, was a good deal of the anecdotal material concerning Dante we have already looked at, and he put this to a far better use than any earlier writer had done. His surmises about Dante are essentially part of an attempt to re-define some of the central problems of Romantic poetic theory, and certain traditional ideas about Dante provided 'the right twigs for an eagle's nest' from the height of which Yeats could look out on the world in all his solitary majesty.

In the excerpt from the Blake essays already quoted there is a suggestion of that 'confrontation' between Blake and Dante which is indeed one of the cardinal points of the essays as a whole: as Yeats puts it, Blake 'was very certain that he and Dante represented spiritual states which face one another in an eternal enmity' (p. 128). This enmity is summed up thus: 'Dante, who deified law, selected its antagonist, passion, as the most important of sins, and made the regions where it was punished the largest. Blake, who deified imaginative freedom, held "corporeal reason" for the most accursed of things' (p. 139). It is clear that Yeats's sympathies lie with Blake, in a piece of writing that celebrates the English poet as the founder-father of the *symboliste* aesthetic Yeats is himself preaching; Dante would hardly have accepted 'passion' – given that Yeats is referring to the 'peccator carnali' ('carnal sinners') of the second circle – as the 'most important' of sins, though one remembers that Yeats's heroines of the nineties are generally 'passion-pale'. What is crucial about the essays is the superficiality they display in Yeats's own position when contrasted with his later philosophy: he, like Blake, takes sides against men like Dante who, 'because of [their] absorption in active life, have been persuaded to judge and to punish', for

> Opposed to this was another philosophy, not made by men of action . . . but by Christ when wrapped in the divine essence, and by artists and poets, who are taught by the nature of their craft to sympathise with all living things, and who . . . come at last to forget good and evil in an absorbing vision of the happy and the unhappy. (pp. 128–9)

What Yeats was later to experience was his own absorption in active life, which brought with it a powerful reminder of good and evil and led him to his own vision of judgement. He never became persuaded to 'punish', but Blake's, and indeed Shelley's, insistence on forgiveness of sin came to seem part of the 'superficiality' of modern writing. In *A Vision* Shelley is measured against Dante and found wanting.

The essays also contain an attack on scholarship, which leads us to a central element in Yeats's thought which was *not* revised in future years. Yeats is objecting to what he misinterprets as John Addington Symonds's preference for Doré's illustrations to Dante, and suggests that 'a temperament, strong enough to explore with unfailing alertness the countless schools and influences of the Renaissance in Italy, is of necessity a little lacking in delicacy of judgement and in the finer substances of emotion' (p. 140). In fact in the essay in question Symonds had directly expressed his admiration for Blake's illustrations which showed, in his own words, 'a spiritual sympathy far beyond the reach of any *improvvisatore* like Doré'.[7] What Yeats particularly admires about Blake is precisely this 'spiritual sympathy', which means, in effect, the liberties Blake has taken with Dante's text. Thus he reproves Botticelli's illustration to *Purgatorio* XXIX: '[his] flames . . . give one no emotion, and his car of Beatrice is no symbolic chariot of the Church led by the gryphon, half eagle, half lion, of Christ's dual nature, but is a fragment of some mediaeval pageant pictured with a merely technical inspiration' (p. 144). Blake's version of the scene forsakes Botticelli's dry accuracy for the sake of an exoticism in which several of Dante's details are omitted and in which the eyes on the wings of the four beasts (XXIX.95) are extended, without Dante's warrant, to the chariot's wheels, in accordance with Ezekiel I.18[8] The resulting decorative abundance of eyes and flame-like wings is, Yeats suggests, more to the taste of a modern world moved 'by the symbolism of bird and beast, of tree and mountain, of flame and darkness' (p. 144); thus we might say Dante's allegory becomes symbolism while passing through Blake's hands. What this symbolism actually symbolises depends, of course, on the disposition of the individual reader.

That the *Commedia*, or indeed any work, permits a 'symbolist' reading or illustrating, as opposed to an 'accurate' or scholarly one, is the core of Yeats's approach to Dante both here and afterwards. It is expressed in a vigorous passage in which the articles come to a climax, and which has to be quoted in its entirety; the 'ordinary student' will suggest that

Doré and Stradanus . . . have given us something of the world of Dante, but Blake and Botticelli have builded worlds of their own and called them Dante's – as if Dante's world were more than a mass of symbols of colour and form and sound which put on humanity, when they arouse some mind to an intense and romantic life that is not theirs; as if it was not one's own sorrows and angers and regrets and terrors and hopes that awaken to condemnation or repentance while Dante treads his eternal pilgrimage; as if any poet or painter or musician could be other than an enchanter calling, with a persuasive or compelling ritual, creatures, noble or ignoble, divine or demonic, covered with scales or in shining raiment, that he never imagined, out of the bottomless deeps of imaginations he never foresaw; as if the noblest achievement of art was not when the artist enfolds himself in

> darkness, while he casts over his readers a light as of a wild and terrible dawn. (p. 141)

Shelley would have had no quarrel with this, nor with Yeats's earlier statement that 'Every philosophy has half its truth from times and generations; and to us one-half of the philosophy of Dante is less living than his poetry' (p. 134), but it was to Blake himself Yeats traced the origins of his approach, a Blake to whom 'The historical Christ was indeed no more than the supreme symbol of the artistic imagination . . .' (p. 137). Thus Yeats is able to conclude that in spite of the 'eternal enmity' between Blake and Dante, the former's

> profound sympathy with passionate and lost souls . . . made [him] the one perfectly fit illustrator for the *Inferno* and the *Purgatorio*; in the serene and rapturous emptiness of Dante's Paradise he would find no symbols but a few abstract emblems, and he had no love for the abstract . . . (pp. 144–5)

He appears to have no qualms about dismembering the *Commedia* of a third of its parts to accommodate Blake's perfect fitness.

When the articles were collected into an edition of his *Essays* (1924), Yeats added in a postscript: 'Now, in reading these essays, I am ashamed when I come upon such words as "corporeal reason", "corporeal law", and think how I must have wasted the keenness of my youthful senses' (p. 145). This hardly amounts to a recantation of the essays, but it does remind us that by 1924 Yeats was very far from seeing Dante through Blake's eyes, however faithful he remained to the symbolist creed.

The next important stage in Yeats's thought about Dante is marked by the publication of a small book of essays entitled *Discoveries* in 1907.[9] Here he expresses a dissatisfaction with the 'dim world' of Rossetti's 'Love's Nocturn': 'we go to it for delight indeed but in our weariness. If we are to sojourn there that world must grow consistent with itself, emotion must be related to emotion by a system of ordered images, as in the *Divine Comedy*' (p. 293). We note that Yeats does not require a system of ordered thoughts or beliefs, but strictly of images, remaining true to the Romantic credo of a poetry that achieves its effects without recourse to a paraphrasable philosophy. Yeats had long had the images; what he needs is the system. *Discoveries* as a whole is an appeal for coherence: 'In literature . . . we have lost in personality, in our delight in the whole man – blood, imagination, intellect, running together' (p. 266); there is a need not only for the whole man, but also for a unity between that man and his native environment: 'Unless the discovery of legendary knowledge and the returning belief in miracle . . . can bring once more a new belief in the sanctity of common ploughland . . . we may never see again a Shelley and a Dickens in the one body, but be broken to the end' (p. 296). This already closely anticipates that call for a harmony between the types of personality Yeats will later dub 'antithetical' and 'primary', a harmony itself entitled 'unity of being'; and the idea of a 'unity of culture' between man and race is likewise already present. It only becomes apparent to Yeats later that Dante achieved both: but the conclusion of *Discoveries* not only hints at this but also redresses the ignorance about the conclusion of the *Commedia* Yeats had shown ten years earlier:

I . . . am certain that a man should find his Holy Land where he first crept upon the floor, and that familiar woods and rivers should fade into symbol with so gradual a change that he may never discover, no, not even in ecstasy itself, that he is beyond space, and that time alone keeps him from Primum Mobile Supernal Eden, Yellow [*sic*] Rose over all. (p. 297)

In 1910 he writes:

A cause for the beauty of the popular writing in old times was that the more subtle emotions of the people were organised by religion. They were not left empty . . . Modern popular poetry is isolated . . . It should be the work of a man of the people expressing himself to the full.[10]

Again and again in his writing he tells us he got 'great pleasure . . . from that tale of Dante hearing a common man sing some stanza from the *Divine Comedy*',[11] but he later accepted that a similar 'unity of culture' in his own day was impossible.

Whatever his respect for the 'system' in Dante, comments from the same period show Yeats retaining the Romantic prejudice against didactic poetry:

Goethe . . . has said 'The poet needs all philosophy, but he must keep it out of his work.' One remembers Dante, and wishes that Goethe had left some commentary upon that saying, some definition of philosophy perhaps; but one cannot be less than certain that the poet, although it may be well for him to have right opinions . . . must keep all opinion that he holds to merely because he thinks it right, out of his poetry, if it is to be poetry at all.[12]

Earlier in this essay he had noted: 'The greater portion of the *Divine*

Comedy is a catalogue of the sins of Italy' (p. 190). Five years later he was still talking of Dante's 'abstract ecstasy' and suggesting that Villon 'in the cry of his ruin . . . touches our compassion more' (*EI*, p. 339). This ambiguity towards the *Commedia*, the idea that the system contained a great deal of extraneous and discordant matter, remains fundamental to Yeats's position and, as we shall see, prompts him to develop a theory that shall explain the poem's flaws. Yeats has no sympathy for the political or religious 'opinion' Dante sets out in the poem, and no interest in Dante's hope to 'removere viventes in hac vita de statu miseriae, et perducere ad statum felicitatis' ('remove those living in this life from a state of wretchedness and to lead them to a state of felicity') (*Ep.* X.15). What Yeats sees in the *Commedia* is the drama of Dante's own battle to rid himself of this opinionatedness; to leave what Yeats calls 'rhetoric' behind him.

Yeats himself more or less managed to keep his philosophy – that is, *A Vision* – out of his poetry. There are indeed poems like 'The Phases of the Moon' (pp. 372–7) and 'The Double Vision of Michael Robartes' (pp. 382–4), and in the preface to *Michael Robartes and the Dancer* (1921) he repeats Goethe's comment above, adding that 'in the excitement of arranging and editing' *A Vision* he 'could no more keep out philosophy than could Goethe himself at certain periods of his life'. 'I have tried to make understanding easy by a couple of notes, which are at any rate much shorter than those Dante wrote on certain of his odes in the *Convito*', he adds wryly, the notes in question being excerpts from *A Vision*'s early stages.[13] What Yeats required was an intimate yet essentially separate relationship between poetry and philosophy, so that the latter might provide the former with both coherence and freedom at the same time:

> I wished for a system of thought that would leave my imagination free to create as it chose and yet make all that it created, or could create, part of the one history, and that the soul's. The Greeks certainly had such a system, and Dante . . . and I think no man since. (*A Vision*, p. xi)

The poems which justify *A Vision* are not, in Yeats's eyes, the 'philosophical' poems just mentioned, but his two greatest volumes, poems whose relationship with *A Vision* is rather more indirect –

> The other day Lady Gregory said to me: 'You are a much better educated man than you were ten years ago and much more powerful in argument.' And I put *The Tower* and *The Winding Stair* into evidence to show that my

poetry has gained in self-possession and power. I owe this change to an incredible experience[14]

– this experience being the system Yeats's supernatural instructors had given him. It is the security or 'self-possession' this system provided him with that bears fruit in Yeats's greatest poetry, as much as any immediate utilisation of the system's images. Thus, although the direct influence of Dante on Yeats's poetry is not extensive, his influence is enormously important through the medium of prose theories in which he figured prominently.[15] But whereas he had incorporated scholastic philosophy directly into his verse, Yeats wished his system to remain in a separate book where it would be less likely to encroach upon the freedom of his imagination.

Yet *A Vision* itself is not so much an explanation of truth as a symbolical presentation of it, 'stylistic arrangements of experience' (1937, p. 25). It is precisely 'a system of ordered images', images that remain a mystical rather than rational means to truth within the master-image of the phasic moon, images that take their ordered place beside each other – 'Hunchback and Saint and Fool'. The system *qua* system relates to the *Commedia* in ways we shall look at, but *qua* philosophy it relates to the completely divergent modern symbolism of the female Image touched upon in the last chapter:

All, all those gyres and cubes and midnight things
Are but a new expression of her body
Drunk with the bitter sweetness of her youth.
And now my utmost mystery is out.
A woman's beauty is a storm-tossed banner;
Under it wisdom stands . . .[16]

In the opening chapter of *Romantic Image*, Kermode describes the danger that the contemplation of images – 'That have the frenzy of our western seas'[17] – possessed for 'The Artist in Isolation' (pp. 13–42). As he argues, no one understood this danger better than Yeats, who described in *A Vision*:

Rodin creating his powerful art out of the fragments of those Gates of Hell that he had found himself unable to hold together – images out of a personal dream, 'the hell of Baudelaire not of Dante', he had said to Symons. (p. 211)

The danger to the artist who had no system or organising

intelligence to hold the images together had already been described by Symons himself:

> The supreme artist . . . is the supreme intelligence. Like Dante, he can pass through hell unsinged. With him, imagination is vision; when he looks into the darkness, he sees. The vague dreamer, the insecure artist and the uncertain mystic at once, sees only shadows, not recognising their outlines. He is mastered by the images which come at his call; he has not the power which chains them for his slaves.[18]

This is the Dantean power Yeats was seeking.

We have run on ahead to *A Vision*, but can now return to the poem 'Ego Dominus Tuus' (1915), which marks the beginning of what one might call the classic phase of Yeats's thinking about Dante. The poem's title, taken from *Vita Nuova* III.3, is the only part of *Amore*'s speech Dante understands, an *Amore* who is 'uno segnore di pauroso aspetto' ('a lord of fearful appearance') henceforth to dominate Dante through Beatrice. According to Yeats's poem, the 'segnore' of Dante's vision is an embodiment of his 'anti-self', and represents that supremely chaste love for Beatrice Dante's poetry celebrates, whereas Dante's life, both now and afterwards, is marked by the lechery 'Guido' (Cavalcanti) 'mocks' him for. It is clear that Yeats is referring to Cavalcanti's sonnet 'I' vegno 'l giorno a te 'nfinite volte'; in *Per Amica Silentia Lunae* (1918), which is prefaced by 'Ego Dominus Tuus' and develops the ideas in it, he quotes some lines from the sonnet in Rossetti's translation, Rossetti himself having suggested that the sonnet rebukes Dante's 'want of constancy in love'.[19] One can hardly, however, justify Yeats's taking Guido's complaint of Dante's 'vil vita' ('ignoble life') as warrant for his outspoken charge of lechery; and the sonnet is hardly a mocking one. What Yeats wants is to set up that opposition between man and poet, self and 'anti-self' that will assume a central position in his theory; Dante is thus equated with Keats in 'Ego Dominus Tuus', whose own 'luxuriant song' persuades us of a *persona* in his poetry again opposite to the actual man, who was, Yeats says, 'poor, ailing and ignorant'. Both Dante and Keats wear then a 'mask' in their writing and in Dante's case particularly it is the mask rather than the 'man' that has come down to us through history and gathered fame:[20]

HIC . . .
Dante Alighieri, so utterly found himself
That he has made that hollow face of his

More plain to the mind's eye than any face
But that of Christ.

ILLE — And did he find himself . . .
is that spectral image
The man that Lapo and that Guido knew?
I think he fashioned from his opposite
An image that might have been a stony face
Staring upon a Bedouin's horse-hair roof
From doored and windowed cliff, or half upturned
Among the coarse grass and the camel-dung.
He set his chisel to the hardest stone.
Being mocked by Guido for his lecherous life,
Derided and deriding, driven out
To climb that stair and eat that bitter bread,
He found the unpersuadable justice, he found
The most exalted lady loved by a man.

(*Poems*, pp. 368–9)

Yeats's equation of the mask with carved stone is notable. Two years later he comments in a note to *At the Hawk's Well* that 'one does grow tired of always quarrying the stone for one's statue';[21] the basic idea of a monumental *persona* created in the artwork who differs from 'the bundle of accident and incoherence that sits down to breakfast', as he later put it (*EI*, p. 509), must have been extraordinarily prompted by the huge 'hieratic head' of Ezra Pound that Gaudier-Brzeska was sculpting in 1913. Pound and Dante become closely associated in Yeats's thought, as we shall see. In the above excerpt, there is an obvious comparison between Dante's face and that of the Sphinx or of Shelley's Ozymandias or some other vast personage of the desert. The Romantic search for monumental parallels for Dante had already led critics to the Middle East: Landor had compared him with 'the strange, mysterious, solitary Nile' (*The Pentameron*, p. 258), and for Maria F. Rossetti 'He rises before us and above us like the Pyramids – awful, massive, solitary . . .'[22]

That Yeats was again thinking seriously of Dante in 1915 must be due, in large measure, to Pound himself who was working as Yeats's secretary at Stone Cottage in the winters between 1913 and 1916 and who had long been a devotee of Dante. Pound may have inspired Yeats, but Yeats's ideas about Dante, far from showing any of Pound's influence, are in fact aimed directly against him, reaching back as they do towards Romantic notions of Dante with which to combat Pound's modernity. This will be discussed at the conclusion of this chapter.

Early on in the first part of *Per Amica Silentia Lunae*, entitled 'Anima Hominis', Yeats gives a longer quotation from that part of the *Vita Nuova* noted above where the seignorial anti-self appears to Dante, again from Rossetti's translation, and also discusses other writers whose work exhibits their anti-selves, including Morris and Landor (pp. 328–30); the latter, for example, 'topped us all in calm nobility when the pen was in his hand, as in the daily violence of his passion when he had laid it down'. F. A. C. Wilson has already noted that a similar dichotomy had been suggested in Dante by Landor himself, in the discussion of the Francesca episode in *The Pentameron*:

> In Francesca, with the faculty of divine spirits, [Dante] leaves his own nature . . . and converts all his strength into tenderness. The great poet . . . is double, possessing the further advantage of being able to drop one half at his option, and to resume it. Some of the tenderest on paper have no sympathies beyond; and some of the austerest in their intercourse with their fellow-creatures, have deluged the world with tears. (p. 41)[23]

Yeats probably read *The Pentameron* with Pound at Stone Cottage early in 1916.[24] When Yeats comes to discuss Dante, we have an illuminating amplification of the ideas in 'Ego Dominus Tuus':

> I am always persuaded that he celebrated the most pure lady poet ever sung and the Divine Justice, not merely because death took that lady and Florence banished her singer, but because he had to struggle in his own heart with his unjust anger and his lust; while, unlike those of the great poets who are at peace with the world and at war with themselves, he fought a double war. (pp. 329–30)

Just as Dante's lust prompted his vision of purity, so another vice, anger, prompted his aspiration towards an elevated vision of impartial justice; but his life was one of violent conflict that impeded his attempts to forgo his own bitter feelings in the contemplation of this 'Divine Justice'. The *Commedia* bears the scars of this tremendous battle to establish the anti-self: as Yeats put it a little further on, 'We make out of the quarrel with others, rhetoric, but of the quarrel with ourselves, poetry' (p. 331), and although he does not specify he obviously regards the harangues of the *Commedia* as belonging to its 'rhetorical' rather than 'poetical' part. *Per Amica* now parts company with 'Ego Dominus Tuus' by marking Dante's work off completely from Keats's brand of wishful thinking:

Some thirty years ago I read a prose allegory by Simeon Solomon . . . and remember or seem to remember a sentence, 'a hollow image of fulfilled desire'. All happy art seems to me that hollow image, but when its lineaments express also the poverty or the exasperation that set its maker to the work, we call it tragic art. Keats but gave us his dream of luxury; but while reading Dante we never long escape the conflict, partly because the verses are at moments a mirror of his history, and yet more because that history is so clear and simple that it has the quality of art. (p.329)

What one might call the 'public function' of Dante's poem is then, for Yeats, negligible: for him the poem is an archetypal record of an individual spiritual struggle, of a history 'so clear and simple that it has the quality of art'. Yeats, like many of his nineteenth-century predecessors, is fascinated by the 'solitary' Dante for reasons that will become clearer.

The dichotomy between man and anti-self leads Yeats to make an astonishing final reference to Dante in his essay:

Saint and hero cannot be content to pass at moments to that hollow image and after become their heterogeneous selves, but would always, if they could, resemble the antithetical self. There is a shadow of type on type, for in all great poetical styles there is saint or hero, but when it is all over Dante can return to his chambering and Shakespeare to his 'pottle-pot'. They sought no impossible perfection but when they handled paper or parchment. (p. 333)

The idea that Dante would willingly sin again after his spectacular course of therapy in the next world represents a strikingly unsympathetic reading of the *Commedia*, especially of the ecstasies of the *Paradiso* and Dante's final prayer to Beatrice –

La tua magnificenza in me custodi,
sì che l'anima mia, che fatt' hai sana,
piacente a te dal corpo si disnodi

(Preserve in me your great power, so that my soul, which you have restored to health, may be pleasing to you when it is loosed from my body) (XXXI.88–90)

–but Yeats would claim as evidence of Dante's daily life not only Cavalcanti's sonnet but also Boccaccio's biography which he has already quoted: '"Always", says Boccaccio, "both in youth and maturity he found room among his virtues for lechery"; or as

Matthew Arnold preferred to change the phrase, "his conduct was exceeding irregular"' (p. 330).[25] Whatever one thinks of Boccaccio's reliability as a biographer (see Chapter II, p. 53), it is not Yeats's declaration of Dante's relapse after his vision that is surprising, as much as the effect of casual vulgarity Yeats deliberately gives: 'Dante can return to his chambering'. At all costs he wants to make this Dante, the Dante that sits down to breakfast, as unmonumental as possible. The movement of Dante's life through chambering–Beatrice–chambering already anticipates the revolution of the individual life through the twenty-eight phases of *A Vision*, in which 'Man seeks his opposite or the opposite of his condition, attains his object so far as it is attainable, at Phase 15 and returns to Phase 1 again' (1937, p. 81).

What relation does Yeats's discussion of Dante bear to his own life at this time? We remember that after Dante lost Beatrice he turned to philosophy for consolation, and similarly Yeats was working out the theory of *Per Amica* coincidentally with his failure to win Iseult Gonne's hand in marriage.[26] Looking ahead to *A Vision* we find a description of how the man of 'Phase 17' – Yeats's and Dante's phase[27] – achieves 'unity of being':

> The being, through the intellect, selects some object of desire for a representation of the *Mask* as *Image*, some woman perhaps, and the *Body of Fate* snatches away the object. Then the intellect (*Creative Mind*) . . . must substitute some new image of desire; and in the degree of its power and of its attainment of unity, relate that which is lost, that which has snatched it away, to the new image of desire, that which threatens the new image to the being's unity. (p. 76)

Just as Beatrice was 'snatched away' by death and replaced as Image by the heavenly Beatrice 'or even the Great Yellow Rose of the *Paradiso*' (p. 76), so Yeats began his meditations on the phasic moon, an Image to which the 'lost' Iseult was related by being associated, in Yeats's mind, with the dancer who would represent the supernatural 'Phase 15' of the lunar circuit.[28] The philosophy is Yeats's attempt to come to terms with personal misfortune, to transcend his anger at adverse circumstance, at a cruel 'Body of Fate', as Dante had done before him. In *Per Amica*, Yeats describes his periodic experience of a sudden, unforeseen 'happy mood': 'It may be an hour before the mood passes, but latterly I seem to understand that I enter upon it the moment I cease to hate. I think the common condition of our life is hatred – I know that this is so with me – irritation with public or private events or persons' (p. 365). The mood is, he adds, 'something about me that, though it makes me love, is more like innocence'. Like Dante, Yeats was struggling with his own 'unjust anger' at this period of his life, with the tone of aggression in his work noticeable since the poems of *Responsibilities* (1914), as in 'Paudeen', 'To a Shade', and 'An Appointment'. It is best illustrated with 'The Fisherman', first published in 1916:

> The living men that I hate,
> The dead man that I loved,
> The craven man in his seat,
> The insolent unreproved,
> And no knave brought to book
> Who has won a drunken cheer,
> The witty man and his joke
> Aimed at the commonest ear,
> The clever man who cries
> The catch-cries of the clown,
> The beating down of the wise
> And great Art beaten down.
> (*Poems*, pp. 347–8)

By 1919 he is writing a more unruffled poetry that celebrates the 'unity of being' he is seeking, as in 'A Prayer for my Daughter' –

> Considering that, all hatred driven hence,
> The soul recovers radical innocence
> And learns at last that it is self-delighting,
> Self-appeasing, self-affrighting,
> And that its own sweet will is Heaven's will
> (p. 405)

– and he seems to catch in the last line here a reminiscence of Piccarda's 'E 'n la sua volontade è nostra pace' ('And in his will is our peace') (*Par.* III.85). The disastrous consequences to a man of 'Phase 17' of being unable to overcome hatred are described in *A Vision*:

> [the being] will avoid the subjective conflict, acquiesce, hope that the *Body of Fate* may die away; and then the *Mask* will cling to it and the *Image* lure it. It will feel itself betrayed, and persecuted till, entangled in *primary* conflict, it rages against all that destroys *Mask* and *Image*. It will be subject to nightmare, for its *Creative Mind* (deflected from the *Image* and *Mask* to the *Body of Fate*) gives an isolated mythological or abstract form to all that excites its hatred.
> (p. 77)

Beneath Yeats's forbidding terminology the thought is already quite clear from *Per Amica*. Dante overcame 'entanglement' to attain the mask of impartiality, the 'Divine Justice', whereas Shelley suffered the 'nightmare' of hatred: 'his political enemies are monstrous, meaningless images' (*A Vision*, p. 77). Dante and Shelley are in *A Vision* types of the success and failure of the man of 'Phase 17', whose duty is to attend to the anti-self and not allow himself to be deflected from it as Shelley was. Yeats's father had anticipated these ideas in a letter to his son of 1915: 'The man who hates is furthest from being a solitary and is a man dependent on having about him the people he hates whether in actual presence or in the mind's eye.'[29] Dante is in fact the only example Yeats can quote of a writer achieving the anti-self, or 'unity of being':

> Yet Dante, having attained, as poet, to Unity of Being, as poet saw all things set in order, had an intellect that served the *Mask* alone, and that compelled even those things that opposed it to serve, was content to see both good and evil. (p. 78)

We note that this remains the achievement of Dante the poet, for Dante the man is, as we know, altogether a lesser being. Yeats's own intervals of 'unity of being' were themselves temporary and fitful: one such is recorded in the poem 'Demon and Beast', whose allegory may owe something to the three beasts Dante meets in the opening canto of the *Commedia*:

> For certain minutes at the least
> That crafty demon and that loud beast
> That plague me day and night
> Ran out of my sight;
> Though I had long perned in the gyre,
> Between my hatred and desire,
> I saw my freedom won
> And all laugh in the sun.
> (pp. 399–400)

But what was the philosophy that was providing Yeats with this 'freedom' and what relation does it bear to Dante's writing? It was basically, in *A Vision*, the understanding and acceptance of reality as 'a continual conflict', which Yeats now offered to the world as 'a Vision of Evil' (p. 78). In the absence of such an understanding modern writing had come to seem superficial to Yeats: as opposed to Shelley, Ruskin and Wordsworth who 'dwell upon good only', 'the strength and weight of Shakespeare, of Villon, of Dante, even of Cervantes, come from their preoccupation with evil . . . for [modern writers] human nature has lost its antagonist'.[30] He adds three years later in *The Trembling of the Veil*: 'Had not Dante and Villon understood that their fate wrecked what life could not rebuild, had they lacked their Vision of Evil, had they cherished any species of optimism, they could but have found a false beauty, or some momentary instinctive beauty' (*Autobiographies*, p. 273). Whereas Dante in *A Vision* was 'content to see both good and evil', Shelley 'lacked the Vision of Evil, could not conceive of the world as a continual conflict, so, though great poet he certainly was, he was not of the greatest kind' (p. 78).

'The world as a continual conflict'. In *A Vision* this conflict is represented as the opposition of forces termed 'Will', 'Mask', 'Creative Mind', and 'Body of Fate'; sublunary human existence is governed by a recurring and regularly determined series of antagonisms between them so that, to take Shelley's case, the Mask's rightful domination over him was usurped, as we saw, by the Body of Fate. Because of this conflict any such optimism as Keats's 'dream of luxury', the resolution of Shelley's *Prometheus Unbound*, or the 'Garden City mind's [denial that] man lives under a curse' ('If I were Four-and-Twenty', p. 276), is woefully inadequate: it is as reasonable to promulgate such beliefs in a world of cyclical instability as it would be in a world governed by the Wheel of Fortune, a mediaeval conception that rather resembles Yeats's. To understand that conflicting forces exist (under whatever symbolism one chooses to regard them), and will be striving to thwart each other's function is to possess the vision of evil; to accept the conditions this involves and to be able to integrate this knowledge into one's life or one's work is to possess 'unity of being', to witness spiritual truth and thus become 'Daimonic'. And Dante exhibits this eminently:

> He who attains Unity of Being is some man, who, while struggling with his fate and his destiny until every energy of his being has been roused, is content that he should so struggle with no final conquest. For him fate and freedom are not to be distinguished; he is no longer bitter, he may even love tragedy like those 'who love the gods and withstand them'; such men are able to bring all that happens, as well as all that they desire, into an emotional or intellectual synthesis and so to possess not the Vision of Good only but that of Evil . . . In the *Convito* Dante speaks of his exile, and

the gregariousness it thrust upon him, as a great misfortune for such as he; and yet as poet he must have accepted, not only that exile, but his grief for the death of Beatrice as that which made him *Daimonic*, not a writer of poetry alone like Guido Cavalcanti. (*A Vision*, pp. 28–9)

Dante's synthesis is of course the *Commedia*, where, to return to another observation from *A Vision*, he 'saw all things set in order'; yet Yeats's continual talk of Dante's 'Vision of Evil', and even of his 'preoccupation' with it, seems strange if we compare Dante's inert, impotent Devil with the effulgence of his Divinity. Like many modern writers, Yeats himself, wanting to hold good and evil in a more antithetical balance, is dissatisfied with Dante's representation of the latter: he notes that in 'early Byzantium' – his ideal of 'unity of culture' – 'Satan [was] the still half divine Serpent, never the horned scarecrow of the didactic Middle Ages' (p. 191). But this inadequacy is not very important, because Yeats is not finally identifying good and evil in the *Commedia* along Christian lines: rather, in postulating Dante's attempt to conceive of the 'unpersuadable' justice of God – the poet's concentration on the Image of the Great Yellow Rose – Yeats identifies evil with all that remains in the poem that might have threatened this concentration, all the private bitterness or 'rhetoric' of Dante the man, the mere politician, his vehemence towards Florence, Boniface VIII or the kings of France. Yeats's theories are the most sophisticated attempt to interpret the *Commedia* in the light of the 'Romantic Image', an Image that must remain the poet's primary pursuit.

But this Image, or Images – the Rose and Beatrice – must be set within a system or synthesis that incorporates evil, otherwise we have mere Shelleyan optimism; after Dante lost his first Image, the earthly Beatrice, and substituted the heavenly one for her, he still had to 'relate . . . that which threatens the new image to the being's unity' (*A Vision*, p. 76); that is, though the sheer order and completeness of the *Commedia* as synthesis soar high above the prejudice and didacticism that remain embedded within it and Dante transcends his everyday self, the synthesis, by definition, must portray the conflict it had to overcome to establish its Images for it to be great art (an 'emotional' synthesis) or great philosophy (an 'intellectual' one). After discussing Beatrice's death and Dante's banishment in *Autobiographies*, Yeats notes: 'In great lesser writers like Landor and like Keats we are shown [the] Image and [the] Mask as something set apart; Andromeda and her Perseus – though not the sea-dragon – but in a few in whom we recognise supreme masters of tragedy, the whole contest is brought into the circle of their beauty' (p. 273). We shall have more to say on why Yeats insists on regarding the *Commedia* as a tragedy. What he does with Dante's poem is to turn it into the ideal Romantic quest, a successful and arduous achievement of that perfect Image which the poet in Shelley's *Alastor* fails to attain; the intimate relation between heaven and earth Dante insists on, the fact that the former is no escape from the latter but the consummation of what the latter, if properly governed, should harmonise with, is sundered by Yeats, as it has been by many moderns, into a poetry of the Image and a non-poetry of outmoded philosophy and politics. Thus, whereas Yeats could find a place in his analysis for, say, St Peter's attack on the corrupt papacy in *Paradiso* XXVII, it is a place that assigns this only a negative value as poetry in throwing the felicitous description of the paradisal Rose into greater relief; but one can only speak for oneself in stating that Dante's passion for earth seems indissoluble from his passion for heaven, and that the *Commedia* would be a lesser object if this were not so. St Peter tells Dante:

e tu, figliuol, che per lo mortal pondo
ancor giù tornerai, apri la bocca,
e non asconder quel ch'io non ascondo.

(and you, my son, who because of your mortal load will go back down [to earth], open your mouth and do not hide what I am not hiding.)
(ll. 64–6)

One would not, perhaps, wish to applaud all Dante's philippics in the *Commedia*, but it seems absurd to write off his political passion as 'rhetoric' when it results in the vigorous and moving drama of a speech like St Peter's; it deprives the poem of half its force to see Dante's concern for the destiny of his fellow-men exchanged for the search for his anti-self, and his examination of the bases of mediaeval society modernised into the Romantic quest, a quest determined by modern assumptions of what is, and what is not, poetry. Of course, Yeats had a deep personal cause for his hatred of 'rhetoric':

Have I not seen the loveliest woman born
Out of the mouth of Plenty's horn,
Because of her opinionated mind

Barter that horn and every good
By quiet natures understood
For an old bellows full of angry wind?
('A Prayer for my Daughter', p. 405)

We can, however, understand Yeats's position more fully by further examination of *A Vision*. He wished for a system that Dante had had 'and I think no man since' (p. xi). His vision is, however, not very similar to Dante's, and we have to rely on his own rather generalising statements to see why he regarded Dante as his forerunner. What impressed Yeats about the *Commedia* was its formal design, its systematisation of images, and there is no reason to believe he ever knew a great deal about its content. The conception of a universe with everything in its place, the achievement of synthesis *per se*, inspired Yeats in his allocation of men to the twenty-eight phases of the lunar cycle in imitation of the pigeon-holing of souls in the *Commedia*. Dante's of course is a moral scheme whereas Yeats's is not; the lunar periods have helped him 'to hold in a single thought reality and justice' (1937, p. 25), but of course his deterministic philosophy 'does justice' to men by abolishing any justification for reward or punishment: men behave as they do because of the phase at which they are situated, and all human beings go round the twenty-eight phases of the cycle in successive reincarnations. In the *Commedia* Yeats saw Dante as attempting to overcome his own idea of justice and as aspiring to an impartial vision of the Divine Justice in which men and friends of his own circle – Yeats might have pointed to Brunetto Latini – are found in Hell. But it was above all in the imposition of regularity on a world of disordered conflict that Yeats felt he was following the Dante who 'saw all things set in order'. Like Dante he felt he had experienced the conflict; and like him he would overcome futile retaliation and concentrate on his synthesis.

But in order to cement his relationship with Dante, Yeats further claims that the idea of 'unity of being' – and indeed the phrase itself – originates with Dante: '. . . I thought that in man and race alike there is something called 'Unity of Being', using that term as Dante used it when he compared beauty in the *Convito* to a perfectly proportioned human body' (*Autobiographies*, p. 190). It is difficult to over-estimate the importance the term came to have for Yeats. 'Much of what follows', he wrote near the beginning of *A Vision*, 'will be a definition or description of this deeper being, which may become the unity described by Dante in the *Convito*' (p. 18). Critics have searched Dante's treatise in vain for the original of Yeats's phrase; Vance and Melchiori have both given it up, and Harper and Hood admit they 'cannot identify its precise source'.[31] I can confirm the elusiveness of its precise source, but it seems clear the following passage of the *Convivio* had a powerful influence on Yeats's ideas:

> l'anima umana . . . più riceve de la natura divina che alcun'altra. E però che naturalissimo è in Dio volere essere . . . l'anima umana essere vuole naturalmente con tutto desiderio; e però che 'l suo essere dipende da Dio e per quello si conserva, naturalmente disia e vuole essere a Dio unita per lo suo essere fortificare. E però che ne le bontadi de la natura si mostra la divina, vèn[e] che naturalmente l'anima umana con quelle per via spirituale si unisce, tanto più tosto e più forte quanto quelle più appaiono perfette . . . E questo unire è quello che noi dicemo amore . . .
>
> (the human soul . . . receives more of the divine nature than any other. And because the will to exist is entirely apposite to the nature of God . . . the human soul naturally wishes to exist too with all its might; and because its existence depends upon God and is preserved by Him, it naturally desires and wishes to be united with God to strengthen its being. And, because in the excellent things of nature the divine nature is seen, it follows that the human soul naturally unites itself with these in a spiritual manner, more quickly and more strongly as these appear the more perfect . . . And this uniting is what we call love . . .) (III.ii.6–9)

In Dante, the soul attempts to 'unite' itself to God to strengthen its being by way of a spiritual union with 'le bontadi de la natura' – as for example Beatrice – through which God is revealed; in Yeats the man attempts to reach the anti-self or Mask in order to 'unify' his being again through an intermediary, the Image, which reveals the Mask: 'The being . . . selects some object of desire for a representation of the *Mask* as *Image*, some woman perhaps' (*A Vision*, p. 76). And this leads to Yeats's definition of 'amore' coinciding with Dante's: 'By *love* is meant love of that particular unity towards which the nature is tending, or of those images and ideas which define it' (*A Vision*, p. 60). As for Dante's linking the term with 'a perfectly proportioned human body', it seems that Yeats is simply conflating the above passage with Dante's observation in *Convivio* I.v.13 that 'pare l'uomo essere bello, quando le sue membra debitamente si rispondono' ('a man seems beautiful when his limbs are in a due proportion to each other'). There is no need to think, however, that Dante would have said with

Owen Aherne 'All dreams of the soul/End in a beautiful man's or woman's body' ('The Phases of the Moon', p. 374).[32]

The phrase 'unity of being' first occurs in Yeats's writings in two essays of 1919, 'A People's Theatre: A Letter to Lady Gregory', and 'If I were Four-and-Twenty' (*Explorations*, pp. 244–59, 263–80). The latter is a plea for a national unity that echoes the theme of *Discoveries* twelve years earlier: the nation would be cultivated 'If we could but unite our economics and our nationalism with our religion' (p. 278); ' . . . I would begin another epoch by recommending to the Nation a new doctrine, that of unity of being' (p. 280). He was to be disappointed in this hope, as we shall see, but the other essay is of more concern to us as exploring the unity in individual terms. In it Yeats complains that the actors and writers who have had the most success at the Abbey Theatre have based their art on 'objectivity', imitation of the world around them: 'it is this objectivity, this making of all from sympathy, from observation, never from passion, from lonely dreaming, that has made our players, at their best, great comedians, for comedy is passionless' (p. 249). He adds: 'Yet we did not set out to create this sort of theatre, and its success has been to me a discouragement and a defeat.' It is at this point that Dante enters the argument as Yeats's opposing ideal:

> His study was unity of being, the subordination of all parts to the whole as in a perfectly proportioned human body – his own definition of beauty – and not, as with those I have described, the unity of things in the world; and like all subjectives he shrank, because of what he was, because of what others were, from contact with many men. (p. 250)

The source for this last observation is again the *Convivio*:

> in describing his poverty and his exile [Dante] counts as his chief misfortune that he has had to show himself to all Italy and so publish his human frailties that men who honoured him unknown honour him no more. Lacking means, he had lacked seclusion, and he explains that men such as he should have but few and intimate friends. (p. 250)

Dante does indeed say 'l'uomo buono dee la sua presenza dare a pochi e la familiaritade dare a meno, acciò che 'l nome suo sia ricevuto, ma non spregiato' ('the worthy man must give his presence to few and his familiarity to even fewer, so that his name may be given acceptance and not scorned') (I.iv.11), but the peculiar conditions forced on Dante by his exile do not at all justify Yeats's labelling Dante as 'subjective', especially since what Yeats means by the phrase is the poet of 'lonely dreaming':

Had [Dante] written plays he would have written from his own thought and passion, observing little and using little, if at all, the conversation of his time – and whether he wrote in verse or in prose his style would have been distant, musical, metaphorical, moulded by antiquity. (p. 250)

In *A Vision*, the analysis of Dante as the archetype of 'Phase 17' has become more sophisticated:

men of this phase are almost always partisans, propagandists and gregarious; yet because of the Mask of simplification, which holds up before them the solitary life of hunters and of fishers and 'the groves pale passion loves', they hate parties, crowds, propaganda. Shelley out of phase writes pamphlets, and dreams of converting the world, or of turning man of affairs and upsetting governments, and yet returns again and again to these two images of solitude, a young man whose hair has grown white from the burden of his thoughts, an old man in some shell-strewn cave whom it is possible to call, when speaking to the sultan, 'as inaccessible as God or thou'. (p. 77)

What Yeats commits himself to finding in Dante's career is then an inability to stay out of public life coupled with the Romantic's fundamental predilection for solitude and its images; a good character assessment of Yeats himself but one that raises difficulties in Dante's case. The preservation of the man/anti-self dichotomy raises no problem on the 'man' side: Yeats snatches at Boccaccio's story that Dante was such a partisan he would even throw stones at women and little children if they denounced the Ghibellines (*A Vision*, p. 78; *Trattatello*, p. 479); but his association of the antithetical Dante with 'the groves pale passion loves', or with the subjective dramatist, 'observing little and using little, if at all, the conversation of his time', involves him in a hopeless neglect of the *Commedia*'s fundamental achievements: its rich observation of human society, of human speech; its celebration of individual friendship, Christian fellowship and social intercourse. This is what we have to set against the idea of the 'solitary' Dante.

It is obvious that Yeats is dependent for his theories not on a familiarity with the *Commedia* but on a patchwork knowledge of Boccaccio's 'Life', the Dante portraits, and the critical tradition these established which we examined in Chapter II. That 'hollow face' of 'Ego Dominus Tuus' is probably a recollection of the

Torrigiani mask, though it could be any of the other portraits already mentioned, which conspired, even as late as 1915, to make Dante's face 'More plain to the mind's eye than any face/But that of Christ'.[33] We have seen how much the face was celebrated in the writing of Macaulay and Carlyle; we also saw Yeats quoting from Matthew Arnold's essay in *Per Amica*, which also insists on Dante as 'a born solitary' ('Dante and Beatrice', pp. 665–6). That 'hollow face' becomes for Yeats an archetypal image of solitude, indeed an Image of his own Mask, to be added to those other 'beautiful lofty things' that commanded his imagination, the Fisherman, Maud Gonne, All the Olympians.

Given that Yeats saw the *Commedia* as exhibiting primarily the quest for solitude, the poem then falls into his own definition of tragedy rather than comedy:

> I have discovered an antagonism between all the old art and our new art of comedy and understand why I hated at nineteen years Thackeray's novels and the new French painting. A big picture of *cocottes* sitting at little tables outside a café, by some follower of Manet, was exhibited at the Royal Hibernian Academy while I was a student at a life class there, and I was miserable for days. I found no desirable place, no man I could have wished to be, no woman I could have loved, no Golden Age, no lure for secret hope, no adventure with myself for theme out of that endless tale I told myself all day long . . . in mainly tragic art one distinguishes devices to exclude or lessen character, to diminish the power of that daily mood . . .
> ('The Tragic Theatre', *EI*, pp. 241–3)

Dante's poem is pressed into service as an antagonist of the modern art of 'observation'; this idea will be emphasised in *A Vision*. Tragic art also attempts to 'lessen character' in order to make the spectator's identification with its simplified heroes easier; the 'True Mask' of 'Phase 17' is labelled 'Simplification through intensity'. In addressing Lady Gregory as an exponent of comedy, Yeats notes 'you have constant humour . . . much observation and a speech founded upon real life' (*Explorations*, p. 253), without realising that these characteristics can be applied to Dante's poem more reasonably than his definition of tragedy can; as Dante says of the *Commedia*: 'Ad modum loquendi, remissus est modus et humilis, quia locutio vulgaris, in qua et mulierculae communicant' ('As for the mode of writing, the style is informal and basic, namely the common tongue that even young girls talk in') (*Ep.* x.10).

Yeats was attempting to construct a solitary 'Mask' in his own work of a similar monumentality to Dante's to offset his 'gregariousness', his involvement with the running of the Abbey Theatre and afterwards his participating, like Dante, in the governing of the state. *A Vision* and *The Tower* are the main attempts – the philosophical fruit of his solitary meditations and a hard-won, and still threatened, Image for them. Thus the fake portrait of 'Giraldus' attached to the first version of *A Vision* and even more the famous etching by Augustus John forming the frontispiece to the second version could easily establish the type of Yeats's physiognomy – the high cheek-bones, arched eyebrows and slanting eyes (Plate 8). In *Per Amica* he wrote:

> Some years ago I began to believe that our culture, with its doctrine of sincerity and self-realisation, made us gentle and passive, and that the Middle Ages and the Renaissance were right to found theirs upon the imitation of Christ or of some classic hero. Saint Francis and Caesar Borgia made themselves overmastering, creative persons by turning from the mirror to meditation upon a mask. (pp. 333–4)

In view of the fact that Yeats was emulating Dante's system and was striving for that state of 'unity of being' which he held that Dante had both achieved and defined, there can be little doubt of his mask's identity, nor of his regarding his life, from 1915 onwards, as an *imitatio Dantis*. When he moved into that 'tumultuous spot', the Tower of Ballylee, in 1919 –

> that after me
> My bodily heirs may find,
> To exalt a lonely mind,
> Befitting emblems of adversity
> ('Meditations in Time of Civil War', p. 420)

– Cacciaguida's lines to Dante, already quoted in 'Ego Dominus Tuus', received an added significance for him –

> Tu proverai sì come sa di sale
> lo pane altrui, e come è duro calle
> lo scendere e 'l salir per l'altrui scale

(You will indeed find how salty other people's bread tastes, and how hard the walk is up and down someone else's stairs)

(*Par.* XVII.58–60)

– even if it was his own tower whose stairs he was toiling up. Whatever one's doubts about Yeats's interpretation of Dante, he does at least rigorously controvert one nineteenth-century tradition. Whereas critics had looked on the 'portraits' and been happy to say, with Carlyle, 'This is Dante', for Yeats the face was precisely a mask. The Dante who chambered and argued his way around Italy may have looked quite different from the Dante whose features have come down to posterity.

In *A Vision* Yeats gives an account of European history from 2000 BC to the time when he was writing, 'circa 1927', and also interprets it according to the cycle of the lunar phases. Each 'era' of two thousand years is a revolution of twenty-eight phases, but within this both periods of a thousand years are also individual revolutions, running from 'primary' society through 'antithetical' and back again to 'primary' (pp. 180–215). 'Primary' society is one in which individualism is scarce; most men follow a common code of behaviour, imposed by some kind of authoritarianism; in 'antithetical' society there are great individuals, or independent elitist groups, as at the courts of the Renaissance. The historical cycle complicates the cycle of personality, so that Dante, a man of 'Phase 17', lived during the historical 'Phase 8'. The crucial periods in any cycle are at phases 8 and 22, when 'primary' dominance passes over into 'antithetical', and vice versa. As these two phases are opposite each other on the Great Wheel, they derive their Masks from one another, and they are allotted dates which immediately strike the eye:

> The period from 1875 to 1927 (Phase 22) – in some countries and in some forms of thought it is from 1815 to 1927 – is like that from 1250 to 1300 (Phase 8) a period of abstraction, and like it also in that it is preceded and followed by abstraction. (p. 209)

There is an exact and diametrical opposition between Yeats's age and Dante's then. The rising tide of contemporary art made 'all from sympathy, from observation, never from passion, from lonely dreaming' is a result of the historical cycle having re-entered the 'primary' phases, beginning at 'Phase 23':

> I find at this 23rd phase which is it is said the first where there is hatred of the abstract, where the intellect turns upon itself, Mr Ezra Pound, Mr Eliot, Mr Joyce, Signor Pirandello, who either eliminate from metaphor the poet's phantasy and substitute a strangeness discovered by historical or contemporary research or who break up the logical processes of thought

by flooding them with associated ideas or words that seem to drift into the mind by chance . . . (p. 211)

The situation had its origins in 'Phase 22':

even before general surrender of the will, there came synthesis for its own sake, organisation where there is no masterful director, books where the author has disappeared, painting where some accomplished brush paints with an equal pleasure, or with a bored impartiality, the human form or an old bottle, dirty weather and clean sunshine. (p. 210)

The crucial difference between phases 8 and 22 is this, that whereas the latter is moving on from its abstraction into a complete 'primary' surrender of individuality – 'a new naturalism that leaves man helpless before the contents of his own mind', as Yeats elsewhere puts it (*EI*, p. 405) – the former was moving from its abstraction into the individualistic, 'antithetical' phases, the transition being exhibited, of course, in Dante:

I prefer, however, to find my example of the first victory of personality where I have more knowledge. Dante in the *Convito* mourns for solitude, lost through poverty, and writes the first sentence of modern autobiography, and in the *Divine Comedy* imposes his own personality upon a system and a phantasmagoria hitherto impersonal; the King everywhere has found his kingdom. (p. 199)

In other words, here there is both 'organisation' *and* 'a masterful director', or a perfect but necessarily fleeting union between the great system and the great individual. Although Yeats is mainly concerned with the individual in Dante's writing, he plainly sees that much of the 'system' was inherited from mediaeval thought and is indispensable to Dante's success. It was precisely the lack of a common system or 'unity of culture' that prevented the other personalities of 'Phase 17' achieving 'unity of being': in Shelley's case 'the age in which [he] lived was in itself so broken that true Unity of Being was almost impossible', while Landor 'had perhaps as much Unity of Being as his age permitted' (pp. 78–9). We saw Yeats in the essay 'If I were Four-and-Twenty' 'recommending to the Nation a new doctrine, that of unity of being', but only three years later he is lamenting in *Autobiographies* that 'Unity of Culture in class or people that is no longer possible at all' (p. 355); on the other hand 'Had not Europe shared one mind and heart, until both mind and heart began to break into fragments a little before Shakespeare's birth?' (p. 191).

Yeats nowhere states that the achievement of 'unity of being' is totally impossible in his own day, even though the difference of historical phase has made it so much harder. Rather the difficulty of achieving it is yet another problem the mind must be schooled to accept, another manifestation of the evil associated with the inexorable circuit of the lunar wheel that the mind must become 'content' to see. The difficulty is then a necessary stage on Yeats's own road to unity and even adds a certain heroic glamour to the undertaking missing in Dante's case. Dante's unity was prepared for him by the unity of society and resulted in something the common man could sing in the street; Yeats had to retire into his own world of images and the cost of his unity is the difficult arcana of *A Vision*.

Yeats's engineering of the opposition between Dante and Pound *et al.* is an attempt to systematise the breach he feels between himself and his contemporaries, to dramatise his isolation in an age he felt unsympathetic towards through his own identification with Dante. For Pound is not only opposed to Dante in *A Vision* – and we remember thirty years earlier Yeats had noted that Blake 'was very certain that he and Dante represented spiritual states which face one another in an eternal enmity' (above, p. 143) – he is also Yeats's own particular antagonist, 'whose art is the opposite of mine, whose criticism commends what I most condemn, a man with whom I should quarrel more than with anyone else if we were not united by affection' (*A Vision*, 1937, p. 3). In the second version of *A Vision* Yeats omits the discussion of Pound and the others at 'Phase 23' given above; but his silence can only be diplomatic since the determinism of the cycle commits him to his original assessment. In any case he makes up for this silence by prefixing to the second version his suggestively entitled *A Packet for Ezra Pound*, from which the last comment has been taken. In the original *Packet* (Dundrum: Cuala, 1929), Pound the poet is again divorced from the man and set up as a type: 'this hard, shining, fastidious modern man, who has no existence, who can never have existence, except to the readers of his poetry . . . having, unlike his character, universability, detachability . . . everywhere his masterful curiosity' (pp. 8–9). The words Yeats applies to Dante and Villon in *Autobiographies* could also be applied to Pound:

We gaze at such men in awe, because we gaze not at a work of art, but at the re-creation of the man through that art, the birth of a new species of man, and it may even seem that the hairs of our head stand up, because that birth, that re-creation, is from terror. (p. 273)

Such men appear then in Yeats's system at cardinal points of history, like great tablets recording the moon's travels. But although the monumentalised Pound and Dante face each other across the lunar-circuit – clutching, one imagines, copies of the *Cantos* and *Commedia* respectively – and although Yeats's sympathies are undoubtedly with the art of the latter, *A Vision* cannot be called a polemic against 'modernism'; it is rather a work of measured and unruffled explication, a demonstration indeed of the author's possession of 'unity of being'; it is also far too obscure to be controversial. Yeats is here announcing his defensive strength, the futility, as it were, of attacks upon him. His implacability is theorised into an impregnable, solitary grandeur.

If Pound ever read *A Vision*, he would have found that the Dante he himself strove to emulate was now at the furthest possible remove from him, an audacious feat of impudence considering that his own knowledge of Dante's work was far greater than Yeats's. Pound had himself anticipated Yeats's appropriation of Dante by trying to establish Dante as the first 'Imagist' poet, a point we shall examine in the next chapter. The Romantic origins of Yeats's thought, his insistence on Dante as the great solitary and on his dramatically unprecedented 'advent' – 'the birth of a new species of man' – deliberately aim to contradict Pound's emphasis, from *The Spirit of Romance* (1910) onwards, on the evolution of Dante's work from the poetry of the troubadours and of the *dolce stil nuovo* poets, especially Cavalcanti, a position that owes something to Rossetti's influence. In *A Packet* Yeats tells us that he and Pound 'discuss Guido Cavalcanti and only quarrel a little' (*A Vision*, 1937, p. 16), but this is surely ironic: Pound's admiration for Guido can hardly be reconciled with Yeats's neglect of him, especially since both writers' views are part of a complex personal historiography. In the earlier *Vision*, Yeats had christened Dante '*Daimonic*, not a writer of poetry alone like Guido Cavalcanti', and this seems to be aimed at Pound (p. 29).

'E 'n la sua volontade è nostra pace.' An echo of this line, 'Thy Will is our freedom', is used in *A Vision* as a motto for 'primary' man, he who, between phases 26 and 4, strives for unity with God or with Nature rather than for the unity of being sought between phases 12 and 18 (pp. 44, 29); the one is obliteration of self, the other aggrandisement of self. But Yeats's re-writing of the *Commedia* in terms of the Romantic theory of the Image means that the self in Dante's poem is very much to the fore – as it was for Shelley and his contemporaries – and the Christian community that that self is absorbed into completely neglected. Yeats's whole approach to the *Commedia* is an attempt to claim this most dogmatic of poems for an anti-didactic formulation of the artwork Shelley would himself have seconded: 'Only that which does not teach, which does not cry out, which does not persuade, which does not condescend, which does not explain, is irresistible' (*EI*, p. 341). The *Commedia* is therefore allegorised into man's successful struggle for the Mask. It is, needless to say, thereby 'de-Christianised': it was this world Dante was bent on coming to terms with even if his synthesis was projected into the next one. This approach to Dante is reminiscent of the mediaeval practice of allegorising classical literature: Yeats had his own beliefs about the afterlife which would rule out a literal acceptance of Dante's journey. There is no need to go into these here, other than to say that they project a cycle of reincarnation which is in part a reaction against Catholicism as the *Commedia* exhibits it:

> Night will fall upon man's wisdom now that man has been taught that he is nothing . . . [he must] blot out the knowledge or half-knowledge that he has lived many times, and think that all eternity depends upon a moment's decision. (*A Vision*, p. 186)

Yeats's historical analysis is here dealing with the beginnings of Christianity and I suggest that he is reproving the damnation of Paolo and Francesca, traced back to 'solo un punto' ('just one moment') in their reading (*Inf.* v.132), or that of Guido da Montefeltro for his decision to advise the Pope (*Inf.* xxvii.106–11).

The Dante Yeats created answered a psychological need in him; the process is illuminated by his discussion of Shakespeare's creation of Richard II:

> One day, as he sat over Holinshed's *History of England*, he persuaded himself that Richard II . . . would be a good image for an accustomed mood of fanciful, impracticable lyricism in his own mind. The historical Richard has passed away for ever and the Richard of the play lives more intensely, it seems, than did ever living man. Yet Richard II, as Shakespeare made him, could never have been born before the Renaissance, before the Italian influence, or even one hour before the innumerable streams that flowed in

on Shakespeare's mind, the innumerable experiences we can never know, brought Shakespeare to the making of him. He is typical not because he ever existed, but because he has made us know of something in our own minds we had never known of had he never been imagined.

He adds in the same essay: 'There is scarcely a man who has led the Irish people, at any time, who may not give some day to a great writer precisely that symbol he may require for the expression of himself.'[34]

'Precisely that symbol he may require for the expression of himself'. The final justification of Yeats's symbolist reading of the *Commedia* lies in the superb self-expression of the poetry he wrote in the second half of his career. One can forgive Yeats both his Dante, and the hieroglyphics of *A Vision*, for this.

VI

Pound, Dante and Cavalcanti

Lappo I leave behind and Dante too,
Lo, I would sail the seas with thee alone!
('Guido Invites You Thus')

With Ezra Pound and T. S. Eliot we move into a more serious and consistent examination of Dante's work than that encountered in any of the writers discussed so far; indeed, the sense that a 'new era', rather than simply a new chapter, has arrived in the history of Dante's *fortuna* amongst English writers is closely associated with the 'modernist' values the two Americans brought into English verse. They publicised Dante to a degree that has no precedent among English poets, each producing a lengthy essay – Pound's chapter in *The Spirit of Romance* (1910), and Eliot's *Dante* (1929) – and each claiming him as the major influence on his own poetry. These claims are, however, of a very dissimilar nature: although Mario Praz long ago set out the common element in their appreciation of Dante ('T. S. Eliot and Dante', pp. 349–56), it now seems, viewing Pound's and Eliot's careers as a whole, that the divergence in their approaches to Dante is not only of fundamental importance but was actually increased by their consciousness of each other's claims upon him.

We may begin the examination of Pound with *The Spirit of Romance*, a book notable for its author's belief in the extreme importance of the *De Vulgari Eloquentia*, a belief Pound seems to have arrived at completely on his own and that no other poet–critic before or since has shared with him.[1] In *Spirit*, Dante's treatise is used as an introductory *Who's Who* to Dante's predecessors in the chapters leading up to the discussion of Dante himself, a neat way of establishing what one might see as the book's main thesis; that is, that Dante's own poetry evolves entirely out of the Provence–Northern Italy heritage. This is summed up at the end of Chapter v, before Pound goes on to deal with 'Il Maestro' himself in Chapter VI:

Seeking, in the works of the centuries immediately preceding him, those elements which Dante's magnanimity has welded into the *Commedia*, we find much of his philosophy or theology in the church fathers. Richard of St Victor had written a prose which becomes poetry, not because of its floridity, but because of its intensity.

The technique of accented poetry had been brought to perfection by Daniel, Guinicelli, and Cavalcanti.

In Rustico di Filippo we find proof that the bitter acid of Italian speech was not first distilled by the Florentine.

Lorris, Clopinel, and Brunetto Latini had already attempted long poems which were not romances or narratives of deed. St Francis had poured forth his religious fervour in the tongue of the people. The means are prepared.

Advenit Magister.[2]

It is not, however, possible to explain the *Commedia*'s 'advent' with reference solely to the mediaeval elements listed above and with particular reference to those mediaeval poets Dante reviews in the *De Vulgari*. One name at least is conspicuously absent from Pound's list: for the purposes of comparison we can set beside the above a comment from Auerbach:

In the first canto . . . Dante says to Virgil: 'Thou alone art he to whom I owe the beautiful style which has done me honor.' This is doubtless correct – and even more in respect to the *Comedy* than to his earlier works and *canzoni*. The motif of a journey to the underworld, a large number of individual motifs, many stylistic turns – for all these he is indebted to Virgil. Even the change in his theory of style from the time of his treatise *De Vulgari Eloquentia* – a change which took him from the merely lyrico-philosophical to the great epic and hence to full-dimensional representation of human events – cannot be accounted for by anything but the influence of classical models and in particular of Virgil. Of the writers we know, he was the first to have direct access to the poet Virgil. Virgil, much more than mediaeval theory, developed his feeling of style and his conception of the sublime. Through him he learned to break the all too narrow pattern of the Provençal and contemporary Italian *suprema constructio*. (*Mimesis*, p. 198)

Pound's complete silence about Virgil in *Spirit* is not simply an instance of that antipathy he showed to the Latin poet throughout his career, as we shall see.[3] That great change in Dante's interests and purposes between his work on the *De Vulgari* and the writing of the *Commedia* which Auerbach refers to is passed over in silence by Pound, who tends to allude to the two works in the same breath, in accordance with his thesis that the *Commedia* is the product and consummation of the 'spirit of romance'.[4] Of course one should not deny the importance of, for example, Arnaut Daniel – the 'miglior fabbro' ('better craftsman') – for the development of Dante's verse; Dante may well have been indebted to his accurate 'observation of Nature' as Pound suggests,[5] but the fact remains that the *Commedia* shows a far greater debt to the poet to whom Dante says quite simply 'Tu se' lo mio maestro e 'l mio autore' ('You are my master and my author') (*Inf.* 1.85).

Another difficulty with *The Spirit of Romance* is its exclusive concentration on questions of poetic technique. Pound's enthusiasm for Dante's treatise as the clearest evidence of the commitment of the 'serious artist' to his art – 'No one who is unprepared to train himself in his art by comparative study of the culture to-day accessible, in the spirit of the author of the *De Vulgari Eloquio*, can expect to be taken seriously', as he later puts it[6] – leads him to imply throughout *Spirit* that the origins of the *Commedia* can be found in Dante's stylistic and philological studies alone. In other words, Pound completely dissociates himself from Dante's biography, since 'Dante's art . . . is really what concerns us' (p. 107). This represents, of course, a radical break with much nineteenth-century thinking about the impetus behind the great poem and anticipates the differences between Pound and Yeats, in whose theories the view persists that the *Commedia* is the outcome, not of Dante's technical studies, but of his much more romantic *fate*: of his tumultuous life of exile, lost love and political involvement. As Carlyle told Dante, 'Florence thou shalt never see: but Hell and Purgatory and Heaven thou shalt surely see! What is Florence . . . and the World and Life altogether? . . . The great soul of Dante, homeless on earth, made its home more and more in that awful other world' ('The Hero as Poet', p. 144). Yeats's insistence on the Romantic notion of Dante's 'advent' representing 'the birth of a new species of man' also runs counter to the entire tenor of *Spirit*, which seeks to place Dante firmly within a mediaeval setting. The Romantic emphasis on the unprecedented Dante was no less common in certain nineteenth-century American writers: Charles Eliot Norton had found 'little that is distinguishingly individual' in

Dante's predecessors, and James Russell Lowell, in describing Dante as 'the first great poet', noted 'Whatever poetry had preceded him, whether in the Romance or Teutonic tongues, is interesting mainly for its simplicity without forethought . . . it shows no trace of the creative faculty either in unity of purpose or style . . .'[7] One only needs to compare Pound's observations on Arnaut – 'those who are trying to trace the sources of Dante's style will do well to consider how much the Tuscan master owes to Daniel's terse vigour of suggestion' (p. 26) – and on Cavalcanti – 'Dante himself never wrote lines more poignant, or more intensely poetic' (p. 97). One such line, 'Vedrai la sua virtù nel ciel salita', we have already noted Pound making extraordinary claims for in the preface to his Cavalcanti translations of 1912 (above, Chapter IV, p. 116).

After the earlier insistence on Dante's struggle in having gone it alone, *The Spirit of Romance* is certainly refreshingly undramatic, but Pound's anti-Romantic correctives seem too stringent in removing *all* biographical impetus from Dante's work. 'He had needed a knowledge for himself and set down a memo', Pound later said of Dante's aims in the *De Vulgari* (*Guide to Kulchur*, p. 107), and indeed those elements in the treatise which seem not altogether in place in a poet's 'memo', or compendium of style, never attract Pound's interest, elements such as the opening picture of a world disharmonious and disunited in its variety of languages after the presumption of Babel, or the attack on the princes of Italy in I.xii.5 for having ceased to patronise men of noble talents. Side by side with the technician we already have the polemicist and apologist of the *Commedia*, but, even though Dante was always willing to interrupt his philosophical works with tirades against his opponents in a manner reminiscent of Pound's own later writing, we never find, in Pound, much attention to Dante the man, or to the events of Dante's life, and this in spite of a certain degree of similarity between the two men's political careers.[8] As Eliot suggested in a comment we shall return to: '[Pound] finds Guido [Cavalcanti] much more sympathetic than Dante, and on grounds which have little to do with their respective merits as poets . . .'[9] The neglect in *Spirit* of Dante's biography and of aspects of his intellectual concerns tends to impair Pound's criticism, because he takes no cognisance of the experiences Dante went through between his *dolce stil nuovo* days and the period of the writing of the *Commedia*: his passage round the courts of Italy, his philosophical and classical studies, his fruitless hopes in

Henry VII establishing the monarchy in Italy. These are the means Dante's predecessors could not prepare.

Nowhere, then, in *Spirit* are we reminded of what Lowell had called the 'utter and disastrous failure' of Dante's life ('Dante' in *Among My Books*, p. 19). Rather, we see Dante writing from a position of maximum stability or consistency practically divorced from extra-literary concerns; from a curious *plenitudo temporis* the tradition had prepared for him – 'Advenit Magister'. It was from just such a position of stability that Dante could 'package' the centuries preceding him, in Pound's later formulation of the *Commedia.*[10]

This tendency to avoid the personal in Dante is very much part of Pound's desire for the production of poetry in his own day to be set upon a 'scientific', impersonal basis. 'It is tremendously important that great poetry be written, it makes no jot of difference who writes it. The experimental demonstrations of one man may save the time of many', he wrote in 1912.[11] *Spirit* attempts to redeem a situation where 'Dante's poetry so overshadows his work in prose that we are apt to forget that he is numbered with Aristotle and Longinus among the great literary critics of past time' (p. 14), but, in rescuing the *De Vulgari* from the shadows, Pound allows the treatise to stand between him and the *Commedia*, rather as Rossetti's admiration for the *Vita Nuova* blurred his understanding of the great poem. Long before Pound attempted to produce his own *De Vulgari* in work that eventually led to the *ABC of Reading* (1934),[12] he was imitating the treatise in *Spirit* itself, where he attempts a Dantesque classification:

> for we find adjectives of two sorts, thus, adjectives of pure quality, as: white, cold, ancient; and adjectives which are comparative, as: lordly. Epithets may also be distinguished as epithets of primary and secondary apparition. By epithets of primary apparition I mean those which describe what is actually presented to the sense or vision. Thus in *selva oscura*, 'shadowy wood'; epithets of secondary apparition or afterthought are such as in '*sage* Hippotades' or '*forbidden* tree' . . . There are also epithets of 'emotional apparition', transensuous, suggestive: thus in Mr. Yeats' line
>
> Under a bitter *black* wind that blows from the left hand . . .
>
> (p. 167)

The measured, formal tone of this is explained by the inspiration behind it coming from one of Pound's favourite passages in the *De*

Vulgari: 'Nam vocabulorum quedam puerilia, quedam muliebria, quedam virilia; et horum quedam silvestria, quedam urbana; et eorum que urbana vocamus, quedam pexa et lubrica, quedam yrsuta et reburra sentimus' ('For some words are childish, some feminine, and some virile; and of these some are rustic, some urbane; and of those I call urbane, some sound combed and smooth, others hairy and bristling') (II.vii.2).[13] Compare 'for we find adjectives of two sorts, thus' with 'Nam vocabulorum quedam puerilia, quedam muliebria', and note the way categories are established and then subdivided in both extracts: 'Epithets may also be distinguished as epithets of primary and secondary apparition. By epithets of primary apparition I mean . . .'; 'horum quedam silvestria, quedam urbana; et eorum que urbana vocamus, quedam pexa . . .' Pound's quoting of Yeats is rather like Dante's practice of illustrating his point with a line from a fellow *stilnovista*.

Returning to Pound's desire to correlate the mediaeval situation with his own position as a modern poet, we find that what *Spirit* and, as Pound would have it, the *De Vulgari* both show is the paramount importance of predecessors. Even if Pound himself were to prove incapable of writing the modern epic, his work could still lead towards it: 'It has been complained, with some justice, that I dump my note-books on the public . . . I am constantly contending that it took two centuries of Provence and one of Tuscany to develop the media of Dante's masterwork', he wrote in 1912 ('Credo', in 'A Retrospect', p. 9). His sense that literary history could be resolved into a series of triads in which 'inventors' lead to 'masters' who are followed by 'diluters', as formulated in the later 'How to Read' (*LE*, p.23), was undoubtedly stimulated by his admiration for Cavalcanti and disgust with Petrarch, with Dante forming a peak of achievement between them. At the outset of his career Pound could not be sure where he fitted into the twentieth-century version of the pattern – whether he was 'inventor' or 'master' – but the kind of schematic historiography we find in *Spirit* guarantees the validity of his own early work in perhaps preparing the way for a greater writer. In the essay on Whitman of 1909 he even casts himself as Petrarch with Whitman:

> Like Dante [writing] in the 'vulgar tongue', in a new metric. The first great man to write in the language of his people.
>
> *Et ego Petrarca in lingua vetera scribo*, and in a tongue my people understand not.[14]

Thus, when Eliot labelled Pound 'il miglior fabbro' in the dedication to *The Waste Land*, he was responding to an invitation Pound had long since issued; but by then, of course, the latter was well into his attempt to emulate Dante himself in the production of an epic.

It seems then that Pound's elevation of Daniel and Cavalcanti into the figures behind the *Commedia* and his dismissal of Virgil are not simply determined by his preferences as a reader of poetry but have a propagandistic element involving his writing of poetry too. His absorbing interest in the *canzone* form, which he calls 'the high mass' of poetry, is amply evidenced by his volume *Canzoni* of 1911, a series of imitations after Arnaut and Dante whom he is careful to link by quoting from the *De Vulgari* (II.x.2) at the head of the opening *canzone*: 'Et huiusmodi stantiae usus est fere in omnibus cantionibus suis Arnaldus Danielis et nos eum secuti sumus' ('And Arnaut Daniel has used a stanza of this kind in almost all his *canzoni*, and I have followed him').[15] However much Pound's interest in the *De Vulgari* owes to the teaching of William P. Shepard at Hamilton College,[16] his early views on Dante might be regarded as an inheritance from Pre-Raphaelitism, in so far as this stresses Dante's place within a circle of gifted contemporaries rather than the immense achievement which separates him from them, and attempts to make an impossible leap straight from his early poetry to the *Commedia*. It is arguable that the two works which had the most profound effect on Pound's conceptions were Rossetti's *Dante and His Circle* and Browning's *Sordello*, in which a near-contemporary of Dante is again elevated into the great precursor. By the time Pound had published his translations of Cavalcanti in 1912 his admiration for the precursor had doubtless begun to increase; by the late 1920s his reworking of these translations for the Genoese edition of Cavalcanti's *Rime* of 1931, together with his work on the 'Donna me prega', led him to retract the expression that Cavalcanti was 'less subtle' than Dante in the revisions he made to *Spirit* in 1929.[17] We have seen the differences this caused between him and Yeats, anxious to keep Dante unprecedented and unparalleled; and we shall return to the differences with Eliot.

Dante's influence on Pound's early verse, *canzoni* aside, has a large Rossettian element, as Pound's note to his poem 'Fortunatus' makes abundantly clear: 'Caught sometimes in the current of strange happiness, borne upon such winds as Dante beheld whirling the passion-pale shapes in the nether-gloom' (*Early Poems*, p. 69). 'Passion-pale' is Yeatsian of course, but the conversion of Paolo and Francesca into examples of 'strange happiness' derives, as Hueffer pointed out (above, p. 123), from Rossetti. The best example of the influence is 'Comraderie', which combines an epigraph from the *Vita Nuova* – 'E tuttoque [*sic*] io fosse a la compagnia di molti, quanto alla vista' ('And although outwardly I was with a lot of people') (IX.2) – with an address to the lady of a 'Blessed Damozel'–'Dante at Verona' parentage:

> Yea sometimes in a bustling man-filled place
> Me seemeth some-wise thy hair wandereth
> Across my eyes, as mist that halloweth
> The air a while and giveth all things grace.
> (*Early Poems*, p. 31)

The movement towards 'Imagism' in Pound's verse, which 'stands . . . for hard light, clear edges', as he put it in 1914,[18] was seen by him as a struggle away from the Rossetti/Swinburne/early-Yeats influence, and this is expressed in the poem 'Revolt', with its subtitle 'Against the Crepuscular Spirit in Modern Poetry', where he rejects the dreams of

> pale flowers,
> Slow-moving pageantry of hours that languidly
> Drop as o'er-ripened fruit from sallow trees.
> (*Early Poems*, p. 96)

It is something of a critical commonplace that Pound's reading in the early Italian poets helped him in this struggle.[19] He had celebrated their 'preciseness . . . of description' and 'clarity of imaginative vision' in *Spirit* (p. 92), and had noted that 'Dante's precision both in the *Vita Nuova* and the *Commedia* comes from the attempt to reproduce exactly the thing which has been clearly seen' (p. 114), long before he converted this two-part process of 'seeing', then 'reproducing exactly', into the first two Imagist formulations worked out 'in the spring or early summer of 1912':

> 1. Direct treatment of the 'thing' whether subjective or objective.
> 2. To use absolutely no word that does not contribute to the presentation.
> ('A Retrospect', p. 3)

Thus it is that an early critic and associate of Pound's, Jean De Bosschère, is able to emphasise the importance of the 'Imagistic' values Pound found in the Tuscans for Pound's own poetry:

the encumbered, heavy rhetoric of *Paradise Lost* must certainly have driven him to the hardness, the incisive form of the *Divine Comedy*. Moreover the clearness and strength of precision struck his imagination from the first. He was always thinking about freeing himself from any indirect construction of phrase, and with a view to this he translated Guido Cavalcanti. He wanted to examine the crude, sincere manner of the poet, and enjoyed studying his keen method of expression . . .[20]

If, however, we examine the Cavalcanti translations that Pound began in 1910 and published in 1912, we find they lead away from Imagism rather than towards it; in fact they represent a complete contradiction of a statement of 1911 in which he declared the type of poetry he wanted to see produced 'during the next decade or so':

It will be as much like granite as it can be . . . it will not try to seem forcible by rhetorical din, and luxurious riot. We will have fewer painted adjectives impeding the shock and stroke of it. At least for myself, I want it so, austere, direct, free from emotional slither.[21]

However, the Cavalcanti translations abound in 'luxurious riot' and indirectness; in the examples which follow I give Pound's translation and the Italian text from the facing page of his edition:

They [my sighs] would return to the eyes in galliard mode

Girieno agli occhi con tanta vertute

(They would go to my eyes with such power) (sonnet XI);

Our style could show unto the least observant,
It beareth mercy for a gonfalon

Puoi di leggier conoscer nostro stile,
Lo quale porta di mercede insegna

(You can easily recognise our style, which bears the insignia of mercy) (sonnet XXIV);

And courtly knights in bright accoutrement

E cavalieri armati, che sian genti

(And armed knights who are noble) (sonnet XVIII);

Till Rumour, courier through the mind, ran crying,
'A vileness in the heart, Oyez! lies dying'

Quando passò ne la mente un romore,
Il qual dicea: Dentro biltà, che more.

(When a voice passed through the mind saying: 'Within is Beauty, who is dying.')
(ballata IV)[22]

Pound repeatedly fits the Italian with heraldic, picturesque trappings. Thus he uses 'sinister side' ('lato manco' – 'left side', sonnet I); 'death-watch' ('per veder morir' – 'to see die', sonnet IV); 'go errant forth' ('vanno' – 'go', sonnet XI); 'thou . . . art sans paragon' ('siete la migliore' – 'you are the best', sonnet XV); 'will sound forloyn' ('Si partira' – 'will leave', sonnet XXIII). The translations revel in what Pound later called the 'embroidery of language' that he saw as characteristic of the Elizabethans ('How to Read', p. 29). In spite then of De Bosschère's assessment, Pound could not, or would not, reproduce Cavalcanti's 'keen method of expression', however much he may have enjoyed studying it.[23]

Of course, the translations make great play with images; but they are far from Imagistic. The ornateness which separates the two types of poetry is obvious if we put side-by-side the opening of sonnet I (together with the original), and Pound's 'stilnovistic', but by now Imagist, 'Gentildonna':

You, who do breach mine eyes and touch the heart,
And start the mind from her brief reveries,
Might pluck my life and agony apart.
Saw you how love assaileth her with sighs,
And lays about him with so brute a might
That all my wounded senses turn to flight.

Voi, che per gli occhi miei passaste al core,
E svegliaste la mente che dormìa,
Guardate a la 'ngosciosa vita mia,
Che sospirando la distrugge Amore.
E' va tagliando di sì gran valore,
Che i deboluzzi spiriti van via . . .

(You, who passed through my eyes to my heart, and awoke the mind which was sleeping, look on my painful life which, sighing, is destroyed by Love. He goes dealing wounds with so much strength that the feeble spirits give way . . .)

She passed and left no quiver in the veins, who now
Moving among the trees, and clinging
in the air she severed,
Fanning the grass she walked on then, endures:
Grey olive leaves beneath a rain-cold sky.[24]

There is a cumbersomeness in the translation which interferes with Cavalcanti's precision, with 'va tagliando' becoming 'lays about him', and 'van via' 'turn to flight'; and then the 'clipped' quality of each line in 'Gentildonna' contrasts with the languid effect of 'reveries' and 'assaileth her with sighs', in Pound's translation. Here Pound has not succeeded, with Cavalcanti's help, in throwing off the 'Crepuscular Spirit' but has rather imbued the Italian writer with it. And, indeed, a moment's thought should enable us to see that the early Italians could hardly be the means of Pound's weaning himself away from nineteenth-century language since they themselves, thanks to Rossetti, had been so heavily invested with it; as Pound wrote in his Introduction: 'In the matter of these translations and of my knowledge of Tuscan poetry, Rossetti is my father and my mother . . .'[25] Later he would prefer to re-phrase this: 'my early versions of Guido are bogged in Dante Gabriel and in Algernon'.[26] Certainly Rossetti's translations do not seem very similar to Pound's: their rhythms are much smoother and they have very little of Pound's rather inflated picturesqueness.[27] The influence would seem to come rather from Rossetti's original poetry, like the sonnet 'Death-in-Love':

There came an image in Life's retinue
That had Love's wings and bore his gonfalon:
Fair was the web, and nobly wrought thereon,
O soul-sequestered face, thy form and hue!
(*Works*, p. 90)

We saw 'gonfalon' used for 'insegna' in Pound's translation of sonnet XXIV. Another factor in his being 'obfuscated by the Victorian language' in the translations ('Cavalcanti', *LE*, p. 193) is undoubtedly his admiration for Browning, particularly for the picturesque mediaevalism of, for example, Browning's celebrated description of the font in Book I of *Sordello* (ll. 410–27). In 1912 he sent off a poem to Harriet Monroe revealingly described as an 'over-elaborate post-Browning "Imagiste" affair' (*Letters*, p. 44), a description that nicely sums up the tussle in his work between the

Victorian language and the desire to 'use absolutely no word that does not contribute to the presentation'. By 1913 he could indeed say of his poems: 'Here they stand without quaint devices', but his work on Cavalcanti could hardly be said to have accelerated the process directly.[28]

I believe that we have to look for the sources of Pound's modernisation in the modern era: to his conversations with Hulme, Ford and Flint, possibly in that order of importance, with Fenollosa's Chinese studies coming along a little later as Imagism's final inspiration. Of course, once this latter had been established, and Pound was producing a 'clear-edged' verse such as in the last line of 'Gentildonna': 'Grey olive leaves beneath a rain-cold sky', his earlier observations on Dante's precision could be reformulated:

> Dante's *Paradiso* is the most wonderful *image*. By that I do not mean it is a perseveringly imagistic performance. The permanent part is Imagisme, the rest, the discourses with the calendar of saints and the discussions about the nature of the moon, are philology.[29]

As applied to Dante, the term Imagism was a modern, rather chic formulation of qualities in his poetry critics had already noted a hundred years earlier. Thus an anonymous review of 1827 compares Milton's 'lofty indistinctness' with Dante's poetical 'materialism': '*Paradise Lost* is a poem which a painter can scarcely touch: the *Divina Commedia* teems with subjects which challenge the bold brush . . .' (Toynbee, *DEL*, II, 472–4); Coleridge, as we saw, complained of Dante's 'occasional fault of becoming grotesque from being too graphic without imagination' (above, p. 49). Sismondi praised the *Commedia* because 'il y a à peine une terzine qui ne pût se rendre avec le pinceau', and made a comparison Pound would have endorsed completely: 'Pétrarque est beaucoup moins poète que le Dante, parce qu'il est beaucoup moins peintre.'[30] Foscolo went a stage further in suggesting that Dante's '[images] are the bold and prominent figures of an *alto rilievo*, which, it seems, we might almost touch . . .'[31] This anticipates Pound's own formulations of poetry's aspiring towards the condition of 'granite', what he later calls 'the "sculpture" of rhyme'.[32] The duality Pound set up between 'the definiteness of Dante's presentation, as compared with Milton's rhetoric' ('A Retrospect', p. 7), was also long established, although a supporter of Milton might easily have replaced the word 'rhetoric' with 'grandiloquence' and decided, as Coleridge did, that Dante was a little too definite at times. This was particularly the case in the Romantic period, with its enthusiasm for the *Inferno* and for Burkean ideas of the sublime: 'clearness of imagery . . . helps but little towards affecting the passions, as it is in some sort an enemy to all enthusiasms whatsoever . . . the obscure idea, when properly conveyed, [is] more affecting than the clear'.[33] For Burke the proper comparison was between poetry and music, not sculpture, and Milton reigned supreme.

Pound had written of the *Commedia* in *Spirit*, 'It is of this sort of poetry that Coleridge says: "Our regard is not for particular passages but for a continuous undercurrent." There are beautiful images in the *Paradiso*, but the chief marvel is not the ornament' (p. 148). The comment already indicates how the *Commedia*'s importance for Pound would not long lie in its providing the stylistic pedigree for the tiny Imagist poems collected into *Lustra* (1916), and how his *Cantos*, which we now turn to, would attempt to establish a far more serious relation with the great poem.

Towards the end of his career Pound explained the purpose of the *Cantos* thus: 'you had six centuries that hadn't been packaged. It was a question of dealing with material that wasn't in the *Divina Commedia*.'[34] The element of 'packaging' in Dante's work was one of the foremost things that drew Pound to it, a Pound greatly alarmed that the excessive amount of printed information available on the shelves of the British Museum Reading Room was no longer packageable (see *Guide to Kulchur*, pp. 53–4). The *De Vulgari* was a sort of mini-package made in preparation for the greater one, evidence that Dante had accepted the artist's obligation to 'master all known forms and systems of metric' ('A Retrospect', p. 9); and we have seen the rather summary equation Pound makes between the two packages above. The *De Vulgari* also provided the older Pound with a favourite catch-phrase – 'directio voluntatis' (II.ii.7) – although at the time of writing *Spirit* his scorn for one of the two poets Dante had referred to as exemplifying this concept, Giraut de Bornelh, seems to rule out any further interest in 'the singers of righteousness, or "direction of the will"; where of a surety the competition [for eminence] was not so keen [compared with that between 'the singers of love']' (p. 15). Pound pays no attention to the fact that in his discussion of the 'directio voluntatis' the second poet Dante refers to is himself; having gone on to celebrate 'righteousness' in poems like 'Doglia mi reca' (*Rime*, 49), 'il Poeta della *Vita Nuova* e di molte rime amorose', in Aristide Marigo's words, 'cede all'amico [Cino da Pistoia] il vanto di poeta d'amore nella lingua nostra, per riservarsi quello più grande di poeta della rettitudine' ('the poet of the *Vita Nuova* and of many love poems cedes to his friend the boast of being the poet of love in our language so as to keep for himself the greater title of poet of righteousness').[35] This is a rather prominent example of Pound's inattention in *Spirit* to the stages of Dante's development, but by *Jefferson and/or Mussolini* (Nott, 1935) 'DIRECTIO VOLUNTATIS' stands at the head of the third chapter in which Pound labels 'The whole of the *Divina Commedia* . . . a study of the "directio voluntatis" (direction of the will). I mean in its basal sense.' This has, however, in Pound's conception little to do with Dante's idea of 'virtus': 'To cut the cackle, you can have an OPPORTUNIST who is RIGHT, that is who has certain convictions and who drives them through circumstance, or batters and forms circumstance with them' (pp. 17–18). Mussolini's overcoming of circumstance in, for example, getting Italian swamp turned into farmland, which 'Italian intellectuals' had talked about doing 'from the time of Tiberius' (p. 23), is equated with Dante's will towards order and light in the sequence of the *Commedia*.[36]

In *A Visiting Card* (1942), which is an extremely useful mini-compendium of many of his main ideas, Pound suggests that 'every book of value contains a bibliography declared or implied. The *De Vulgari Eloquio* refers us to Richard of St Victor, Sordello, Bertran de Born, and Arnaut Daniel' (p. 292). The *Cantos* themselves are a kind of *De Vulgari–Commedia* hybrid, poem and bibliography combined: in the vital need to package and to get ideas into action, it was not always practicable to 'poeticise' the bibliographical elements, or the extracts from books, letters and diaries Pound gave. In *A Visiting Card*, Pound notes 'Dante was content to cite the first lines of certain *canzoni* [in the *De Vulgari*]' (p. 294), a practice Pound copies in Canto v:

> For the gossip of Naples' trouble drifts to North,
> Fracastor (lightning was midwife) Cotta, and Ser D'Alviano,
> Al poco giorno ed al gran cerchio d'ombra,
> Talk the talks out with Navighero,
> Burner of yearly Martials . . .[37]

Here, apart from its 'bibliographical function' in referring us to Dante's *canzone*, the inclusion of the Italian line functions poetically in emphasising the moonlit scene of Giovanni Borgia's cloak floating on the Tiber after his assassination.

What Pound admired about the middle ages was a unity that made them more easily packageable, although he must have noted that that unity was very much in question in the *Commedia* itself:

> Who set the Church against the Empire? Who destroyed the unity of the Catholic Church with this mud-wallow that serves the Protestants in the place of contemplation? Who decided to destroy the mysteries within the Church so as to be able to destroy the Church itself by schism? Who has wiped the consciousness of the greatest mystery out of the mind of Europe – to arrive at an atheism proclaimed by Bolshevism, in Russia but not of Russia?
>
> Who has received honours by putting argumentation where before there had been faith? (*VCd*, p. 287)

The *De Vulgari* shows that the vital channels of communication were still comparatively intact in the middle ages however; also '"Cogitatio, meditatio, contemplatio."/Wrote Richardus, and Dante read him' (Canto LXXXVII, p. 570); likewise 'Guido C. had read "Monologion"' which 'Anselm . . . scripsit, 1063' (CV, pp. 746–7), and 'Dante had read that Canzone' (XCVII, p. 678; presumably the *canzone* on Fortune Pound had accepted as Cavalcanti's in *Spirit* (p. 98)). Earlier in Canto XCVII, we had the modern situation: 'And by curious segregation Brooks Adams ignores him, Del Mar' (p. 673). Thus Pound was conscious of writing his poem against the grain of his time, when the first of the two forces found in history: 'one that divides, shatters, and kills, and one that contemplates the unity of the mystery' (*VCd*, p. 276), had firmly got the upper hand. But the differences in structure between the *Cantos* and *Commedia* cannot simply be reduced to what Eliot called Dante's 'luck' in living in an age that possessed a common and coherent 'system of thought',[38] to the fact that, as Pound told Creekmore in 1939, Dante had an 'Aquinas map' and he did not (*Letters*, p. 418). Such a view is in accordance with the technical, 'scientific' emphasis of *The Spirit of Romance*, in which Dante's predecessors had laid all the foundations and Dante's job was simply to erect the poem on top of them. A glance at Dante's biography is again pertinent here: the *Commedia* was written over a period of from fifteen to twenty years whereas the *Cantos* took over fifty;

moreoever, the opening canto of Dante's poem represents an acknowledgement that the turning point of his life, as represented by the horror of the 'selva oscura', is behind him, and that the pilgrimage has now begun which will take him back 'home' ('a ca', *Inf.* xv.54) to God. The general form of the *Commedia* seems to have been firmly established at the start, whereas the *Cantos* were begun with the most dramatic episodes in Pound's life lying far in the future. Those first three *Cantos* 'of a poem of some length' published in 1917[39] deliberately establish a 'wait-and-see' sort of form flexible enough to incorporate the unpredictable in its author's reading and experience. Thus the epic poem Pound had in mind at the outset, which 'begins "In the Dark Forest", crosses the Purgatory of human error, and ends in the light, and "fra i maestri di color che sanno" ["among the masters of those who know"]',[40] was to be loose enough in its 'Dantean' structure to accommodate whatever unexpected guests the world was found to have an 'immediate need' of, like Confucius, Del Mar, or Sir Edward Coke. As Pound said of Jefferson and Mussolini: 'In neither man of genius was preconception or theory strong enough to blind the leader to the immediate need' (p. 73). Thus, although Wilhelm finds 'the same general pattern' in the two poets' careers and 'both epics fall[ing] into' this pattern, one must insist on the marked differences in 'The Rhythms of Two Lives', to quote the same author's chapter-heading (*Dante and Pound*, pp. 10, 24).

Within Pound's basic 'directio' from darkness to light[41] there are what one might call epicycles. Thus the Hell-Cantos, xiv–xv, were followed by a 'purgatorio' in xvi and a 'general paradiso' in xx (Letter to Homer L. Pound, 1927, p. 285), but there are plenty of subsequent references to hell throughout the poem since 'The hells move in cycles,/No man can see his own end' (cxiii, p. 787). Cantos xiv and xv are the first in the poem where an inspiration from Dante is seriously felt; although *Usura* is mentioned in xv, Pound's relative lack of attention to it here is interesting in view of his later thinking, his interest centring rather on

> the perverts, the perverters of language
>   the perverts, who have set money – lust
> Before the pleasures of the senses . . .
>
> (xiv, p. 61)

where Dante's disdain for the 'lupa' is evoked though 'the pleasures of the senses' are not what Dante himself would set against it; and on

> the swill full of respecters,
> bowing to the lords of the place,
> explaining its advantages,
> and the laudatores temporis acti
> claiming that the sh-t used to be blacker and richer . . .
> (xv, p. 64)

where the precedent in Dante's second *bolgia* and its flatterers ('gente attuffata in uno sterco/che da li uman privadi parea mosso' – 'people plunged in excrement that seemed taken from human cess-pits' – *Inf.* XVIII.113–14) is obvious. Indeed, the disgusting atmosphere of this *bolgia* dominates both Pound's Hell-Cantos, even though it receives the *least* attention of any section of Hell in the *Commedia* (only thirty-seven lines, *Inf.* XVIII.100–36). Pound's conception of Hell was to change in 1934 after reading Binyon's translation: only then did he realise more clearly 'how the whole hell reeks with money' ('Hell', *LE*, p. 211); indeed, *The Fifth Decad of Cantos XLII–LI*, published in 1937, might be in part an outcome of this reading, showing the most obvious unity of any section of the poem up till then in its concentration on financial good and evil, this last represented by 'Geryon twin with usura' (LI, p. 251).[42]

The Hell-Cantos indicate a certain restriction in Pound's interest in Dante's Hell which in *Spirit* he had given a rather summary account of, noting 'One hears far too much about Dante's Hell, and far too little about the poetry of the *Purgatorio* and *Paradiso* . . .' (p. 117). In them he re-creates the squalor of certain of the *bolge* to produce a hell 'without dignity, without tragedy' (XIV, p. 63); one might also note the absence of any order or division, since clear demarcation is a positive value for Pound of the highest importance; he thus emphasises hell's meanness by dumping all his sinners together in one boundless ooze. This provides a striking contrast to the extraordinarily systematic ethical divisions of Dante's Hell, explained in *Inferno* XI, a division referring us to a divider working with a complex but precise judicial 'arte' which Dante *personaggio* very much admires; and Eliot doubtless had this in mind when he made his well-known objection that 'a Hell altogether without dignity implies a Heaven without dignity also' (*After Strange Gods*, p. 43). Pound himself was very much aware of this 'arte' in the

Inferno: 'The scale and proportion of evil, as delimited in Dante's hell (or the catholic hell) was obliterated by the Calvinist and Lutheran churches . . . the effect of Protestantism has been semiticly to obliterate values, to efface grades and graduations' (*Guide to Kulchur*, p. 185). His hell was therefore intentionally, and symptomatically, 'modern'. We must return to Eliot's protests in the following chapter; whether or not they indicate a deficiency in Pound's hell, they very much illuminate Eliot's own religious concerns. For me, Pound's Hell-Cantos constitute some of the most extraordinary and impressive verse he ever wrote, a sustained and highly imaginative essay in coprology that indeed rivals the hideous atmosphere of Dante's *basso inferno*, a 'mediaeval world, blind with its ignorance, its violence, and its filth' (*Spirit*, p. 122), though in the last resort we are perhaps reminded of Hieronimus Bosch rather than of anything in Dante:

> their wrists bound to
> their ankles,
> Standing bare bum,
> Faces smeared on their rumps,
> wide eye on flat buttock,
> Bush hanging for beard,
> Addressing crowds through their arse-holes . . .
>
> (XIV, p. 61)

Pound sees the *Inferno* itself from a rather eccentric angle: 'the whole hell reeks with money', is one of his claims, together with the assertion that *usura* and its 'twin' Geryon are Hell's dominant motifs: 'Deep hell is reached via Geryon (fraud) of the marvellous patterned hide, and for ten cantos thereafter the damned are all of them damned for money'; and, with reference to *Inferno* XXV: 'These low circles are not for simple carnality, the damned here have always a strong stain of meanness, cheating though not, I admit, brought into strong relief: *fraudulent* homicide, Cacus for "furto *frodolente*". It begins with the usurers in canto XI' ('Hell', p. 211). Pound's lack of interest in certain important features of the *Inferno* was already apparent in *Spirit*: he tends to ignore figures like Ulysses or Guido da Montefeltro in these lower circles, or rather tends to ignore the enormous ethical and dramatic resonance of Dante's meetings with them, in his concentration on the 'strong stain of meanness'. The drama of Dante's own discovery of sin, the realisation that some of his own affections and admirations have to be surrendered to a higher conception of 'virtute e canoscenza' ('virtue and knowledge') (*Inf.* XXVI.120), and the ambiguity and complexity this involves in presenting some of the damned are features Pound hardly remarks upon. Thus, although Wilhelm has suggested that the *Cantos* and *Commedia* may both be regarded as 'epics of judgement' (pp. 157–9), Pound's judgement seems rather more straightforward; it does not partake of that powerful narrative dimension in the *Commedia* in which the protagonist – at some cost to himself – comes to understand what judgement is. Pound experienced judgement, in no uncertain manner of course, at Pisa and after; but his poem is not an education in the discriminations of judging others to the extent that Dante's is. Again, in Eliot's words, Pound's Hell was 'a Hell for . . . *other people* . . . not for oneself and one's friends' (*After Strange Gods*, p. 43). Moreover, although one is aware of Dante's frequent complaints about the lust for money in the *Commedia*, Geryon cannot be made into an image of strictly *financial* fraud: there are plenty of sinners in the *basso inferno* not damned for money – the soothsayers, Guido da Montefeltro, Ugolino and, of course, Brutus and Cassius – so that Pound tends to belittle the diversity of Dante's conception of man's attempts to frustrate God's will, ignoring Dante's religious and political concerns by 'promoting' Geryon over the head of Satan. This reduced view of the *Inferno* had been strikingly anticipated by Ruskin, as Bidney has shown:

> All along, as we have seen, Ruskin has been making Dante's *Inferno* into a Hell for the misusers of wealth. He has equated Ulysses' fate with that of those who love wealth [noting that the siren in *Purgatorio* XIX.22–23 deceived Ulysses with her song (*Works*, ed. Cook and Wedderburn, XVII, 214) and equating her with the 'Wealth-Siren' (*Ibidem*, 215)] . . . he has equated Geryon with '*avaricious* fraud' [*Ibidem*, 100] . . . and has tended to transform [him] into an aspect or manifestation of Plutus . . . he has converted the sand-stretches running parallel with the Phlegethon into the '*quick*sand' of 'Speculation' . . . So here [in *Ethics of the Dust*] it is hardly surprising to find that the 'king of the valley' – clearly a modified Plutus – is taking over Satan's central role [*Works*, XVIII, 215] . . .
>
> ('Ruskin's Uses of Dante', p. 117)

Pound's assessment of Dante's Hell has important consequences for the part played in the *Cantos* by the *Paradiso*, as we shall see.

It is hardly surprising that in *Spirit* Pound asserts that the Dante who visits Hell is 'a more impersonal figure than he is usually accounted' (p. 126); or that he dismisses a famous encounter like the following in one short sentence: 'In Canto xv we find Brunetto Latini still anxious for the literary immortality of his "Tesoro"' (p. 123); no reference here to Brunetto's disclosures about Dante's fate! It is of course a measure of Pound's rejection of Romantic interests in Dante that there is so little in his work about Brunetto, Ulysses, Ugolino or Dante himself, who, in De Sanctis's words, 'towered' above all the rest, 'il piú infernale, il piú vivente di tutti' ('the most infernal, the most vivid of them all') (*Storia della letteratura italiana*, I, 232). This fresh, 'impersonal' look at the *Commedia* forms a great contrast with Eliot's interest in the poem's depiction of individual souls after death, the souls who seemed to him less dead than the living;[43] throughout his poetry Eliot exploits a rich vein of irony and paradox in juxtaposing the two orders of 'life' and 'death' with examples and images borrowed from the *Commedia*, to arrive finally at the recreation of the Brunetto episode in *Little Gidding*. Similarly Arnaut Daniel was important for Eliot as a spirit undergoing the purgatorial fire, whereas Pound quotes his speech to Dante (*Purg*. XXVI.140–7) without a thought for its religious significance (*Spirit*, p. 16), but simply as Dante's acknowledgement of a poetic debt. This neglect of the significance of the *Commedia*'s characterisation helped Pound in his formulation of the poem as a 'packaging' of the previous era and of Dante as a reactionary ('Cavalcanti', *LE*, p. 149), for, as we have seen in previous chapters, it was frequently in the creation of the realistic literary character that Dante's progressiveness was felt to reside.[44]

Pound then secularises the *Commedia*, and, taking Dante's journey as 'a symbol of mankind's struggle upward out of ignorance into the clear light of philosophy' (*Spirit*, p. 116), models his own epic journey upon it towards a non-transcendent light as in the comment quoted above (p. 186). In the meantime, his prose writings and comments on Dante continue a programme of ignoring Christian meanings in the original, as in his commentary on Dante's phrase 'il ben de l'intelletto' (*Inf*. III.18) – 'Homely English would get that down to "use of your wits", but I reckon Dante meant something nearer to Mencius's meaning . . . the sense of justice or equity . . .'[45] Though Pound had little enthusiasm for Christianity itself, he respected what it had provided, the greater unity of thought and culture in the middle ages, together with its images and buildings. But, as he told the old nun, ' . . . I wasn't Christian . . . I believed in a more ancient and classical system with a place for Zeus and Apollo' (*Jefferson and/or Mussolini*, p. 31). In establishing the *Cantos*' destination as a *paradiso terrestre*, Pound was perfectly well aware that his conception of the light of knowledge diverged from that in the *Commedia*, where it had been assigned only a relative value: 'Dante uses *che sanno* in his passage on Aristotle in limbo. He uses *intendendo* for the angels moving the third heaven' (*Guide to Kulchur*, p. 315).

The way knowledge or understanding is presented through images of light in the later parts of the two poems seems to offer the most fertile ground for purposes of comparison and contrast. In the *Paradiso* Dante's arrival at understanding as Beatrice leads him towards God is presented as an entry into brighter and brighter depths of light, so that there is an exact parallel between his physical and mental illumination. In the post-Pisan *Cantos* Pound does not present his light of knowledge similarly, that is as a total ambience; it is there in marvellous passages but it is not sustained. The movement towards unity in the *Commedia* and the final vision of it in the 'luce etterna' –

> Nel suo profondo vidi che s'interna
> legato con amore in un volume,
> ciò che per l'universo si squaderna:
> sustanze e accidenti e lor costume
> quasi conflati insieme, per tal modo
> che ciò ch'i' dico è un semplice lume

(I saw enfolded in its depth, bound with love in one volume, all that is scattered through the universe: substances and accidents and their relations, as it were fused together in such a way that what I am saying is a mere glimmer [of the truth]) (*Par.* XXXIII.85–90)

– had been prepared for from the beginning by the design and proportion prevailing in the universe Dante had been travelling through, whereas when Pound states

> I have brought the great ball of crystal;
> who can lift it?
> Can you enter the great acorn of light?
>
> (CXVI, p. 795)

his image of unity offsets, rather than embraces, 'ciò che per l'universo si squaderna'; he is aware, that is, that the intractable in human existence remains:

> Le Paradis n'est past artificiel
>   but is jagged,
> For a flash,
>   for an hour.
> Then agony,
>   then an hour,
>   then agony . . .
>
> (XCII, p. 620)

Dante's presentation of the grades and graduations of light in the *Paradiso* parallels the careful planning of penal divisions in the *Inferno*; within the splendour of the former exists a divinely appointed series of ratios between love, understanding and grace, as Solomon explains:

> La sua chiarezza séguita l'ardore;
> l'ardor la visïone, e quella è tanta,
> quant'ha di grazia sovra suo valore.

([The soul's] brightness depends on its ardour; its ardour on the extent of its vision, and this depends on how much grace it has over and above its own merit) (XIV.40–2)

These obvious differences in unity between the *Commedia* and *Cantos* start to reveal themselves most fully as Pound enters his *paradiso* in the post-Pisan *Cantos*, when references to the *Commedia* itself become more abundant and sustained. The earlier *Cantos* had assumed a paternity in Dante without troubling themselves unduly to substantiate it, and hardly offer enough evidence in themselves – the Hell-Cantos aside – to allow one to make any detailed comparison with Dante's first two *cantiche*. To call the *Cantos*, as one critic has, 'a nonteleological rehorizontalised Dantesque *commedia*' makes too summary an equation between the general form of the two poems, even if one can understand what exactly remains 'Dantesque' about any *commedia* that has had the teleology and 'verticality' taken out of it.[46]

The *Cantos* as a whole read like a review of the intractability of history, of the very fact that it cannot be packaged. Indeed, the 'sun and serenitas' (CXIII, p. 786) that are more to the fore in the later *Cantos*, with the long review of Confucian teaching in XCIX (pp. 694–712), or the contemplation of the goddesses in CVI (pp. 753–5), derive not from a gradual Dantesque entry into fulfilment but rather from the acceptance that the Dantesque plan is not workable: there can be no final arrival or stationing in the light of knowledge in a world whose presiding genius is *Fortuna*, a prominent goddess in the later *Cantos*:

> to know beauty and death and despair
> and to think that what has been shall be,
> flowing, ever unstill.
> Then a partridge-shaped cloud over dust-storm.
> The hells move in cycles,
> No man can see his own end.
> The Gods have not returned. 'They have never left us'.
> They have not returned.
> Cloud's processional and the air moves with their living.
> (CXIII, p. 787)

This is more the philosophy of Yeats's *Vision* than of Dante's –

> Thru the 12 Houses of Heaven
> seeing the just and the unjust,
> tasting the sweet and the sorry,
> Pater Helios turning.
> 'Mortal praise has no sound in her ears'
> (Fortuna's) . . .
> (*Ibidem*, p. 786)

– but it is a disorder that seeks to locate itself within a wider order suggestive of Dante's cosmology:

> above the Moon there is order,
> beneath the Moon, forsitan.
> (XCVII, p. 677)

The reader of the *Cantos* will have already anticipated this conclusion, since it was exhaustively illustrated by the Chinese Cantos (LII–LXI), which open with a marvellous account of the labours of the seasons as regulated by the sun's passage through the 'Houses of Heaven' (LII, pp. 258–61) and then proceed with the less desirable cycle of political stability and instability, of honest and corrupt administrations, within the history of the Chinese Empire. The impression we take away from 3,500 years of Chinese history is one of constant and inconclusive repetition: 'yet now came again eunuchs, taozers and hochang' (LVII, p. 312). Thus the three divisions of 'the permanent, the recurrent, the casual', into which

Pound had suggested to Drummond the *Cantos* might be divided in 1932 (*Letters*, p. 321), are accepted in the later *Cantos* as inseparable, with 'the mind as Ixion, unstill, ever turning' (CXIII, p. 790). This acquiescence in the 'unpackageability' of history remains, however, only partial, for in the later *Cantos* themselves the mind is turning afresh to the histories of other civilisations, to Byzantium in XCVI, to Renaissance England in CVII–CIX; it is as if Pound cannot rid himself of the hope that one of the threads of history will lead him to a finality akin to Dante's vision of 'La forma universal di questo nodo' ('The universal form of this knot') (*Par.* XXXIII.91).

Thus several of the references to the *Commedia* in the final decads of the *Cantos* emphasise the distance between the two poems: 'The *Cantos* are but footnotes to the *Commedia*', Pound remarked in 1952,[47] footnotes which refer us to a unity his own poem cannot re-establish:

> by the silk chords of the sunlight,
> Chords of the sunlight (*Pitagora*)
>   non si disuna (xiii)
> Splendor . . .
>
> (XCVIII, p. 693)

When we trace this reference –

> Ciò che non more e ciò che può morire
> non è se non splendor di quella idea
> che partorisce, amando, il nostro Sire;
> ché quella viva luce che sì mea
> dal suo lucente, che non si disuna
> da lui né da l'amor ch'a lor s'intrea,
> per sua bontate il suo raggiare aduna,
> quasi specchiato, in nove sussistenze,
> etternalmente rimanendosi una

(That which does not die and that which does is nothing but the effulgence of that idea which our Lord, in an act of love, gave birth to; because that living light, which radiates from a source that remains united to God and the love that completes the Trinity, concentrates its rays through its goodness into nine substances which are, as it were, reflected in a mirror, itself remaining eternally one) (*Par.* XIII.52–60)

– we are straight into the mathematical and metrical precision characteristic of the *Commedia*'s presentation of its ordered universe, and straight into the complex yet clear theological 'content' of Dante's light. The unity of the 'viva luce' is not simply stated in the *Commedia* but is inherent in the structure of the entire work, as suggested above, through the subordination one to another of souls in varying degrees of grace. This aspect of the poem, of great importance to Eliot as we shall see, has tended to be passed over by Pound, whose own conception of light as what one may call an ethical substance has little in common with Dante's.

In the later *Cantos*, Pound 'tried to make a paradiso/terrestre' (Notes for CXVII *et seq.*, p. 802):

> And in thy mind beauty, O Artemis,
> as of mountain lakes in the dawn,
> Foam and silk are thy fingers,
> Kuanon,
> and the long suavity of her moving,
> willow and olive reflected,
> Brook-water idles,
> topaz against pallor of under-leaf
> The lake waves Canaletto'd
> under blue paler than heaven . . .
> (CX, p. 778)

This had long been a cherished ambition: in *Spirit* he quotes at length from Dante's description of the *paradiso terrestre* (pp. 130–44), and in the early poem '"Blandula, Tenulla, Vagula"' he asks:

> What hast thou, O my soul, with paradise?
> Will we not rather, when our freedom's won,
> Get us to some clear place wherein the sun
> Lets drift in on us through the olive leaves
> A liquid glory?
> (*Early Poems*, p. 150)

He was aware of the differences between his own marvellous colour-effects in the *Cantos* and the more 'monochrome' scintillations of the *Paradiso* –

> Light, cubic
> by volume
> so that Dante's view is quite natural;
> (Tenth, Paradiso, nel Sole)
> non per color, ma per lume parvente . . .
> (CVII, p. 756)

– the reference here being to *Paradiso* X.42: the blessed stand out against the sun, as Dante explains, because of their greater brightness, not because of a difference in colour. Pound's admiration for these effects is combined in the *Cantos* with a beauty absent from the *Commedia*, the

> color prediletto
> the crystal body of air
> deep green over azure . . .
> (*Ibidem*, p. 762)

– a delicacy of chromatic and phenomenological effect, 'Firm even fingers held to the pale firm stone' (IV, p. 13), reminiscent of *quattrocento* art rather than of anything earlier. But, as he says, Dante *was* in the circuit of the sun, so his view 'is quite natural'; he is careful to dissociate Dante from those whose

> mania is a lusting for farness
> Blind to the olive leaf
> not seeing the oak's veins.
> (*Ibidem*, pp. 762–3)

As Pound pointed out, Dante often achieves his effects in the *Paradiso* using natural analogies: his essay on Cavalcanti celebrates that 'radiant world' of 'magnetisms that take form, that are seen, or that border the visible, the matter of Dante's *paradiso*, the glass under water, the form that seems a form seen in a mirror . . .' (p. 154). Like any reader of the *Paradiso* he appreciated Dante's concern, even during the moments of highest ecstasy, to express supernatural experience in natural images. Pound's prayer to the light in the addendum to Canto C –

> pure Light, we beseech thee
> Crystal, we beseech thee
> Clarity, we beseech thee . . .
> (p. 799)

– remains, however, the consummation of a classicism that has been constant throughout the poem from Canto III, in Pound's desire for a 'system with a place for Zeus and Apollo':

> Gods float in the azure air,
> Bright gods and Tuscan, back before dew was shed.
> Light: and the first light, before ever dew was fallen.
> (p. 11)

But the relationship between the 'pure Light' and those who might be said to deny it in Pound's poem – notably the usurers – remains much more unspecified than the situation that obtains in the *Commedia*, where the light Dante prays to at the end is the consummation of a moral system the rest of the poem makes explicit.

In *A Visiting Card* an ambiguity is suggested in Pound's response to the *Commedia*'s 'light' in his practice of setting up an opposition between the religious image and the 'dogmatic definition' (p. 292): 'the images of the gods, or Byzantine mosaics, move the soul to contemplation and preserve the tradition of the undivided light' (p. 277). Thus he suggests,

> To replace the marble goddess on her pedestal at Terracina is worth more than any metaphysical argument.
>
> And the mosaics in Santa Maria in Trastevere recall a wisdom lost by scholasticism, an understanding denied to Aquinas. A great many images were destroyed for what they had in them.
>
> Ma dicon, ch'*è* idolatra, i Fra Minori,
> per invidia, che non *è* lor vicina.[48]
>
> (p. 290)

The quotation used here ('But the Franciscans say it is idolatry, out of envy that she doesn't live near them') from Cavalcanti's sonnet 'Una figura della Donna mia' (Marti, *Poeti . . .*, pp. 245–6; Pound, *Translations*, p. 94) indicates one way in which the friend of Dante became more sympathetic to Pound than Dante himself: his poetry communicated a similarly 'radiant world' to that found in the *Paradiso* without that radiance's dogmatic component; a radiance that was also more manageable, more 'imagistic', compressed into single lines rather than accumulated through a four-thousand-plus line *cantica*:

> Dante himself never wrote lines more poignant, or more intensely poetic than did this Cavalcanti. The single line is, it is true, an insufficient test of a man's art, but it is a perfect test of his natural vigour, and of his poetic nature. (*Spirit*, p. 97)

The line from Canto IV, 'Shaking, air alight with the goddess' (p. 14), is obviously inspired by one of Pound's favourite lines from Cavalcanti: 'che fa di clarità l'aer tremare' ('who makes the air pulse with brightness'), from the sonnet 'Chi è questa che vèn'.[49] The celebration of the lady in Dante's *dolce stil nuovo* poetry is quieter in tone, less 'brilliant': compare the sonnet just mentioned with

Dante's 'Ne li occhi porta la mia donna Amore' ('My lady bears Love in her eyes') (*VN* XXI), where the *virtù* of the subject has of course a fundamental Christian significance, as it has not in Cavalcanti. Observing that Rossetti 'had made a remarkable translation of the *Vita Nuova*', Pound added: 'there was something in Guido that escaped him . . . A *robustezza*, a masculinity' ('Cavalcanti', p. 193). Besides, we may note in the *Vita Nuova*, to quote Eliot's words once more, 'the Catholic philosophy of disillusion', as expressed in its not 'expect[ing] more from *life* than it can give' (*Dante*, p. 275), whereas the qualities of Cavalcanti which Pound admired included his celebration of terrestrial beauty, his belief in 'goddesses' who remain strictly phenomenological. Thus Pound's reference at the end of Canto IV to the same sonnet quoted above in *A Visiting Card* –

> Across the Adige, by Stefano, Madonna in hortulo,
> As Cavalcanti had seen her
>
> (p. 16)

– presents one of the religious images of the 'undivided light' seen through Cavalcanti's eyes; that is, with sufficiently little of Christianity in Cavalcanti's adoration of her as to draw down the reproaches of the 'Fra' Minori'. It was, suggested Eliot, the fact that Guido 'was very likely a heretic, if not a sceptic' that drew the 'individualist' and 'libertarian' Pound to him (*After Strange Gods*, p. 42); through Cavalcanti the images could be retained and the dogma jettisoned. (See Pound's reference to the 'blasphemous intention' of the sonnet, 'Cavalcanti', p. 181).

The 'Donna me prega' is of course the crucial document here, positing Love in terms of images of light – 'Formed like a diafan from light on shade' (from Pound's translation in Canto XXXVI, p. 177) – which participate in the radiance, but not in the ethics, of the *Paradiso* (Marti, pp. 183–91). The changes Pound made to his translation between its first appearance in the *Dial* for July 1928 and in Canto XXXVI emphasise the light's autonomy and indivisibility: thus the earlier translation's 'Spreading its rays, it tendeth never down/By quality, but is its own effect unendingly' (reprinted in 'Cavalcanti', p. 156; the Italian, from Pound's edition in the same essay, is: 'Perchè da qualitatde non disciende/Risplende/in sé perpetuale effecto', p. 164) becomes tightened into 'Descendeth not by quality but shineth out/Himself his own effect unendingly' (p.

177); similarly 'Love doth not move, but draweth all to him' (p. 157, for 'E non si mova/perch'a llui si tirj', p. 166) becomes 'He himself moveth not, drawing all to his stillness' (p. 178). Christine Brooke-Rose has noted that in this last example Pound 'marvellously mistranslates' Cavalcanti,[50] but it is worth remarking that the 'mistranslation' of the *canzone* as a whole has the effect of completely inverting Cavalcanti's intentions. The 'Donna me prega' is of course a notoriously difficult poem and has been the subject of much controversy, complicated by the variant manuscript readings that Pound himself had to cope with; but Nardi's point that Cavalcanti is presenting love as a dangerous and disruptive passion that obscures the light of the intellect and man's rational faculties seems now generally accepted.[51] Hence Pound seems to identify *Amore* with a diaphanous light without realising that Cavalcanti is using the 'diafan' at l. 17 of the *canzone* only as a term of comparison for an emotion which is entirely antithetical: in Nardi's words, 'Come un corpo diafano è reso luminoso dalla luce che l'attraversa e l'informa, così l'amore, che è passione cieca dell'appetito sensibile, consiste in un'oscurità che è cagionata da una maligna influenza di Marte sull'anima sensitiva, e in questa risiede' ('Like a diaphanous body is made luminous by light passing through it and informing it, so love, which is a blind passion of the sensory appetite, consists of a darkness cast by a malign influence of Mars on the sensory faculty, which it thereafter inhabits') ('L'Averroismo del "primo amico"', p. 106). The 'Donna me prega' further emphasises at its conclusion that *Amore*, 'assiso/'n mezzo scuro, luce rade' ('situated in the dark medium [of the *anima sensitiva*] shuts out light') (l. 68, Marti, p. 191; Pound's reading is 'Asciso/mezzo schuro luce rade', 'Cavalcanti', p. 167). Pound translates this rather confusingly in Canto XXXVI; in the earlier translation the confusion again suggests *Amore*'s positive value: 'In midst of darkness light light giveth forth' ('Cavalcanti', p. 157). In Pound's formulation the Cavalcantian *Amore* seems to become identified once more with the Romantic Image, 'considered as having "a life of its own", supplying its own energy, and possessing no detachable meanings – yielding to no analysis, containing within itself all that is relevant to itself' (Kermode, p. 107). It is particularly in the fact that the 'white light that is allness' of Pound's translation in Canto XXXVI seems unyielding to analysis that sets it off from the light of the *Paradiso*, into which Dante penetrates both physically and mentally as he gathers instruction from Beatrice and the other spirits. Thus the Image present in Imagism as an exemplar of a correct poetic technique takes on, in the translation, an absolute philosophical value.

For Pound then, if not for Cavalcanti himself, the Cavalcantian *Amore*, as the object of the mind's mystical pilgrimage, 'moves the soul to contemplation' in a manner that is frequently re-enacted in his own verse, especially in the *Pisan Cantos* –

> nothing matters but the quality
> of the affection –
> in the end – that has carved the trace in the mind
> dove sta memoria
>
> (LXXVI, p. 457)

– where Cavalcanti's poem is the source of inspiration for the meditation that turns *inward*, either on love –

> IN quella parte
> dove sta memoria
> Prende suo stato
> sí formato
> chome
> Diafan dal lume
>
> (Where memory liveth,
> it takes its state
> Formed like a diafan from light on shade
> Pound's translation, Canto XXXVI, p. 177)

– or on the image that provokes it:

> [Amore]
> VIEN da veduta forma ches s'intende
> Che 'l prende
> nel possibile intelletto
> Chome in subgetto
> locho e dimoranza.
>
> (Cometh from a seen form which being understood
> Taketh locus and remaining in the intellect possible . . .
> Pound's translation, Canto XXXVI)

We find Pound's celebration of 'certain images . . . formed in the mind/to remain there/formato locho' (LXXIV, p. 446) to be a particular feature of the poetry of his imprisonment, when his mind was one of the few sources of inspiration left to him. Although a characteristic range of 'vedute forme' is found throughout the *Cantos* – the stone eyes that look seaward, the marble column, the granite stair – from the *Pisan Cantos* onwards one senses Pound's mind dwelling upon them more; thus the movement towards the *paradiso terrestre* in his poem differs importantly from Dante's progress in the *Commedia*, where ecstasy remains no less than sin and damnation an experience Dante wishes to communicate to his readers through common, exoteric images and descriptions. But what Pound's paradisal images communicate is not a common system of thought but the aesthetic values of clarity and precise delineation, as opposed to a hell where 'with usura the line grows thick/with usura is no clear demarcation' (Canto XLV, p. 229). Thus the presentation of that paradise rests ultimately on the rather esoteric communicability of the Image and of 'Imagist' values: 'an expert, looking at a painting . . . should be able to determine the degree of tolerance of usury in the society in which it was painted' (*VCd*, p. 293). What began as an enthusiasm for the *De Vulgari* develops, in the later writings and in the *Cantos* themselves, into the veritable apotheosis of technique. Pound's early elevation of manner over matter –

> It makes no difference *in kind* whether the artist treat of heaven and hell . . . or of Love appearing in an ash-grey vision . . . there is to the artist a like honourable opportunity for precision, for that precision through which alone can any of these matters take on their immortality[52]

– remains a key to his philosophy and a measure of the distance between him and Dante. 'I can "cure" the whole trouble simply by criticism of style', he says in *Jefferson and/or Mussolini*. 'I have been saying so for some time' (p. 17). No one was more aware than Pound about the existence of 'a modern Eleusis being possible in the wilds of a man's mind only' (*Guide to Kulchur*, p. 294), given that, to use Yeats's phrase, the 'unity of culture' Dante drew upon had disappeared; but he also realised that the modern tendency – one thinks of Shelley – to present a private, individual *paradiso* had no just precedent in the *Commedia* in which even Beatrice 'belongs' to a community rather than to the poet who celebrated her: 'personal love poetry neither in the *Cantos* nor in any Epos . . . even (say) Beatrice in the *Commedia*', he observed in 1932, when his own epos was barely a third under way (*Letters*, p. 322), and when the movement inwards towards the mind's carved traces had still to become prominent.

There is, then, no expression of intimacy towards Dante in Pound's writing to compare with that in Canto LXXIII in which Cavalcanti appears to the narrator: 'Sono quel Guido che amasti/pel mio spirito altiero/E la chiarezza del mio intendimento' ('I am that Guido whom you loved for my proud spirit and the brightness of my understanding').[53] The 'new thing in medieval work' that he attempts to define in the Cavalcanti essay, what he calls the 'medieval clean line', has 'nothing to do with Christianity'; in the same essay he comes down against the devising of hells 'to punish, not to heal, the individual sufferer', and labels their devisers 'European Hindoos' (p. 150). Eliot commented drily: '... [Pound] is attracted to the Middle Ages, apparently, by everything except that which gives them their significance' (*After Strange Gods*, p. 41). His protest against the belief 'that the body is evil' also alerts us to his sympathy with the more forceful sexual elements in Cavalcanti's poetry, compared, that is, with Dante's, as in the *ballata* 'In un boschetto' (Marti, pp. 240–2; Pound, *Translations*, pp. 116–17). Pound's own 'vera imago' for *Amore* throughout the *Cantos* is frequently Venus, especially from the *Pisan Cantos* onwards:

> in coitu inluminatio
> Manet painted the bar at La Cigale or at Les Folies in that year
> she did her hair in small ringlets, à la 1880 it might have been,
> red, and the dress she wore Drecol or Lanvin
> a great goddess, Aeneas knew her forthwith ...
> (LXXIV, p. 435)

In Canto XCVII, Venus is the 'Dea libertatis' (p. 681), and XCI ends with an invocation to her, 'O Queen Cytherea,/che 'l terzo ciel movete' (p. 617). Pound here rather flies in the face of Dante, who takes pains at the opening of *Paradiso* VIII to dissociate his Christian conception of the third sphere from the dangerous idolatry of the ancients:

> Solea creder lo mondo in suo periclo
> che la bella Ciprigna il folle amore
> raggiasse, volta nel terzo epiciclo ...

(The world used to believe to its cost that the beauteous Venus, turning in the third epicycle, radiated down mad [sensual] love ...) (1–3)

Dante's blessed in this sphere are no longer aflame with the 'folle amore' but with the greater love that enables them to put it into perspective:

Non però qui si pente, ma si ride,
non de la colpa, ch'a mente non torna,
ma del valor ch'ordinò e provide.

(Not that we repent here, for we smile, not at the fault, which does not come back to our minds, but at the Power which ordained and foresaw.)
(*Par.* IX.103–5)

Pound's references to one of the inhabitants of this sphere, Cunizza da Romano, nevertheless continue to associate her with the pagan Venus, as in LXXIV (pp. 443–4); her libertine biography, which Dante shows no interest in dwelling on (see *Paradiso* IX.31–6), is given fully in Canto XXIX (p. 142). One feels Pound must have been aware of the contradiction here: that he was recruiting images for his *paradiso* from what Dante negates rather than endorses.

Throughout the later *Cantos* Pound draws heavily on Dante's cosmology – his various 'cieli':

And to know interest from usura
(Sac. Cairoli, prezzo giusto)
In this sphere is Giustizia.
(CXIII, p. 789)

The reference is to the sphere of Jupiter, of which Justice is described as an 'effetto' in *Paradiso* XVIII.116–17. In Canto XCIII, Pound refers to the 'Nine knowledges':

The 8th being natural science, 9th moral
8th the concrete, 9th the agenda,
Agassiz with the fixed stars, Kung to the crystalline . . .
(p. 625)

Although he said in 1962, 'One can't follow the Dantesquan cosmos in an age of experiment' (*Paris Review*, pp. 48–9), he is periodically forced, as here, to resort to it in lieu of a more satisfactory framework in which to station his own great men, the reference being to Dante's allocation of the eighth sphere to 'Fisica' and 'Metafisica' and the ninth to 'Morale Filosofia' in *Convivio* II.xiv. In the same interview Pound explained that the *Thrones de los Cantares* (XCVI–CIX) were inspired by the thrones in the *Paradiso* in their presentation of 'those [people] who have some part of the divine vision'. These *Cantos* attempt 'to establish some definition of an order possible or at any rate conceivable on earth' (*Ibidem*, p. 49). Pound will, however, only accept Dante's 'terzo ciel' if it is re-invested with its pre-Christian significance. We remember the designation of Dante's glorification of Beatrice in *Spirit* as the 'consummation' of what is there presented as Mariolatry's 'pagan lineage' (1952 ed., pp. 91–2). Earlier in the *Cantos* Pound had transferred Helen of Troy from the 'bufera infernal' ('infernal storm') of *Inferno* V to his own 'general paradiso' (above, p. 186) of Canto XX: 'cosi Elena vedi,/In the sunlight, gate cut by the shadow ...' (p. 92).

Pound's ignoring of Dante's religious beliefs may have been stimulated in the later *Cantos* at least by a re-reading of the *Convivio*, which is suddenly thrust upon our attention in XCIII. Here Pound presents us with Dante the philosopher, the follower of Aristotle: 'E però dice lo Filosofo che l'uomo naturalmente è compagnevole animale' ('And therefore the Philosopher says that man is by nature a social animal') (*Convivio* IV.iv.1), an observation Pound refers to twice on page 626; as he says, 'Dant' had it/Some sense of civility', prefacing the lines with the quotation 'non fosse cive' (p. 624), a reference that takes us to *Paradiso* VIII.116 where Aristotle is again named a few lines later as the 'maestro' of political theory (see above, p. 29). The lines 'and mentions distributive justice, Dante does, in Convivio/Four, eleven ...' (p. 627) again suggest a Dante of predominantly civic concerns, while Pound tends to be rather cavalier in his blending of references to the *Convivio* and *Commedia*:

> 'non sempre' (in the 3rd of Convivio)
> or as above stated 'jagged'[54]
>   l'amor che ti fa bella
> ('ut facias' – Goddeschalk – 'pulchram')
>   That love is the 'form' of philosophy,
> is its shape (è forma di Filosofia) ...
>   (p. 626)

The 'amor' 'che mi fa bella' ('that makes me beautiful') is the charity that induces St Bonaventura to give his eulogy on St Dominic in *Paradiso* XII.31ff, whereas the two quotations from *Convivio* III.xiii (3, 10) represent a completely different stage in Dante's development, when that love of wisdom celebrated in the *Convivio* seemed to be taking on a greater and greater extra-religious autonomy in his thought. In Canto XCIII Pound seems to be emphasising that 'other Dante' of Kenelm Foster's formulation (see p. 250 n. 37), a much more suitable candidate for a place 'fra i maestri di color che sanno' in the *paradiso terrestre*. Indeed, as Pound admits, Dante's admiration for Philosophy in the *Convivio* exceeds Pound's own enthusiasms: '[Dante] puts knowledge higher than I should' (XCIII, p. 626), a reasonable assessment bearing in mind the fervent celebration of knowledge's 'nobile perfezione' (*Conv.* IV.xiii.9) found particularly in the treatise's last two books. In the above excerpt Pound's quotations from Dante are components of an 'ideogram' of 'amor', and subject to the inevitable dislocation from context the ideogrammatic method involves.

Canto XCIII has by far the greatest number of references to Dante of any of the *Cantos*; thus an ideogram of 'amor' is succeeded by an ideogram of light, beginning with the Chinese 'hsien' character:

> hsien
> nuova vita
> e ti fiammeggio.
> Such light is in sea-caves
> e la bella Ciprigna
> where copper throws back the flame
> from pinned eyes, the flames rise to fade
> in green air.
> A foot-print? alcun vestigio?
>
> (pp. 630–1)

If we trace the context of 'ti fiammeggio' ('I flame on you') we immediately find ourselves back inside the *Paradiso*'s totally consistent equation of this flame with the vision of, and consequent love of, God: Beatrice's increased brightness in Dante's eyes comes from the 'perfetto veder' ('perfect vision') she enjoys (*Par.* V.1–6), and is obviously completely at the opposite pole from the flame investing 'la bella Ciprigna'. Pound seems to be aware that in combining the Christian and pre-Christian here he is dismantling the hierarchy of values established in the *Commedia*, for he seems to question Beatrice's subsequent statement from the same speech:

> e s'altra cosa vostro amor seduce,
> non è se non di quella [l'etterna luce] alcun vestigio,
> mal conosciuto, che quivi traluce.

(and if anything else seduces your love, it is no other than a foot-print of that which shines here, imperfectly understood.) (10–12)

For Pound 'la bella Ciprigna' is no foot-print of anything else, but an absolute in her own right, 'a great goddess', whom we must not, of course, identify with mere sensualism: her beauty is rather a symbol of what Pound sought to establish in the Cavalcanti essay as 'the Tuscan aesthetic':

> It is more than the simple athleticism of the *mens sana in corpore sano*. The conception of the body as perfect instrument of the increasing intelligence pervades. (p. 152)

She is ideal unity, or balance. The canto ends with a coalescence or ideogram of female beauty evoked within an atmosphere of entranced contemplation: we have the 'Tre donne intorno alla mia mente' ('Three ladies encircling my mind') again from Canto LXXVIII (p. 483), although their identities have changed:

> You are tender as a marshmallow, my Love,
> I cannot use you as a fulcrum.
> You have stirred my mind out of dust.
> Flora Castalia, your petals drift thru the air,
> the wind is ½ lighted with pollen
> diafana,
> e Monna Vanna . . . tu mi fai rimembrar.
> (p. 632)

The 'tre donne' are all in fact the same, the fertility goddess, Spring: Cavalcanti's Monna Vanna or Primavera from the *Vita Nuova*, XXIV (where Dante of course prefers to interpret her name as 'prima verrà' ('she will come first') the Baptist figure), the Matelda who makes Dante remember Proserpine at the entrance to the *paradiso terrestre* (*Purg.* XXVIII.49), and Flora herself. Thus what one can call the Dante Canto ends with Pound's own concept of *amore* and with the Cavalcantian 'diafana' there once more to emphasise it; Beatrice is, one might say, conspicuously absent. Indeed, in Canto LXXIII Cavalcanti's spirit is described as having returned from the 'terzo cielo' to revisit the Romagna, and like Cunizza he confesses that while on earth 'De la ciprigna sfera/Conobbi il fulgore' ('I knew the brightness of the sphere of Venus') (p. 12). Again Pound tends to take over the structure of Dante's cosmology only to negate what is contained within it: Cavalcanti's spirit shows no interest in forsaking his past practices but recounts his infatuation with a modern Romagna beauty who 'cantava amore/senz' aver bisogno d'andar in cielo' ('was singing of love without needing to go to heaven') (p. 12). Of all Dante's 'cieli', then, it is the third that Pound shows the most interest in, though for reasons Dante himself would not have recognised. One might describe the *Cantos* as presenting a *Commedia* that has been truncated at both ends: the Hell goes as far down as Geryon/hyperusura, most in evidence in XLV, where Dante's explanation of how usury is an offence against both nature and human arts and industry (*Inf.* XI.97–111) inspires Pound's marvellous description of how it 'gnaweth the thread in the loom', and 'lyeth/between the young bride and her bridegroom' (p. 230); whereas his *paradiso* tends to locate itself in Dante's third sphere in which, for Pound, 'natura' is apotheosised. 'After the eighth canto of the *Paradiso*, who understands the meaning?', he asks in *A Visiting Card* (p. 302).

Eliot's suggestion that Pound had a higher regard for Cavalcanti than for Dante would seem then to have some justification. Yet if we return to *The Spirit of Romance* we can be left in no doubt that to begin with his admiration for 'Il Maestro' was both humble and boundless, and in this work Cavalcanti himself is referred to only rather briefly. One paragraph is worth quoting in full:

> One might indefinitely continue the praise of Dante's excellence of technique and his splendours of detail; but beneath these individual and separate delights is the great sub-surge of his truth and his sincerity: his work is of that sort of art which is a key to the deeper understanding of nature and the beauty of the world and of the spirit. From his descriptions of the aspects of nature I have already quoted the passage of the sunlight and the cloud shadows; for the praise of that part of his worth which is fibre rather than surface, my mind is not yet ripe, nor is my pen skilled. (p. 172)

The later *Cantos* show a return, I think, to a cognition of Dante's 'worth' if not frequently of his ideals, to an awareness of that 'great sub-surge of his truth and his sincerity', as expressed particularly in the references to Dante's 'sense of civility'; moreover, however much Pound disagreed with the substance of Dante's faith in 'cose non parventi' –

> fede è sustanza di cose sperate
> ed argomento de le non parventi;
> e questa pare a me sua quiditate

(faith is the substance of things hoped for, and evidence of things not seen; and this seems to me its quidity) (*Par.* XXIV.64–6)

– he applauds the majestic expression it gave rise to in the *Commedia*:

> quidity!
> Have they heard of it?
> 'Oh you', as Dante says
> 'in the dinghy astern there' . . .
> (XCIII, p. 631)

However useful Cavalcanti might be in providing details for Pound's formulation of the Image, only Dante could provide the inspiration for an epic. That Pound was later to say of Eliot 'His was the true Dantescan voice' reflects, perhaps, his inability to reconcile what the two Italian poets stood for in his own mind.[55]

Thus one senses in Pound's career a turning back towards Dante after a pronounced Cavalcantian 'aberration' that took place especially during the late twenties and early thirties, and that centres, from this point of view, around his edition of Cavalcanti's *Rime* of 1931. We remember Yeats recording his discussions with Pound about Cavalcanti in *A Packet for Ezra Pound* (1929), a Yeats who had already made Dante his own particular forerunner; at the same time, Eliot was beginning to find in Dante his primary source of inspiration, as reflected by the *Dante* essay of 1929 and *Ash-Wednesday* of 1930. It is little to wonder at if Pound, with his self-confessed 'nomadic predisposition' (*Guide to Kulchur*, p. 243), began to find the Dante-field a little overcrowded, and had returned to and expanded his earlier work on the individualist and free-thinking Cavalcanti described in his essay as a counter to the increasing 'orthodoxy' of Eliot, an orthodoxy that, moreover, insisted on an orthodox interpretation of Dante as well. Since Pound's 'discovery' of Daniel and Cavalcanti and his attempt, discussed above, to correlate their relationship with Dante with his own search for a poetic identity, the practice of finding such parallels had been taken up by Yeats and Eliot in turn, *The Waste Land*'s dedication affording the most famous example. A modern battle with mediaeval names; at any rate one cannot help feeling that Pound saw his own relationship with Eliot reflected in his statement that Cavalcanti 'shows himself much more "modern" than his young friend Dante Alighieri, *qui était diablement dans les idées reçues . . .*' ('Cavalcanti', p. 149). And it is with the young, or at any rate younger, friend Eliot that we conclude this study, which has moved from Shelley's admiration for the 'heretical' in Dante to this new emphasis that no such element exists in his work.

VII

T. S. Eliot: the return to reality

We perceive a pattern behind the pattern . . . at rare moments of inattention and detachment, drowsing in sunlight.

('John Marston')

'We look, in a poet as well as in a novelist, for what Henry James called the Figure in the Carpet.'[1] In bringing Dante forward to help us detect this Figure in Eliot's own work we are entering upon an argument that has already been much discussed from various viewpoints and sustained by Eliot's declaration in 1950 that Dante's poetry exercised 'the most persistent and deepest influence upon my own verse . . .'[2] We may begin *nel mezzo* with the *Dante* essay of 1929, an essay that can be regarded as noticeably orthodox in a sense we shall be returning to; in Eliot's own words the essay 'pretends no more than it professes: to be a simple account of my own experience . . . My only original contribution is possibly a few hints about the *Vita Nuova*, which seems to me a work of capital importance for the discipline of the emotions . . .'[3] Eliot's pages on the *Vita Nuova* are indeed the most striking and polemical part of the essay, centring as they do around the suggestion that the childhood meeting between Dante and Beatrice described in the second chapter of the 'libello' represented for Dante a 'type of *sexual* experience' (my italics) in an account that may therefore be described as 'a very sound psychological treatise on something related to what is now called "sublimation"'.[4] In an essay of two years earlier Eliot had described the *Vita Nuova* as a record of Dante's 'brave attempts to fabricate something permanent and holy out of his personal animal feelings';[5] his attitude is greatly illuminated by the essay on Baudelaire of 1930, where he states, 'the recognition of the reality of Sin is a New Life . . .' (*SE*, p. 427). This last statement is the basis of his reading of the *Vita Nuova* itself: the beatitude Beatrice represents for Dante is not the straightforward rejoicing in God's handiwork which others experience – 'benedetto sia lo Segnore, che sì mirabilemente sae adoperare!' ('blessed be the Lord, who can work so miraculously!') (xxvi.2) – but a much more strenuous achievement based on the disciplining of his 'animal' responses to her: in the words of Dante's 'spirito naturale', 'Heu miser, quia frequenter impeditus ero deinceps!' ('Alas, wretch, how I shall be frequently obstructed from now on!') (ii.6). What Beatrice's appearance first awoke in Dante was then, to put it simply, not Virtue but Vice, and in order to get to the former he had to go by the way of the latter. It is little wonder, with this emphasis, that Dante should point out that his *donna* 'fu chiamata da molti Beatrice li quali non sapeano che si chiamare' ('was called Beatrice by many who did not know why she was thus named') (ii.1). This uncompromising interpretation of the *Vita Nuova*'s 'agony/Of death and birth', to use a phrase from *East Coker*,[6] relies above all on Eliot's sensitivity to the 'libello''s opening chapters, with Dante's dream in the third embodying for him a 'moment which is unique, of shock and surprise, even of terror (*Ego Dominus Tuus*)' (*Dante*, p. 250), that 'awful daring of a moment's surrender' (*The Waste Land*, l. 403) which the protagonists of his poems from *Prufrock* onwards are continually approaching and evading in their uncertain recognitions of its significance. It seems likely that Yeats's speculations on Dante, as they exist in their more assimilable form in the poem 'Ego Dominus Tuus', had some influence on Eliot, reminding him as they did of the tradition that Dante's animal instincts were a force to be reckoned with; but the utter seriousness with which Eliot takes the *Vita Nuova* and his sense of the agony of the battle between the new life and the old have no precedent in the pages of this study.

On the contrary, Eliot's interpretation is a deliberate corrective to a series of nineteenth-century formulations of the place occupied by Beatrice in Dante's life and work. The 'anti-Rossettian' stance is of course explicit: '. . . Rossetti's *Blessed Damozel*, first by my rapture and next by my revolt, held up my appreciation of Beatrice by many years' (*Dante*, p. 262), and Eliot's own definition of the *Vita Nuova*'s 'anti-romantic' philosophy – 'not to expect more from *life* than it can give or more from *human* beings than they can give; to look to *death* for what life cannot give' (p. 275) – has already been contrasted with the extraordinary expectations in Shelley's *Epipsychidion*. Eliot noted how 'in much romantic poetry the sadness is due to the exploitation of the fact that no human relations are adequate to human desires, but also to the disbelief in any further object for human desires than that which, being human, fails to satisfy them' ('Baudelaire', *SE*, p. 428), an observation that seems particularly applicable to Rossetti's work. Eliot's ideas are no less a reaction, however, to the other Victorian conception of Beatrice examined in Chapter IV, to that ideal of female domesticity championed by Theodore Martin which Eliot dismissed in the Clark Lectures as the 'bankruptcy' of the 'Tennysonian happy marriage'.[7] Although Eliot acknowledges the help received from Santayana's *Three Philosophical Poets* (1910) in the preface to the original 1929 *Dante* (p. 13), Santayana's attitude to Dante's depiction of love in the *Vita Nuova*, which he describes as 'not normal or healthy', remains, if one may so put it, extremely 'Martinesque': 'if the love in question had been natural and manly, it would have offered more resistance to so mystical a transformation. The poet who wishes to pass from love to philosophy should accordingly be a hearty and complete lover' (pp. 129–30). Santayana's study, which looks forward to the day when what the author calls 'a natural comedy' will be written, 'as much surpassing Dante's divine comedy in sublimity and richness as it will surpass it in truth' (p. 210), smacks not a little of that 'cheerfulness, optimism, and hopefulness' which, as Eliot continues, 'stood for a great deal of what one hated in the nineteenth century' (*Dante*, p. 262), though here Eliot seems to have had particularly in mind statements like Tennyson's own assessment of *In Memoriam*: 'It begins with a funeral and ends with a marriage – begins with death and ends in promise of a new life – a sort of *Divine Comedy*, cheerful at the close' (quoted above, p. 135). This equation of Dante's work with the Victorian parlour and nursery was a great obstacle to Eliot's enjoyment of it: 'It took me many years to recognize that the states of improvement and beatitude which Dante describes are still further from what the modern world can conceive as cheerfulness, than are his states of damnation' (*Dante*, p. 262).

In Eliot's mind the *Vita Nuova* properly embodies what he calls 'the Catholic philosophy of disillusion' (*Dante*, p. 275). Most of what he regarded as poetically valuable in the nineteenth century came to him from France rather than from England, and especially, during the 1920s and after, from Baudelaire, whose work is undoubtedly responsible for some interference in Eliot's reception of Dante. He discovered more explicitly in Baudelaire's work the recognition that 'the reality of Sin is a New Life', and the possibility of damnation is so immense a relief in a world of electoral reform, plebiscites, sex reform and dress reform, that damnation itself is an immediate form of salvation – of salvation from the ennui of modern life, because it at last gives some significance to living.

('Baudelaire', p. 427)

He also discovered from the same source that to conceive of 'the sexual act as evil is more dignified, less boring, than as the natural, "life-giving", cheery automatism of the modern world' (p. 429). In order to help the reader to recognise the presence of this sense of evil in the *Vita Nuova*, Eliot insists it be read after the *Commedia*, where the good and evil varieties of *amor* are fully displayed: we are thus able to spot what Eliot claims is inherent in the 'libello' through Dante's later amplification of it, and thus resist its 'Pre-Raphaelite quaintness' (*Dante*, p. 276). Dante's awakening to sin antedates by many years, then, his foundering in the *selva oscura*, which in part represents a type of sin – Dante's intellectual and political aberrations – which engrossed Eliot less, so to speak, than the evil of the sexual act.

Eliot would have contested Santayana's suggestion that Dante was not a 'complete' lover, though he understood the adjective very differently. The *Commedia* and *Vita Nuova* represented for him the consummate adjustment 'of the natural to the spiritual, of the bestial to the human and the human to the supernatural' ('Baudelaire', p. 428). Dante was an expert of *amor* in all its forms and of the adjustment between these forms, as confirmed most obviously by the presence of Paolo and Francesca in Hell. What Eliot missed in Virgil, for example, was not only the idea of Love as 'a principle of order in the human soul' and as moving the sun and the stars, but also the 'intensity of physical passion' which made Virgil more 'tepid than some other Latin poets'.[8] Eliot also suggests that in Dante's work we have the contrast between 'higher and lower carnal love' (*Dante*, p. 275), interpreting it would seem Dante's words on seeing Beatrice in the *paradiso terrestre*: 'conosco i segni de l'antica fiamma' ('I know the marks of the ancient flame') (*Purg.* XXX.48), as signifying a recrudescence of emotions that include the sexual: 'in the dialogue that follows we see the passionate conflict of the old feelings with the new; the effort and triumph of a new renunciation, greater than renunciation at the grave, because a renunciation of feelings that persist beyond the grave' (p. 263).

With the above in mind we may turn to *Ash-Wednesday*, which

Eliot described in the letter to More already referred to as 'a first attempt at a sketchy application of the philosophy of the *Vita Nuova* to modern life'. We should note that Eliot specifies the *Vita Nuova* here, even though much of *Ash-Wednesday*'s imagery derives from the *Commedia*, notably the purgatorial stair of part III and the three leopards of part II which are partly inspired by the three beasts Dante meets in *Inferno* I. In his poem Eliot closely combines references to Dante's two works, and he would see nothing inconsistent in this since the disciplining of the emotions seems to have been, at the time of the Dante essay and the writing of *Ash-Wednesday*, the most conspicuous feature of both: the Dante of the 'libello' battling to fabricate something holy out of his animal feelings is identified in the poem with Arnaut Daniel, also preparing for holiness by being purged in the flame of his lust. Eliot talks of an 'application' of the *Vita Nuova*'s philosophy; this sense of willed, rather dour travail, 'having to construct something/Upon which to rejoice', is plainly apparent, informed as it is by the complex frustrations of that sense 'of the timeless and of the temporal together',[9] which is the most obvious staple of all Eliot's poetry.

In part I Eliot formally accepts the conditions of man's exile from eternity into time, gradually investing Cavalcanti's song of secular exile (Marti, pp. 211–13) and Shakespeare's dismissal of earthly glory (sonnet 29) with a religious significance: he renounces both 'the blessèd face' and the Garden 'where trees flower, and springs flow'. We learn however that there are moments 'out of time', the moments of 'consciousness' of *Burnt Norton*, in which the *paradiso terrestre* can be re-entered, or at least inspected, as in part IV. 'Teach us to care and not to care/Teach us to sit still': this note of exhausting but inevitable tension recurs throughout the poem, a condition of the protagonist having to straddle, as best he may, these two orders of existence.

This acceptance of the exile is necessary before Eliot can embark upon the New Life in part II of the poem in which the three white leopards figure 'the recognition of the reality of Sin', which, we remember from the Baudelaire essay, is a condition of the New Life. There are, of course, no such beasts in Dante's own *Vita Nuova*, but there are, Eliot insists, Dante's 'personal animal feelings' which Beatrice awoke in Dante and which led Dante to the knowledge of good and evil; his spiritual adoration of Beatrice represents his determination to follow the former. Likewise, through sin, Eliot has achieved spiritual contact with his 'Lady' in part II of the poem. We do not need to suppose that Eliot has any particular woman in mind here, though it is probable that the episode in the hyacinth garden in the first part of *The Waste Land* and that recounted by the waiter in 'Dans le Restaurant' do refer to actual experiences from Eliot's youth akin to that he saw in the childhood meeting of the *Vita Nuova*.[10] The Lady has rather been 'constructed' as a representation of the New Life, and undoubtedly Dante's own Beatrice has contributed to her; she 'honours the Virgin in meditation' just as Beatrice held the Virgin 'in grandissima reverenzia' ('in the greatest reverence') (*VN* XXVIII.1), and Eliot adores her both 'in terra' here and, in part IV 'in Eden', following Dante's precedent.

In discussing the three beasts from *Inferno* I in the Dante essay, Eliot suggested: 'What we should consider is not so much the meaning of the images, but the reverse process, that which led a man having an idea to express it in images' (p. 242). *Ash-Wednesday* gives us some help in this consideration: to see oneself as being eaten by three white leopards instead of describing oneself with a bare epithet such as 'lecherous'; to imagine the old life being wheeled away in a 'gilded hearse' by 'jewelled unicorns', as in part IV; these devices give a sense of dignity, order and significance to the experience of sin and wastage, since it is through this experience that the New Life has been discovered which will redeem the old. The aimless copulation of Eliot's typist and clerk and Tiresias' guilty participation in the same are transferred to the realm of what Eliot calls the 'high dream' (*Dante*, p. 262). Moreover, this 'high dream' comes to one, as it were, from outside, whereas 'We take it for granted that our dreams spring from below: possibly the quality of our dreams suffers in consequence' (p. 243). Allegory's fundamental importance for Eliot was precisely the opportunity it offered for escaping from self – and especially the self that is located 'below' – into a common, external order, and thus the opportunity for appeasing the extraordinary burden of self we are presented with throughout the early poems and essays: 'only those who have personality and emotions know what it means to want to escape from these things' ('TrIT', p. 21). It is, to use an obvious phrase, the 'objective correlative' in a more extended and significant form, that which Shakespeare so badly needed as he 'attempted to express the inexpressibly horrible' ('Hamlet', *SE*, pp. 145–6). In *The Spirit of Romance* Pound had noted how 'In the allegory [the mediaeval author] learns to separate himself, not yet from complete moods, but from simple qualities and passions, and to visualize them' (1910 ed., p. 85), but Pound makes no reference to what one might call the therapeutic value of allegory which is a feature that develops in Eliot's writing and that leads to the 'separation' described in *Ash-Wednesday* II. As Harry tells Mary in *The Family Reunion*: 'There is only one way for you to understand/And that is by seeing' (p. 309), and it marks Harry's 'salvation' when he realises that what he sees is external; as he tells the Eumenides:

> you shall not think that I am afraid to see you.
> This time, you are real, this time, you are outside me,
> And just endurable.
>
> (p. 336)

In part II, then, we have the adoration of the Lady 'in time'; the part was originally entitled 'Salutation' on its first and independent appearance in 1927,[11] a reference to Beatrice's greeting ('saluto') in the *Vita Nuova* which Dante described as 'lo fine del mio amore' ('the aim of my love') (XVIII.4; the 'saluto' is the agency of Dante's 'salute', or salvation). A title Eliot originally chose for the part was 'Jausen lo Jorn' ('[I see] joyously the day')[12] from Arnaut's speech (*Purg*. XXVI.144), an Arnaut who, still held in a time-bound purgation, anticipates his entry into the *paradiso terrestre*. Part III takes us to the 'som de l'escalina' ('top of the stair') – the part's original title[13] – which Arnaut envisages and to the entry into the *paradiso*, itself presented in part IV. We are reminded in this section of Eliot's emphasis on the *Commedia* as an 'adjustment' of different aspects of *amor* to each other; the distracting flute-player in the window who would divert the protagonist from his destination strongly recalls the musician Casella of *Purgatorio* II, who delays Dante's progress up the mountain with his singing of 'Amor che ne la mente mi ragiona' ('Love which discourses to me in my mind') (ll. 112–23). Eliot would have been very much aware here of the celebration of one type of love holding Dante back from the fuller experiencing of it 'al som de l'escalina' and he may have recalled a pertinent comment by Grandgent in another book Eliot pays tribute to in the 1929 preface to *Dante* (p. 12), namely that in Bunyan the 'alluring' musician Casella would have been replaced by a character called 'Turnabout'.[14]

As it is Eliot does 'turn about' in part III: while he is spiralling

1. The Tofanelli Dante. Frontispiece to Cary's translation of the *Inferno*. Vol. 1 (1805).

2. Stothard's Dante: Frontispiece to Boyd's translation of the *Commedia*. Vol. I (1802).

3. Engraving after Kirkup's drawing of the Bargello Dante. From Lyell's *Poems of the 'Vita Nuova' and 'Convito'* (1842).

5. Dante Gabriel Rossetti, *The Salutation of Beatrice* (1859).

6. Giotto, Dante, Innocent III. Stained-glass window, Truro Cathedral, Cornwall.

7. Plaster cast of the Torrigiani 'death-mask' of Dante.

8. W. B. Yeats. Etching by Augustus John (1907). Frontispiece to *A Vision* (1937).

towards the stair-top he turns back to see an earlier unpurged self 'struggling with the devil of the stairs' at a lower level. We remember that when Dante enters the actual gate of Purgatory in canto IX the angel warns him not to look back; it is a warning not to return to the way of sin after the completion of the sacrament of confession, which the entry represents (ll. 131–32). This double movement in part III, the turning back towards an earlier self still struggling on the stair combined with the turning upwards towards redemption, is entirely symptomatic of the religious tension at the heart of the poem which centres round the bewildering ambiguities of the word 'turn'. The poem of course completes a circle: after the vision out of time in part IV we are back in the period of 'exile' in parts V and VI, though the truncated phrase from the Catholic Mass which completes part IV does, in its complete form, look forward to the ending of that exile. But the protagonist returns to the dimension of time and sin to resume all the contradictory impulses of acceptance and rejection that that dimension entails, to

> affirm before the world and deny between the rocks
> In the last desert between the last blue rocks
> The desert in the garden the garden in the desert
> Of drouth, spitting from the mouth the withered apple-seed.

It is true that in this last phrase we have a redemption from sin following the Incarnation presented in part V; but what an agony of tension in the turning to God those words 'spitting' and 'withered' convey! And, although after the note of 'rebellion' in part VI the poem ends on a simple, affirmative prayer, we go back round the circle to part I of the poem not with any composed acquiescence in the divine will but with the consciousness that the battle to achieve the New Life never lets up; that the Mass and the prayers from it which, as in the *Purgatorio*, punctuate the poem, remain the main allies in this Dantesque sequence of exercises aimed at 'the discipline of the emotions'. An inevitable, ceaseless turning then, though this takes place about the still, axial point of Christ, who is always there but always divided by the temporal barrier; the poem recognises in its circular form that 'in time' one must sacrifice the possibility of 'sitting still' prayed for in part I, a repose that is, in *Four Quartets*, the prerogative of the saint's *imitatio Christi*, or that is approached by the poem itself which formally circumscribes an area of human experience.

Meanwhile, back out of time in part IV of the poem, we have a re-enactment, of sorts, of the procession in *Purgatorio* XXIX–XXX:

> Here are the years that walk between, bearing
> Away the fiddles and the flutes, restoring
> One who moves in the time between sleep and waking, wearing
>
> White light folded, sheathed about her, folded.

The temporal barrier of the years passes in front of the protagonist's eyes like the twenty-four elders in Dante's poem (*Purg.* XXIX.82–90) who herald Beatrice; it is followed by the unicorns, the 'gilded hearse', and the Lady from part II who, now restored *sub specie aeternitatis*, has exchanged her terrene 'white gown' for a sheath of white light, just as the red dress in which Beatrice first appeared to Dante as a child (*VN* II.3) becomes the 'colour of living flame' when he sees her in the *paradiso terrestre* (*Purg.* XXX.33). 'The silent sister veiled in white and blue' of parts IV and V seems to fulfil a role analogous to that of Matelda in Dante's poem, in introducing the protagonist to this vision and in commentating, albeit silently, upon it; in her station 'between the slender/Yew trees' in part V and in her function there of praying for those 'torn on the horn between season and season, time and time' she surely allegorises the Church.

Ash-Wednesday is Dante very much stripped to the bone; a restrained, still rather dry intuition of the earthly paradise always weighed upon by the exile into time the protagonist labours under elsewhere. Thus the details of the 'higher dream' we are given in part IV are not very high at all compared with that surfeit of beauty and happiness that is inaugurated by the appearance of Matelda in Dante's poem. The veiled sister with her colours of violet, white and blue is an ascetic, watercolour copy of Dante's illumination. This introduces us to a crucial difference in the religious and political outlook of the two men. In the last two cantos of the *Purgatorio* Beatrice shows Dante an allegorical pageant of the history of the Church; the tale is one of increasing corruption, but the time is at hand in which an emperor will arrive to set this to rights by resuming all secular rule himself, including that which the Church has usurped (*Purg.* XXXIII. 37–45). Dante believed that the realm of the temporal was not the unmitigated, 'ridiculous' misfortune Eliot presents throughout his poetry but was in part redeemable through

Imperial rule; the earthly paradise is not outside time but is a terrestrial ideal, a figure of a felicity some men might achieve by being free to exercise the moral and intellectual virtues unimpededly under the Imperial peace. In short, Dante believed in a 'beatitudinem . . . huius vitae' ('blessing . . . of this life') (*Mon.* III.XV.7), and Matelda represents man having achieved it. In writing *Ash-Wednesday* it is not surprising then that Eliot should have kept before his eye the *Vita Nuova* as his model, not in its images but in its 'philosophy of disillusion' in which the battle between sin and restoration is devoid of ideas of secular restoration, an infinitely more condensed and solitary battle than that found in the social and political dimension of the *Purgatorio*. Rather like Rossetti, Eliot tends here to be squeezing the *Commedia* into the miniature frame provided by the *Vita Nuova*, though for completely different reasons. *Ash-Wednesday* centres entirely on its protagonist's sense of personal sin and unworthiness, and I shall return shortly to Eliot's neglect of Dante's public and political concerns.

'Poetry is not a turning loose of emotion, but an escape from emotion; it is not the expression of personality, but an escape from personality', Eliot wrote in 'Tradition and the Individual Talent' (p. 21), and we have seen how allegory provided him with an escape-route, though it was no longer, as in the middle ages, a *tradition* into which his individual talent was escaping; the worse luck for us, who have to contend with the unfamiliarity of *Ash-Wednesday*. In the same essay we find another famous dictum: 'the more perfect the artist, the more completely separate in him will be the man who suffers and the mind which creates . . .' (p. 18), and Dante again expressed the division perfectly, for, as Eliot phrased it in the Clark Lectures, 'The experience which forms the material of the *Vita Nuova* is the material of adolescence; but it is handled by a mature man with a philosophy which assigned a place to such experience' (III, 22). This division is again present in the *Commedia* of course, as Eliot suggests when he states that 'Canto XV of the *Inferno* (Brunetto Latini) is a working up of the emotion evident in the situation' ('TrIT', p. 18), a formulation that indicates his attention to the *personaggio–poeta* distinction. Indeed, Eliot's sensitivity to the *Commedia* as a hierarchical ordering of experiences and emotions undergone is crucial for my interpretation of his own work.

Eliot's categorisation of the sexual act as 'evil' in the Baudelaire essay shows his desire to recognise that spiritual forces were still operating in the modern world, a marked concern of his writing during the late twenties and thirties. His search for this kind of significance had been curiously anticipated a few years earlier by Yeats's attempts to recover a 'vision of evil', as we saw in Chapter V, but for Eliot, of course, 'Mr Yeats's "supernatural world" was the wrong supernatural world . . . not a world of real Good and Evil' (*After Strange Gods*, p. 46). In this same book we also saw him criticising Pound's Hell-Cantos:

> I find one considerable objection to a Hell of this sort: that a Hell altogether without dignity implies a Heaven without dignity also. If you do not distinguish between individual responsibility and circumstances in Hell, between essential Evil and social accidents, then the Heaven (if any) implied will be equally trivial and accidental. (p. 43)

Eliot seems to have found the presence of 'a circle of lady golfers' in Pound's Hell (Canto XV, p. 64) one example of its general triviality, to judge from the 'non ragionam di lor' ('let us not talk of them') (*Inf.* III.51) tone of these lines from the third Chorus from *The Rock*:

> The nettle shall flourish on the gravel court,
> And the wind shall say: 'Here were decent godless people:
> Their only monument the asphalt road
> And a thousand lost golf balls.'
>
> (*CP*, p. 155)

This alerts us to a certain narrowness in Eliot's approach to the *Inferno*, a certain adulation of Dante's damned which, in the first essay on Dante, is directed in a typical polemic against the 'limbo-dwellers' of his own day: 'in Dante's Hell souls are not deadened, as they mostly are in life; they are actually in the greatest torment of which each is capable'.[15] Fourteen years later, in *After Strange Gods*, a book in which the author is 'reproaching a world in which blasphemy is impossible' (p. 52), we are still being told, in explanation of this, that 'most people are only very little alive; and to awaken them to the spiritual is a very great responsibility: it is only when they are so awakened that they are capable of real Good, but that at the same time they become first capable of Evil' (p. 60). As opposed to 'Questi sciaurati, che mai non fur vivi' ('These wretches, who were never alive'), in Dante's phrase (*Inf.* III.64), Eliot could point to only a very few moderns who were truly 'awake', notably Baudelaire:

The worst that can be said of most of our malefactors, from statesmen to thieves, is that they are not men enough to be damned. Baudelaire was man enough for damnation . . . ('Baudelaire', p. 429)

It will be apparent then why certain crucial features of Dante's *Inferno* are never brought out in Eliot's discussions of it: for example, the undignified brawl between maestro Adamo and Sinon in canto XXX which Eliot would have found, if one may so put it, rather too Poundian. There can be no doubt that Adamo is, in Eliot's sense of the word, very much 'alive'; but one is not sure Eliot would have really found him 'man enough for damnation', for it is quite clear that Adamo has ended up in Hell not through a deliberate and 'awakened' choice between 'real' Good and Evil, but through an ignorant and instinctive reliance on the belief that forging money is easier than earning it. We can be fairly sure that a thirteenth-century 'malefactor' was pretty much the same as a twentieth-century one. Eliot's admiration is, however, all for characters like Ulysses who 'preserve any degree of beauty or grandeur that ever rightly pertained to them [which] intensifies and also justifies their damnation' ('Dante', p. 167). But not all the inhabitants of Dante's Hell are Ulysses or Farinata, or even Brunetto Latini, whose 'excellence in damnation' – 'so admirable a soul, and so perverse' – is rather curiously emphasised by Eliot (*Ibidem*, p. 166). Eliot's own description of Manichaeanism as 'the desire for a devil to worship' comes to mind here;[16] he certainly expressed a desire for damned to admire, and also joins his voice to that recurring protest about the inadequacy of Dante's Devil – we have seen previous complaints from Coleridge and Yeats – which in his case results in the drastic suggestion that we should 'omit the last canto' on our first reading of the *Inferno* (*Dante*, p. 251). 'It is true to say that the glory of man is his capacity for salvation; it is also true to say that his glory is his capacity for damnation', Eliot noted in the Baudelaire essay (p. 429), making, it seems, a rather strange application of Dante's lines on the 'sciaurati' of *Inferno* III who are not permitted to enter Hell proper lest 'alcuna gloria i rei avrebber d'elli' ('the damned should get any glory out of them') (l. 42).

Eliot's objection to *Inferno* XXXIV centres round its Devil's imperfect representation of what he calls the 'Essence' or 'Spirit' of evil (*Dante*, p. 251), and we have seen his concern in *After Strange Gods* to 'distinguish between individual responsibility and circumstances in Hell, between essential Evil and social accidents'. 'Essential' evil is then the individual's deliberate rejection of Good, whereas to Eliot an evil that is merely the result of circumstances, as, let us say, Adamo's unlucky association with the Conti Guidi (*Inf.* XXX.76–90), is much more trivial. But Eliot's glamorous picture of evil as a deliberate and informed choice takes no account of Dante's emphasis throughout the *Commedia* – and this is surely why the work is so moving – that damnation is all too easily within the reach of ordinary men and women who have very little conception of what a proper choice between good and evil consists of. In a properly governed society, with the Church attending to its educational role and the Empire imposing a set of laws directing man's attention to the common good, it is difficult to imagine the thought of 'essential Evil' causing Dante too much anxiety, since evil – at least as embodied in the *Inferno* – is not as it was for Eliot an ineradicable aftermath of Original Sin but largely a remediable malfunctioning of social institutions. It is thus appropriate that the Devil should not be an embodiment of that independent malevolent force Eliot seems so sensitive to, but rather an inert effigy of what would be powerless did not ordinary human stupidity and ignorance assist it. As Kenelm Foster puts it:

> the sin [Dante] encounters [in the *Inferno*] is . . . largely sin against the light of reason alone, apart from any 'higher' considerations. It is wrongdoing very much on the human level and in the give and take of ordinary social intercourse. A strong social emphasis marks the *Inferno* . . . the measure of right and wrong that governs, immediately, the greater part of it is a rational, not a specifically Christian, measure; it is drawn from moral philosophy (especially Aristotle's) rather than from the Gospels.[17]

This social emphasis governs Pound's concentration on the poem as we saw, to the exclusion of its religious concerns; and it seems Eliot's approach goes too far in the opposite direction. The difference between Eliot and Dante with regard to the belief in man as a 'compagnevole animale' is perhaps best illustrated in Eliot's poem 'Animula' (1929), which takes its opening line '"Issues from the hand of God, the simple soul"' from line 85 of Marco Lombardo's speech in *Purgatorio* XVI, a speech which contends that bad guidance, 'la mala condotta', 'è la cagion che 'l mondo ha fatto reo' ('is the reason why the world has become wicked'), and which outlines the need to remedy this by keeping the civil and ecclesiastical jurisdictions separate (ll. 103–14). Eliot's poem, however, proposes no remedies for what he calls 'The pain of living'; human existence has no potential to organise itself satisfactorily 'in time' which is looked upon, as in *Four Quartets* and *Ash-Wednesday*, as a profoundly unsuitable and distorting medium into which the soul is exiled on issuing 'from the hand of God'; thus the soul '[lives] first in the silence after the viaticum' (*CP*, pp. 107–8). It is extremely difficult to imagine Dante having any sympathy with this belief that life is death and that only in death we achieve life; and this must lead us to make reservations about Frank Kermode's expression of a common 'faith in the Empire' between the two poets, since Eliot's 'mystique of Empire' neither aspires to nor even envisages a *paradiso terrestre*.[18] This is not to deny that Eliot's 'Imperialism' owes a good deal to Dante, as we shall see; but he seems to have been misled by the form of Dante's vision into a belief in the Empire as wholly visionary. He elected, in A. D. Moody's words, 'to be the citizen of no earthly city: to be a voluntary alien in human society, and to be at home only in the City of God'. According to the same author, 'That made his criticism of *all* existing political systems essentially negative' (p. 324).

That also means that there is no response in his writings to the *Commedia*'s politics; in his identification of his own sense of sin with Arnaut Daniel's or with Dante's in the *Vita Nuova*, or in his categorisation of modern society as one vast limbo, he is totally concerned with the other-worldly dimension in Dante's writing. His belief that 'the great majority of people' were living in a spiritual 'no man's land'[19] is perhaps first obvious in the poem 'Gerontion' and expressed most starkly in *The Hollow Men* (1925). These latter give corporate voice to the thesis already referred to that human existence is a living death and that only after death will reality begin. It is not clear how early Eliot was committed to such a view; Lyndall Gordon suggests that he 'began to measure his life by the divine goal as far back as his student days, in 1910 and 1911',[20] and certainly by 1917 in the dialogue 'Eeldrop and Appleplex' he is positing that juxtaposition of the two orders of existence which remains a favourite device in his poetry:

> With the decline of orthodox theology and its admirable theory of the soul, the unique importance of events has vanished . . . a man murders his mistress. The important fact is that for the man the act is eternal . . . For the 'enlightened public' the case is merely evidence for the Drink question or Unemployment, or some other category of things to be reformed. But the

mediaeval world, insisting on the eternity of punishment, expressed something nearer the truth.[21]

As in *The Hollow Men*, the important thing is not man's appearance *sub specie temporis*; life itself is merely 'death's dream kingdom' in the poem (part II), simply a reflex of 'death's other Kingdom' which is God's, as in the prayer in part V. Whereas Dante's souls who pass through limbo on their way to damnation 'pronti sono a trapassar lo rio' ('are eager to cross the river') (*Inf.* III.124) in order to take their place in a divine scheme which alone gives them significance, the hollow men

> grope together
> And avoid speech
> Gathered on this beach of the tumid river
>
> Sightless, unless
> The eyes reappear
> As the perpetual star
> Multifoliate rose
> Of death's twilight kingdom
> The hope only
> Of empty men.
>
> (*CP*, p. 85)

It is not really important whether the eyes are, so to speak, those of the Beatrice described in *Inferno* II – 'Lucevan li occhi suoi più che la stella' ('Her eyes shone more brightly than the stars') (l. 55) – who induced Virgil to leave his fellow 'sospesi' and commence Dante's salvation, or the 'occhi di bragia' ('eyes like glowing coals') of Charon (*Inf.* III.109) who ferries souls into Hell proper, since both pairs of eyes are passports to reality, whether of salvation or damnation. As Eliot expressed it in the Baudelaire essay, 'so far as we do evil or good, we are human; and it is better, in a paradoxical way, to do evil than to do nothing: at least, we exist' (p. 429). And yet, as we have seen, Eliot's conception of what it is to do evil or good seems to be more 'elevated' than Dante's, whose treasured conception of the State made him sensitive to civil, no less than to religious, malpractices, and who therefore awards damnation to those who, in Eliot's eyes, do not seem to earn it. Hence Eliot's projection of a limbo-state that is more pervasive and therefore more dreadful than Dante's, that 'ennui of modern life' from which damnation itself can be 'an immediate form of salvation', and which is glimpsed as continuing after death in *Murder in the Cathedral*:

> behind the face of Death the Judgement
> And behind the Judgement the Void, more horrid than active shapes of hell;
> Emptiness, absence, separation from God;
> The horror of the effortless journey, to the empty land
> Which is no land, only emptiness, absence, the Void,
> Where those who were men can no longer turn the mind
> To distraction, delusion, escape into dream, pretence,
> Where the soul is no longer deceived, for there are no objects, no tones,
> No colours, no forms to distract, to divert the soul
> From seeing itself, foully united forever, nothing with nothing . . .
>
> (*CP*, p. 272)

The hollow men, as remarked, are present from Eliot's earliest verse, in 'Gerontion' – 'I was neither at the hot gates/Nor fought in the warm rain' – and of course in 'The Love Song of J. Alfred Prufrock'. The difference between these early protagonists and those of the 1925 poem lies in Eliot's gradual movement towards stripping them of any glamour they might possess; the stark economy of *The Hollow Men* can leave us with no doubts about the soul having finally arrived at 'seeing itself, foully united forever, nothing with nothing', whereas in the early poems, as Hugh Kenner has said, words themselves, 'numinous and substantial, strain to make human speakers sound more significant than they are'.[22] *The Waste Land* is an important intermediary stage here, for it first gives us a definite indication of the limbo-setting, 'I had not thought death had undone so many', yet is still inhabited by exotic characters like Madame Sosostris and decked with language of an extraordinary resonance, as in the opening description in part II. Similarly, devices remain which serve to add a measure of aggrandisement to the scenes of modern ennui, such as Tiresias' commentary which places sexual sterility in, so to speak, a classical perspective. In *The Hollow Men* the narrator is no longer screening his own involvement in the modern limbo by resorting to such a *persona*: he is finally anatomising his own sterility by keeping a tight rein on the 'distraction' of language. The poem might be regarded as the beginning of Eliot's New Life, in its association, which we shall return to, of what might be called a 'purged' language with the possibility of Purgation proper.

In his first essay on Dante, Eliot is already concerned to point out that sense of a correlation of parts in the *Commedia* which remained for him one of the work's most significant achievements:

no emotion is contemplated by Dante purely in and for itself. The emotion of the person, or the emotion with which our attitude appropriately invests the person, is never lost or diminished, is always preserved entire, but is modified by the position assigned to the person in the eternal scheme, is coloured by the atmosphere of that person's residence in one of the three worlds. (p. 167)

'Not all succeed as did Dante in expressing the complete scale from negative to positive. The negative is the more importunate', he adds (p. 169). It is difficult to assess how early Eliot was conscious of the movement along a similar scale in his own work; certainly, as I have suggested, *The Hollow Men* would seem to invite us to make some modifications to our response to the potent appeal of, for example, J. Alfred Prufrock. The epigraph from Dante the *Prufrock* volume now carries – not in the original 1917 edition but added on the re-appearance of the *Prufrock* poems in *Ara Vus* [*sic*] *Prec* (1920) – would seem to confirm that Eliot saw the poems as an expression of the 'importunate negative':

Or puoi la quantitate
comprender de l'amor ch'a te mi scalda,
quand'io dismento nostra vanitate,
trattando l'ombre come cosa salda.

(Now you can understand the extent of the love which burns in me for you, when I forget our emptiness and treat shadows like solid things.)
(*Purg.* XXI.133–6)

Eliot addressed Statius' words to Virgil to his friend Verdenal, killed in the first world war, and he imposes a new meaning on the words by expressing the familiar paradox that life is death and human beings mere shadows, not solid things. We thus come to Prufrock having been alerted, as it were, to his provisionality: the extraordinary imaginative appeal of this particular 'episode' in the scale corresponds somewhat to the positioning of Paolo and Francesca in the *Commedia*, for, by the time we have reached *The Hollow Men* and arrived at the deepest and most uncompromising stage of Eliot's journey through limbo, we are ready, perhaps, to see

Prufrock in a new light and re-examine our own response to him.

There is, however, an indication of the movement of Eliot's career in the poem itself: I refer to the poem's epigraph, the six lines from Guido da Montefeltro's speech to Dante in *Inferno* XXVII (61–6). I take the lines as suggesting not so much an identification between Prufrock and Guido but as indicating a way out of Prufrock's '*fin-de-siècle* inferno', to use Kenner's phrase (see his superb description of this in *The Invisible Poet*, pp. 9–11), by 'descending lower' into the *Inferno* itself; the epigraph reminds us that an order of spiritual reality exists into which the escape from limbo can be made. The epigraph represents, then, a typical Eliotic juxtaposition of Dante's 'real world' with Eliot's own apprehension of the *vanitas* of life itself. 'Dante . . . does not analyse the emotion so much as he exhibits its relation to other emotions', Eliot reminds us in *The Sacred Wood* (p. 168), and we are certainly better able to understand Eliot's attitude to Prufrock's emotion by investigating the emotion in the episode in Dante Eliot has chosen to relate to it. In *After Strange Gods* Eliot suggested that

> with the disappearance of the idea of intense moral struggle, the human beings presented to us both in poetry and in prose fiction to-day . . . tend to become less and less real. It is in fact in moments of moral and spiritual struggle depending upon spiritual sanctions . . . that men and women become nearest to being real. (p. 42)

One is certainly reminded here of that struggle reported by Guido da Montefeltro between his duty to the Pope and to his Franciscan vows (*Inf.* XXVII.94–111), and one becomes no less aware that the environment Prufrock operates in affords no significance whatsoever to any 'decisions' he might make; the result is the protagonist's consciousness of the terrible futility of deciding:

> Time for you and time for me,
> And time yet for a hundred indecisions,
> And for a hundred visions and revisions,
> Before the taking of a toast and tea.
> (*CP*, p. 14)

As opposed to the unreality of Prufrock's world, the apprehension of an order that can give significance to human decisions is then voiced in the epigraph. Once this is apprehended,

> The awful daring of a moment's surrender
> Which an age of prudence can never retract

becomes a reality; 'By this, and this only, we have existed/Which is not to be found in our obituaries' (*The Waste Land*, part v), and it is quite possible that Eliot had Guido in mind again here, whose 'surrender' to an existence in Hell was of course not recorded in all his obituaries after his supposedly 'model' conversion to the Franciscan order in 1296.[23] The use of the epigraph in 'Prufrock' to point a contrast with the poem's protagonist is repeated in the use of Conrad's 'Mistah Kurtz – he dead' as epigraph to *The Hollow Men*. Kurtz of course comes to be regarded in Conrad's story as precisely *not* one of the hollow men: Marlow reports that his cry of 'The horror!' 'was an affirmation, a moral victory paid for by innumerable defeats, by abominable terrors, by abominable satisfactions. But it was a victory!' And when Marlow returns to civilisation he finds himself 'back in the sepulchral city resenting the sight of people hurrying through the streets to filch a little money from each other, to devour their infamous cookery, to gulp their unwholesome beer, to dream their insignificant and silly dreams'.[24] It is clear, then, that Eliot's repudiation of Pound's Hell derives from his need to believe in a damnation that is not a continuation of human triviality but a way out from it.

The proper definition of reality and of 'individuality' might be described as the trajectory pursued by Eliot's career. From Grandgent especially, Eliot seems to have derived the paradox that the modern era's stress on 'self-development, self-realization, self-assertion' was in fact a poor makeshift for the 'admirable theory of the soul' that, in the middle ages, guaranteed each individual's importance; as Grandgent wryly put it:

> Now that we no longer (in theory) regard the earth as the centre of the universe, we are apt (also in theory) to doubt the all-importance of man. We dream of other planets inhabited by other beings; of countless other suns . . . No such fancies disturbed the mediaeval mind. Man alone was the centre. (*Dante*, pp. 59–60, 196–7)

Individuality was, for Eliot, an acceptance of this centrality; of the undergoing of the 'agony/Of death and birth' which a relationship with God entails and of the consequent absorption into an order greater than self in which alone the self has its reality:

> O world! forget your glories and your quarrels,
> Forget your groups and your misplaced ambitions,
> We speak to you as individual men;

As individuals alone with GOD.
Alone with GOD, you first learn brotherhood with men.[25]

This absorption had long been the staple of Eliot's literary theories: 'No poet, no artist of any art, has his complete meaning alone. His significance, his appreciation is the appreciation of his relation to the dead poets and artists. You cannot value him alone . . .' ('TrIT', p. 15), a statement that recalls his insistence that in the *Commedia* 'no emotion is contemplated . . . purely in and for itself'. The search in both cases is for an order that defines individuals by bringing them into a relation with each other. The modern tendency to reject such an order in favour of unmitigated self-expression is diagnosed particularly in Eliot's writings of the 1920s, and comes increasingly under fire in his doubts about the writer whom he sets up as the originator of this cult of 'personality', John Donne. Looking back on the beginning of his career, Eliot accepted an opposition between Dante and Donne: 'In my youth, I think that Dante's astonishing economy and directness of language . . . provided for me a wholesome corrective to the extravagances of the Elizabethan, Jacobean and Caroline authors in whom I also delighted' ('To Criticize the Critic', p. 23), but his common delight in the two writers in the face of what he regarded as a not-very-helpful Victorian poetic tradition seems to have delayed, to begin with, his perception of this opposition. Thus, in his essay on 'The Metaphysical Poets' (1921), he notes that Donne and his contemporaries were 'simple, artificial, difficult, or fantastic . . . no less nor more than Dante, Guido Cavalcanti, Guinicelli, or Cino' (*SE*, pp. 287–8). As he worked towards the economy of *The Hollow Men*, the opposition began to be formulated, and was undoubtedly confirmed by his reading of Mario Praz's *Secentismo e Marinismo in Inghilterra* (Florence: 'La Voce', 1925), a book referred to in the Clark Lectures of 1926, which are Eliot's first serious examination of the Dante–Donne question. Praz had noted the absence of 'un sistema [o] un pensiero centrale' ('a systematic or unifying philosophy') in Donne's poetry: 'non di convincimenti metafisici si tratta, ma di divertimenti metafisici' ('we are not dealing with metaphysical convictions but metaphysical diversions'), and had suggested that

la differenza fra il Donne e Dante è questa: che mentre Dante intende fare sul serio poesia didattica e discorsiva, risolvendo dubbi, refutando ipotesi, allegando ragioni, il Donne introduce tutta quella disquisizione in una lirica . . . è attore e spettatore insieme, la ragione non esclude in lui la passione, ma ne è come il lambicco . . .

(the difference between Donne and Dante is this: that while Dante intends to produce a serious didactic and discursive poetry, clearing up doubts, refuting hypotheses, adducing arguments, Donne incorporates all this learning into a lyric . . . he is at once actor and spectator, reason does not exclude passion in him but is a kind of chemical retort for it . . .)

(pp. 105–6)

Eliot noted in the Clark Lectures that

with Donne . . . the peculiarity is the absence of order, the fraction of *thought* into innumerable *thoughts*. Donne is a poet, a true poet, perhaps even a very great poet, of chaos . . . the only thing that holds his poems, or any one poem, together, is what we call unsatisfactorily the personality of Donne. In this, he is a modern poet. (v, 17)

With Dante, however,

as I have said again and again, you get a system of thought and feeling; every part of the system felt and thought in its place, and the whole system felt and thought; and you cannot say that it is primarily 'intellectual' or primarily 'emotional', for the thought and the emotion are reverse sides of the same thing. In Donne you get a sequence of thoughts which are felt . . .

(vi, 22)

In his collection *For Lancelot Andrewes* (1928), with its significant subtitle *Essays on Style and Order*, Eliot spends a large part of the opening essay on Andrewes exposing Donne's fascination; his concern to 'exorcise' Donne testifies to his having experienced such a fascination powerfully:

[Donne] is dangerous only for those who find in his sermons an indulgence of their sensibility, or for those who, fascinated by 'personality' in the romantic sense of the word – for those who find in 'personality' an ultimate value – forget that in the spiritual hierarchy there are places higher than that of Donne.[26]

The modernity and appeal of Donne's work lies then in its sense of an individual having escaped from an order whose fragments yet remain in the work as a means to self-expression; what Eliot elsewhere calls 'a puzzled and humorous shuffling of the pieces', an absence of organisation that is 'perhaps one reason why Donne has appealed so powerfully to the recent time', with its 'more conscious awareness of the apparent irrelevance and unrelatedness of things'.[27]

The Donne who 'picked up, like a magpie, various shining fragments of ideas as they struck his eye, and stuck them about here and there in his verse' ('SSS', pp. 138–9) might be regarded as Eliot's 'duca e segnore' in *The Waste Land*; but like Dante's Virgil he can take his pupil only so far, and in the second half of the twenties Eliot rather dramatically takes leave of him.

The consequence is an increased commitment to Dante and a more profound exploration of the qualities of Dante's poetry, a new sense of the connexion between 'style' and 'order'. There are the famous pages from the *Dante* essay defending the *Vita Nuova* against the charge of being a modern 'confession' –

> . . . Dante, I believe, had experiences which seemed to him of some importance; not of importance because they had happened to him and because he, Dante Alighieri, was an important person who kept press-cutting bureaux busy, but important in themselves; and therefore they seemed to him to have some philosophical and impersonal value (pp. 272–3)

– and there is the emphasis, which will dominate Eliot's thinking about the *Commedia* from this point on, on Dante's language as 'the perfection of a common language' (p. 252). Dante's 'simplicity' is explained in the essay as the result of his 'economy of words' and 'austerity in the use of metaphor, simile, verbal beauty, and elegance' (p. 252); it derives from the closeness of the Italian in which he wrote to mediaeval Latin which, unlike modern languages which '*tend* to separate abstract thought', 'tended to concentrate on what men of various races and lands could think together' (p. 239). This 'universality' is the reason why 'more can be learned about how to write poetry from Dante than from any English poet . . . Most great English poets are *inimitable* in a way in which Dante was not' (p. 252).

This insistence on Dante's preference of a common to an individual language, undoubtedly stimulated by Dante's search for the *volgare illustre* in the *De Vulgari Eloquentia*, but applicable to the very different 'Florentine speech' used in the *Commedia* because 'the localization ("Florentine" speech) seems if anything to emphasize the universality, because it cuts across the modern division of nationality' (p. 239), is conspicuously absent from the earlier Dante essay in *The Sacred Wood*. But, indeed, some of Eliot's earlier critical pronouncements represent a complete abnegation of the kinds of significance Dante will come to have for him: as opposed to the need to take one's language and imagery from 'outside', from the traditions of allegory and the common language, we are told in the essay on the Metaphysical Poets that 'to "look into our hearts and write" . . . is not looking deep enough; Racine or Donne looked into a good deal more than the heart. One must look into the cerebral cortex, the nervous system, and the digestive tracts' (*SE*, p. 290). Eliot's picture of himself 'dissembled' into a heap of bones and organs at the beginning of *Ash-Wednesday* II represents a forgetfulness of self as he concentrates on the Lady, and an acknowledgement that one has to look deeper still, not simply into the cerebral cortex (and the rest) but through and beyond it. Similarly, the statement in this same essay that 'poets in our civilisation . . . must be difficult . . . more and more comprehensive, more allusive, more indirect, in order to force, to dislocate if necessary, language into [their] meaning' (p. 289) is something Eliot violently rejects later, most obviously in the first Milton essay (1936), where Milton's highly individualistic style, its tortuousness, artificiality, and the 'dislocation' between 'inner meaning' and 'surface', 'may still be considered as having done damage to the English language from which it has not wholly recovered' (*OPAP*, p. 145). We shall return shortly to Eliot's 'classicism' and its concomitant theory of style, but since this will take us to the *Four Quartets* it may be best to make a few final considerations here about Eliot's writing in the 1920s.

It will be obvious that the excerpts from the Clark Lectures quoted above indicate a serious re-thinking of the celebrated 'dissociation of sensibility' question discussed in the Metaphysical Poets essay: 'Tennyson and Browning are poets, and they think; but they do not feel their thought as immediately as the odour of a rose. A thought to Donne was an experience; it modified his sensibility' (p. 287). What began to worry Eliot increasingly was, as we have seen, the quality of the thought available to Donne, the fact that the system Dante had had behind him now existed only in fragments, and that while Donne enjoyed the 'odour' of these fragments he had no interest in attempting to re-assemble them:

Dante, for example, held, I believe, a more or less consistent theory of love which informs all of his poetry. But the conviction has more and more grown on me in reading Donne that he was interested in philosophy, but very little in the discovery of truth through philosophy . . . it is feeling transformed by thought, and thought transformed by feeling, that interests Donne, not the question whether the thought forms a consistent theory.[28]

The 'association' of sensibility apparent in Donne comes then to take on only a relative value, whereas Dante's work, which 'you cannot say . . . is primarily "intellectual" or primarily "emotional", for the thought and the emotion are reverse sides of the same thing' (above, p. 230), exhibits a much more authentic unity. Donne is labelled 'a modern poet' in the Clark Lectures and hence the gap between him and Dante is seen as wider than that between him and ourselves. It is only a philosophy that exists in fragments which can be manipulated into an expression of 'personality' in the Donne manner: for the thought and the emotion to be 'reverse sides of the same thing' the thought needs to be sufficiently vigorous to resist the personality's encroachment.

In Dante's time, of course, this was the case:

thought was orderly and strong and beautiful, and . . . was concentrated in one man of the greatest genius . . . the thought behind [Dante's poetry] is the thought of a man as great and lovely as Dante himself: St Thomas. ('SSS', p. 136)

Eliot's anxiety to emphasise Dante's 'orthodoxy', his acquiescence in an external authority and the suppression in his work of any individual impurities, results in the striking claim that Dante's poem 'corresponds point to point' with the Aquinan system and that there is no reason to believe that Dante (or Shakespeare) 'did any thinking on his own' (pp. 135–6). We have already witnessed one example of Eliot's neglect of Dante's original thinking in his silence over Dante's political vision; and there are several passages in the *Commedia* where Dante parts company with the thought of St Thomas.[29] It is of course a measure of Eliot's desire to de-Romanticise the *Commedia* that he should be so wary of acknowledging Dante's freedom of thought within it; but beyond this we see the familiar desire for order, the desire for thought and emotion to be united but separate, the two sides of one coin: poetry and philosophy are 'better performed inside two skulls than one', with Coleridge serving as an example of the failure of one skull to co-ordinate them.[30] Eliot's insistence on this point takes on, at times, an extraordinary rhetorical tone: in one essay of 1924 'A poet who is also a metaphysician' is branded a 'monster':

It is more convenient to use, if necessary, the philosophy of other men, than to burden oneself with the philosophy of a monstrous brother in one's own bosom. Dante and Lucretius used other men's philosophies cheerfully without bothering too much about verifying them for themselves.[31]

A year later, of course, Yeats's *A Vision* appeared, which Eliot no doubt viewed with increasing alarm ever since he admitted to finding himself 'quite lost' when reviewing *Per Amica Silentia Lunae*.[32] Then there was Yeats's mentor Blake, whose 'indulging in a philosophy of his own' Eliot had complained of in *The Sacred Wood* (p. 143); in the Clark Lectures his complaint against Blake is that, whereas Dante's thought and poetry are 'quite distinct', 'my enjoyment is not as with Dante a double enjoyment, but a confused enjoyment, the direct emotional enjoyment of an idea which I do not understand, and which if I understood, I should enjoy as an idea rather than as poetry' (VII, p. 21). The monsters are responsible for a monstrous confusion of the faculties in their readers. Ultimately then, though Eliot would have agreed with Croce about 'la mediocrità della . . . politica e la nessuna originalità della scienza' ('the mediocrity of the . . . political thought and complete unoriginality of the learning') of Dante,[33] his aim is not the Romantic dismissal of didactic poetry but rather the compartmentalisation and ordering of human activity.

The *Dante* essay of 1929 shows an Eliot 'nel mezzo del cammin' in the sense that, while he effortlessly repudiates the position just discussed – 'Dante's debt to St Thomas Aquinas, like his debt (a much smaller one) to Virgil, can be easily exaggerated' (p. 257) – he has not yet arrived at the conception of the Classic which stresses the importance of the Virgil–Dante link, and which is presented in the marvellous essay of 1944, 'What is a Classic?'. Here he discusses

> the new seriousness – *gravity* I might say – the new insight into history, illustrated by the dedication of Aeneas to Rome, to a future far beyond his living achievement . . . So we may think of Roman literature . . . universal as no other literature can be; a literature unconsciously sacrificing, in compliance to its destiny in Europe, the opulence and variety of later tongues, to produce, for us, the classic . . . the maintenance of the standard is the price of our freedom, the defence of freedom against chaos.
> (*OPAP*, p. 70)

In the *Dante* essay we saw that Dante's 'universality' had been inherited from mediaeval Latin, and that it was there brought into contrast with the 'opulence and variety' of the language of later writers like Shakespeare; but the conception of the classical standard being handed on through history, like a runner's baton, became apparent to Eliot only after a further consideration of Virgil, and of the role assigned to him in the *Commedia*:

as it was his function to lead Dante towards a vision he could never himself enjoy, [Virgil] led Europe towards the Christian culture which he could never know; and who, speaking his final words in the new Italian speech, said in farewell

> 'il temporal foco e l'eterno
> veduto hai, figlio, e sei venuto in parte
> dov'io per me più oltre non discerno'

['the temporal and eternal fire you have seen, my son, and have come to the place where I, by myself, can see no further'].
(*OPAP*, pp. 70–1)

Virgil and Dante – 'in the *Divine Comedy*, if anywhere, we find the classic in a modern European language' (p. 60) – are the inspiration behind the insistence in Eliot's later writing that 'the poet should be the servant of his language, rather than the master of it' ('What Dante Means to Me', p. 133). This sense of historical responsibility and service, embodied by Aeneas and summed up in the Virgilian concepts of *labor*, *pietas* and *fatum* celebrated by Eliot in 'Virgil and the Christian World' (p. 125), is described as:

one of the marks of the *classical* poet . . . Shakespeare himself takes liberties [with his native language] which only his genius justifies; liberties which Dante, with an equal genius, does not take. To pass on to posterity one's own language, more highly developed, more refined, and more precise than it was before one wrote it, that is the highest possible achievement of the poet as poet. ('What Dante Means to Me', p. 133)

Before going on to discuss how these ideas operate in *Four Quartets*, it may be a good idea to make a short summary of Dante's significance for Eliot as outlined in these pages. The 1929 essay might be described as orthodox in its relative restraint: Eliot was no doubt aware of the rather eccentric approaches to Dante of several of his predecessors as portrayed in this study; and, as opposed to the more extreme statements of Yeats and Pound, there is very little in the essay which most readers of Dante would object to, apart, perhaps, from the peculiar emphasis on the *Vita Nuova* with which we began this chapter. Moreover, the orthodoxy of Dante himself is at the centre of the essay: 'He not only thought in a way in which every man of his culture in the whole of Europe then thought, but he employed a method which was common and commonly understood throughout Europe' (p. 242). Apart from allegory, which may be called the language of orthodoxy, Dante also used a simple, 'universal' style, characterised by its economy and austerity. These values, representing a participation in an order that stands outside the individual, are first clearly apparent in Eliot's verse in *The Hollow Men*; Dante's presence in the earlier poetry is far more fragmentary, interrupted, as it is, by a powerful need to testify to the sense of individual and social chaos, the 'importunate negative'. This is not to suggest of course that Eliot's earlier poetry is to be repudiated in favour of the later, for his work expresses a 'scale' from negative to positive, in which Prufrock and his companions are as integral (and powerful) a part as the *Inferno* is in Dante's poem. Eliot was acutely conscious of the completeness of this scale in Dante from an early stage in his career; and I believe he had hopes, from a similarly early stage, of moving in a similar direction from negative to positive.

The episode in *Little Gidding* imitative of an encounter in the *Commedia* has been widely celebrated: 'many would consider [it] the finest passage in *Four Quartets*', in Dame Helen Gardner's words.[34] Yet it is not altogether clear, perhaps, in what its superiority consists, and one may well have some sympathy with A. C. Charity's suggestions of various 'flaws' in the episode that derogate from its success as an 'equivalent to a canto of the *Inferno* or the *Purgatorio*', as Eliot subsequently described it ('What Dante Means to Me', p. 128).[35] For me, the power of the episode lies in the peculiar centrality it has in Eliot's oeuvre: it embodies and condenses so many of the themes in his work presented in this chapter and re-explored in the *Quartets* themselves, and this through a personal encounter where these themes take on flesh, as it were. Perhaps one may borrow Eliot's own expression from the essay 'Shakespeare and the Stoicism of Seneca' in which he claims '. . . Dante's poetry receives a boost which in a sense it does not merit' from having Aquinas' thought behind it (*SE*, p. 136), and say that the poetry receives a 'boost' here simply from the importance of the thought that stretches out behind it in Eliot's own career. Unfortunately for the explicator, this means that the episode is highly complex and can be analysed on several levels. It is to begin with a 'point of intersection of the timeless/With time' (*DS* v),[36] as was Dante's journey, that intersection which the *Quartets* strive to communicate and which is here dramatised. We have suggested that, throughout Eliot's work, the apprehension of two orders of existence, set in juxtaposition to each other, has been constant, one order of 'real' beings who exist outside time, after death – the world of Dante's *Commedia* – and the other in the here and now prompting Eliot's painful consciousness of its provisionality and even absurdity: 'Ridiculous the waste sad time/Stretching before and after' (*BN* v). The theme of the *Quartets* is the return to that order of reality, of which we are given glimpses in the moments of 'sudden illumination'. In the encounter in *Little Gidding*, Eliot's lament for the entire race's exile in time after the fall of man takes on an urgent personal note: the 'intersection' (of which the Incarnation is the prototype and condition) is no longer the difficult intuition of *Burnt Norton* or *East Coker* – the

> Whisper of running streams, and winter lightning.
> The wild thyme unseen and the wild strawberry,
> The laughter in the garden, echoed ecstasy . . .
>
> (*EC* III)

– but is a visitation, a sustained conjunction. The communication of the 'dead master' is 'tongued with fire beyond the language of the living' (*LG* I) in the painful disclosure he makes to Eliot about 'the gifts reserved for age'; in this insistence on *vanitas mundi* he is associated with the Pentecostal tongues of fire of the 'dark dove' as it unleashes destruction. *Little Gidding*'s affirmative position, the fact that 'All manner of thing shall be well' (part III) and that a return to the rose-garden lies in prospect at the end of the poem, is reached through an acceptance of the fiery tongues as reminders and implementers of the transitoriness of existence in time, and of the need to purge oneself of the temporal in preparation for the 'reality'. A great deal then depends on this interview with the 'dead master', who has stepped out of God's fire in the afterlife – and it would seem, by the final lines of his speech at least, that he comes from the 'refining fire', the 'foco che li affina' of *Purgatorio* (XXVI.148), the final barrier to the *paradiso terrestre* – into God's fire in this one; the two worlds having 'become much like each other'. His passage between the two worlds has taken place just before morning, when, as Dante agreed, 'la mente nostra . . . a le sue visïon quasi è divina' ('our mind . . . is almost divine in its visions') (*Purg.* IX.16–18).

The figure Eliot meets, 'Both intimate and unidentifiable', is, on one level, himself, the Eliot as he will exist in his reality after death, undergoing purgation proper; the Eliot who meets him is then a kind of *figura* of the 'dead master'. The idea of the two selves was introduced into the *Quartets* at the beginning, in *Burnt Norton* I: one exists in the world of 'what might have been', the other in 'what has been', but the two orders are 'always present' to the mind; the two selves have continuous and parallel existences. The 'what might have been' is the world of the rose-garden, of man's prelapsarian state before 'time' existed; this world is also envisaged as man's destination after time in the poem, time then seen as a 'ridiculous' interruption of man's real existence, though this existence, because it occurs outside time, has never ceased: the result is a ghostly doubling of our lives, though of course it is we here on earth who are the ghosts, or, as Harry tells Agatha in *The Family Reunion*, insisting on the continuous reality of our lives in the rose-garden, 'phantasms':

> what did not happen is as true as what did happen
> O my dear, and you walked through the little door
> And I ran to meet you in the rose-garden.
>
> (p. 335)

In moments of consciousness – 'To be conscious is not to be in time' (*BN* II) – we make contact with our real selves, as in the rose-garden in *Burnt Norton*: the momentary glimpse of this paradisal self – 'they were behind us, reflected in the pool' – is perhaps intended to evoke Dante's first sight of the blessed in the *Paradiso*, when he mistakenly believes, from their faintness, that they are reflections of something behind him: 'quelle stimando specchiati sembianti/per veder di cui fosser, li occhi torsi' ('thinking those were reflections in a mirror I turned my eyes to see whose they were') (III.20–1).[37] The meeting with the 'dead master' in *Little Gidding* is a similar though more tangible encounter between self and real self; its results are more tangible too, because it indicates that there can be no return to the 'first world' of the garden other than via what one might call the 'detour' of time and the Purgatory consequent upon time; *Little Gidding* gives then fuller voice to the knowledge that 'the way forward is the way back' (*DS* III).

The 'compound ghost' then occupies a place in that arrangement of the individual souls after death which alone constitutes their reality; Eliot's first rough note for *Little Gidding* is extraordinarily illuminating on this point:

> They vanish, the individuals, and
> our feeling for them sinks into the
> flame which refines. They emerge
> in another pattern & recreated &
> reconciled
> redeemed, having their meaning to-
> gether not apart, in a union
> which is of beams from the central
> fire. (quoted in Gardner, p. 157)

This sense of the 'pattern' in the afterlife, the having 'meaning together not apart', was, as we saw, Eliot's insistence as early as *The Sacred Wood* with regard to the souls in the *Commedia*: 'Dante . . . does not analyse the emotion so much as he exhibits its relation to other emotions' (p. 168), and I have suggested that even in 'Prufrock' we have a trace of Eliot's absorbing interest in the pattern in his choice of epigraph. In *Little Gidding* Eliot seems to have based his Dantesque episode, to begin with, on Dante's meeting with Brunetto Latini because nowhere else in the *Commedia* do we find such a striking illustration of the different pattern that prevails in death: the Brunetto who was Dante's master is now 'colui che perde' ('the one who loses') while Dante will reach the 'gloroso porto' ('glorious port') (*Inf.* xv.124,56); and Dante's feeling for Brunetto's 'cara e buona imagine paterna' ('dear and kind paternal image') (l. 83) will be adjusted and 'refined' by his understanding of how inadequate is Brunetto's conception of 'come l'uom s'etterna' ('how man makes himself eternal') (l. 85) in relation to the life eternal after time. The shock of seeing Brunetto not as man was used to see him but as God sees him, and the necessary adjustments Dante is called upon to make – this would be the best exemplar of those lines from *Little Gidding* III:

> See, now they vanish,
> The faces and places, with the self which, as it could, loved them,
> To become renewed, transfigured, in another pattern.

But this theme of the purifying of one's earthly attachments involves Eliot in a rather strange coalescing of Dante's first two *cantiche*; the 'irresolute' moral attitude to the ghost this implies has been explored at some length by Charity ('T. S. Eliot: the Dantean Recognitions', pp. 143–6). The letter to Hayward accompanying Eliot's second revision of the episode (quoted in Gardner, pp. 64–5) shows that the ghost began to be identified in Eliot's mind with Yeats; and that with this identification grew Eliot's desire that the episode as a whole should be Purgatorial. Thus the Brunetto figure, who represents an earthly relationship which will need to be purified, is also a figure actually undergoing purgation: he is both what the earthly self has to escape from and what it has to escape to; and in this latter sense, as remarked above, he is Eliot's own realised self. Apart from his place in what one might call the timeless, 'vertical axis' of the pattern of souls after death, the ghost also occupies a place in the 'horizontal axis' of the poetic tradition, and it is clear that the ghost began to assume Yeats's features when the task of 'purify[ing] the dialect of the tribe' assumed far more importance in the episode than it now does in the final version (see the early drafts in Gardner, pp. 186–7). Less than a year before he began *Little Gidding*, Eliot had delivered the first annual Yeats Lecture, in 1940; indeed, preliminary notes for part of the poem were written on a sheet of paper earlier used for some of the lecture notes (see Gardner, p. 65). In the lecture, Eliot had called attention to Yeats as an exponent of the classical values of writing we have looked at, the passing on to posterity of a more 'refined' language:

> another, and important, cause of improvement is the gradual purging out of poetical ornament. This, perhaps, is the most painful part of the labour . . . The course of improvement is towards a greater and greater starkness. The beautiful line for its own sake is a luxury . . . What is necessary is a beauty which shall not be in the line or the isolable passage, but woven into the dramatic texture itself . . . ('Yeats', *OPAP*, pp. 259–60)

It would seem at first, then, that the Dantesque episode in *Little Gidding* began to move from an Infernal to a Purgatorial setting under purely secular pressures, so to speak: the purging of poetry, not of the soul, the pain of forgoing poetic luxuries as opposed to the *lussuria* which is purged on Dante's seventh terrace. Eliot is fervent in his praise of these services to language in the Yeats Lecture: 'an artist, by serving his art with entire integrity, is at the same time rendering the greatest service he can to his own nation and to the whole world' (p. 262), and *Four Quartets* as a whole, of course, attempts to synthesise services to the Word and to the word, notably in the final section of *Little Gidding*. But at some point in the composition of the Dantesque episode the need arose to subordinate the secular to the religious in Dante's own manner, as described in the essay 'Poetry and Drama':

it is ultimately the function of art, in imposing a credible order upon ordinary reality, and thereby eliciting some perception of an order *in* reality, to bring us to a condition of serenity, stillness, and reconciliation; and then leave us, as Virgil left Dante, to proceed toward a region where that guide can avail us no farther. (*OPAP*, p. 87)

Art can take us only so far; the secular 'purgatory' must give way to Purgatory proper. Eliot began his final re-writing of the second part of the episode with a prose draft in which '. . . Yeats as the poet of old age replaces Yeats as the "fighter for language"' (Gardner, p. 189). He can now be properly associated with Arnaut Daniel as, from within his flame, he sees 'la passada folor' ('the past folly') (*Purg.* XXVI.143), and communicates his knowledge to his interlocutor: 'Let me disclose the gifts reserved for age . . .' In this, Eliot's identification with him as poet and penitent is now complete: he had quoted Yeats's poem 'The Spur' in his lecture (Yeats, *Poems*, p. 591) and had asked of the sentiments of 'lust and rage' expressed in it: 'To what honest man old enough, can these . . . be entirely alien?' ('Yeats', pp. 257–8).

The episode itself is written in Eliot's stark, 'purged' style, as befits its theme:

And he: 'I am not eager to rehearse
  My thoughts and theory which you have forgotten.
  These things have served their purpose: let them be.
So with your own, and pray they be forgiven
  By others, as I pray you to forgive
  Both bad and good. Last season's fruit is eaten
And the fullfed beast shall kick the empty pail.
  For last year's words belong to last year's language,
  And next year's words await another voice.
But, as the passage now presents no hindrance
  To the spirit unappeased and peregrine
  Between two worlds become much like each other,
So I find words I never thought to speak
  In streets I never thought I should revisit
  When I left my body on a distant shore . . .'

One may set beside it the following lines of Brunetto:

Ed elli a me: 'Se tu segui tua stella,
non puoi fallire a glorïoso porto,
se ben m'accorsi ne la vita bella;

e s'io non fossi sì per tempo morto,
veggendo il cielo a te così benigno,
dato t'avrei a l'opera conforto.
Ma quello ingrato popolo maligno
che discese di Fiesole *ab* antico,
e tiene ancor del monte e del macigno,
ti si farà, per tuo ben far, nimico;
ed è ragion, ché tra li lazzi sorbi
si disconvien fruttare al dolce fico.
Vecchia fama nel mondo li chiama orbi;
gent' è avara, invidiosa e superba:
dai lor costumi fa che tu ti forbi.
La tua fortuna tanto onor ti serba
che l'una parte e l'altra avranno fame
di te; ma lungi fia dal becco l'erba . . .'

(And he to me: 'If you follow your star you cannot fail to reach a glorious port, if in the fair life I understood correctly; and if indeed I had not died too early, seeing heaven so well-disposed towards you I would have comforted you in your work. But that malign, ungrateful people who came down from Fiesole in ancient times and still smack of mountain and rock will become your enemy in return for your good work; and with reason, since the sweet fig shouldn't fruit among bitter sorbs. The world has long reputed them blind; they are a greedy, envious and proud people: make sure you cleanse yourself of their customs. Your destiny reserves so much honour for you that one party and the other will hunger after you; but the grass will be far from the goat . . .') (*Inf.* XV.55–72)

Leaving aside the metaphor of the beast and the pail which is, one imagines, an attempt at the periodical homeliness of Dante's *locutio vulgaris*, it is clear that the diction in these two excerpts is not very similar: the *gravitas* of Eliot's ghost is apparent in the studied formality of a phrase like 'unappeased and peregrine', whereas Brunetto's speech, as he warms to his theme of haranguing the Florentines, has a more colloquial, energetic vocabulary. Even so, the rhythm of the two extracts is rather similar in the frequency of end-stopped lines and of lines beginning with conjunctions which accommodate the metre to the syntax; similarly the correlation of the three-line unit with an introductory subordinate clause and the delaying of the main verb to the following tercet – 'But, as the passage . . . So I find words . . .'; 'Ma quello ingrato popolo maligno/che discese . . . ti si farà . . .' – show that Eliot genuinely had Dante's episode in mind. Throughout Eliot's writing, however, as we have seen, there is an over-emphasis on the 'austerity' of

Dante's style, an ignoring of the changes of register, particularly in the *Inferno*; as Mario Praz remarks: '. . . Dante fits his language to the theme so that examples of all kinds of style may be found in him . . .'[38] The most famous example of this is probably in canto XXXII of the *Inferno*, where he employs the 'rime aspre e chiocce' ('harsh and grating rhymes') as a style befitting the description of the bottom of Hell, a style which, in the eyes of Italian critics from Bembo to Bettinelli, had made Dante anything but a model for future poets.[39] Eliot's insistence on Dante as a classic writer, on the clarity and 'universality' of his style, can indeed claim our sympathy; but it does leave out of account some of the most conspicuous features of that style, its vivacity, at times vulgarity, and its communication of a Dante *personaggio* whose energy, spontaneity and commitment are such memorable experiences in our reading of the *Commedia*. But, just as Eliot's sense of evil required a Hell that was predominantly dignified, so he shied away from the less elevated aspects of Dante's style.

What *Little Gidding* noticeably introduces into *Four Quartets* is the theme of *Amor*. It is at this point that Dante parted company with Virgil, for whom the world 'had order and dignity', but who was denied the higher vision of a universe 'legato con amore in un volume' (*Par.* XXXIII.86).[40] The theme of *Little Gidding* is an attempt to intuit this unity, and the *Quartet*'s key-word is reconciliation. We have our meaning 'together not apart', and the combatants of the Civil War now 'folded in a single party', are a symbol of this reconciliation after time to those now undergoing another, European, war. But all shall be well: the foreign bombs with their 'flickering tongues' are a reminder of God's love at Pentecost, when the apostles were visited by the tongues of fire which enabled them to cope with these divisions between nations and their languages (Acts ii.1–11). *Little Gidding* ends on a reliance on the time when

> the tongues of flame are in-folded
> Into the crowned knot of fire
> And the fire and the rose are one

when the disunity of individuals and nations shall be over; and the tutelary genius of the poem is, of course, Dante Alighieri, who not only preached such a vision but preached it in a tongue that all Europe could share in.

Conclusion

In this study it was found convenient to make certain generalisations and conclusions at appropriate points in the various chapters: for example, the (largely negative) effect of the gradual growth in Dante scholarship on the poets' conceptions of Dante was referred to in Chapter II (pp. 55–6); and we have paid a good deal of attention to the novel, 'anti-romantic' emphasis in Pound's and Eliot's writing on Dante, which contrasts so forcibly with the consummation of Romantic thought that Yeats's Dante represents; indeed, Yeats's claim to be one of the 'last romantics' is perhaps nowhere better illustrated than in his picture of Dante. The contrasts that have been produced by this juxtaposition of viewpoints have enabled us, I hope, to see more easily what is peculiarly distinctive about each poet's response to Dante: the next poet of stature to busy himself in the matter will doubtless cause us to make some modification in the judgements reached so far by bringing a fresh emphasis into play.[1] One becomes more aware of what one writer misses in Dante by noting what another sees, and thus there can be no final judgement.

What one may conclude with safety then is that the 'poets' Dantes' that have been discussed are at bottom neither very similar to one another nor to Dante himself; no poet seems to have been able to hold in a balance the 'two' Dantes, the Aristotelian Dante of the secular world, with his concern for the ordering of human society on earth, and the Dante who presents his Catholic visions of eternity; Shelley and Pound, for example, allow the former to eclipse the latter, whereas Browning and Eliot, more excusably, do the reverse. Yet we can hardly complain about these partial views, nor wish that several of the poets in question had had a less conspicuous disregard for Dante scholarship: we can accuse Yeats, for example, of an ignorance about Dante while acknowledging that few men's understanding has been so fruitful. But the differences between the work of Dante and the modern poets considered in this study should, I think, be insisted upon: in the field of 'comparative literature' one frequently comes across suggestions that, for example, Pound's later *Cantos* or Eliot's *Four Quartets* are modern *Paradisos*, which makes one wonder what has befallen the faculty of comparison in the critics who make such claims. Several studies referred to in these pages which make more or less unqualified correlations between various modern poems and aspects of the *Commedia* do justice to neither Dante himself nor to the poets they attempt to link him with; often both the mediaeval and the modern works are trimmed and squeezed into some formulation that supposedly unites them but in fact deprives them of much of their significance.

One may also confirm here the magnitude of Dante's work, the fact that so many writers have been able to interpret it so differently. I am not of course referring to the quantity of writing Dante produced, but rather to the number of elements his work combines, especially in the *Commedia*. When two works such as Antoine Ozanam's *Dante et la philosophie catholique au treizième siècle* (Paris, 1839) and Eugène Aroux's *Dante hérétique, révolutionnaire et socialiste* (1854) can claim within fifteen years of each other Dante's support for two entirely differing ideologies, for everything in the title of Aroux's study contradicts Ozanam's emphasis on Dante's Catholicism, then it is clear that we are dealing with a classic that embodies no ordinary adaptability. Dante's story, in fact, 'has everything': whereas other works of literature may display a comparable range, such as the Homeric epics or Shakespeare's plays, Dante affords the added attraction of having led such an extraordinary life, one that had, as Yeats said, 'the quality of art' and that takes on a quasi-legendary quality, aided by the portraits, in the nineteenth century particularly. Perhaps Milton is the only writer who can approach Dante in this respect, but even Milton's political, religious and romantic experiences have not afforded the same fascination for modern writers.

Guidubaldi suggested that Eliot saw in Dante's work a 'sintesi completa (quale "riassunto" del mondo antico ed "anticipo" del mondo moderno) dei duemila anni da salvare' ('complete synthesis (as it were a "summary" of the ancient world and "anticipation" of the modern one) of the two thousand years to be salvaged') (*Dante europeo*, I, 243), taking his cue from Eliot's talk on 'The Unity of European Culture' which ends on the appeal to the European nations to

try to save something of those goods of which we are the common trustees; the legacy of Greece, Rome and Israel, and the legacy of Europe throughout the last 2,000 years. In a world which has seen such material devastation as ours, these spiritual possessions are also in imminent peril.[2]

Guidubaldi continues: 'È cosa talmente chiara quest'indole *ricapitolativa* di Dante da farsi contemplare tutto intero in lui (*legato con amore in un volume*, vien fatto da dire) ciò che nei duemila anni troveremo *squadernato*' ('It is so clear, this *summarising* character of Dante which allows us to contemplate complete in him (*bound with love in one volume*, in other words) that which we shall find *scattered* through the two thousand years') (p. 246). This suggestion is supported by Eliot's statement in the Dante essay that the last canto of the *Paradiso* 'is to my thinking the highest point that poetry has ever reached or ever can reach' (p. 251), a kind of 'still point' of a 2,000-year circle. Guidubaldi notes the existence of the 2,000-year cycle in the historiography of Curtius and Spengler, and we can of course parallel this with the cycle in Yeats's *A Vision*, and may note again Pound's attitude to Dante's work as a 'package' or 'riassunto' of the centuries preceding it. In short, the *Divine Comedy*, like a great landmark on the horizon of time, has helped modern writers to make sense of the sequential unfolding of history, to find their own place within it; and it seems unlikely, given 'the darkness into which we peer', that this function of Dante's poem and his poetry in general will become any less an inspiration or a support for the future. Men will be continually looking back to a time when all things could be seen as 'legato con amore in un volume'.

Notes

The place of publication of books in the notes and bibliography is London unless otherwise stated.

Introduction

1 'The Influence of Dante on the Nineteenth-Century English Poets', Diss. Harvard 1922.
2 'What Dante Means to Me', in *To Criticize the Critic* (Faber, 1965), p. 132.
3 Martin Bidney, 'Ruskin's Uses of Dante', Diss. Indiana 1971; Mary T. Reynolds, *Joyce and Dante: The Shaping Imagination* (Princeton: Princeton Univ. Press, 1981).

I Shelley, Dante and freedom

1 Benedetto Croce, *La poesia di Dante*, 7th ed. (Bari: Laterza, 1952). See especially the Introduction and Chapter II, 'La Struttura della *Commedia* e la poesia'.
2 For earlier studies of Dante's influence on Shelley, see Halley, 'The Influence of Dante', and John V. Saly, 'Dante and the English Romantics', Diss. Columbia 1959, pp. 86–216. Other studies will be referred to at relevant points in the text.
3 See *The Letters of Percy Bysshe Shelley*, ed. Frederick L. Jones, 2 vols. (Oxford: The Clarendon Press, 1964), II, 94, 163–4.
4 See *Mary Shelley's Journal*, ed. Frederick L. Jones (Norman: Univ. of Oklahoma Press, 1947), pp. 97, 123. It is unlikely that Shelley had much knowledge of Dante before his departure for Italy in 1818. Two letters of December 1817 request the *Purgatorio* and *Paradiso* from his booksellers (*Letters*, I, 575, 586).
5 For the sake of convenience Thomas Hutchinson's edition of Shelley's *Poetical Works*, rev. G. M. Matthews, 2nd ed. (Oxford: Oxford Univ. Press, 1970) has been used, though this will be superseded by Neville Rogers's edition of *The Complete Poetical Works*, 4 vols. (Oxford: The Clarendon Press), Vols. I and II of which have appeared to date (1972, 1975).
6 See *Dante in English Literature*, compiled by Paget Toynbee, 2 vols. (Methuen, 1909), II, 436. This will henceforth be abbreviated to *DEL* where it is necessary to distinguish it from Toynbee's other works.
7 'Essay on the Devil and Devils', in *Shelley's Prose*, ed. David Lee Clark, 2nd ed.

(Albuquerque: Univ. of New Mexico Press, 1966), p. 273. A glance through Toynbee's anthology will reveal the predominant Romantic interest in the *Inferno*.

8 The *Convivio* notes are printed in Neville Rogers, *Shelley at Work*, 2nd ed. (Oxford: The Clarendon Press, 1967), pp. 340–1. Shelley's pencil markings to his copies of the *Vita Nuova* and *Inferno* are published in Walter Edwin Peck, *Shelley: His Life and Work* (Boston: Houghton Mifflin, 1927), II, 355–61.

9 *A Defence of Poetry*, *Shelley's Prose*, p. 289.

10 *Poetical Works*, pp. 188–9. Mrs Shelley's notes on Shelley's poems are reprinted by Hutchinson from her own editions (1839) of the poems.

11 Robert Browning, 'Essay on Shelley', in *The Browning Society's Papers, 1881–4*, Pt. I, i (1881), p. 15.

12 See for example Leigh Hunt's discussion of the place occupied by the Paolo and Francesca episode in an *Inferno* described by him as 'a kind of sublime nightmare':

> We even lose sight of the place, in which the saturnine poet, according to his summary way of disposing both of friends and enemies, has thought proper to put the sufferers; and see the whole melancholy absurdity of his theology, in spite of itself, falling to nothing before one genuine impulse of the affections.

Preface to *The Story of Rimini* (1816), p. viii. The involvement of the 'primo amore' in the foundation of Hell sets it off from the Shelleyan conception of love which, as Rogers points out (p. 54 – quoting from Shelley's translation of the *Symposium*), 'neither inflicts nor endures injury in its relations either with Gods or men'. Shelley's translation is in *The Complete Works of Percy Bysshe Shelley*, ed. Roger Ingpen and Walter E. Peck, Julian Edition, VII (Benn, 1930), 157–220.

13 *Shelley e Dante* (Milan: Sandron, 1922), p. 158.

14 *Dante* (Faber, 1929), p. 67; rpt. in *Selected Essays*, 3rd ed. (Faber, 1951), p 275.

15 'The Role of Dante in *Epipsychidion*', *Comparative Literature*, 30 (1978), 233. Beatrice of course was never a native of Dante's third heaven, though Brown's mistake is a continuation of a practice originating in the fourteenth century, and found again in Rossetti, of imagining Dante and Beatrice involved in a private Paradisal love-match: see for example Boccaccio's sonnet beginning 'Dante, se tu nell'amorosa spera,/com'io credo, dimori riguardando/la bella Bice' ('Dante, if you dwell in the amorous sphere, as I believe, gazing on the beautiful Bice [Beatrice]') in *Opere in versi . . .*, ed. Pier Giorgio Ricci (Milan: Ricciardi, 1965), p. 11 (sonnet XIV). See also sonnet XX, p. 16, and Cino da Pistoia's two *canzoni* on Beatrice's and on Dante's deaths in Mario Marti, ed., *Poeti del dolce stil nuovo* (Florence: Le Monnier, 1969), pp. 724, 862. This practice might be said to represent a 'Vita-Nuovising' of the *Commedia* and is suggested by *Epipsychidion* itself which coalesces the Beatrices of the two works.

16 See 'Shelley and Keats', *The Use of Poetry and the Use of Criticism*, 2nd ed. (Faber, 1964), p. 92.

17 For earlier instances of this kind of claim among 'i riformatori inglesi . . . [che] hanno potuto vantare [Dante] come loro campione' ('the English reformers . . . who have been able to vaunt Dante as their champion'), see E. R. Vincent, 'Fortuna di Dante in Inghilterra', in the *Enciclopedia Dantesca*, 6 vols. (Rome: Istituto della Enciclopedia Italiana, 1970–8), III, 446.

18 *The Marriage of Heaven and Hell*, in *William Blake's Writings*, ed. G. E. Bentley, Jr (Oxford: The Clarendon Press, 1978), I, 80; M. H. Abrams, *The Mirror and the Lamp* (New York: Oxford Univ. Press, 1953), p. 251.

19 Shelley's approach to the poetry of the past is similar to what Frank Kermode describes as the process of 'accommodation' 'as a way of maintaining the relevance of the classics', a practice in which the classic is seen as 'a more or less open text from which new readings may generate . . . meanings contemporary with us which, quite possibly, an informed contemporary [or the original author himself] could not have discovered'. *The Classic* (Faber, 1975), pp. 72, 75.
20 Preface to *Prometheus Unbound*, p. 207.
21 'Essay on Christianity', *Shelley's Prose*, pp. 197, 204.
22 *The Spirit of Romance*, revised ed. (Peter Owen, 1952), p. 127.
23 See 'Johnson as Critic and Poet', in *On Poetry and Poets* (Faber, 1957), p. 169.
24 Ugo Foscolo, *Discorso sul testo del poema di Dante*, [ed. F. S. Orlandini], in *Opere edite e postume* (Florence, 1850), III, 375, quoted by Luciana Martinelli, *Dante*, Storia della critica, 4 (Palermo: Palumbo, 1966), p. 172. Martinelli's book forms a convenient introduction to the history of Dante criticism, particularly in Italy.
25 As early as the fourteenth century itself we have the attempt, according to Martinelli, to enjoy the poetry in the *Commedia* without the politics in the commentary on the poem by the Guelph writer Graziolo Bambaglioli, who concentrates on the 'operazione di progressivo perfezionarsi del poeta medesmo . . . il centro motore della vicenda è posto nell'interno moto del personaggio–poeta . . .' ('operation of the gradual perfecting of the poet himself . . . the driving force of the affair is seen in this internal movement of the poet–protagonist') (*Dante*, pp. 9–10).
26 *Browning: Poetical Works 1833–1864*, ed. Ian Jack (Oxford: Oxford Univ. Press, 1970), p. 17, ll. 403–4.
27 See for example E. G. Parodi, 'La *Divina Commedia*, Poema della libertà dell'individuo e il canto XXVII del *Purgatorio*', in *Dante: Raccolta di studi*, ed. Alojzij Res (Gorizia: Paternolli, 1921), pp. 31–41.
28 The *Monarchia* remained on the Index till 1881 (see 'Monarchia', *Enciclopedia Dantesca*, III, 1002). For the eighteenth-century disapproval of Dante's social and ecclesiastical censures see Martinelli, *Dante*, pp. 113–15.
29 'A parallel between Dante and Petrarch', *Essays on Petrarch* (1821; rpt. 1823), pp. 187–8.
30 [Thomas] Medwin, *Conversations of Lord Byron*, ed. Ernest J. Lovell, Jr (Princeton: Princeton Univ. Press, 1966), p. 160.
31 See the note on Cato in his edition of the *Commedia*, La letteratura italiana: storia e testi, IV (Milan: Ricciardi, 1957), p. 339.
32 William Hazlitt, 'On Poetry in General', *Lectures on the English Poets* (1818), p. 34.
33 This admiration for the radical Dante is not found among all Shelley's contemporaries; thus Coleridge's assessment is so exactly opposed to Shelley's as to be worth quoting here:

This comparative failure of Dante, as also some other peculiarities of his mind, *in malam partem*, must be immediately attributed to the state of North Italy in his time, which is vividly represented in Dante's life: a state of intense democratical partizanship, in which an exaggerated importance was attached to individuals, and which whilst it afforded a vast field for the intellect, opened also a boundless arena for the passions, and in which envy, jealousy, hatred, and other malignant feelings, could and did assume the form of patriotism, even to the individual's own conscience.

'Lecture x: Donne–Dante–Milton–*Paradise Lost*', in *Notes and Lectures upon Shakespeare . . . with other Literary Remains*, ed. Mrs H. N. Coleridge (1849), II, 100.

34 Erich Auerbach, *Mimesis*, trans. Willard R. Trask (Princeton: Princeton Univ. Press, 1953), p. 202.

35 'Dante', *The Sacred Wood* (Methuen, 1920), p. 150.

36 'Dante and the English Romantic Poets', *English Miscellany*, 2 (1951), 145–7.

37 One should note, however, that in the fourth book of the *Convivio* and in the *Monarchia* we find adumbrated, as Kenelm Foster has stressed, 'a humanist ethic for life in time, based on man's inherent "nobility" and capacity for a "virtue" that is self-achieved'. This obviously contrasts with the *Commedia*'s emphasis 'on a personal union with God beyond and outside time; and as regards the way to that end, on the need for accepting divinely appointed guides'. Indeed, Foster goes on to suggest that 'the deep [humanist] strain' of what he calls this 'other Dante' 'never wholly conformed to the new pattern imposed by [the] shift towards other-worldliness and the surrender of autonomy', and then traces contradictions this leads to in the *Commedia.* See 'The Two Dantes', in *The Two Dantes and Other Studies* (Darton, Longman and Todd, 1977), p. 161.

38 As far as I know, the only important contemporary of Shelley to acknowledge (and object to) Dante's attacks on the Italian city-states and his monarchical projects is Walter Savage Landor. See *The Pentameron and Pentalogia* (1837), pp. 167ff.

39 *The Life of Lorenzo de' Medici*, 4th ed. (1800), I, 420. This seems to be the book Shelley ordered from Rickman in 1812 under the title 'History of the Houses of Medicis' (*Letters*, I, 345). Poliziano's lines are in his *Sylvae*, part IV, 'Nutricia' (ll. 720–8), in *Prose volgari . . . e poesie latine e greche*, ed. Isidoro Del Lungo (Florence, 1867), pp. 422–3.

40 *Remarks upon M. Voltaire's 'Essay on the Epick Poetry of the European Nations'* (1728), p. 30, quoted in Toynbee, I, 215.

41 Shelley's admiration for Florence is also revealed in his *A Philosophical View of Reform, Shelley's Prose*, p. 231.

42 On the importance of mediaeval Florence to the English liberals in the Romantic period and their associating it with Athens, see Marilyn Butler, *Peacock Displayed* (Routledge & Kegan Paul, 1979), pp. 63–5. For the different kind of appeal Florence had in Victorian England, see my Chapter IV, pp. 117–19.

43 W. B. Yeats, *A Vision*, 2nd corrected ed. (Macmillan, 1962), p. 143.

44 Canto XCIII, *The Cantos of Ezra Pound*, revised collected ed. (Faber, 1975), p. 624.

45 [John Taaffe], *A Comment on the 'Divine Comedy' of Dante Alighieri* (1822); see Shelley, *Letters*, II, 303. Plentiful references to the *Commedia* have been traced in *The Triumph* by A. C. Bradley, 'Notes on Shelley's *Triumph of Life*', *Modern Language Review*, 9 (1914), 441–56.

46 *The Use of Poetry and the Use of Criticism*, p. 90.

47 'What Dante Means to Me', in *To Criticize the Critic*, pp. 132, 130.

48 *Ibidem*, p. 132.

49 The contrast between the Romantic response to Dante as the poet of liberty and some twentieth-century responses, including Eliot's, is touched upon in Egidio Guidubaldi, *Dante europeo*, I (Florence: Olschki, 1965), pp. 225–56.

50 See Roland A. Duerkson, *Shelleyan Ideas in Victorian Literature* (The Hague: Mouton, 1966), Chap. I.

II Dante as the Byronic hero

1 (Turin: Bocca, 1922).
2 *Lord Byron e L'Italia* (Palermo: Sandron, 1919), pp. 99–100.
3 The edition of Byron's poetry in *The Works of Lord Byron*, Vols. I–VII, ed. Ernest Hartley Coleridge (John Murray, 1898–1904), is used throughout this chapter.
4 *'Born for Opposition': Byron's Letters and Journals*, ed. Leslie A. Marchand, VIII (1821) (John Murray, 1978), 39–40. Schlegel's comment (quoted in Toynbee, II, 278) is from his *Lectures on the History of Literature* (trans. J. G. Lockhart) (1818), II, 15–16.
5 Medwin, *Conversations*, pp. 161–2; the episode is also reported in Medwin's *The Life of Percy Bysshe Shelley* (1847), ed. H. Buxton Forman (Oxford: Oxford Univ. Press, 1913), pp. 376–7.
6 Saverio Bettinelli's notorious conversations between Virgil and other shades in Elysium deriding the *Commedia* were published in 1756. They seem to have inspired several of the observations on Dante in Landor's *Pentameron*.
7 See Frederick L. Beaty, 'Byron and the Story of Francesca da Rimini', *PMLA*, 75 (1960), 395–401.
8 A classic example is from Alfred de Musset's 'Souvenir', in *Poésies nouvelles*:

> Dante, pourquoi dis-tu qu'il n'est pire misère
> Qu'un souvenir heureux dans les jours de douleur?
> Quel chagrin t'a dicté cette parole amère,
> Cette offense au malheur?
> . . .
> Ce blasphème vanté ne vient pas de ton coeur,
> Un souvenir heureux est peut-être sur terre
> Plus vrai que le bonheur.
>
> Et c'est à ta Françoise, à ton ange de gloire,
> Que tu pouvais donner ces mots à prononcer,
> Elle qui s'interrompt, pour conter son histoire,
> D'un éternel baiser!

Poésies complètes, ed. Maurice Allem ([Paris]: Gallimard, 1957), pp. 406–7; quoted in George Santayana, *Three Philosophical Poets* (Cambridge, Mass.: Harvard Univ. Press, 1910), p. 118 note.
9 Francesca's fate is rectified, however, at the end of Hunt's poem on her, where her sleep seems to be peaceful enough:

> But no more of sorrow.
> On that same night, those lovers silently
> Were buried in one grave, under a tree.
> There side by side, and hand in hand, they lay
> In the green ground: – and on fine nights in May
> Young hearts betrothed used to go there to pray.
> (*Story of Rimini*, p. 111)

10 Compare Hazlitt's:

There is one subject on which Lord Byron is fond of writing, on which I wish he would not write – Buonaparte. Not that I quarrel with his writing for him, or against him, but with his writing both for him and against him. What right has he to do this? Buonaparte's character, be it what else it may, does not change every hour according to his Lordship's varying humour.

(*Lectures on the English Poets*, p. 304)

11 Not that Byron embraced any particular creed. See for example C. M. Woodhouse, 'The Religion of an Agnostic', *The Byron Journal*, 6 (1978), 26–33.

12 H. F. Cary, *The Vision . . . of Dante Alighieri*, 2nd ed. (1819), I, xv. The original reads:

> per le parti quasi tutte a le quali questa lingua si stende, peregrino, quasi mendicando, sono andato, mostrando contra mia voglia la piaga de la fortuna, che suole ingiustamente al piagato molte volte essere imputata. Veramente io sono stato legno sanza vela e sanza governo, portato a diversi porti e foci e liti dal vento secco che vapora la dolorosa povertade . . .

13 *The History of English Poetry* (1774–81; rpt. 1824), IV, 77; quoted in Toynbee, I, 296. Warton's reference is to *Paradise Lost* II. 719–20.

14 *Edinburgh Review*, June 1815, p. 47. This review of Sismondi's *De la littérature du Midi de l'Europe* was taken over almost verbatim for Hazlitt's section on Dante in the *Lectures*, though the statement referred to was omitted. A large part of it is included in Toynbee, II, 176–8, where several mistakes in Hazlitt's reading of the *Commedia* are pointed out.

15 *Dissertazione accademica sopra Dante* (1800), in *Lettere virgiliane e inglesi e altri scritti critici*, ed. V. E. Alfieri (Bari: Laterza, 1930), pp. 284–5 note.

16 For an interesting and perceptive contemporary disagreement on this preference of Milton's Devil to Dante's as an expression of evil, see the unsigned essay 'On the German Drama. No. 1: Oehlenschlaeger', in *Olliers Literary Miscellany*, I (London, 1820), 119–21 note.

17 'Criticisms on the Principal Italian Writers: No. 1: Dante', in *Works*, ed. Lady Trevelyan (1871), VII, 609. The article originally appeared in *Knight's Quarterly Magazine* (January 1824).

18 J. B. Merian, *Dissertazione sulla 'Divina Commedia'* (1782–84), in R. Zotti's edition of the *Commedia* and *Canzoni e sonetti* of Dante (1808–9), IV, lxii.

19 Holbrook suggests the Tofanelli portrait derives from an original that was only painted after *c.* 1450, while the Stothard seems to derive from the frontispiece to the edition of the *Convivio* published at Venice in 1521. See Richard Thayer Holbrook, *Portraits of Dante from Giotto to Raffael* (Lee Warner, 1911). This study is a good summary of the vexed question of the various portraits and their authenticity.

20 *Trattatello in laude di Dante*, ed. Pier Giorgio Ricci, in Giovanni Boccaccio, *Tutte le opere*, ed. Vittore Branca, III ([Milan]: Mondadori, 1974), 477. Compare the sober picture of Dante in Cary's 'Life', pp. xxv–xxvi.

21 R. Frattarolo, 'Dante nella critica fra tre e cinquecento', *Letture classensi*, III (Ravenna: Longo, 1970), 68.

22 This inattention to the energy of Dante's style must surely have been abetted by the popularity of Cary's translation, whose author, in a letter of 1844, could talk of Dante's 'grave and sedate character' (quoted in Toynbee, I, 499). Although the translation was generally received extremely favourably – notably by Coleridge – Taaffe's objections to it seem exactly right: 'whatever be its literal merits, it does not give, nor pretend to give any of the melody of its Original. Dante writes in rhyme and in a metre whose chief characteristics are pliancy and concision. Mr Cary in blank verse imitative of the stateliness and occasional prolixity of Milton' (*A Comment*, p. xix). A few examples picked at random from the translation tend to show a Dante under sedation:

'Even so glittering and so round' said I,
'I not a whit misdoubt of its assay.'

Ond'io: 'Sì, ho, sì lucida e sì tonda,
che nel suo conio nulla mi s'inforsa.'

(Whereupon I: 'Yes, I have, so bright and round that I have no doubts about its coining.') (*Par.* XXIV.86–7)

And, 'Whither is she vanish'd?' straight I ask'd.

E 'Ov'è ella?', sùbito diss'io.
(And 'Where is she?', I asked at once) (*Par.* XXXI.64)

when he rests
Within the temple of his vow, looks round
In breathless awe, and hopes some time to tell
Of all its goodly state.

che si recrea
nel tempio del suo voto riguardando,
e spera già ridir com'ello stea . . .

(who feels refreshed looking round the temple of his vow and already hopes to tell how it was . . .) (*Par.* XXXI.43–5)

23 *Rerum Memorandum Libri*, ed. Giuseppe Billanovich, in *Opere* (Edizione nazionale), v (Florence: Sansoni, 1943), Book II. 83.
24 Ralph Waldo Emerson, *Society and Solitude: Twelve Chapters, Complete Works* (Centenary edition), VII (Boston: Houghton Mifflin, 1912), 7.
25 The *Athenaeum*, 19 March 1864, p. 410.
26 'Milton', *Works* v, 20–1; originally in the *Edinburgh Review*, August 1825.
27 Dante is then a notable omission from Peter L. Thorslev, Jr's *The Byronic Hero: Types and Prototypes* (Minneapolis: Univ. of Minnesota Press, 1962).
28 'What seems certain is that Dante sought and found a relative security and peace in the last years of his life. He was able to have his children with him, and whatever may be thought to the contrary, probably even his wife.' Michele Barbi, *Life of Dante*, trans. and ed. Paul G. Ruggiers (Berkeley and Los Angeles: Univ. of California Press, 1954), p. 28.
29 I follow Michele Barbi in his dating of the *Convivio* to between 1304 and 1307. See his Introduction to the *Convivio*, ed. G. Busnelli and G. Vandelli, 2nd ed., I, *Opere di Dante*, ed. Barbi, IV (Florence: Le Monnier, 1953), xvi–xix.
30 See also Beverly Taylor, 'Byron's Uses of Dante in *The Prophecy of Dante*', *Keats–Shelley Journal*, 28 (1979), 102–19.
31 'The Hero as Poet', *On Heroes, Hero-Worship, & the Heroic in History* (1841), pp. 139–40. The lectures were delivered in 1840, published in 1841.
32 A.-F. Rio, *Epilogue à l'art chrétien* (1879), II, 339, quoted in Alan Carey Taylor, *Carlyle et la pensée latine* (Paris: Boivin, [1937]), p. 31.
33 See the 'Life of Giotto' in *The Lives of the Artists*, select. and trans. George Bull (Harmondsworth: Penguin, 1965), p. 58.

III Browning, Dante and the two Sordellos

1 *The Early Italian Poets from Ciullo d'Alcamo to Dante Alighieri . . . together with Dante's 'Vita Nuova'* (1861), p. xi.
2 'Tennyson, Browning, and a Romantic Fallacy', *University of Toronto Quarterly*, 13 (1943–4), 195.
3 M. Y. Mason, 'A Study of Browning's Poem *Sordello*', Diss. Oxford 1965, p.

293. Mason's thesis is, as far as I know, the most comprehensive single study of the poem written in recent years.
4 'The Sources of Browning's *Sordello*', *Studies in Philology*, 34 (1937), 467–96.
5 The first edition of *Sordello* (Moxon, 1840) is used throughout this chapter.
6 Browning made major revisions to the poem for the 1863 edition of his *Poetical Works*, and minor changes of punctuation for the editions of 1868 and 1888–9. The final text is quoted here from *Poetical Works 1833–1864*, ed. Ian Jack (Oxford: Oxford Univ. Press, 1970). This volume, subsequently abbreviated to *PW*, is used for the rest of Browning's poetry quoted in this chapter, other than *The Ring and the Book*, where Richard D. Altick's edition (Harmondsworth: Penguin, 1971) has been used.
7 *Strafford: An Historical Tragedy* (1837), III.ii (p. 69).
8 T. E. McCrory, 'Browning and Dante', Diss. University of Pennsylvania 1958, p. 103. McCrory's thesis has a useful introductory chapter on Browning's early reading of Dante and makes some interesting points on *Sordello*, but tends to be swollen by redundant suggestions of Dante's influence on, for example, *Pauline* and '"Childe Roland to the Dark Tower Came"'. Its treatment of *The Ring and the Book* is also rather incomplete.
9 Dedication to the 1863 edition, *PW*, p. 156.
10 *The Letters of Robert Browning and Elizabeth Barrett Barrett 1845–1846*, ed. Elvan Kintner (Cambridge, Mass.: Harvard Univ. Press, 1969), I, 336.
11 Thus McCrory states that Browning's poem 'owes a good deal to Dante's interpretation of Sordello' (p. xxxiv), whilst in Mason's words 'Dante's picture of Sordello . . . seems to have had little influence on Browning's conception of his hero' ('A Study', p. 9 note).
12 See Robert Langbaum, *The Poetry of Experience* (Chatto and Windus, 1957), pp. 79, 89–91.
13 *The Poems of Tennyson*, ed. Christopher Ricks (Longman, 1969), pp. 565–6.
14 *University of Toronto Quarterly*, 18 (1948–9), 234.
15 *Storia della letteratura italiana* (1870–1), introd. Natalino Sapegno, ed. Niccolò Gallo, in *Opere*, ed. Carlo Muscetta, VIII (Turin: Einaudi, 1958), 283.
16 See for example De Sanctis:

Non è un tempio greco; è un tempio gotico, pieno di grandi ombre, dove contrari elementi pugnano, non bene armonizzati. Or rozzo, or delicato. Ora poeta solenne, or popolare. Ora perde di vista il vero e si abbandona a sottigliezze, ora lo intuisce rapidamente e lo esprime con semplicità. Ora rozzo cronista, ora pittore finito . . .
(It is not a Greek, but a Gothic temple, full of great shadows, where contrary elements, not very well harmonised, conflict with one another. Now it is rough, now delicate. Now he is a solemn poet, now a vulgar one. Now he loses sight of the truth and abandons himself to sophistries, now he intuits it quickly and expresses it with simplicity. Now a crude chronicler, now a finished painter . . .)
(*Storia della lett. it.*, pp. 194–5).

17 See C. M. Bowra, 'Dante and Sordello', *Comparative Literature*, 5 (1953), 1–15.
18 Notes to *Par.* IX, *The Vision*, III, 78.
19 *Mimesis*, p. 196. Auerbach's fuller essay on 'Figura', trans. Ralph Manheim, can be found in his *Scenes from the Drama of European Literature* (Gloucester, Mass.: Smith, 1973), pp. 11–76.
20 'Donne in Our Time', in *A Garland for John Donne, 1631–1931*, ed. Theodore Spencer (Cambridge, Mass.: Harvard Univ. Press, 1931), p. 8.
21 'The "Donna Angelicata" in *The Ring and the Book*', *PMLA*, 41 (1926), 55–81.

22 'Browning's "Childe Roland" and Dante's *Inferno*', *Victorian Poetry*, 5 (1967), 296–302.

23 Indeed, Fairchild would see this as a further illustration of Browning's imperfect Christianity, of the wearisomeness of an 'eternally complete and unimperiled' consummation to a man who was 'eternally falling and rising, striving and thriving, speeding and fighting toward a goal which, if it ever were attained, would thereby lose its power to stimulate his appetite for boundlessness . . . In the last analysis, one is tempted to conclude, he cannot bear stoppage on either side of the grave.' *Religious Trends in English Poetry*, IV (New York: Columbia Univ. Press, 1957), 160–1.

IV Rossetti and the cult of the *Vita Nuova*

1 *Italy and the English Romantics* (Cambridge: Cambridge Univ. Press, 1957), p. 72.

2 See the 'Chronological List of Translators', in G. F. Cunningham, *The 'Divine Comedy' in English* Vol. 1, 1782–1900 (Edinburgh and London: Oliver and Boyd, 1965), p. 6.

3 Paget Toynbee, comp., *Britain's Tribute to Dante in Literature and Art* (British Academy, 1921), p. 106.

4 Cunningham, *The 'Divine Comedy'*, pp. 6–10.

5 Paget Toynbee, 'Dante in English Art', pp. 28–100, supplement to the *Thirty-Eighth Annual Report of the Dante Society (Cambridge, Mass.) 1919* (Boston: Dante Society, 1921).

6 *The Stones of Venice*, III.iii.67, in *Works*, ed. E. T. Cook and Alexander Wedderburn, XI (George Allen, 1904), 187. Quoted in *Comments of John Ruskin on the 'Divina Commedia'*, comp. G. P. Huntington, introd. C. E. Norton (Boston, Mass.: Houghton Mifflin, 1903), p. 3.

7 Twenty-five sonnets survive from Hallam's translation. See *The Writings of Arthur Hallam*, ed. T. H. Vail Motter (New York: Modern Language Association; Oxford: Oxford Univ. Press, 1943), pp. 113–30. The editor dates these translations to *c.* 1828–32. See also Charles Lyell, *The Canzoniere of Dante, including the Poems of the 'Vita Nuova' and 'Convito'* (1835), p. viii.

8 For Dante's influence on *In Memoriam*, see the appendix to this chapter.

9 *Works* (1846), II, 233.

10 Cf. *Don Juan* III.x.

11 *Fraser's Magazine*, 65 (Jan.–June 1862), 581.

12 For the fullest recent discussion of the authenticity of the portrait, and one which makes a very persuasive case for not accepting it, see E. H. Gombrich, 'Giotto's Portrait of Dante?', *Burlington Magazine*, 121 (1979), 471–83.

13 Letter of 12 September 1840, in Gabriele Rossetti, *A Versified Autobiography*, trans. and supplemented by William Michael Rossetti (Sands, 1901), p. 146; quoted in Toynbee, *DEL*, II, 640.

14 'The *Vita Nuova* of Dante', *Dublin University Magazine*, 29 (Jan.–June 1847), 412.

15 'Dante and Beatrice', *Hood's Magazine*, 3 (Jan.–June 1845), 226.

16 *The 'Vita Nuova' of Dante* (1862), p. xxv.

17 'Dante and Beatrice', *Fraser's Magazine*, 67 (Jan.–June 1863), 666.

18 *Dublin University Magazine*, p. 427.

19 F. T. Palgrave, *Idyls and Songs* (1854), pp. 62–4; [D. M. Mulock], *Poems by the Author of 'John Halifax, Gentleman'* [1859], pp. 168–9.

20 *Fraser's Magazine*, 65, 587–8.

21 Only the first of the work's nine parts was published. The complete study appeared in 1935, ed. Maria Luisa Giartosio de Courten (Imola: Galeati).
22 *Works*, ed. William Michael Rossetti (Ellis, 1911), p. 208.
23 Plate 51 in Virginia Surtees, ed., *The Paintings and Drawings of Dante Gabriel Rossetti: A Catalogue Raisonné*, 2 vols. (Oxford: Oxford Univ. Press, 1971).
24 *Letters of Dante Gabriel Rossetti*, ed. Oswald Doughty and John Robert Wahl (Oxford: The Clarendon Press, 1965), I, 197–8.
25 According to William Rossetti's notes to Rossetti's *Works*, 'The translation of the *Vita Nuova* had been done . . . at a very early date, probably 1847–8 . . .' (p. 676).
26 Paull Franklin Baum, ed., *Dante Gabriel Rossetti: An Analytical List of Manuscripts in the Duke University Library* (Durham, N. Carolina: Duke Univ. Press, 1931), p. 14. Baum prints twelve early sonnets written to *bout-rimés* and not included in the *Works*, pp. 56–65.
27 Rossetti refers to Carlyle's lecture in *Letters*, I, 204.
28 Letter to Joseph Severn (1847), *Works*, XXXVI (1909), 69; quoted in M. P. Bidney, 'Ruskin's Uses of Dante', Diss. Indiana 1971, p. 21.
29 *The Poems of Tennyson*, p. 409.
30 For Rossetti's paintings from Dante see also Paget Toynbee, 'Chronological list, with notes, of paintings and drawings from Dante by Dante Gabriel Rossetti', in *Scritti varii . . . in onore di Rodolfo Renier* (Turin: Bocca, 1912), pp. 135–66; and A. I. Grieve, *The Art of Dante Gabriel Rossetti No. 3: The Watercolours and Drawings of 1850–1855* (Norwich: Real World, [1978]), pp. 4–31.
31 William Michael Rossetti, 'Notes on Rossetti and his Works', *Art Journal*, 43 (July 1884), 205.
32 Rossetti frequently records the actual date of Beatrice's death in his paintings, as if to insist on the reality of her historical existence. His father, however, by taking the 'perfetto numero' ('perfect number') of *Vita Nuova* XXIX.1 to be nine – 'nella tavola pittagora il supremo de' caffi semplici' ('in the pythagorean table the highest simple odd number') – instead of ten, calculates that Beatrice 'died' in 1281: 'dunque Dante incontrava bella e viva per le vie una donna ch'era già nella tomba da due anni . . . [queste] son cifre sibelline da lui espressamente concertate per avvertirci che quella donna non è reale ma figurata . . .' ('so Dante used to meet in the streets a real, live woman who had already been in the tomb for two years . . . these are sibylline cyphers expressly put together by him to warn us that that woman is not real but imaginary . . .') (*La Beatrice di Dante* (1842 ed.), pp. 63–65).
33 Poems by Rossetti, Scott and Tupper addressed to the members of the PRB are given in Appendix 6 of William E. Fredeman's edition of William Rossetti's *The P.R.B. Journal* (Oxford: The Clarendon Press, 1975), pp. 121–9; other poems by the circle are in Kineton Parkes, ed., *The Painter-Poets* [1890].
34 Foscolo had anticipated both Browning and Rossetti by publishing an account of Sordello's career in the *European Review*, September 1824, and an article on Cavalcanti in the *New Monthly Magazine*, 5, No. 19 (1822), 1–9.
35 Introduction to *Sonnets and Ballate of Guido Cavalcanti* (1912), in *The Translations of Ezra Pound*, introd. Hugh Kenner (Faber, 1970), p. 19. For Cavalcanti's poem, see Pound, pp. 106–7, Marti *Poeti . . .*, pp. 181–2. For a discussion of *virtù*, see again Pound's Introduction, pp. 18–19.
36 William notes, concerning the Rossetti children's contact with their father's studies: 'The *Convito* was always a name of dread to us, as being the very essence of arid unreadableness'. *Dante Gabriel Rossetti: His Family Letters*, with a Memoir by William Michael Rossetti (1895), I, 64.

37 The watercolour of this subject (1852), now lost, is illustrated in H. C. Marillier, *Dante Gabriel Rossetti* (Bell, 1901), facing p. 34, and in Grieve, *The Art of Dante Gabriel Rossetti*, p. 13. A very similar sketch is in Surtees, plate 45.
38 The statement by the fourteenth-century chronicler Antonio Pucci that Giotto was seventy when he died in 1337 is now generally accepted as confirmation of his having been born *c.* 1267.
39 In Carlo Del Balzo, ed., *Poesie di mille autori intorno a Dante Alighieri*, VIII (Rome: Forzani, 1903), 391–566. The text is accompanied by a French translation.
40 *Discorso sul testo*, pp. 377–8.
41 *The Stones of Venice*, II.viii.86, in *Works*, X (1904), 400. Quoted in Martin Bidney, 'The "Central Fiery Heart": Ruskin's Remaking of Dante', *Victorian Newsletter*, No. 48 (Fall 1975), p. 12. On Ruskin and the *Vita Nuova* see also Beatrice Corrigan, ed., *Italian Poets and English Critics, 1755–1859* (Chicago and London: Univ. of Chicago Press, 1969), Introd., pp. 20–7.
42 We might note that Innocent's success in restoring the temporal authority of the Holy See between 1198 and 1216 can hardly have endeared him to Dante.
43 Grieve (p. 19) thinks the figure may be Cavalcanti, but he looks more like the Cimabue from the later sketch of *Giotto painting Dante's Portrait* (plate 45). Round his neck he wears a chain of linked 'C's, which is not of much help, and a pen and inkwell, which could again refer to poetry or drawing (Dante is shown drawing with pen and ink; the medium of Rossetti's sketch itself is the same). If this were Cimabue then the small boy with him holding his master's sketchbook would, of course, be Giotto.
44 'Dante Gabriel Rossetti and Dante Alighieri', *Englische Studien*, 68 (1933–4), 230.
45 Kirkup's original drawing of the Bargello portrait is reproduced in Grieve, p. 14; for a discussion of the mask, see Holbrook, *Portraits of Dante* pp. 36–52. The illustration given here shows a plaster cast of the mask, discussed in Chapter V.
46 *Essays and Studies* (1875), p. 71.
47 Specific examples of Dantesque borrowings in *The House of Life* not mentioned in this chapter can be found in Paull Franklin Baum's commentary in his edition of the sequence (Cambridge, Mass.: Harvard Univ. Press, 1928), and in R. D. Waller's excellent chapter on Rossetti's poetry in *The Rossetti Family 1824–1854* (Manchester: Univ. of Manchester, 1932), pp. 181–207. Rossetti's sequence is hereafter abbreviated in notes to *HL*.
48 'T. S. Eliot and Dante', in *The Flaming Heart* (New York: Doubleday, 1958), pp. 365–6. The essay first appeared in the *Southern Review*, 2, No. 3 (1937).
49 'Rossetti and Dante', *The Last Romantics* (Duckworth, 1949), p. 80.
50 *Rossetti Dante and Ourselves* (Faber, 1947), pp. 33–4. A more recent examination of 'The Importance of Dante' for Rossetti which in fact adds very little to the argument can be found in Joan Rees, *The Poetry of Dante Gabriel Rossetti: Modes of Self-Expression* (Cambridge: Cambridge Univ. Press, 1981), pp. 127–40.
51 To Rossetti's claim that in *The House of Life*: 'all the passionate and just delights of the body are declared – somewhat figuratively, it is true, but unmistakably – to be as naught if not ennobled by the concurrence of the soul at all times', Buchanan replied: 'My complaint precisely is, that Mr Rossetti's "soul" *concurs* a vast deal too easily.' Robert Buchanan, *The Fleshly School of Poetry* (1872), p. 58 and note.
52 See also the conclusion to his poem 'Parted Presence' (*Works*, p. 224).

53 Ford Madox Hueffer, *Ancient Lights and Certain New Reflections* (Chapman and Hall, 1911), p. 63.
54 See also the seventh stanza of 'The Portrait', and the second of 'Plighted Promise' (*Works*, pp. 170, 209). For Rossetti's translation of the *canzone*, see *Works*, pp. 432–3. The original is in Marti, *Poeti* . . ., pp. 57–62.
55 'Prose Paraphrase of *The House of Life*', *Dante Gabriel Rossetti as Designer and Writer* (1899), p. 261. See also R. Bentley, 'Religious Themes and Images in the Work of D. G. Rossetti', Diss. London 1974, pp. 534–51. William noted of his brother: 'I cannot say with any accuracy what he supposed immortality to consist of' but suggested it included for him 'a period of purgation . . . comparable more or less to the purgatory of Roman Catholics.' *Family Letters*, I, 381.
56 Browning commented amusingly in a letter: 'how I hate [Rossetti's] "Love", as a lubberly naked young man putting his arms here & his wings there, about a pair of lovers, – a fellow they would kick away, in the reality.' *Dearest Isa*, ed. and introd. Edward C. McAleer (Edinburgh: Nelson, 1951), p. 337.
57 'The Blood's Winter', in Baum, *Analytical List*, pp. 61–2.
58 *An Essay on the 'Vita Nuova'* (1949; rpt. Baltimore: Johns Hopkins, 1977), Chap. III, 'From Love to Caritas', pp. 63–74.
59 Rossetti took the original from *Poeti del primo secolo della lingua italiana* (Florence, 1816), I, 319.
60 *Letters*, I, 39. Hunt's letter is quoted in *Family Letters*, I, 122–3.
61 *Romantic Image* (1957; rpt. Fontana, 1971), pp. 71, 56–7.
62 John Keats, *The Complete Poems*, ed. John Barnard, 2nd ed. (Harmondsworth: Penguin, 1976), p. 442.
63 John Livingston Lowes, '"Hyperion" and the *Purgatorio*', Letter, *TLS*, 11 Jan. 1936, p. 35; see also Robert Gittings, 'Keats's Debt to Dante', *The Mask of Keats* (Heinemann, 1956), p. 43.
64 See for example Bruno Nardi, 'Il concetto dell'Impero nello svolgimento del pensiero dantesco', in *Saggi di filosofia dantesca*, 2nd ed. (Florence: 'La Nuova Italia', 1967), p. 266.
65 Lowes's equation of Beatrice and Moneta on the grounds that the former also enjoys an 'inner vision which she alone could see', replaces the allegorical Beatrice with a modern symbolical one. This is achieved by omitting any reference to the *Paradiso* in which Beatrice communicates at least part of her vision.
66 'For Our Lady of the Rocks: By Leonardo da Vinci', *Works*, p. 171.
67 See Ricks's Introduction to the poem in *The Poems of Tennyson*, pp. 855–8.
68 See John D. Rosenberg, 'The Two Kingdoms of *In Memoriam*', *Journal of English and Germanic Philology*, 58 (1959), 228–40.
69 Reported by Sir James Knowles in 'Aspects of Tennyson: A Personal Reminiscence', *Nineteenth Century*, 33 (Jan.–June 1893), 182; quoted in *Poems*, p. 859. Dante explains in his letter to Can Grande that his poem can be called a comedy because it begins in adversity but ends happily (*Ep.* X.10).
70 Dante does in fact make clear that there is no loss of individuality as such in Heaven: the spirits may 'lose themselves' in light initially, but we are told in canto XIV that the blessed will repossess their bodies after the Last Judgement (see *Paradiso* XIV.43–66).
71 A greater but rather generalising claim for Dante's influence on *In Memoriam*, through the medium of Hallam's own interest in Dante, is made out by Gordon D. Hirsch, 'Tennyson's *Commedia*', *Victorian Poetry*, 8 (1970), 93–106.

V W. B. Yeats and Dante's Mask

1 *The Variorum Edition of the Poems of W. B. Yeats*, ed. Peter Allt and Russell K. Alspach (New York: Macmillan, 1957), p. 154. All references to Yeats's poems are to this edition.
2 Quoted in Richard Ellmann, *The Identity of Yeats*, 2nd ed. (Faber, 1964), p. 72.
3 *A Vision* (Laurie, 1925), pp. 28–9. This first version of *A Vision*, with which we are mainly concerned, has been re-issued as *A Critical Edition of Yeats's 'A Vision' (1925)*, ed. George Mills Harper and Walter Kelly Hood (Macmillan, 1978).
4 Collected in *Essays and Introductions* (Macmillan, 1961), pp. 116–45, to which all references are made; henceforth abbreviated to *EI*.
5 *The Trembling of the Veil* (1922), in *Autobiographies* (Macmillan, 1955), p. 261.
6 *Per Amica Silentia Lunae* (1918), in *Mythologies* (Macmillan, 1959), p. 329. C. L. Shadwell's translation of the *Purgatorio* was published in two parts in 1892 and 1899, and his *Paradiso* in 1915.
7 Preface to *Illustrations to the 'Divine Comedy' of Dante . . . by Stradanus*, introd. Guido Biagi (1892), no pag.
8 Albert S. Roe says of this illustration: 'while the scene at first glance appears much as Dante describes it, the symbolism is entirely Blake's own and very different from that of the poem. Detailed study will show that, of all the illustrations, this is perhaps the one in which Blake's personally contrived mythological system figures to the greatest extent'. See *Blake's Illustrations to 'The Divine Comedy'* (Princeton: Princeton Univ. Press, 1953), p. 166 and plate 88.
9 In *EI*, pp. 261–97.
10 *Memoirs*, ed. Denis Donoghue (Macmillan, 1972), p. 249.
11 *Autobiographies*, p. 191. The 'tale' is told by the fourteenth-century writer Franco Sacchetti. See his *Il Trecentonovelle*, ed. Emilio Faccioli (Turin: Einaudi, 1970), Nos. 114–15 (pp. 298–302).
12 'The Irish Dramatic Movement: *Samhain*: 1905', in *Explorations*, select. Mrs W. B. Yeats (Macmillan, 1962), pp. 198–9.
13 Preface to *Michael Robartes and the Dancer* (Dundrum: Cuala, 1920), no pag.; rpt. in *Poems*, p. 853.
14 *A Packet for Ezra Pound* (1929), in *A Vision*, 2nd version (1937; corrected and rpt. Macmillan, 1962), p. 8. This second version is henceforth referred to by its date, 1937.
15 Some instances of Dante's influence on Yeats's poetry have been well discussed by David Spurr, 'A Celtic *Commedia*: Dante in Yeats' Poetry', *Rackham Literary Studies*, 8 (1977), 99–116.
16 'The Gift of Harun Al-Rashid', *Poems*, p. 469; *A Vision*, pp. 126–7.
17 'The Double Vision of Michael Robartes', p. 384.
18 Arthur Symons, *The Symbolist Movement in Literature* (1899), introd. Richard Ellmann (New York: Dutton, 1958), p. 14.
19 *Mythologies*, p. 330; Rossetti, *Works*, pp. 370, 368 note. The sonnet is in Marti, *Poeti . . .*, pp. 228–9. *Per Amica* is dated in the text February and May 1917, but was published the following year.
20 Yeats may have coupled Dante and Keats in the poem because celebrated death-masks survived of them both; on the walls of the famous salon at Casa Guidi 'Dante's grave profile' hung on the other side of the chimney-breast to 'a cast of Keats's face and brow taken after death'. See W. W. Story's description of the room in William Sharp, *Life of Robert Browning* (1890), p. 155.

21 *The Variorum Edition of the Plays of W. B. Yeats*, ed. Russell K. Alspach and Catharine C. Alspach (Macmillan, 1966), p. 417.
22 *A Shadow of Dante*, 4th ed. (1884), p. 1.
23 See F. A. C. Wilson, *Yeats's Iconography* (Gollancz, 1960), p. 210.
24 Pound's letter to Iris Barry, 27 July 1916: 'Yeats and I spent our last winter's months on Landor.' *The Letters of Ezra Pound 1907–1941*, ed. D. D. Paige (Faber, 1951), p. 140.
25 'Tra cotanta virtù . . . in questo mirifico poeta, trovò ampissimo luogo la lussuria, e non solamente ne' giovani anni, ma ancora ne' maturi' ('But among so much virtue . . . in this wondrous poet, lust occupied a large place, not only when he was young but in the mature man as well'). Boccaccio, *Trattatello*, p. 480; Arnold, 'Dante and Beatrice', p. 668.
26 See Joseph Hone, *W. B. Yeats 1865–1939*, 2nd ed. (Macmillan, 1962), pp. 304–6.
27 For direct evidence of Yeats's assigning himself to 'Phase 17', see the editorial notes in Harper and Hood's re-issue of *A Vision*, p. 21.
28 See A. Norman Jeffares, *W. B. Yeats: Man and Poet*, 2nd ed. (Routledge and Kegan Paul, 1962), p. 212.
29 J. B. Yeats, *Letters to His Son W. B. Yeats and Others 1869–1922*, ed. Joseph Hone, pref. Oliver Elton (Faber, 1944), p. 207.
30 'If I were Four-and-Twenty', *Explorations*, p. 275.
31 Thomas Vance, 'Dante, Yeats and Unity of Being', *Shenandoah*, 17, No. 2 (1966), 73–85; Giorgio Melchiori, 'Yeats and Dante', *English Miscellany*, 19 (1968), 153–79; Harper and Hood, p. 12. Neither Vance nor Melchiori seems to me to penetrate very deeply into the relationship Yeats set up between himself and Dante. The same objection can be levelled at a more recent examination of the question by George Bornstein, 'Yeats's Romantic Dante', *Colby Library Quarterly*, 15 (1979), 93–113.
32 There were four English translations of the *Convivio* available to Yeats, by E. P. Sayer (1887), Katharine Hillard (1889), P. H. Wicksteed (1903) and W. W. Jackson (1909). It is possible that Dante's description of love a few sentences before the passage discussed above, at *Convivio* III.ii.3, also caught Yeats's eye: 'Amore . . . non è altro che unimento spirituale de l'anima e de la cosa amata; nel quale unimento di propia sua natura l'anima corre tosto e tardi, secondo che è libera o impedita' ('Love . . . is no other than the spiritual union of the soul with the thing that is loved; into which union the soul by its very nature runs sooner or later, depending on whether it is free or impeded'). It is possible that the words 'unimento di propia sua natura' are the origin of Yeats's phrase: Sayer's translation of the latter half of the sentence is: 'into which union, of its own nature, the Soul hastens sooner or later, according as it is free or impeded' (*The Banquet of Dante Alighieri*, p. 102). Could 'union, of its own nature' have become 'union of its own nature' and hence 'unity of being'? Shelley had made a memorandum on this same passage (see Rogers, *Shelley at Work*, p. 341).
33 Kirkup presented a cast of Dante's mask to the Oxford Dante Society in 1879 (Plate 7); this was loaned to the Bodleian Library in 1916 and exhibited from 1917 onwards with Toynbee's collection of portraits, busts and masks of Dante. See *The Oxford Dante Society: A Record of Forty-four Years (1876–1920)*, comp. Paget Toynbee (Oxford: printed for private circulation, 1920), pp. 50, 85, 86 note.
34 'The Irish Dramatic Movement: *Samhain*: 1904: First Principles', in *Explorations*, pp. 145–8.

VI Pound, Dante and Cavalcanti

1 As Pound stated in *Guide to Kulchur* (Faber, 1938), p. 107: 'Whether anyone between 1321 and 1905 in the year of our Lord considered that treatise as text book I as yet know not.'
2 *The Spirit of Romance* (Dent, [1910]), p. 104.
3 See for example his essay 'The Renaissance', in *Literary Essays of Ezra Pound*, ed. T. S. Eliot (Faber, 1954), p. 215: '. . . Virgil . . . has no story worth telling [in the *Aeneid*], no sense of personality. His hero is a stick who would have contributed to *The New Statesman*.' The *Literary Essays* is henceforth abbreviated to *LE*.
4 Compare Cecil Grayson's observation on how, in the sixteenth century, 'Florentines . . . like Machiavelli, tried to identify the theory of the [*De Vulgari*] with the language of the *Comedy* and with their own speech, and failed to realise that in his great poem Dante had turned his back on the refined and selective language of his treatise, preferring to use his more varied and vigorous native Florentine mingled with other external elements.' 'Dante and the Renaissance', in *Italian Studies Presented to E. R. Vincent*, ed. C. P. Brand *et al.* (Cambridge: Heffer, 1962), pp. 70–1.
5 'I gather the Limbs of Osiris' (1911–12), in *Selected Prose 1909–1965*, ed. William Cookson (Faber, 1973), p. 27.
6 *A Visiting Card* (1942), in *Selected Prose*, p. 294. Pound's booklet is hereafter abbreviated to *VCd*.
7 Norton, *The 'New Life' of Dante: An Essay, with Translations* (Cambridge, Mass., 1859), p. 13; Lowell, 'Dante', *Among My Books*, second series (Boston, 1876), p. 94. Although Norton included with his essay a translation of Cavalcanti's 'Donna me prega' by Charles T. Brooks, he did so for its curiosity-value alone, noting, 'For us it has little intrinsic worth; but it is of interest . . . as exhibiting how truly Dante was the chief author of the *dolce nuovo stile*, and how wide a difference lay between his love poems and those [of Cavalcanti]' (pp. 97–8). For Dante in America, see Angelina La Piana, *Dante's American Pilgrimage* (New Haven: Yale Univ. Press, 1948).
8 This is not at all brought out in James J. Wilhelm's *Dante and Pound: The Epic of Judgement* (Orono: Univ. of Maine Press, 1974).
9 *After Strange Gods* (Faber, 1934), p. 42.
10 See for example his interview with Donald Hall in the *Paris Review*, 28 (1962), p. 24. I return to Pound's discussion of Dante's 'packaging' later.
11 'A Retrospect', *LE*, p. 10.
12 See Giovanni Giovannini, *Ezra Pound and Dante* (Nijmegen: Dekker and Van de Vegt, [1961]), p. 7.
13 Cf. 'You have to go almost exclusively to Dante's criticism to find a set of OBJECTIVE categories for words. Dante called words "buttered" and "shaggy" because of the different NOISES they make. Or *pexa et hirsuta*, combed and hairy.' *ABC of Reading* (1934; rpt. Faber, 1951), p. 37.
14 'What I feel about Walt Whitman', *Selected Prose*, p. 116.
15 *Collected Early Poems of Ezra Pound*, ed. Michael John King, introd. Louis L. Martz (Faber, 1977), pp. 305, 133.
16 See his tribute to Shepard's teaching of Dante in *VCd*, p. 289.
17 See the revised edition of *Spirit* (Peter Owen, 1952), p. 110.
18 See his letter to Amy Lowell (1 August 1914), in *The Letters of Ezra Pound 1907–1941*, ed. D. D. Paige (Faber, 1951), p. 78.
19 See for example Martz's description in his Introduction to the *Collected Early*

Poems of how 'the medieval poets showed [Pound] a way of escaping from the Swinburnian twilight' (p. xiv).

20 'Ezra Pound', *Egoist*, 4 (1917), 7–8.

21 'Credo', from 'Prolegomena', dated 'Dec. 1911' in the footnote on p. 12 of *LE*, originally published in the *Poetry Review*, 2 (February 1912), 76.

22 *Sonnets and Ballate of Guido Cavalcanti* (Swift, 1912). The translation of 'biltà', 'vileness' (= 'viltà'), in the last example quoted is presumably a simple mistake on Pound's part.

23 For favourable assessments of Pound's translations see Anne Paolucci, 'Ezra Pound and D. G. Rossetti as Translators of Guido Cavalcanti', *Romanic Review*, 51 (1960), 256–67, an article that insists on Pound's 'unerring taste' (p. 261); and G. Singh, 'Pound and Cavalcanti', in *Essays in Honour of John Humphreys Whitfield*, ed. H. C. Davis *et al.* (St George's Press for the Italian Department, University of Birmingham, 1975), pp. 268–84. More doubtful judgements are expressed by Donald Davie, *Ezra Pound: Poet as Sculptor* (Routledge and Kegan Paul, 1965), pp. 102–12, and Christine Brooke-Rose, *A ZBC of Ezra Pound* (Faber, 1971), pp. 81ff.

24 'Gentildonna' is in *Collected Shorter Poems*, 2nd ed. (Faber, 1968), p. 101.

25 *Sonnets and Ballate*, p. 6; rpt. in *The Translations of Ezra Pound*, introd. Hugh Kenner (Faber, 1970), p. 20. Subsequent references to Pound's Introduction are to this edition.

26 'Cavalcanti', *LE*, p. 194.

27 Paolucci's article (above, note 23) has a good analysis of the differences between the two translations, though her argument seems unduly weighted in favour of Pound's.

28 'Salutation the Second', from 'Contemporania', *Poetry*, 2 (April–Sept. 1913), 6; rpt. in *Shorter Poems*, p. 94.

29 *Gaudier-Brzeska* (1916), new edition (Hessle: Marvell Press, 1960), p. 86.

30 J. C. L. Simonde de Sismondi, *De la littérature du Midi de l'Europe* (Paris, 1813), I, 391, 409.

31 *Essays on Petrarch*, p. 174; quoted in Toynbee, II, 169.

32 'Hugh Selwyn Mauberley', *Collected Shorter Poems*, p. 206. See also Symons's comment on the pathological tendency of decadent art, as represented by the inability of the 'vague dreamer' to recognise outlines compared with the clarity of Dante's 'seeing', quoted above, p. 149.

33 Edmund Burke, *A Philosophical Enquiry into the Origin of our Ideas of the Sublime and Beautiful*, ed. J. T. Boulton (Routledge and Kegan Paul, 1958), pp. 60–1.

34 *Paris Review* interview, p. 24.

35 See the commentary to his edition of the *De Vulgari*, *Opere di Dante*, ed. Michele Barbi, VI (Florence: Le Monnier, 1938), 178.

36 Cf. *A Visiting Card*, p. 282: 'What counts is the direction of the will . . . The name of the Fascist era is *Voluntas*.'

37 *The Cantos of Ezra Pound*, revised collected ed. (Faber, 1975), p. 20.

38 'Shakespeare and the Stoicism of Seneca', *Selected Essays*, p. 136.

39 In the first American edition of *Lustra*.

40 'An Introduction to the Economic Nature of the United States', *Selected Prose*, p. 137.

41 Ronald Bush regards ' . . . Cantos I to XXX (or perhaps to XLI) . . . [as] the poem's "inferno"', partly because they present a series of characters 'stranded in mid-life, dreaming of their renascence'. Thus Pound's admiration for Malatesta is only provisional and might be compared with Dante's 'heroic' presentation

of Farinata. See *The Genesis of Ezra Pound's 'Cantos'* (Princeton: Princeton Univ. Press, 1976), p. 16 note, pp. 86–7. Another similarity between the two poems might be seen in the harmony between Church and Empire and State and Bank the *Commedia* and *Cantos* propose respectively.

42 See Gabrielle Barfoot, 'The Theme of Usury in Dante and Pound', *Rivista di letterature moderne e comparate*, 30 (1977), 254–83.

43 See his comment in *The Sacred Wood*, p. 150, quoted above, p. 24.

44 For an outspoken Italian criticism of Pound's discussion of the *Inferno* in *Spirit* see Napoleone Orsini, 'Ezra Pound, critico letterario', *Letterature moderne*, 7 (1957), 38–40.

45 'Blast', *'Ezra Pound Speaking': Radio Speeches of World War II*, ed. Leonard W. Doob (Westport, Conn.:Greenwood Press, 1978), p. 109. 'Il ben de l'intelletto' – 'the good of the intellect' – is truth, and here means the highest truth of all, namely God.

46 Georg M. Gugelberger, '"By No Means An Orderly Dantescan Rising"', *Italian Quarterly*, 16 (1973), 42.

47 Quoted by Angela C. Y. Jung Palandri, 'Italian Images of Ezra Pound', *Italian Quarterly*, 16 (1973), 21, note 3.

48 Wilhelm notes (*Dante and Pound*, p. 140) that in the later *Cantos* '. . . Dante is seen as the Roman or western end-product of the Byzantine development. Instead of regarding Dante as a pre-Renaissance idealist and kinsman of Aquinas, Pound views him as a member of that fraternity of Neoplatonic nature disciples who preached love in the Apollonian tradition . . .'

49 Marti, *Poeti . . .*, pp. 133–4; Pound, *Translations*, p. 38. Marti's is the accepted reading of this line, 'che far tremar di chiaritate l'ârc . . .', a reading Pound inveighs against in his Introduction (p. 24). His own reading is also quoted in Canto LXXIV, p. 448.

50 *A ZBC of Ezra Pound*, p. 214. Concerning the first excerpt from the 'Donna me prega' quoted here, Marti in his commentary (p. 186) follows Bruno Nardi in taking as the subject of 'disciende' (to retain Pound's reading) not 'Amore' but the 'possibile intelletto' of l. 22; thus the lines would mean that Love does not station itself in the 'possible intellect' 'Because this does not derive from the qualities [of the four elements but is a separate, incorruptible substance] and in it only eternal ideas [not passions] shine'. Brooke-Rose explains the second excerpt (where Pound has again taken 'Amore' as the subject) as meaning 'he [the lover] doesn't move when he is being shot at' because 'love has so benumbed' him; Marti takes it to mean that the lover cannot move so as to approach (and conquer, the object of his love) (p. 189).

51 See Bruno Nardi, 'L'Averroismo del "primo amico" di Dante' and 'Di un nuovo commento alla canzone del Cavalcanti sull'amore', in *Dante e la cultura medievale*, 2nd ed. (Bari: Laterza, 1949), pp. 93–152. A previous examination of Pound's use of the 'Donna me prega' can be found in Georg M. Gugelberger, 'The Secularization of "Love" to a Poetic Metaphor: Cavalcanti, Center of Pound's Medievalism', *Paideuma*, 2 (1973), 159–73. Gugelberger rather uncritically adopts Pound's interpretation of the *canzone*, adducing J. E. Shaw's study, *Guido Cavalcanti's Theory of Love* (Toronto: Univ. of Toronto Press, 1949), to support him at several points in the argument. Shaw's approach to the *canzone* had itself been criticised by Nardi (pp. 100–1).

52 From the added chapter to the 1952 edition of *Spirit*, 'Psychology and Troubadours', p. 88. The chapter was originally published in the *Quest* (October 1912).

53 *Cantos LXXII and LXXIII*, still not included in the collection *Cantos*, were

published in a limited edition by The Estate of Ezra Pound (Washington D.C., 1973). The quotation is from p. 11.

54 See Canto XCII, p. 620.

55 'For T. S. E.', *Selected Prose*, p. 434; originally in the *Sewanee Review*, 74 (1966), 109.

VII T. S. Eliot: the return to reality

1 'Rudyard Kipling', in *On Poetry and Poets* (Faber, 1957), p. 235. This book is henceforth abbreviated in the notes to *OPAP*.

2 'What Dante Means to Me', in *To Criticize the Critic* (Faber, 1965), p. 125.

3 Letter to Paul Elmer More, 2 June 1930, quoted in James Sullivan Torrens, 'T. S. Eliot and the Contribution of Dante towards a Poetics of Sensibility', Diss. Michigan 1968, p. 155.

4 *Dante*, rpt. in *Selected Essays*, 3rd ed. (Faber, 1951), p. 275; this volume is henceforth abbreviated to *SE*.

5 'Shakespeare and the Stoicism of Seneca', *SE*, p. 137. Henceforth 'SSS'.

6 *The Complete Poems and Plays of T. S. Eliot* (Faber, 1969), p. 180. Henceforth *CP*.

7 Clark Lectures (1926), unpublished, Lecture III, p. 20. The typescript of the lectures is in the library of King's College, Cambridge.

8 'Virgil and the Christian World', *OPAP*, p. 131.

9 'Tradition and the Individual Talent', *SE*, p. 14. Henceforth 'TrIT'.

10 See, for example, A. D. Moody, *Thomas Stearns Eliot: Poet* (Cambridge: Cambridge Univ. Press, 1979), pp. 77–8.

11 In the *Saturday Review of Literature*, 10 December 1927, p. 429.

12 See Moody, *Thomas Stearns Eliot*, p. 139.

13 On its appearance in *Commerce*, 21 (Autumn 1929), pp. 99–103.

14 C. H. Grandgent, *Dante* (Harrap, 1920), p. 273. Exaggerated claims of the affinities between part III of the poem and the *Purgatorio* can be found in Sister M. Cleophas, '*Ash-Wednesday*: The *Purgatorio* in a Modern Mode', *Comparative Literature*, 11 (1959), 329–39.

15 'Dante', *The Sacred Wood* (Methuen, 1920), p. 150. This is enclosed within inverted commas in documentation and thus distinguishable from the *Dante* essay of 1929.

16 'Niccolo Machiavelli', in *For Lancelot Andrewes* (1928; rpt. Faber, 1970), p. 51. At the same time we can distinguish Eliot's admiration for Dante's damned from, say, the Romantic hero-worship of Milton's Satan with its predominantly political emphasis, in which the rights of the individual are upheld against an autocratic ruler. In welcoming the potential for damnation as a sign of spiritual life Eliot is hardly condoning insurrection in this world or the next.

17 'An Introduction to the *Inferno*', *The Two Dantes*, p. 3.

18 See the Introduction to his edition of *Selected Prose of T. S. Eliot* (Faber, 1975), p. 21; and, for a longer discussion of Eliot's and Dante's Imperialism, the first chapter of *The Classic*, pp. 15–45.

19 *The Idea of a Christian Society* (Faber, 1939), p. 49.

20 *Eliot's Early Years* (Oxford: Oxford Univ. Press, 1977), p. 1.

21 *Little Review*, 4, No. 1 (1917), 9.

22 *The Invisible Poet: T. S. Eliot* (Allen, 1960), p. 104.

23 See Paget Toynbee, *A Dictionary of Proper Names and Notable Matters in the Works of Dante*, rev. Charles S. Singleton (Oxford: The Clarendon Press, 1968), p. 344, where Angioli's *Storia del convento d'Assisi* is quoted to the effect

that Guido 'in ordine pie ac umiliter vixit, errata lacrimis et jejuniis diluens, et religiosissime in sacra Assisiensi domo obiit' ('lived piously and humbly within the order, cleansing his sins with tears and fasting, and died most religiously in the sacred church at Assisi'). Dante seems at first to have accepted that Guido's last years were spent entirely *religiosissime*, to judge from *Convivio* IV.xxviii.8.

24 Joseph Conrad, *Heart of Darkness* (Harmondsworth: Penguin, 1973), pp. 101–2. For a sound account of Eliot's poem see Everett A. Gillis, 'The Spiritual Status of T. S. Eliot's Hollow Men', *Texas Studies in Literature and Language*, 2 (1960–1), 464–75.

25 *The Rock* (Faber, 1934), p. 46.

26 1970 ed., p. 26; rpt. in *SE*, p. 352.

27 'Donne in Our Time', in *A Garland for John Donne 1631–1931*, ed. Theodore Spencer (Cambridge, Mass.: Harvard Univ. Press, 1931), p. 8.

28 'Rhyme and Reason: The Poetry of John Donne', *Listener*, 19 March 1930, p. 503.

29 The most conspicuous example is in his elevation of the Averroist thinker Siger of Brabant, whom Aquinas had publicly refuted in 1266, to the *cielo del sole*, together with St Thomas himself (*Par.* x.133–8). See Etienne Gilson, *Dante the Philosopher*, trans. David Moore (Sheed and Ward, 1948), pp. 257–81.

30 *The Use of Poetry and the Use of Criticism*, 2nd ed. (Faber, 1964), p. 99.

31 Eliot's Introduction to Paul Valéry, *Le Serpent*, trans. Mark Wardle (*The Criterion*, 1924), p. 13.

32 The *Egoist*, 5 (1918), 87.

33 'L' "Utilità" di Dante pel mondo moderno', in *Pagine sparse*, 2nd ed. (Bari: Laterza, 1960), II, 335.

34 *The Composition of 'Four Quartets'* (Faber, 1978), p. 64.

35 A. C. Charity, 'T. S. Eliot: The Dantean Recognitions', in '*The Waste Land' in Different Voices*, ed. A. D. Moody (Edward Arnold, 1974), pp. 141–8.

36 The *Quartets* are abbreviated to their respective initials in the notes from this point on.

37 The parallel is also noted by Wayne H. Hoffmann-Ogier, in a long, thorough discussion of 'Dantean Parallels in T. S. Eliot's Description of a Mystical Experience in "Burnt Norton I" ', *Studia Mystica*, 2 (Fall 1979), 24–58.

38 'T. S. Eliot as a Critic', *Sewanee Review*, 84 (1966), 269.

39 For Bettinelli, see above, Chapter II, note 6; Bembo's strictures are in the second Book of his *Prose della volgar lingua*, ed. Mario Marti (Padua: Liviana, 1955), p. 56.

40 'Virgil and the Christian World', p. 131.

Conclusion

1 It is interesting to note in Seamus Heaney's latest collection *Field Work* (Faber, 1979) recreations of episodes from the *Inferno*, as in 'An Afterwards' (p. 44) and 'Leavings' (p. 57), together with his translation of the Ugolino episode (pp. 61–4).

2 *Notes towards the Definition of Culture*, 2nd ed. (Faber, 1962), p. 124.

Bibliography

1. General

Abrams, M. H. *The Mirror and the Lamp*. New York: Oxford Univ. Press, 1953.
Auerbach, Erich, 'Figura'. Trans. Ralph Manheim. In his *Scenes from the Drama of European Literature*. Gloucester, Mass.: Smith, 1973, pp. 11–76.
Mimesis. Trans. Willard R. Trask. Princeton: Princeton Univ. Press, 1953.
Carlyle, Thomas. 'The Hero as Poet'. In *On Heroes, Hero-Worship, & the Heroic in History*. 1841, pp. 126–85.
Hazlitt, William. *Lectures on the English Poets*. 1818.
Kermode, Frank. *The Classic*. Faber, 1975.
Romantic Image. 1957; rpt. Fontana, 1971.
Landor, Walter Savage. *The Pentameron and Pentalogia*. 1837.
Langbaum, Robert. *The Poetry of Experience*. Chatto and Windus, 1957.
Marti, Mario, ed. *Poeti del dolce stil nuovo*. Florence: Le Monnier, 1969.

2. Dante

I. Editions and translations of Dante

Barbi, Michele, introd. Dante Alighieri, *Il Convivio*. Ed. G. Busnelli and G. Vandelli. 2nd ed. Vol. I. In *Opere di Dante*. Ed. M. Barbi. Vol. IV. Florence: Le Monnier, 1953.
Boyd, Henry, trans. *The Divina Commedia*. 3 vols. 1802.
Cary, H. F., trans. *The Vision: or Hell, Purgatory and Paradise of Dante Alighieri*. 2nd ed. 3 vols. 1819.
Dante Alighieri. *La Commedia*. Ed. Giorgio Petrocchi. *Le Opere di Dante Alighieri*. Edizione nazionale, 7. 4 vols. [Milan]: Mondadori, 1966–7.
Il Convivio. Ed. Maria Simonelli. Bologna: Pàtron, 1966.
De Vulgari Eloquentia. Ed. Pier Vincenzo Mengaldo. Vol. I. Padua: Antenore, 1968.
Epistolae. Ed. Paget Toynbee. 2nd ed. Oxford: The Clarendon Press, 1966.
Monarchia. Ed. Pier Giorgio Ricci. Edizione nazionale, 5. [Milan]: Mondadori, 1965.
Rime. Ed. Gianfranco Contini. 3rd ed. Turin: Einaudi, 1973.
Vita Nuova. Ed. Domenico De Robertis. Milan: Ricciardi, 1980.
Garrow, Joseph, trans. *The Early Life of Dante Alighieri*. Florence, 1846.

Lyell, Charles, trans. *The Canzoniere of Dante, including the Poems of the 'Vita Nuova' and 'Convito'.* 1835. New editions, 1840, 1842, 1845.
Marigo, Aristide, ed. *De Vulgari Eloquentia.* In *Opere di Dante.* Ed. Michele Barbi. Vol. VI. Florence: Le Monnier, 1938.
Martin, Theodore, trans. *The 'Vita Nuova' of Dante.* 1862.
Norton, Charles Eliot. *The 'New Life' of Dante: An Essay, with Translations.* Cambridge, Mass. 1859.
Oelsner, Hermann, ed. *The 'Divina Commedia', with an English Prose Translation.* Temple Classics. Vol. I. *Inferno.* (Trans. J. A. Carlyle. Rev. H. Oelsner). Vol. II. *Purgatorio.* (Trans. T. Okey). Vol. III. *Paradiso.* (Trans. P. H. Wicksteed). Dent, 1899–1900.
Sapegno, Natalino, ed. *La Divina Commedia.* La letteratura italiana: storia e testi. Vol. IV. Milan: Ricciardi, 1957.
Sayer, E. P., trans. *The Banquet of Dante Alighieri.* 1887.
Shadwell, Charles Lancelot, trans. *The Paradise of Dante Alighieri.* Introd. J. W. Mackail. Macmillan, 1915.
trans. *The Purgatory of Dante Alighieri.* Introd. Walter Pater. 2 vols. 1892 and 1899.

II. Dante biography and criticism – General

Arnold, Matthew. 'Dante and Beatrice'. *Fraser's Magazine*, 67 (Jan.-June 1863), 665–9.
Aroux, Eugène. *Dante hérétique, révolutionnaire et socialiste.* Paris, 1854.
Barbi, Michele, *Life of Dante.* Trans. and ed. Paul G. Ruggiers. Berkeley and Los Angeles: Univ. of California Press, 1954.
Boccaccio, Giovanni. *Trattatello in laude di Dante.* Ed. Pier Giorgio Ricci. In *Tutte le opere.* Ed. Vittore Branca. Vol. III. [Milan]: Mondadori, 1974.
Bowra, C. M. 'Dante and Sordello'. *Comparative Literature*, 5 (1953), 1–15.
Chabanon, Michel. *Vie du Dante.* Amsterdam, 1773.
Coleridge, S. T. 'Donne–Dante–Milton–*Paradise Lost*'. In *Notes and Lectures upon Shakespeare . . . with other Literary Remains.* Ed. Mrs H. N. Coleridge. 1849. Vol. II, 91–126.
Croce, Benedetto. *La poesia di Dante.* 7th ed. Bari: Laterza, 1952.
'L' "Utilità" di Dante pel mondo moderno". In *Pagine sparse.* 2nd ed. Bari: Laterza, 1960. Vol. II, 329–35.
De Sanctis, Francesco. *Storia della letteratura italiana.* Introd. Natalino Sapegno. Ed. Niccolò Gallo. In *Opere*. Ed. Carlo Muscetta. Vol. VIII. Turin: Einaudi, 1958.
Foscolo, Ugo. *Discorso sul testo del poema di Dante.* (Ed. F. S. Orlandini). In *Opere edite e postume.* Florence, 1850. Vol. III.
Essays on Petrarch. 1821; rpt. 1823. In *Opere*. Edizione nazionale. Vol. x. Ed. Cesare Foligno. Florence: Le Monnier, 1953, 1–147.
Foster, Kenelm. *The Two Dantes and Other Studies.* Darton, Longman and Todd, 1977.
Frattarolo, R. 'Dante nella critica fra tre e cinquecento'. In *Letture classensi.* Vol. III. Ravenna: Longo, 1970.
Gilson, Etienne. *Dante the Philosopher.* Trans. David Moore. Sheed & Ward, 1948.
Gombrich, E. H. 'Giotto's Portrait of Dante?'. *Burlington Magazine*, 121 (1979), 471–83.
Grandgent, C. H. *Dante.* Harrap, 1920.

Grayson, Cecil. 'Dante and the Renaissance'. In *Italian Studies Presented to E. R. Vincent*. Ed. C. P. Brand *et al.* Cambridge: Heffer, 1962, pp. 57–75.

Guidubaldi, Egidio. *Dante europeo.* Vol. 1. Florence: Olschki, 1965.

Holbrook, Richard Thayer. *Portraits of Dante from Giotto to Raffael.* Lee Warner, 1911.

La Piana, Angelina. *Dante's American Pilgrimage.* New Haven: Yale Univ. Press, 1948.

Lowell, James Russell. 'Dante'. In *Among My Books.* Second series. Boston: 1876, pp. 1–124.

Macaulay, Thomas Babington, Baron Macaulay. 'Criticisms on the Principal Italian Writers: No 1: Dante'. In *Works.* Ed. Lady Trevelyan. 1871. Vol. VII, 601–18.

[Martin, Theodore]. 'The *Vita Nuova* of Dante'. *Dublin University Magazine*, 29 (Jan.-June 1847), 412–27.

Martinelli, Luciana. *Dante.* Storia della critica, 4. Palermo: Palumbo, 1966.

Mather, Frank Jewett, Jr. *The Portraits of Dante compared with the Measurements of His Skull and Reclassified.* Oxford: Oxford Univ. Press, 1921.

Merian, J. B. *Dissertazione sulla 'Divina Commedia'.* In Dante Alighieri, *Canzoni e sonetti.* Ed. R. Zotti. 1809, pp. vii-ccx.

Nardi, Bruno. *Dante e la cultura medievale.* 2nd ed. Bari: Laterza, 1949.

Saggi di filosofia dantesca. 2nd ed. Florence: 'La Nuova Italia', 1967.

Ozanam, Antoine Frédéric. *Dante et la philosophie catholique au treizième siècle.* Paris: 1839.

Parodi, E. G. 'La *Divina Commedia*, Poema della libertà dell'individuo e il canto XXVII del *Purgatorio*'. In *Dante: Raccolta di studi.* Ed. Alojzij Res. Gorizia: Paternolli, 1921, pp. 31–41.

Ricci, Pier Giorgio. 'Monarchia'. *Enciclopedia Dantesca.* 6 vols. Rome: Istituto della Enciclopedia Italiana, 1970–8.

Rossetti, Gabriele. *La Beatrice di Dante.* 1842. New ed. Ed. Maria Luisa Giartosio de Courten. Imola: Galeati, 1935.

Sullo spirito antipapale che produsse la Riforma, e sulla segreta influenza ch'esercitò nella letteratura d'Europa e specialmente d'Italia. 1832. Trans. C. Ward as: *Disquisitions on the Antipapal Spirit which produced the Reformation . . .* 2 vols. 1834.

Rossetti, Maria F. *A Shadow of Dante.* 4th ed. 1884.

Ruskin, John. *Comments of John Ruskin on the 'Divina Commedia'.* Comp. G. P. Huntington. Introd. C. E. Norton. Boston Mass.: Houghton Mifflin, 1903.

Santayana, George. *Three Philosophical Poets.* Cambridge, Mass.: Harvard Univ. Press, 1910.

Singleton, Charles S. *An Essay on the 'Vita Nuova'.* 1949; rpt. Baltimore: Johns Hopkins, 1977.

Solerti, Angelo, comp. *Le Vite di Dante, Petrarca e Boccaccio scritte fino al secolo decimosesto.* Milan: Vallardi, [1904].

[Taaffe, John]. *A Comment on the 'Divine Comedy' of Dante Alighieri.* 1822.

Toynbee, Paget. *A Dictionary of Proper Names and Notable Matters in the Works of Dante.* Rev. Charles S. Singleton. Oxford: The Clarendon Press, 1968.

comp. *The Oxford Dante Society: A Record of Forty-four Years (1876–1920).* Oxford: privately printed, 1920.

'The *Vita Nuova* of Dante'. *Fraser's Magazine*, 65 (Jan.-June 1862), 580–94.

Wicksteed, P. H. *The Early Lives of Dante.* Moring, 1904.

Yates, Frances A. 'Transformations of Dante's Ugolino'. *Journal of the Warburg and Courtauld Institutes*, 14 (1951), 92–117.

III. Dante in English literature – General

Bidney, Martin. 'The "Central Fiery Heart": Ruskin's Remaking of Dante'. *Victorian Newsletter*, 48 (Fall 1975), 9–15.

'Ruskin's Uses of Dante'. Diss. Indiana 1971.

Brand, C. P. *Italy and the English Romantics.* Cambridge: Cambridge Univ. Press, 1957.

Corrigan, Beatrice, ed. *Italian Poets and English Critics, 1755–1859.* Chicago and London: Univ. of Chicago Press, 1969.

Cunningham, G. F. *The 'Divine Comedy' in English.* Vol. I, 1782–1900. Vol. II, 1901–66. Edinburgh and London: Oliver & Boyd, 1965–6.

De Sua, William. *Dante into English: A Study of the Translation of the 'Divine Comedy' in Britain and America.* Chapel Hill: Univ. of North Carolina Press, 1964.

Doughty, Oswald. 'Dante and the English Romantic Poets'. *English Miscellany*, 2 (1951), 125–69.

Farinelli, Arturo. *Dante in Spagna, Francia, Inghilterra, Germania.* Turin: Bocca, 1922.

Flick, Adrian John. 'Dante in English Romanticism'. Diss. Cambridge 1978.

Friederich, Werner P. *Dante's Fame Abroad 1350–1850.* N.p.: Univ of North Carolina Press, 1950.

Gittings, Robert. 'Keats's Debt to Dante'. In *The Mask of Keats.* Heinemann, 1956, pp. 5–44.

Halley, A. R. 'The Influence of Dante on the Nineteenth-Century English Poets'. Diss. Harvard 1922.

Hirsch, Gordon D. 'Tennyson's *Commedia*'. *Victorian Poetry*, 8 (1970), 93–106.

Lowes, John Livingston. '"Hyperion" and the *Purgatorio*'. Letter. *TLS*, 11 Jan. 1936, 35.

Reynolds, Mary T. *Joyce and Dante: The Shaping Imagination.* Princeton: Princeton Univ. Press, 1981.

Saly, John V. 'Dante and the English Romantics'. Diss. Columbia 1959.

Toynbee, Paget, comp. *Britain's Tribute to Dante in Literature and Art.* British Academy, 1921.

comp. *Dante in English Literature: From Chaucer to Cary (c. 1380–1844).* 2 vols. Methuen, 1909.

Vincent, E. R. 'Fortuna di Dante in Inghilterra'. *Enciclopedia Dantesca.*

3. Shelley

Bradley, A. C. 'Notes on Shelley's *Triumph of Life*'. *Modern Language Review*, 9 (1914), 441–56.

Brown, Richard E. 'The Role of Dante in *Epipsychidion*'. *Comparative Literature*, 30 (1978), 223–35.

Duerkson, Roland A. *Shelleyan Ideas in Victorian Literature*. The Hague: Mouton, 1966.

Holmes, Richard. *Shelley: The Pursuit.* Weidenfeld and Nicolson, 1974.

Medwin, Thomas. *The Life of Percy Bysshe Shelley*. Ed. H. Buxton Forman. Oxford: Oxford Univ. Press, 1913.

Peck, Walter Edwin. *Shelley: His Life and Work.* Boston: Houghton Mifflin, 1927. Vol. II.

Rogers, Neville. *Shelley at Work.* 2nd ed. Oxford: The Clarendon Press, 1967.

Shelley, Mary. *Mary Shelley's Journal*. Ed. Frederick L. Jones. Norman: Univ. of Oklahoma Press, 1947.
Shelley, Percy Bysshe. *The Letters of Percy Bysshe Shelley*. Ed. Frederick L. Jones. 2 vols. Oxford: The Clarendon Press, 1964.
Poetical Works. Ed. Thomas Hutchinson. Rev. G. M. Matthews. 2nd ed. Oxford: Oxford Univ. Press, 1970.
Shelley's Prose. Ed. David Lee Clark. 2nd ed. Albuquerque: Univ. of New Mexico Press, 1966.
trans. *The Symposium*. In *The Complete Works of Percy Bysshe Shelley*. Ed. Roger Ingpen and Walter E. Peck. Julian Edition. Vol. VII. Benn, 1930, 157–220.
Webb, Timothy. *The Violet in the Crucible: Shelley and Translation*. Oxford: The Clarendon Press, 1976.
Zacchetti, Corrado. *Shelley e Dante*. Milan: Sandron, 1922.

4. Byron

Beaty, Frederick L. 'Byron and the Story of Francesca da Rimini'. *PMLA*, 75 (1960), 395–401.
Byron, George Gordon, Lord Byron. *'Born for Opposition': Byron's Letters and Journals*. Ed. Leslie A. Marchand. Vol. VIII (1821). John Murray, 1978.
The Works of Lord Byron. Vols. I-VII. Ed. Ernest Hartley Coleridge. John Murray, 1898–1904.
Medwin, Thomas. *Conversations of Lord Byron*. Ed. Ernest J. Lovell, Jr. Princeton: Princeton Univ. Press, 1966.
Taylor, Beverly. 'Byron's Uses of Dante in *The Prophecy of Dante*'. *Keats–Shelley Journal*, 28 (1979), 102–19.
Thorslev, Peter L, Jr. *The Byronic Hero: Types and Prototypes*. Minneapolis: Univ. of Minnesota Press, 1962.
Woodhouse, C. M. 'The Religion of an Agnostic'. *The Byron Journal*, 6 (1978), 26–33.
Zacchetti, Corrado. *Lord Byron e L'Italia*. Palermo: Sandron, 1919.

5. Browning

Browning, Robert. *Dearest Isa: Robert Browning's Letters to Isabella Blagden*. Ed. Edward C. McAleer. Edinburgh: Nelson, 1951.
'Essay on Shelley'. *The Browning Society's Papers, 1881–4*. Pt. I, i (1881), 5–19.
The Letters of Robert Browning and Elizabeth Barrett Barrett 1845–1846. Ed. Elvan Kintner. Cambridge, Mass.: Harvard Univ. Press, 1969. Vol. I.
Poetical Works 1833–1864. Ed. Ian Jack. Oxford: Oxford Univ. Press, 1970.
The Ring and the Book. Ed. Richard D. Altick. Harmondsworth: Penguin, 1971.
Sordello. 1840.
Strafford: An Historical Tragedy. 1837.
Fairchild, Hoxie N. 'Browning'. In his *Religious Trends in English Poetry*. Vol. IV. New York: Columbia Univ. Press, 1957, 132–67.
'Browning the Simple-Hearted Casuist'. *University of Toronto Quarterly*, 18 (1948–9), 234–40.
Holmes, Stewart W. 'The Sources of Browning's *Sordello*'. *Studies in Philology*, 34 (1937), 467–96.
McCrory, T. E. 'Browning and Dante'. Diss. Pennsylvania 1958.
Mason, M. Y. 'A Study of Browning's Poem *Sordello*'. Diss. Oxford 1965.

Sharp, William. *Life of Robert Browning*. 1890.
Shaw, J. E. 'The "Donna Angelicata" in *The Ring and the Book*'. *PMLA*, 41 (1926), 55–81.
Stevenson, Lionel. 'Tennyson, Browning, and a Romantic Fallacy'. *University of Toronto Quarterly*, 13 (1943–4), 175–95.
Sullivan, Ruth Elizabeth. 'Browning's "Childe Roland" and Dante's *Inferno*'. *Victorian Poetry*, 5 (1967), 296–302.

6. Rossetti

Banerjee, Ron D. K. 'Dante through the Looking Glass: Rossetti, Pound, and Eliot'. *Comparative Literature*, 24 (1972), 136–49.
Bentley, R. 'Religious Themes and Images in the Work of D. G. Rossetti'. Diss. London 1974.
Gray, Nicolette. *Rossetti Dante and Ourselves*. Faber, 1947.
Grieve, A. I. *The Art of Dante Gabriel Rossetti No. 3: The Watercolours and Drawings of 1850–1855*. Norwich: Real World, [1978].
Hough, Graham. 'Rossetti and Dante'. In *The Last Romantics*. Duckworth, 1949, pp. 67–82.
Morse, B. J. 'Dante Gabriel Rossetti and Dante Alighieri'. *Englische Studien*, 68 (1933–4), 227–48.
Rees, Joan. *The Poetry of Dante Gabriel Rossetti: Modes of Self-Expression*. Cambridge: Cambridge Univ. Press, 1981.
Rossetti, Dante Gabriel, trans. *Dante and His Circle: With the Italian Poets Preceding Him (1100–1200–1300)*. 1874.
Dante Gabriel Rossetti: An Analytical List of Manuscripts in the Duke University Library. Ed. Paull Franklin Baum. Durham, N. Carolina: Duke Univ. Press, 1931.
Dante Gabriel Rossetti: His Family Letters. Memoir by W. M. Rossetti. 2 vols. 1895.
trans. *The Early Italian Poets from Ciullo d'Alcamo to Dante Alighieri (1100–1200–1300) in the Original Metres, Together with Dante's 'Vita Nuova'*. 1861.
The House of Life. Ed. Paull Franklin Baum. Cambridge, Mass.: Harvard Univ. Press, 1928.
Letters of Dante Gabriel Rossetti. Ed. Oswald Doughty and John Robert Wahl. 4 vols. Oxford: The Clarendon Press, 1965–7.
The Paintings and Drawings of Dante Gabriel Rossetti: A Catalogue Raisonné. Ed. Virginia Surtees. 2 vols. Oxford: Oxford Univ. Press, 1971.
Works. Ed. William Michael Rossetti. Ellis, 1911.
Rossetti, William Michael. *Dante Gabriel Rossetti as Designer and Writer*. 1899.
'Notes on Rossetti and his Works'. *Art Journal*, 41, 42, 43 (1884), 148–52, 165–8, 204–8.
The P.R.B. Journal. Ed. William E. Fredeman. Oxford: The Clarendon Press, 1975.
Swinburne, Algernon Charles. 'The Poems of Dante Gabriel Rossetti'. In *Essays and Studies*. 1875, pp. 60–109.
Toynbee, Paget. 'Chronological list, with notes, of paintings and drawings from Dante by Dante Gabriel Rossetti'. In *Scritti varii . . . in onore di Rodolfo Renier*. Turin: Bocca, 1912, pp. 135–66.
Waller, R. D. *The Rossetti Family 1824–1854*. Manchester: Univ. of Manchester, 1932.

7. Yeats

Bornstein, George. 'Yeats's Romantic Dante'. *Colby Library Quarterly*, 15 (1979), 93–113.
Ellis, Stephen Paul. 'Yeats and Dante'. *Comparative Literature*, 33 (1981), 1–17.
Ellmann, Richard. *The Identity of Yeats*. 2nd ed. Faber, 1964.
Hone, Joseph. *W. B. Yeats 1865–1939*. 2nd ed. Macmillan, 1962.
Jeffares, A. Norman. *W. B. Yeats: Man and Poet*. 2nd ed. Routledge and Kegan Paul, 1962.
John, Brian. '"To Hunger Fiercely after Truth": Daimonic Man and Yeats's Insatiable Appetite'. *Éire–Ireland*, 9, No. 1 (1974), 90–103.
Melchiori, Giorgio. 'Yeats and Dante'. *English Miscellany*, 19 (1968), 153–79.
Spurr, David. 'A Celtic *Commedia*: Dante in Yeats' Poetry'. *Rackham Literary Studies*, 8 (1977), 99–116.
Vance, Thomas. 'Dante, Yeats and Unity of Being'. *Shenandoah*, 17, No. 2 (1966), 73–85.
Wade, Allan. *A Bibliography of the Writings of W. B. Yeats*. 3rd ed. Rev. Russell K. Alspach. Hart-Davis, 1968.
Wilson, F. A. C. *Yeats's Iconography*. Gollancz, 1960.
Yeats, J. B. *Letters to His Son W. B. Yeats and Others 1869–1922*. Ed. Joseph Hone. Pref. Oliver Elton. Faber, 1944.
Yeats, W. B. *Autobiographies*. Macmillan, 1955.
Essays. Macmillan, 1924.
Essays and Introductions. Macmillan, 1961.
Explorations. Select. Mrs W. B. Yeats. Macmillan, 1962.
Memoirs. Ed. Denis Donoghue. Macmillan, 1972.
A Packet for Ezra Pound. Dundrum: Cuala, 1929.
Per Amica Silentia Lunae. In *Mythologies*. Macmillan, 1959, pp. 317–69.
The Variorum Edition of the Plays of W. B. Yeats. Ed. Russell K. Alspach and Catharine C. Alspach. Macmillan, 1966.
The Variorum Edition of the Poems of W. B. Yeats. Ed. Peter Allt and Russell K. Alspach. New York: Macmillan, 1957.
A Vision. Laurie, 1925. Re-issued as *A Critical Edition of Yeats's 'A Vision' (1925)*. Ed. George Mills Harper and Walter Kelly Hood. Macmillan, 1978.
A Vision. Macmillan, 1937. 2nd corrected ed. Macmillan, 1962.

8. Pound

Barfoot, Gabrielle. 'The Theme of Usury in Dante and Pound'. *Rivista di letterature moderne e comparate*, 30 (1977), 254–83.
Brooke-Rose, Christine. *A ZBC of Ezra Pound*. Faber, 1971.
Bush, Ronald. *The Genesis of Ezra Pound's 'Cantos'*. Princeton: Princeton Univ. Press, 1976.
Davie, Donald. *Ezra Pound: Poet as Sculptor*. Routledge and Kegan Paul, 1965.
De Bosschère, Jean. 'Ezra Pound'. *Egoist*, 4 (1917), 7–8, 27–9, 44.
Ellis, Stephen Paul. 'Dante in Pound's Early Career'. *Paideuma*, 8 (1979), 549–61.
Fussell, Edwin. 'Dante and Pound's *Cantos*'. *Journal of Modern Literature*, 1 (1970), 75–87.
Gallup, Donald. *A Bibliography of Ezra Pound*. 2nd ed. Hart-Davis, 1969.
Giovannini, Giovanni. *Ezra Pound and Dante*. Nijmegen: Dekker and Van de Vegt, [1961].

Gugelberger, Georg M. '"By No Means An Orderly Dantescan Rising"'. *Italian Quarterly*, 16 (1973), 31–48.
'The Secularization of "Love" to a Poetic Metaphor: Cavalcanti, Center of Pound's Medievalism'. *Paideuma*, 2 (1973), 159–73.
Jung Palandri, Angela C. Y. 'Italian Images of Ezra Pound'. *Italian Quarterly*, 16 (1973), 11–22.
Kenner, Hugh. *The Pound Era*. Faber, 1972.
Orsini, Napoleone. 'Ezra Pound, critico letterario'. *Letterature moderne*, 7 (1957), 34–51.
Paolucci, Anne. 'Ezra Pound and D. G. Rossetti as Translators of Guido Cavalcanti'. *Romanic Review*, 51 (1960), 256–67.
Pleynet, Marcelin. 'La compromission poétique'. *Tel Quel*, 70 (Summer 1977), 11–26.
Pound, Ezra. *ABC of Reading*. 1934; rpt. Faber, 1951.
The Cantos of Ezra Pound. Revised collected ed. Faber, 1975.
Cantos LXXII and LXXIII. Washington D.C.: Estate of Ezra Pound, 1973.
Collected Early Poems of Ezra Pound. Ed. Michael John King. Introd. Louis L. Martz. Faber, 1977.
Collected Shorter Poems. 2nd ed. Faber, 1968.
'Ezra Pound Speaking': Radio Speeches of World War II. Ed. Leonard W. Doob. Westport, Conn.: Greenwood Press, 1978.
Gaudier-Brzeska. 1916. New edition, Hessle: Marvell Press, 1960.
Guide to Kulchur. Faber, 1938.
ed. *Guido Cavalcanti: Rime*. Genoa: Marsano, [1931].
Interview with Donald Hall. *Paris Review*, 28 (1962), 22–51.
Jefferson and/or Mussolini. Nott, 1935.
The Letters of Ezra Pound 1907–1941. Ed. D. D. Paige. Faber, 1951.
Literary Essays of Ezra Pound. Ed. T. S. Eliot. Faber, 1954.
Selected Prose 1909–1965. Ed. William Cookson. Faber, 1973.
Sonnets and Ballate of Guido Cavalcanti. Swift, 1912.
The Spirit of Romance. Dent, [1910]. Revised ed. Peter Owen, 1952.
The Translations of Ezra Pound. Introd. Hugh Kenner. Faber, 1970.
Singh, G. 'Pound and Cavalcanti'. In *Essays in Honour of John Humpreys Whitfield*. Ed. H. C. Davis *et al.* St George's Press for the Italian Department, Univ. of Birmingham, 1975, pp. 268–84.
Wilhelm, James J. *Dante and Pound: The Epic of Judgement*. Orono: Univ. of Maine Press, 1974.

9. Eliot

Charity, A. C. 'T. S. Eliot: The Dantean Recognitions'. In *'The Waste Land' in Different Voices*. Ed. A. D. Moody. Edward Arnold, 1974, pp. 117–62.
Cleophas, Sister M. '*Ash-Wednesday*: The *Purgatorio* in a Modern Mode'. *Comparative Literature*, 11 (1959), 329–39.
Eliot, T. S. *After Strange Gods*. Faber, 1934.
Ara Vus [*sic*] *Prec*. Ovid Press, [1920].
Clark Lectures, Unpublished, 1926.
The Complete Poems and Plays of T. S. Eliot. Faber, 1969.
Dante. Faber, 1929.
'Dante as a "Spiritual Leader"'. Rev. of *Dante*, by H. D. Sedgwick. *Athenaeum*, 2 April 1920, 441–2.

'Donne in Our Time'. In *A Garland for John Donne, 1631–1931*. Ed. Theodore Spencer. Cambridge, Mass.: Harvard Univ. Press, 1931, pp. 1–19.
'Eeldrop and Appleplex'. *Little Review*, 4, No. 1 (1917), 7–11.
For Lancelot Andrewes: Essays on Style and Order. 1928; rpt. Faber, 1970.
The Idea of a Christian Society. Faber, 1939.
Notes towards the Definition of Culture. 2nd ed. Faber, 1962.
On Poetry and Poets. Faber, 1957.
'Rhyme and Reason: The Poetry of John Donne'. *Listener*, 19 March 1930, 502–3.
The Rock: A Pageant Play. Faber, 1934.
The Sacred Wood. Methuen, 1920; 2nd ed. Methuen, 1928.
Selected Essays. 3rd ed. Faber, 1951.
introd. *Le Serpent*. By Paul Valéry. Trans. Mark Wardle. The Criterion, 1924.
To Criticize the Critic. Faber, 1965.
Unsigned rev. of *Per Amica Silentia Lunae*, by W. B. Yeats. *Egoist*, 5 (1918), 87.
The Use of Poetry and the Use of Criticism. 2nd ed. Faber, 1964.
The Waste Land: A Facsimile and Transcript of the Original Drafts including the Annotations of Ezra Pound. Ed. Valerie Eliot. Faber, 1971.
Gallup, Donald C. *T. S. Eliot: a Bibliography*. Faber, 1969.
Gardner, Dame Helen. *The Composition of 'Four Quartets'*. Faber, 1978.
Gillis, Everett A. 'The Spiritual Status of T. S. Eliot's Hollow Men'. *Texas Studies in Literature and Language*, 2 (1960–1), 464–75.
Gordon, Lyndall. *Eliot's Early Years*. Oxford: Oxford Univ. Press, 1977.
Hoffmann-Ogier, Wayne H. 'Dantean Parallels in T. S. Eliot's Description of a Mystical Experience in "Burnt Norton I"'. *Studia Mystica*, 2 (Fall 1979), 24–58.
Kenner, Hugh. *The Invisible Poet: T. S. Eliot*. Allen, 1960.
Kermode, Frank, introd. *Selected Prose of T. S. Eliot*. Faber, 1975.
Moody, A. D. *Thomas Stearns Eliot: Poet*. Cambridge: Cambridge Univ. Press, 1979.
Praz, Mario. 'T. S. Eliot and Dante'. In *The Flaming Heart*. New York: Doubleday, 1958, pp. 348–74.
'T. S. Eliot as a Critic'. *Sewanee Review*, 84 (1966) (T. S. Eliot Special Issue), 256–71.
Torrens, James Sullivan. 'Charles Maurras and Eliot's "New Life"'. *PMLA*, 89 (1974), 312–22.
'T. S. Eliot and the Contribution of Dante towards a Poetics of Sensibility'. Diss. Michigan 1968.

10. Miscellaneous

Barlow, H. C. Letter. *Athenaeum*, 19 March 1964, p. 410.
Bembo, Pietro. *Prose della volgar lingua*. Ed. Mario Marti. Padua: Liviana, 1955.
Bettinelli, Saverio. *Lettere virgiliane e inglesi e altri scritti critici*. Ed. V. E. Alfieri. Bari: Laterza, 1930.
Blake, William. *The Marriage of Heaven and Hell*. In *William Blake's Writings*. Ed. G. E. Bentley, Jr. Oxford: The Clarendon Press, 1978. Vol. I.
Boccaccio, Giovanni. *Opere in versi*. In La letteratura italiana: storia e testi. Vol. IX. Ed. Pier Giorgio Ricci. Milan: Ricciardi, 1965.
Buchanan, Robert. *The Fleshly School of Poetry*. 1872.
Burke, Edmund. *A Philosophical Enquiry into the Origin of our Ideas of the Sublime and Beautiful*. Ed. J. T. Boulton. Routledge and Kegan Paul, 1958.
Butler, Marilyn. *Peacock Displayed*. Routledge & Kegan Paul, 1979.

Chaytor, H. J., ed. *The Troubadours of Dante*. Oxford: The Clarendon Press, 1902.
Conrad, Joseph. *Heart of Darkness*. Harmondsworth: Penguin, 1973.
Eliot, George. *Middlemarch*. Ed. W. J. Harvey. Harmondsworth: Penguin, 1965.
Emerson, Ralph Waldo. *Society and Solitude: Twelve Chapters*. In *Complete Works* (Centenary edition). Vol. VII. Boston: Houghton Mifflin, 1912.
Foscolo, Ugo. 'Guido Cavalcanti'. *New Monthly Magazine*, 5, No. 19 (1822). In *Opere*. Vol. X, 423–35.
'Italian Literature: Epoch First. From the year 1180 to 1230'. *European Review*, September 1824. In *Opere*. Vol. XI, Pt. 1. 1958, 73–97.
Hallam, Arthur. *The Writings of Arthur Hallam*. Ed. T. H. Vail Motter. New York: Modern Language Association; Oxford: Oxford Univ. Press, 1943.
Hazlitt, William. Rev. of *De la littérature du Midi de l'Europe*, by J. C. L. Simonde de Sismondi. *Edinburgh Review*, June 1815, 31–63.
Heaney, Seamus. *Field Work*. Faber, 1979.
Hueffer, Ford Madox. *Ancient Lights and Certain New Reflections*. Chapman and Hall, 1911.
Hunt, Leigh. *The Story of Rimini*. 1816.
Keats, John. *The Complete Poems*. Ed. John Barnard. 2nd ed. Harmondsworth: Penguin, 1976.
Kollman, Ignaz. *Dante*. In Carlo Del Balzo, ed. *Poesie di mille autori intorno a Dante Alighieri*. Vol. VIII. Rome: Forzani, 1903, 391–566.
Landor, Walter Savage. 'Dante and Beatrice'. *Hood's Magazine*, 3 (Jan.-June 1845), 225–30. Rpt. *Works*. 1846. Vol. II, 152–4.
'Dante and Gemma Donati'. *Works*. 1846. Vol. II, 232–4.
Macaulay, Thomas Babington, Lord Macaulay. 'Milton'. *Works*. Vol. V, 1–45.
[Mulock, Dinah Maria]. *Poems by the Author of 'John Halifax Gentleman'*. [1859].
'On the German Drama. No. 1: Oehlenschlaeger'. *Olliers Literary Miscellany*, 1 (1820), 90–153.
Ormond, Leonee and Richard. *Lord Leighton*. New Haven and London: Yale Univ. Press, 1975.
Palgrave, F. T. *Idyls and Songs*. 1854.
Parkes, Kineton, ed. *The Painter-Poets*. [1890].
Patmore, Coventry. *The Angel in the House*. In *The Poems of Coventry Patmore*. Ed. Frederick Page. Oxford: Oxford Univ. Press, 1949, 59–208.
Petrarch, Francesco. *Rerum Memorandum Libri*. Ed. Giuseppe Billanovich. In *Opere*. Edizione nazionale. Vol. V. Florence: Sansoni, 1943. Book II.
Poeti del primo secolo della lingua italiana. Florence, 1816. Vol. I.
Poliziano, Angelo Ambrogini. 'Nutricia'. Part IV of *Sylvae*. In *Prose volgari inedite e poesie latine e greche edite e inedite*. Ed. Isidoro Del Lungo. Florence, 1867.
Praz, Mario. *Secentismo e Marinismo in Inghilterra*. Florence: 'La Voce', 1925.
Read, Sir Herbert. *Reason and Romanticism*. Faber and Gwyer, 1926.
Roe, Albert S. *Blake's Illustrations to the 'Divine Comedy'*. Princeton: Princeton Univ. Press, 1953.
Roscoe, William. *The Life of Lorenzo de' Medici*. 4th ed. 1800. Vol. I.
Rosenberg, John D. 'The Two Kingdoms of *In Memoriam*'. *Journal of English and Germanic Philology*, 58 (1959), 228–40.
Ruskin, John. *The Stones of Venice*. In *The Works of John Ruskin*. Ed. E. T. Cook and Alexander Wedderburn. Vols. IX-XI. Allen, 1903–4.
Sacchetti, Franco. *Il Trecentonovelle*. Ed. Emilio Faccioli. Turin: Einaudi, 1970. Nos. 114–15.

Sismondi, J. C. L. Simonde de. *De la littérature du Midi de l'Europe.* Paris: 1813. Vol. I.
Symonds, John Addington, pref. *Illustrations to the 'Divine Comedy' of Dante . . . by Stradanus.* Introd. Guido Biagi. 1892.
Symons, Arthur. *The Symbolist Movement in Literature.* Introd. Richard Ellmann. New York: Dutton, 1958.
Taylor, Alan Carey. *Carlyle et la pensée latine.* Paris: Boivin, [1937].
Tennyson, Alfred, Lord Tennyson. *The Poems of Tennyson.* Ed. Christopher Ricks. Longman, 1969.
Toynbee, Paget. 'Dante in English Art'. Supplement to the *Thirty-Eighth Annual Report of the Dante Society (Cambridge, Mass.) 1919.* Boston: Dante Society, 1921.
Vasari, Giorgio. 'Life of Giotto'. In *The Lives of the Artists.* Select. and trans. George Bull. Harmondsworth: Penguin, 1965, pp. 57–81.

Index